The economics of trade protection

The economics of trade protection

NEIL VOUSDEN
Australian National University

CAMBRIDGE UNIVERSITY PRESS

Cambridge
New York   Port Chester   Melbourne   Sydney

Published by the Press Syndicate of the University of Cambridge
The Pitt Building, Trumpington Street, Cambridge CB2 1RP
40 West 20th Street, New York, NY 10011, USA
10 Stamford Road, Oakleigh, Melbourne 3166, Australia

© Cambridge University Press 1990

First Published 1990

Printed in the United States of America

Library of Congress Cataloging-in-Publication Data
Vousden, Neil, 1947–

The economics of trade protection / Neil Vousden.

p. cm.
Includes bibliographical references.
ISBN 0-521-34661-4. – ISBN 0-521-34669-X (pbk.)
1. Protectionism. I. Title.
HF1713.V68   1990
382'.73–dc20   89-25195
                                                   CIP

British Library Cataloguing in Publication Data
Vousden, Neil

The economics of trade protection.

1. Foreign trade. Protection
I. Title
382.7

ISBN 0-521-34661-4 hardback
ISBN 0-521-34669-X paperback

To my parents

Contents

Preface

During the last two decades, there has been a gradual but fundamental change in the nature of world protectionism. While various rounds of international trade negotiations have succeeded in reducing tariffs to very low levels, national governments have resorted to a range of increasingly intricate policies to protect their domestic industries from foreign competition. Direct quantitative restrictions on international trade have become particularly widespread and have made it difficult for newly industrializing countries to access new export markets. In addition, it has become clear that these non-tariff trade barriers often have very different effects from tariffs and require careful analysis in their own right. This has spawned a voluminous, if scattered, literature on the properties of policies as wide ranging as import quotas, voluntary export restraints, variable import levies and export subsidies, content protection schemes and government procurement schemes.

Economists have also become increasingly aware of the importance of imperfect competition and economies of scale in many of the more heavily protected manufacturing industries (e.g. steel and automobiles). Canadian economists, in particular, had long felt that one of the most significant costs of protection was its effect in inhibiting firm scale, by promoting excessive entry of domestic firms. Proponents of protection had often spoken vaguely of the need to increase the market share of domestic firms, a proposal which only has meaning when applied to non-competitive industries. However, most of these ideas were not to find formal expression until the late 1970s and early 1980s when a series of important papers by trade theorists subjected the full range of non-competitive market structures to formal analysis. In the process, many ideas from industrial organization theory permeated the trade literature, and a range of new arguments for and against protection were given prominence.

The same period also saw many economists becoming disenchanted with their traditional role of identifying and advocating socially efficient policies. After several decades of pointing to the social costs of most impediments to free trade, they were beginning to realize that imperfections in the political process were likely to favour the adoption of inefficient policies by governments wishing to retain office. This awareness led a number of public economists to develop the "political markets" approach to government policy, based on the idea that redistributional tools such as tariffs and import quotas are "prices" which equilibrate markets for political support. The idea that trade barriers were actually endogenous to the system found immediate favour with protection economists, who were looking for a framework which would explain the growth of protectionism in the 1970s and the shift from tariffs to other forms of trade restriction.

These developments have been accompanied by greater awareness of the other constraints and costs faced by even the most altruistic policy makers. For example, in an economy which is riddled with distortions, some unalterable, the question of "which way is up?" is so informationally demanding that most will opt for the status quo. Such considerations led to the development of the theory of "piecemeal reform", which attempts to identify simple welfare-improving rules for reducing tariffs and other distortions. Of course, most reductions in protection are not achieved unilaterally but as the outcome of a process of collusion or negotiation between countries. Accordingly, much recent attention has been devoted to modelling the possible outcomes of such negotiations with or without the presence of piecemeal rules. This research is now shedding new light on the vexed question of why countries have negotiated tariffs to such low levels only to erect new and usually more costly trade barriers in their place.

The aim of this book is to present these new developments in a thorough and systematic manner as part of a comprehensive overview of the theory of protection. The need for a text of this type became apparent to me while I was teaching a graduate course on the theory of trade policy at the Australian National University. Despite the existence of many good international trade texts and some noteworthy books on various aspects of protection, there was no book which fully covered all of the main theoretical issues of modern trade policy in sufficient detail. In writing the book, I have been conscious of the need to make the material accessible to a wide class of readers including the non-specialist. For this reason, diagrams and intuition have been used extensively, and an introductory chapter on basic trade theory has been included to make the text as self-contained as possible. Material which is technically more demanding is included in the final two chapters and also in appendices.

Even though the book is primarily concerned with the theory, the reader also should be aware of the empirical studies which have motivated and informed that theory. Of special interest is the growing number of applied general equilibrium models, which have been used to simulate the effects of trade-liberalization exercises such as the U.S.–Canada Free Trade Agreement and the proposals considered in the Tokyo Round of GATT negotiations. The findings of a number of these studies are detailed and discussed at various points throughout the book, with particular emphasis on the newer models incorporating imperfect competition and economies of scale. An important feature of these models is their finding that the gains from trade liberalization can be dramatically increased when economies of scale are present.

The book is suitable for a one-term course at the advanced undergraduate or graduate level. It assumes a background in intermediate micro theory and, the more difficult material in the appendices and Chapters 9 and 10 presupposes a knowledge of multivariate constrained optimization, some duality theory and simple matrix algebra.

Outline of book

This book consists of four parts plus mathematical appendices. Part I (Chapters 1–4) presents the standard competitive markets model. The first chapter offers an overview of the basic two-sector trade model for readers who are unfamiliar with trade theory; for others, a cursory reading of this chapter may be sufficient. Appendix 1 provides a mathematical version of the material in Chapter 1 for the reader who would like to see the model written down explicitly. Chapter 2 considers the effects of tariffs and compares them with other types of protection (e.g. import quotas, content protection schemes and export subsidies) for a country which is too small to influence its own terms of trade. It is shown that such a country will necessarily lose by restricting trade. The measurement of the cost of such trade restriction is discussed, and a number of empirical estimates of this cost are cited. Although many of these estimates are very low, a number of reasons are offered why they are likely to underestimate the true cost of protection, even in the competitive case. Of course, protection will often be used in spite of its costs as a means of achieving certain income distributional objectives. In such a second-best context, the important question is, What is the least-cost means of achieving such an objective? It is shown that the most appropriate instrument to use is the one which directly affects the target variable. Finally, the chapter takes a critical look at the use of effective rates of protection for measuring assistance to industries with several tiers of intermediate goods.

Although tariffs and quantitative trade restrictions are equivalent under static perfect competition, casual observation suggests that the two types of policy differ markedly in the real world. One of the main reasons for this is the presence of uncertainty. Continuing to focus on the case of a small country, Chapter 3 compares tariffs and import quotas when there is uncertainty with respect to world price and demand. For the most part, tariffs are found to be a less costly tool than quotas for restricting imports. The two policies also differ in their effects when agents expend resources competing for the scarce quota rents or the tariff revenue (so-called rent or revenue seeking). Once again, tariffs emerge as the less costly alternative. The chapter also addresses the important question of how conventional measures of the cost of protection must be modified when resources are being dissipated in rent-seeking activity.

If the country imposing a tariff is large enough to affect its own terms of trade, then it can gain by restricting trade. This observation forms the basis for Chapter 4, which considers trade policy in a large-country context. If a large country can be confident of restricting trade without any retaliation from its trading partners, then it can maximize its own welfare by imposing the so-called optimal tariff which balances the gain from an improved terms of trade against the domestic consumption and production costs of the tariff. In practice, it is likely that imposition of such a tariff would induce retaliation by other large countries. It is shown that the outcome of such a trade war will depend on whether the instrument of trade restriction is a tariff or a quota. In particular, a quota war is likely to lead to a greater degree of trade restriction than a tariff war. Two other policies which have become increasingly important for large countries are voluntary export restraints and variable import levies. Both of these have had a profound effect on international trade in the last two decades; they are considered in detail in Chapter 4.

Although the economies considered in Chapter 4 are large enough to have market power at the world level, this market power resides at the industry rather than the firm level. In Chapter 4, as in the rest of Part I, industries satisfy the perfectly competitive model, with individual firms having no ability to affect price. However, in the real world, many heavily protected industries consist of a small number of firms, each having significant price-setting ability. In addition, their production processes are typically characterized by substantial scale economies. Part II (Chapters 5–7) is devoted to these cases, which have been the subject of so much theoretical research in the last decade.

Chapter 5 considers the simplest type of imperfect competition, pure monopoly. International trade serves to limit the market power of a domestic monopolist, whereas sufficient protection from import competition restores some or all of the firm's monopoly power. In this respect, import quotas differ fundamentally from tariffs because they render the supply of imports inelastic and confer greater monopoly power on the domestic firm. Thus domestic monopoly provides another instance of the non-equivalence of tariffs and quotas; once again, quotas tend to emerge as the inferior policy. If economies of scale are also present, the costs of protection will be increased further, particularly if the protection is essential to the domestic firm's viability. In contrast, if the domestic market is supplied solely by a foreign monopolist, then even a small country stands to gain by using a trade tax to capture some of the foreign firm's repatriated rents for domestic taxpayers. This observation forms the basis of the so-called rent-shifting argument for protection, which occupies a large part of Chapter 6.

When a single domestic firm competes with a single foreign firm in the home market, a tariff will not only shift rents from the foreign firm to domestic taxpayers. It can also shift some foreign rents to the domestic firm. In such an oligopoly framework, the role of protection is to pre-commit the domestic firm to a more aggressive output or price policy than it would be able credibly to achieve on its own, thereby capturing additional foreign rents for the domestic economy. Similarly, an export subsidy may be contemplated as a means of increasing the home firm's market share (and rents) in the foreign market. As can be seen in Chapter 6, this argument is quite sensitive to the assumptions in the underlying model. An alternative model with free entry of firms (hence no rents) and an integrated world market for the protected good yields quite different results: protection is seen as encouraging inefficient entry of firms with no offsetting gains from rent shifting. This latter type of model has been the basis for a number of applied studies of trade liberalization, some of which are discussed at the end of Chapter 6.

In Chapter 7 we depart temporarily from the assumption of homogeneous goods and allow for production of different varieties of the same product. Such product differentiation gives rise to a market structure called *monopolistic competition*. This is characterized by free entry (or exit) of firms to (or from) an industry in which each firm produces a different variety of the good, and production of each variety exhibits economies of scale. An important implication of this case is that in a two-country world, each variety will be produced in only one country; consequently, international trade will serve to increase the number of varieties available to consumers in both countries. The type of trade which occurs in such an industry is termed *intra-industry trade* and is now known to be an important component of total world trade. The implication is that protection is harmful because it reduces the volume of such trade and also reduces the product variety available to consumers in each country. It may also lead to shorter production runs, higher unit costs and higher prices.

Part III (Chapter 8) is concerned with the "political markets" view of protection: the idea that the various forms of protection are no more than prices which equilibrate the markets for political support. Because there is limited scope for lump-sum interpersonal compensation, various distortionary taxes, subsidies and regulations are used to redistribute income among different groups in the political system. This chapter considers how tariff levels are determined as the outcome of a process involving voters, pressure groups and political parties. Of course, political markets determine not only the level of protection but also the form of protection. Models of the choice between tariffs and import quotas are presented in the last section of the chapter with a view to explaining the apparent preference of governments for quantitative trade restrictions.

Part IV, which deals with the task of reducing protection, is presented at a higher level than the rest of the book and requires a knowledge of simple duality theory, calculus and matrix algebra. Nevertheless, readers without such a background would benefit by skimming through the intuitive discussions that accompany the various results. Chapter 9 is concerned with unilateral aspects of reducing protection, with particular emphasis on the "piecemeal" approach to reform. The starting point of the analysis is the observation that governments are unlikely to dismantle immediately all of the economy's distortions. The question posed is, How can they improve matters by only reducing some distortions? After noting the type of second-best problems which complicate the business of partial reform, the chapter proceeds to consider the main piecemeal tariff-reduction rules. These are (i) reduce all trade taxes in the same proportion and (ii) reduce the highest tax first. Piecemeal reform of quotas is also considered. The conditions under which the various rules will improve community welfare are noted and discussed. A related issue, which is analysed using the same model, is the crucial question of intertemporal reform: Should protection be reduced in a single step or gradually over time? The framework of Chapter 9 is also used to derive more general formulae for measuring the cost of protection.

Chapter 10 considers the reform issue in a multilateral setting. One of the obstacles to multilateral reform is the difficulty of making intercountry transfers. Without such transfers, some piecemeal reform proposals can make matters worse rather than better. One resolution of the problem is for groups of countries to realize mutual benefits by forming so-called trading clubs, such as free-trade areas and customs unions. One section of the chapter is devoted to the case of customs unions, which are trading clubs in which there is free trade among a group of countries, with each member imposing a common tariff on imports from outside the group. Conditions are derived for customs-union formation to be beneficial for the member countries. The final section of the chapter is devoted to recent developments in the theory of trade negotiations.

Acknowledgements

I particularly wish to thank Stephen Magee of the University of Texas at Austin, Ed Tower of Duke University and Graeme Wells of the Australian National University for their thorough reading of the manuscript and their detailed comments. I am also indebted to Steve Husted, Luke Nottage, Rohan Pitchford, Bijit Bora and Brian Copeland for comments and suggestions and to Richard Cornes, Ted Sieper, Albert Schweinberger and Alan Woodland for helpful discussions.

PART I

Protection with competitive markets

CHAPTER 1

Basic international trade theory

This introductory chapter develops basic analytical tools that are commonly used in trade and protection theory. It will also serve as a compendium of some of the better known results in the field, which will be useful for reference in later chapters. Much of this material is familiar to students who have completed a course in the pure theory of international trade; such students may find a cursory reading of the chapter to be adequate.

The main model to be considered here was originally formulated by Swedish economists E. Heckscher and B. Ohlin, with a view to explaining the pattern of trade between countries. It is perhaps ironic that, although the model has had limited success in explaining the determinants of trade, subsequent developments (most notably by Paul Samuelson) have made it a popular general equilibrium framework for analysis of impediments to trade in competitive markets. On the other hand, it is less easily adapted to analysing situations in which markets are not perfectly competitive and in which production may exhibit economies of scale. In such cases (which we consider in Chapters 5–7), it is often more expeditious to employ a partial equilibrium framework. Nevertheless, the two-sector model presented in this chapter serves as a useful reference point for our analysis.

Our approach to presenting the basic model is necessarily heuristic, using diagrams and verbal intuition wherever possible. More advanced students may want a more rigorous treatment. For these students, Appendix 1 contains a full mathematical specification of the model together with proofs of the main results obtained in this chapter.

1.1.   The Heckscher–Ohlin–Samuelson model

The main features of this model for a single country are as follows. The economy is assumed to produce two goods, food and cloth, using two factors of production, capital and labour, which are perfectly mobile between sectors. This factor-mobility assumption is central to the Heckscher–Ohlin–Samuelson (HOS) model, distinguishing it from the Ricardo–Viner specific-factors model, which we consider in Section 1.4. Production functions for both goods are assumed to exhibit constant returns to scale, with diminishing returns to each factor. All markets are perfectly competitive, and it is assumed that the economy's balance of payments is zero (i.e. income = expenditure). We shall begin by considering the consumption side of the model.

(a)   Consumers

The appropriate starting point for consideration of the demand side of the economy is the preferences of individual consumers. Figure 1.1 illustrates a set of indifference curves for a typical individual in the economy. As is well known to any undergraduate microeconomics student, all points along a given indifference curve (say u_1) yield the consumer the same level of welfare. Moreover, it is customary to assume that these curves are strictly convex to the origin, downward sloping, and that higher curves correspond to higher levels of utility. The underlying utility function is generally assumed to be *ordinal* (i.e. it is defined up to a strictly increasing monotonic transformation). A consumer maximizes her utility, subject to a budget constraint (line *AB* in Figure 1.1), the result being an equilibrium for the consumer at the tangency point *E*.

In moving from the individual to the community as a whole, we encounter the problem of defining and establishing the existence of a set of *community-indifference curves,* which (one might hope) have the same properties (e.g. convexity) as those for the individual consumer. Unfortunately, the mere existence of a set of well-defined community-indifference curves depends on a set of very restrictive assumptions. For example, if each individual's consumption of each good is constrained to be non-negative, and if there are no restrictions on prices and the distribution of incomes among consumers, then a necessary and sufficient condition for the existence of an aggregate utility function is that all consumers have *identical homothetic preferences.*[1] At the same time, much expositional simplicity is gained by using community-indifference curves. With this in mind, we shall assume throughout the book that (i) society can maximize its welfare as if it were a single individual with a well-behaved convex indifference map, and (ii) a higher level of community welfare can be translated into higher welfare for each individual in the community by means of appropriate lump-sum transfers between individuals. We should, however, be careful not to lose sight of the strong assumptions underpinning this approach.

(b)   Production

Figure 1.2 illustrates the economy's production possibilities frontier (or production-transformation curve). This frontier (curve *AB* in the diagram) shows the maximum output of each good which can be produced with the economy's existing factor supplies for any given output of the other good. Clearly, such things as factor growth and technical change can make it possible to produce more of either good, thus shifting the curve outwards. Similarly, wasteful or non-productive use of resources shift it in and to the left.

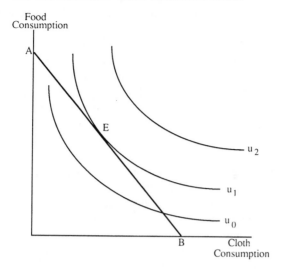

Figure 1.1

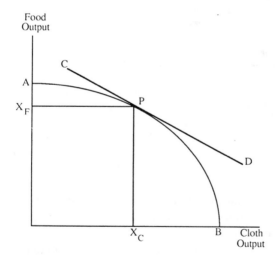

Figure 1.2

The bowed-out or concave form of the curve reflects the particular assumptions of the supply side of the model: that is, competitive good and factor markets, constant-returns-to-scale technology, with diminishing returns to each factor, and the additional assumption that the factor intensities (the ratio of capital input to labour input) are different in the two sectors. Here we assume without loss of generality that food production employs a higher ratio of capital to labour than cloth, at all relevant output levels (i.e. food is relatively capital intensive). Then as, say, the capital-intensive sector (food) expands and the labour-intensive sector (cloth) contracts, declining cloth output releases relatively more labour and relatively less capital than the expanding food sector requires; this leads to an excess demand for capital and an excess supply of labour, which drives the wage–rental ratio down and thus reduces the unit cost of cloth (which uses labour more intensively) and increases the unit cost of food. That is, as food output increases, the opportunity cost of an additional unit of food rises. This explains why the production frontier has the concave form illustrated in Figure 1.2.[2]

Figure 1.2 also illustrates the determination of the economy's equilibrium output levels for the two goods. The slope of line CD represents the relative price of cloth faced by producers. Under the assumption of competitive markets, production occurs at point P, where the price line CD is tangent to the production frontier. Output of food and cloth are X_F and X_C, respectively. This tangency reflects the fact that, in competitive equilibrium, the relative price of cloth and the marginal rate of transformation of food into cloth are equal. The equilibrium production point has the property that, at the existing relative prices, the total value of national output cannot be increased by any feasible change in sectoral outputs. The prices associated with the price line CD are sometimes said to *support* production at point P.

(c)   Autarky and free-trade equilibrium

Having seen how consumers and producers optimize subject to a given price, we now consider the equilibrium which results from the interaction of the two groups. In a situation of autarky in which the economy does not trade with the rest of the world, equilibrium prices are those at which consumer demand equals producer supply for each good (we assume that these equilibrium prices exist and are unique). The equilibrium price ratio for the two-good economy is given by the slope of the price line p_A, which is tangential to both the production frontier and the community indifference curve u_A at point A in Figure 1.3a. This separating price line supports equilibrium consumption (and production) of food C_F ($=X_F$) and of cloth C_C ($=X_C$).

Now suppose that the economy is opened to trade with the rest of the world. The equilibrium price no longer is determined so as to clear markets in the domestic economy (unless that economy is such a large part of the world economy for the problem to be uninteresting). Instead, relative prices adjust to equate world supply and demand for each good; indeed, if the country we are considering is small in the world market, its demands and supplies do not affect the world price at all. Figure 1.3b shows both the autarkic equilibrium A and the free-trade equilibrium for the country in question. Price line p^* represents the market-clearing world price ratio. We shall not concern ourselves here with

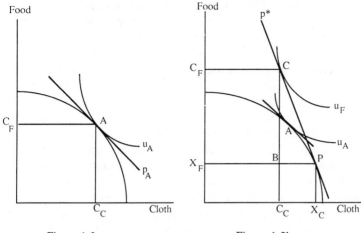

Figure 1.3a   Figure 1.3b

how world prices are determined, leaving the details of that problem until Section 1.5. To make our point, it is sufficient that free-trade relative prices p^* differ from the country's autarkic relative prices p_A. Faced with relative prices p^*, we know that producers will produce where p^* is tangential to the economy's production frontier, at point P in Figure 1.3b. It remains for us to identify the economy's consumption point. To do this, we must make use of another assumption of the model: the economy's income equals its expenditure. This is the same as assuming that the economy always balances its trade. Of course, we know that this does not happen in reality, but it is both a natural and a relatively harmless assumption in the present context. It is justified here because our central concern is the effects of trade (and protection) on the *real* economy. A non-zero trade balance would imply that the economy's stock of wealth is changing over time via monetary inflows and outflows, international capital flows and so on; we want to abstract from such transitory wealth effects and focus on long-run equilibrium, where wealth levels have adjusted to restore a zero trade balance.

Accordingly, the economy's consumption must equal the value of its output (P) at world prices p^*; that is, the free-trade consumption point must lie on the world price line p^* through P. Given that p^* is effectively the budget line facing consumers, the economy's consumption point is at point C in Figure 1.3b, where a community indifference curve is tangential to p^*. Given the absence of any domestic distortions such as tariffs, taxes and subsidies, this equilibrium involves equality between relative prices, the marginal rate of substitution in consumption and the marginal rate of transformation in production. The economy produces X_C and X_F units of cloth and food, and consumes C_C and C_F. It exports its excess supply of cloth $(X_C - C_C)$ in return for imports equal to its excess demand for food $(C_F - X_F)$. These exports and imports are also given by the sides of the triangle CBP, which is often referred to as the "trade triangle." In this case, CB measures imports and BP measures exports.

The level of community utility associated with the free-trade equilibrium is u_F, which is seen to be higher than the level of utility u_A under autarky; that is, the economy has gained from trade.[3] Of course, we are referring here to an aggregate gain (see the preceding discussion of community indifference curves). Concealed behind the move from community indifference curve u_A to curve u_F are the gains and losses of different agents in the economy. In particular, domestic sellers of the importable and buyers of the exportable are made worse off by the change in relative prices associated with the move to free trade (just as domestic buyers of the importable and sellers of the exportable are made better off). However, for the move from u_A to u_F to be interpreted as a strict Pareto improvement for the economy (no individual worse off and at least one individual better off), it would have to be accompanied by an appropriate set of redistributions between agents, such that the losers are compensated by the gainers and in the final equilibrium no one is made worse off. Moreover, insofar as there are no commodity taxes or subsidies in the model of Figure 1.3, it is implicitly assumed that the necessary redistributions are effected by means of lump-sum transfers. Unfortunately, the use of such lump-sum compensation is fraught with difficulties, primarily because the appropriate transfer is different for each individual, giving each individual an opportunity and an incentive to mislead the tax authorities by overstating her loss or understating her gain from a particular policy. Accordingly, interest has recently shifted to the question of whether the potential Pareto improvement associated with trade liberalization can be achieved by employing a set of commodity taxes and subsidies which are the same for all individuals and are thus relatively immune to the preceding problem. At this stage, it would appear that under certain conditions an appropriate set of taxes and subsidies *can* be found (see Dixit and Norman, 1980, 1986; Kemp and Wan, 1986). Nevertheless, the issue of how the gains from trade are distributed in the absence of lump-sum compensation remains a promising area for future research.

Let us now abstract from the problem of how the gains from trade are distributed and consider the aggregate gain (the increase in community utility from u_A to u_F in Figure 1.3b). What is the source of this gain? It has come about because the economy is no longer constrained to consume exactly what it produces of each good; it can now be a net seller (exporter) of one good and a net buyer (importer) of the other good, with its opportunity set enlarged from the area enclosed by the production frontier and the axes to the area enclosed by the world price line p^* and the axes (i.e. the economy can now transform one good into another by international trade as well as by production). Only if the

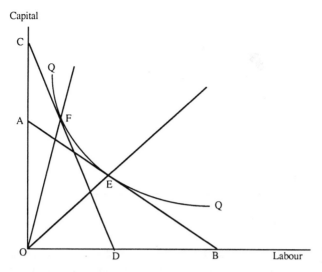

Figure 1.4

world price ratio just happens to equal the economy's equilibrium autarky price ratio, will the economy be no better off from trade. In such a case, its opportunity set is still larger than under autarky, but its chosen consumption point in that set is the autarky equilibrium A.

This completes our specification of trading equilibrium for a single country. In Section 1.5 we shall consider how equilibrium is determined in a world consisting of two such countries, and in subsequent chapters we shall also consider how a trading equilibrium is affected by various distortions such as tariffs and import quotas. However, before proceeding to other questions, it is worth pausing to derive some important results which flow from the production structure of the HOS model.

1.2. Factor intensities, factor prices and product prices

We now consider the relationships between product prices, factor prices and factor intensities in the HOS model. These relationships (which are subsumed in the production equilibrium already derived) constitute some of the better known "theorems" of pure trade theory.

We begin by noting that, for a constant-returns-to-scale production function, a rise in the relative price of a factor causes that factor to be used less intensively in both sectors. This is readily seen with the aid of Figure 1.4, which illustrates the choice of input mix for either of the goods produced in the economy. Suppose one unit of the good is being produced. The isoquant for this output

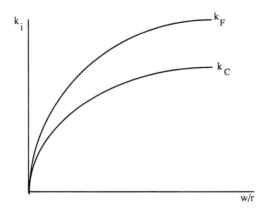

Figure 1.5

(the unit isoquant) is represented by the convex curve QQ in Figure 1.4. This shows the different combinations of capital and labour which produce one unit of the good. The least-cost combination of these factors is where the ratio of the factor prices (the slope of an isocost line) equals the marginal rate of substitution of one factor for another (the slope of the isoquant) – that is, a point of tangency between the unit isoquant and an isocost line. Point E is one such tangency when the ratio of the price of labour to the price of capital (the wage–rental ratio, w/r) is given by the slope of isocost line AB. The cost-minimizing ratio of capital to labour is given by the slope of the ray OE. Now, suppose that the wage–rental ratio increases. This implies steeper isocost lines, with one such line (CD) touching the isoquant at the cost-minimizing point F. Clearly the ray OF is steeper than OE, implying an increase in the capital–labour ratio. Finally, we note that, for constant returns to scale production functions, a given factor price ratio implies the same factor input ratio at all scales of output, so the result (just proven for the case of unit output) is true at all levels of output. Figure 1.5 illustrates this relationship between the capital–labour ratio in each sector (k_i for sector i) and the economy's wage–rental ratio (w/r).

Let us now consider how changes in the economy's product price ratio affect factor prices. The way in which changes in product prices feed through to factor rewards is of particular relevance when we are considering the income-distribution implications of protection. Tariffs, production subsidies and so on all change the producer price of the protected good, and it is of interest to see how a particular factor gains or loses as a result. Such information may be of help in explaining the pro- and anti-protectionist positions that different groups adopt.

For simplicity, we shall confine our attention to the case in which both goods are produced in equilibrium. Given that both sectors are perfectly competitive, equilibrium entails zero profits in both sectors. It is these zero-profit conditions

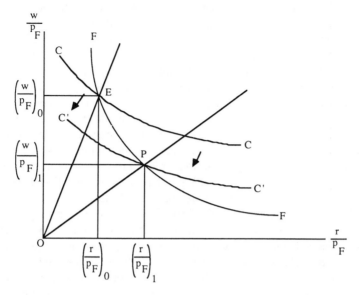

Figure 1.6

which determine the relationship between product and factor prices. A rise in the relative price of food due to, say, a tariff on food creates positive profits in the food sector. This attracts new firms into the sector, which, you will recall, is more capital-intensive than the cloth sector ($k_F > k_C$). As food production expands and cloth production contracts, relatively more capital is demanded by the food sector than is being released by the cloth sector (equivalently, the cloth sector is releasing relatively more labour than the food sector wants to take up). This implies an excess demand for capital and an excess supply of labour. To clear the factor markets, the real return to capital must rise, and the real return to labour must fall. In other words, a rise in the relative price of food leads to an increase in the real return to the factor used intensively in food production. This result may be stated more generally as:

The Stolper–Samuelson theorem: A rise in the relative price of a commodity leads to a rise in the real return to the factor used intensively in producing that commodity and to a fall in the real return to the other factor.

Figure 1.6 offers a fairly simple diagrammatic proof of the Stolper–Samuelson theorem (an algebraic proof can be found in Appendix 1). Loci *FF* and *CC* in Figure 1.6 represent the combinations of real factor rewards (expressed in food units) that yield zero real profits per unit (also measured in food units) in the food and cloth sectors, respectively. In this figure, w is the nominal wage, r is the nominal return to a unit of capital and p_F is the price of a unit of food; so w/p_F and r/p_F are the real factor returns measured in units of food. Both loci are downward sloping because, at given relative product prices, a higher price of one factor yields negative profits in either sector unless it is offset by a lower price of the other factor. Furthermore, the higher the capital–labour ratio in a sector, the greater is the fall in profits caused by a rise in the price of capital, and hence the larger is the fall in the price of labour needed to restore profits to zero in that sector. In other words, a sector's iso-profit curve is steeper the higher its capital–labour ratio.[4] This has two implications for the curves in Figure 1.6. First, it means that at any given wage–rental ratio, the zero-profit locus of the more capital-intensive sector (FF) must have a steeper absolute slope than that of the other sector (CC). Second, it implies that the loci are convex to the origin. This is because as we move to the right along either locus, the wage–rental ratio (w/r) is falling, leading to a fall in the capital–labour ratio of both sectors (as illustrated in Figure 1.5). Moreover, as a sector becomes less capital intensive, its zero-profit locus becomes flatter; it thus follows that the two loci are convex to the origin as shown. Given that both goods are produced, profits are zero in both sectors, and the equilibrium is at the point of intersection of FF and CC (E in Figure 1.6).

Now suppose there is a rise in the relative price of food. This does not affect real food profits measured in food units, so the FF locus does not shift. However, the real price of a unit of cloth has fallen, so real cloth profits will be negative unless the real return to either factor falls; thus the CC locus shifts down and to the left to position $C'C'$. The new equilibrium is at point P where $C'C'$ intersects FF. In the move to the new equilibrium, the real wage has fallen from $(w/p_F)_0$ to $(w/p_F)_1$ while the real return to capital has risen from $(r/p_F)_0$ to $(r/p_F)_1$. The wage–rental ratio, which is given by the slope of the ray joining the equilibrium point to the origin, also clearly falls. Given that capital's return has increased relative to the food price, it must also have increased relative to the price of cloth. If we had made cloth the numeraire instead of food in Figure 1.6, we would have seen that the wage measured in cloth units also falls (the reader may like to check this as an exercise). Thus, the real return to capital unambiguously rises and the real return to labour unambiguously falls in terms of both goods: regardless of how each factor allocates its spending between food and cloth, capital is clearly better off and labour is worse off as a result of the rise in the relative price of food.

One possible implication of the Stolper–Samuelson theorem is that the imposition of a tariff (which raises the domestic relative price of the importable good) benefits the factor used intensively in the importables sector and hurts the other factor.[5] However, such a conclusion would, in turn, imply that labour and capital would be expected to take opposite sides in lobbying for and against protection, something which is rarely observed (if at all). This has led a number of economists to question the HOS model's underlying assumption of perfect inter-sectoral factor mobility. An alternative model, which seems better suited to explaining the income distributional effects of tariffs and subsidies (and the observed responses of pressure groups), assumes that production in each sector combines a single mobile factor (labour) with industry-specific factors which are immobile between sectors. This model (the Ricardo–Viner–Jones specific factors model) is considered in detail in Section 1.4 and appears to offer a more satisfactory explanation of observed events. Nevertheless the Stolper–Samuelson result may have some value as a description of the longer run when factors are relatively mobile between sectors.

Before we proceed, it is worth noting another implication of Figure 1.6: that the economy's relative product prices uniquely determine factor prices. Given that free international trade in commodities will equate relative commodity prices across countries, it is clear from the preceding discussion that factor prices will also be equalized across countries that have the same technology, even though the factors in question are not mobile internationally. This observation is the substance of another well-known result of trade theory, the *factor–price equalization theorem* (for a rigorous proof of this theorem and a critical discussion of its interpretation see Dixit and Norman, 1980).

1.3. Factor endowments and the Rybczynski theorem

During the 1950s, trade theorists became interested in the effects of factor growth on the structure of industry. In particular, they wished to know how changes in an economy's relative factor supplies would affect sectoral outputs at any given commodity price ratio. We know from the previous section that, at fixed relative product prices, factor prices and input ratios are also fixed. Thus, factor substitution, while still a technical possibility, can be ignored in this case. The effects of factor growth may then be illustrated using Figure 1.7. Lines KK and LL represent the combinations of outputs of cloth and food which yield full employment of given endowments of capital and labour, respectively.[6] Each is negatively sloped because, for given factor endowments, higher output and factor demand in one sector must be offset by lower factor demand and lower output in the other sector. Both curves have constant slope[7] because input–output ratios in both sectors are fixed by product prices; thus, the amount by which output of one sector must contract in order to release enough of a particular factor to produce an extra unit of the other good is independent of output levels. In addition, the KK line is flatter than the LL line.[8] This is because a given rise in cloth output reduces food output less via the economy's capital constraint KK than via its labour constraint LL (because cloth requires relatively less capital).

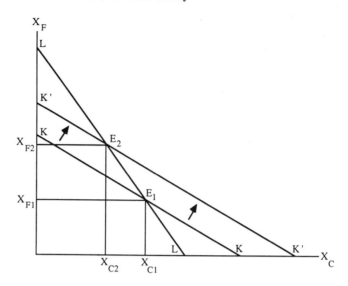

Figure 1.7

Initial equilibrium occurs where both factors are fully employed, at the intersection of *LL* and *KK* at point E_1 in Figure 1.7. Now suppose the economy's endowment of capital increases. This leaves *LL* unaffected but shifts *KK* out and to the right to position $K'K'$ (because more of either output can now be produced at a given level of the other output without exceeding the economy's supply of capital). The equilibrium shifts to E_2, where $K'K'$ cuts *LL*. Food output rises from X_{F1} to X_{F2} while cloth output contracts from X_{C1} to X_{C2}. This result can be more generally stated as:

Rybczynski's theorem: If an economy's endowment of one factor increases while the other factor is in fixed supply, the output of the good using the augmented factor intensively will increase while the output of the other good will contract.

It is straightforward to extend the Rybczynski result to cases in which endowments of both factors are changing. In particular, it can be shown (see Appendix 1) that:

A rise in the endowment of one factor relative to the other will increase the output of the good using that factor intensively relative to output of the other good.

The reader can check this result using Figure 1.7. An increase in the endowments of both capital and labour shift both *KK* and *LL* out and to the right. If both factors increase in the same proportion, the two lines shift by the same proportion, with the new equilibrium lying along the same ray through the origin as the original equilibrium. In such a case, the relative outputs of the two sectors are unchanged by the factor growth. On the other hand, if, say, the endowment of capital increases proportionately more than the endowment of labour, KK will shift out by a greater proportion than LL, and equilibrium will move onto a steeper ray through the origin, implying an increase in the relative output of the capital-intensive good (food).

Results of the Rybczynski type are of particular interest in situations where resources are being withdrawn from productive use (negative factor growth), as might be the case for certain government projects, rent-seeking activity and so on. In such cases, the results of this section need only be applied in reverse. We shall consider such an application when we analyse rent seeking in Chapter 3.

1.4.   Specific factors and income distribution in the short run

We now consider an alternative to the HOS framework, the so-called Ricardo–Viner specific factors model as developed by Jones (1971a, 1975), Mayer (1974) and Mussa (1974). As we observed in Section 1.2, the HOS model's assumption of perfect mobility of factors between sectors leads to results such as the Stolper–Samuelson theorem, which appear to be at odds with observed behaviour. In particular, the Stolper–Samuelson theorem implies that any tariff is unequivocally supported by one factor (the factor used intensively in the industry protected by the tariff) and opposed by the other factor (whose real return is reduced by the tariff). However, such a conflict of interest between factors in an industry sits uneasily with the frequently observed pro-protection coalitions of capital and labour within industries (see Magee, 1978, for empirical evidence). As we shall see in this section, such instances of commonality of interest within an industry can be explained by the immobility (or specificity) of certain factors in the short run. We shall now examine the effects of introducing specific factors into the basic two-sector model. Apart from the different approach to factor mobility, the model is formally identical to the HOS model outlined in Section 1.1.

The model assumes that one factor (labour) is perfectly mobile between sectors. Each sector's output is produced by combining this mobile factor with its own sector-specific factor (capital), which, by definition, is immobile between sectors. Thus, food is produced using labour L_F and food-specific capital K_F, whereas cloth is produced using labour L_C and cloth-specific capital K_C. Because labour is freely mobile between sectors, the economy's total labour supply L is allocated so that the value of the marginal product of labour in each sector is equated to the money wage w. The nominal rental rate for food capital is denoted by r_F, and the rate for cloth capital is r_C. Because each type of capital

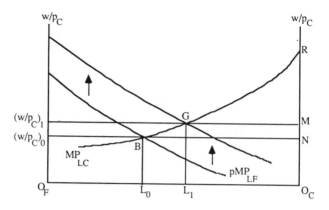

Figure 1.8a

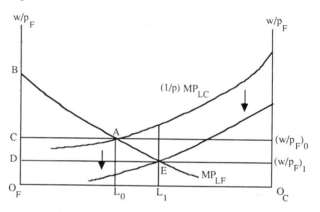

Figure 1.8b

is locked into its own sector, r_F and r_C are not, in general, equal. As in the Stolper–Samuelson case, we are interested in finding the effects of a rise in the relative price of food (due, for example, to a tariff on food) on the real returns to both factors.

The two diagrams in Figure 1.8 illustrate the determination of these real factor returns expressed in units of cloth and food, respectively. The mobile factor, labour, is measured along the horizontal axis, L_F being measured to the right of origin O_F and L_C to the left of O_C. The length of the axis, $O_F O_C$, is the economy's total labour supply L. In Figure 1.8a, both vertical axes measure variables in units of cloth (e.g. w/p_C). The two curves in the diagram represent the *value of the marginal product of labour,* measured in units of cloth, in the food and cloth sectors, respectively. These can be written as

$$\frac{\text{VMP}_{\text{LF}}}{p_C} = \left(\frac{p_F}{p_C}\right) \text{MP}_{\text{LF}} = p\text{MP}_{\text{LF}}$$

$$\frac{\text{VMP}_{\text{LC}}}{p_C} = \left(\frac{p_C}{p_C}\right) \text{MP}_{\text{LC}} = \text{MP}_{\text{LC}}.$$

where $p \equiv p_F/p_C$ is the relative price of food. Both curves slope downwards relative to their respective axes, reflecting the fact that the marginal product of labour in a sector declines as more labour is applied to a fixed quantity of the sector's specific factor.

As noted, labour is allocated between the two sectors to the point at which the value of its marginal product is the same in both sectors. Thus, in Figure 1.8a, the equilibrium labour allocation and the real wage w/p_C which clears the labour market are determined by the intersection of the curves $p\text{MP}_{\text{LF}}$ and MP_{LC} at point B. The initial equilibrium wage measured in cloth units is $(w/p_C)_0$. Now suppose there is an increase in p, the relative price of food. This shifts $p\text{MP}_{\text{LF}}$ up and to the right while MP_{LC} is unaffected. In Figure 1.8a, the equilibrium shifts from B to G.

Figure 1.8b is the same as Figure 1.8a except that the vertical axes measure variables in units of food (e.g. w/p_F). In this case, the curves represent

$$\frac{\text{VMP}_{\text{LF}}}{p_F} = \text{MP}_{\text{LF}} \quad \text{and} \quad \frac{\text{VMP}_{\text{LC}}}{p_F} = \left(\frac{p_C}{p_F}\right) \text{MP}_{\text{LC}} = \left(\frac{1}{p}\right) \text{MP}_{\text{LC}}.$$

Initial equilibrium occurs where the two curves intersect at A. An increase in p shifts the cloth curve $(1/p)\text{MP}_{\text{LC}}$ down but does not affect the food curve MP_{LF}. Equilibrium moves from A to E.

What can we conclude about movements in real factor returns? From Figure 1.8a, we see that w/p_C goes up from $(w/p_C)_0$ to $(w/p_C)_1$ whereas Figure 1.8b tells us that w/p_F falls from $(w/p_F)_0$ to $(w/p_F)_1$. In other words, the nominal wage goes up but proportionately less than the price of food. What happens to a worker's real wage depends on the proportions in which she consumes the two goods. If we suppose that "food" is a small part of the consumer's budget, "cloth" being a "composite" of all other goods, then it seems reasonable to suppose that the real wage rises and that workers in both sectors stand to gain from a tariff on food.

In analysing the movements of the real returns to the specific factors, we are assisted by the fact that the quantities of K_F and K_C are fixed. Hence the direction of change in the aggregate return to the specific factor indicates the direction of change of the return per unit of the factor. In addition, the assumption of constant returns to scale implies that total factor rewards in each sector just exhaust the value of output. The value of output in a sector is just the area under the relevant VMP curve up to the labour employed in the sector. Subtracting the sector's wage bill from this yields the return to the specific factor. Thus, in Figure 1.8a, the total payment to K_C in terms of cloth falls from area RBN ($=RBL_0O_C - NBL_0O_C$) to RGM ($=RGL_1O_C - MGL_1O_C$). Thus, r_C/p_C falls, and because p_C/p_F also falls, we see that

$$\frac{r_C}{p_F} = \left(\frac{r_C}{p_C} \right) \cdot \left(\frac{p_C}{p_F} \right)$$

falls. Hence the real return to cloth-specific capital falls unambiguously. From Figure 1.8b, the total payment to K_F rises from BAC to BED, r_F/p_F rises and so

$$\frac{r_F}{p_C} = \left(\frac{r_F}{p_F} \right) \cdot \left(\frac{p_F}{p_C} \right)$$

also rises. The real return to food-specific capital unambiguously rises.

In summary, the factor which is specific to the sector whose relative price has risen unambiguously gains (because no other units of the factor can move into the sector and drive down the return); and the factor specific to the other sector unambiguously loses (because it cannot move to take advantage of higher returns in the other sector). The mobile factor can gain or lose in real terms depending on the share of the protected good in that factor's budget. Insofar as any single good is a small proportion of the consumer budget, it seems likely that the mobile factor will gain from higher tariffs on a particular good, its interests coinciding with those of the specific factor in the protected sector.

The specific-factors model is seen to provide at least a partial explanation of why labour and capital in a particular sector may find it in their short-run interests to collude in seeking tariff protection (even though it may be against the long-run interests of one of them). Various writers have attempted to synthesise this model and the mobile factors model. Mayer (1974), Mussa (1974) and Neary (1978) all consider the adjustment path of the economy with sector-specific capital gradually becoming mobile in the longer run. Grossman (1983) adopts a somewhat different approach, assuming that capital has some intersectoral mobility even in the short run. He defines a measure of this intersectoral mobility, the magnitude of which determines the effect of a tariff on factor incomes. The Stolper–Samuelson and specific-factor results then emerge as special cases.

1.5.   Determination of world prices

So far, we have confined our attention to the case of a single country facing given world prices. Although many important questions can be answered in this context (e.g. the effects of trade policy in a small country), other situations and

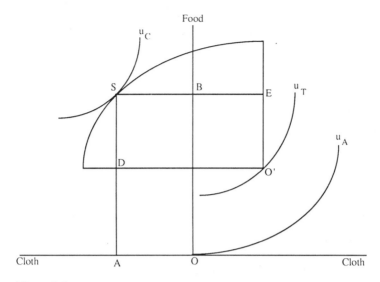

Figure 1.9

problems make it necessary to look at the world market as a whole. For example, the trade policies of large countries such as the United States and Japan usually have significant effects beyond their borders, which require explicit analysis. Accordingly, we now bring the rest of the world into the model and consider how world prices are determined.

To facilitate the analysis, we must first introduce some new analytical tools: *trade-indifference curves* and *offer curves*. Both are motivated by the observation that world prices are the outcome of amounts offered for trade (i.e. exports and imports). It is thus convenient to redefine our social indifference map and the aggregate consumer problem in terms of excess demands and supplies. The trade-indifference curve, a geometric device devised by Meade, does precisely this (see Meade, 1952). At the same time, it gives us a simple way of defining offer curves. Figure 1.9 illustrates the basic idea.

Consumption of cloth is measured along the horizontal axis to the left of the origin O. Consumption of food is measured on the vertical axis above O. Let u_C be an arbitrarily chosen community-indifference curve in the top left-hand quadrant, a locus of bundles of food and cloth that the community regards as equally desirable. Now (the reason will become clear shortly), shift the production frontier up and to the right (initially, its origin is at O and its location is the same quadrant as u_C) until it touches u_C at a consumption point S on u_C. The new origin of the production frontier is at O'. It is then possible to show that if one slides the production block along so that it is always tangential to u_C, its

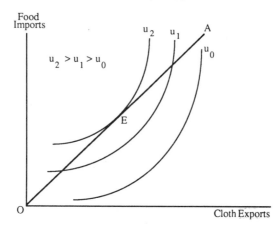

Figure 1.10

origin generates a "trade-indifference curve", which gives the combinations of excess demands and supplies of food and cloth yielding utility u_C. This curve is illustrated as u_T in Figure 1.9.

To see that O' (for example) gives a combination of exports and imports which society regards as equivalent to consumption at S (given the production frontier), we note that

   i.   Food production $= DS$ and food consumption $= AS$, so food imports $= AD$.

   ii.   Cloth production $= O'D = ES$ and cloth consumption $= BS$, so cloth exports $= BE$.

In other words, the co-ordinates of the new origin (O') of the translated production block are, respectively, the imports of food and the exports of cloth associated with consumption point S, given the economy's technology. Clearly, if we slide the production block tangential to u_C, the origin O' traces the locus of points u_T in the import-export plane; and these points all involve utility u_C. Furthermore, if we shift the production block so that it is tangent to higher community-indifference curves, trade-indifference curves involving higher utility levels than u_C can be mapped. In particular, we note that the trade-indifference curve through the origin corresponds to the level of utility associated with autarky and is therefore labelled u_A.

A typical trade-indifference map is illustrated in Figure 1.10. It can be shown (see Appendix 1 for a formal proof) that these curves have the same curvature properties as the underlying consumption-indifference map. Curves which are higher and to the left correspond to higher levels of welfare. We can also use Figure 1.10 to illustrate how the economy's actual imports and exports are determined. If the free-trade consumption point were at S in Figure 1.9, then S would be a point at which both the indifference curve u_C and the shifted production block through S have a slope equal to the world relative price of food. At point O', u_T has this same slope. Thus, the actual import–export point is a point of tangency between a world price line and a trade-indifference curve. The world price line satisfying the zero balance of trade condition is a ray through the origin with the equation

$$p_F M_F = p_C E_C, \quad \text{that is,} \quad M_F = \left(\frac{p_C}{p_F} \right) E_C$$

where M_F denotes food imports, E_C denotes cloth exports and p_F and p_C are the world prices of food and cloth, respectively. The graph of this equation is sometimes called the economy's terms of trade line (because its slope is the economy's terms of trade p_C/p_F). The equilibrium trade point for the economy in Figure 1.10 is therefore at point E where the terms-of-trade line (OA) is tangent to a trade-indifference curve (u_2).

It is now possible to generate the economy's *offer curve*. To understand the concept of an offer curve it may be helpful to refer to Figure 1.3b. At the terms of trade (relative world prices) assumed in that diagram, domestic equilibrium was achieved with consumption at C and production at P, implying that, at those relative prices, the home country wished to export (or offer) BP units of cloth in exchange for BC units of food imports. Clearly, by rotating the terms of trade line p^*, one could generate the equilibrium offers (cloth exports) by the home country and graph them against the associated level of food imports for different relative prices. In terms of Figure 1.10, this same price–consumption curve can be generated by rotating the terms-of-trade line through the origin and tracing its points of tangency with trade-indifference curves. This relationship, when graphed in the import–export plane, is termed the *domestic offer curve*. Such a curve is illustrated in Figure 1.11.

Once again we note that the slope of a ray from the origin to a point on the offer curve (such as OT in Figure 1.11) gives the terms of trade at that point (because it measures the amount of food OF which can be obtained by exporting a particular quantity of cloth OC) and that steeper rays correspond to better terms of trade for the country in question. A useful property of the offer-curve diagram (which we shall be using in our analysis of trade wars in Chapter 4) is that any point on the offer curve can be socially ranked relative to any other simply by comparing the trade-indifference curves through the two points. Thus, in the case illustrated, point T_2 is seen to be preferred to T_1 (because the trade-indifference curve u_2 lies above curve u_1), which is, in turn, preferred to T.

Before we proceed, it is worth pausing to consider the shape of the offer curve illustrated in Figure 1.11. Suppose the terms of trade improve from, say, OT to OT_1. We can distinguish three effects of this higher relative price of cloth:

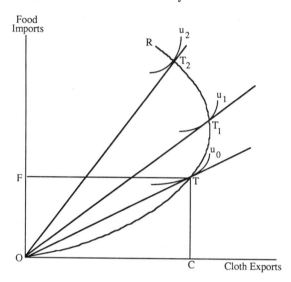

Figure 1.11

i. *A production effect* as resources move out of the food sector into the cloth sector in response to higher relative prices in that sector.
ii. *A substitution effect* as consumers switch demand from cloth to food.
iii. An *income effect* (due to the improved real income associated with higher relative export price) leading to increased consumption of both goods (assuming no inferior goods).

Effects (i) and (ii) both serve to increase cloth exports and food imports. Effect (iii), on the other hand, though it reinforces any increase in food imports, tends to reduce cloth exports. If the output and substitution effects [(i) and (ii)] dominate, then the net effect is an increase in both imports and exports. This is the case illustrated as the upward-sloping segment (OT_1) of the offer curve in Figure 1.11. In this region, the offer curve is said to be *elastic*. If the terms of trade improve further (from OT_1 to, say, OT_2) and the income effect (iii) dominates the production and substitution effects, then a higher quantity of imports is associated with a *reduced* quantity of exports, and the curve is negatively sloped. This backward-bending part of the curve $(T_1T_2R$ in Figure 1.11) is termed the *inelastic* region. This "elasticity" terminology derives from the fact that the offer curve has a positive slope if and only if the home country's elasticity of demand for imports (with respect to the relative price of the importable) exceeds unity (see Appendix 1 for proof).

It is now a routine matter to derive the equilibrium world terms of trade from

Home country's food imports
Foreign country's food exports

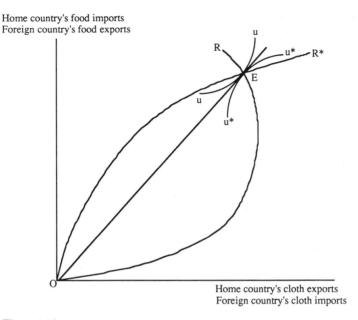

Figure 1.12

an offer-curve diagram (Figure 1.12). Assume that the world consists of two countries, the home country and the "rest of the world" (the foreign country). Curve OR is the home country's offer curve as just defined; OR* is the foreign country's offer curve, similarly derived. The intersection of these two curves at *E* in Figure 1.12 determines the world equilibrium relative price, as given by the slope of *OE*. Moreover, given the definition of the offer curves, the price line *OE* is tangent at *E* to trade-indifference curves in both countries (*u* and *u** are the trade-indifference curves of the home country and the foreign country, respectively).

The equilibrium world price usually changes if either country's offer curve shifts. Shifts in a particular country's offer curve can be caused by changes in its basic production and demand parameters (e.g. changes in factor endowments and changes in tastes) or by imposition of tariffs, subsidies and other distortions. Of course, such shifts do not affect world relative prices if the country in question is small in world markets. A small country faces a *perfectly elastic foreign offer curve*, which is represented by a straight line through the origin (e.g. *OE*); that is, the foreign offer curve defines the terms of trade, and shifts in a small country's own offer curve serve only to change the quantities traded at that terms-of-trade. We shall return to the offer-curve diagram when we analyse the effects of trade restrictions imposed by a large country in Chapter 4.

1.6.   Summary

Our aim has been to introduce some tools of trade theory that we shall be using in subsequent chapters. The basic two-sector trade model has been presented in two forms: (i) the version with two factors that are freely mobile between sectors (the Heckscher–Ohlin–Samuelson model), and (ii) the version with three factors, of which one is mobile between sectors and the other two are sector specific (the Ricardo–Viner–Jones specific-factors model). The two models have very different implications for income distribution, with the mobile-factors model predicting that one factor gains and the other loses from a policy such as a tariff and the specific-factors model predicting that both the specific factor in the protected sector and the mobile factor probably gain from a tariff. Thus, the specific-factors model appears to correspond more closely to observed protectionist positions adopted by various pressure groups.

The proposition that an economy can gain from trade is also fundamental to any analysis of protection policies. The result is quite robust to various generalizations of the model. In particular, the gains from trade do not depend on the presence of inter-sectoral factor mobility and therefore apply to both versions of the model presented in this chapter. We shall return to this point in the next chapter when we consider the welfare costs of a tariff.

The reader should be sure to have a good grasp of the basic indifference curve–production frontier diagram (Figure 1.3) and the offer curve–trade-indifference curve diagram (Figures 1.11 and 1.12) before proceeding.

CHAPTER 2

Protection for a small country

In the modern world, national governments have at their disposal a wide range of policies for restricting international trade and protecting domestic industries. These include production subsidies, price support schemes, tariffs on imports, export subsidies and taxes, import quotas and local content schemes. Some of these policies also serve as sources of government revenue. In this chapter and the next we analyse a range of these policies in the competitive framework of the HOS model developed in Chapter 1. Because the case of tariffs is sufficient to illustrate all of the basic principles, we look at tariffs first. However, later we consider some of the many other policies which are frequently used. These non-tariff distortions to trade have in recent years assumed increasing importance as the principal impediments to free trade while tariffs themselves have been negotiated to a very low level.

Here and in Chapter 3, we confine our attention to the case of a country which is "small" in all relevant world markets, facing a perfectly elastic supply of imports and a perfectly elastic demand for its exports. In other words, the country cannot affect its terms of trade. Of course, there are many interesting cases in which countries are large enough to affect the price at which they buy or sell certain commodities, and these are considered in Chapter 4. The model of this chapter provides a convenient starting point and serves to identify the domestic effects of protection which arise independently of any market power a country may have in particular commodities.

2.1. Tariffs in the HOS model

We begin by considering the effects of a tariff in the two-sector HOS model, starting from a situation of free trade. We assume that there are no distortions (other than the tariff) in the economy. In Figure 2.1, points P_F and C_F represent free-trade production and consumption, respectively. Line p^* represents the economy's consumption possibilities at world prices. Now suppose that a tariff is imposed on imports of food. Given the fixed terms of trade and perfect competition in domestic markets, the immediate effect of the tariff is to increase the price of food for domestic producers and consumers by the amount of the tariff per unit of food, with the new domestic price line flatter than p^*, say p_T. This increase in the relative price of food induces resources to move from the

25

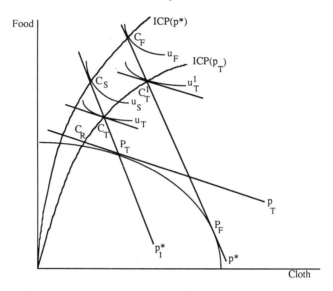

Figure 2.1

cloth sector into the food sector with the economy's production point shifting to P_T, the point of tangency between the price line p_T and the production frontier.

Identification of the new consumption point is less straightforward, but is simplified if we keep in mind the following points:

i.   Trade between the home country and the rest of the world is at world prices.

ii. The economy's expenditure equals its income at world prices (it can only consume a bundle of goods equal in value, at world prices, to what it produces).

iii. Domestic consumers face the tariff-distorted domestic price ratio.

Putting this information together we see that the economy's consumption point under the tariff is on the world-price line (see i) through production point P_T (see ii) and on an indifference curve tangent to a domestic price line (see iii). Thus, in Figure 2.1, the consumption point is at C_T on price line p_1^*, where that line intersects the income consumption path for relative prices p_T [ICP(p_T)]. ICP(p_T) lies to the right of ICP(p^*), the income consumption path for the world price ratio p^*, because at a higher relative price of food a smaller proportion of a given income is spent on food.

The effects of the tariff can now be listed as follows:

i.   The tariff causes resources to be shifted from the unprotected sector (cloth) to the protected sector (food).

ii. Consumption of the importable good falls, with income and substitution effects reinforcing each other (assuming food is non-inferior); consumption of the exportable good may rise or fall depending on the relative strengths of opposing income and substitution effects (assuming cloth is non-inferior).

iii. There is a fall in imports of food as a result of effects i and ii.

iv. There is a fall in community welfare under the tariff compared with free trade (from u_F to u_T in Figure 2.1).

v. Even if resources are immobile between sectors, with production remaining at P_F under the tariff, there is nevertheless a fall in both consumption and imports of food and an associated welfare loss (from u_F to u_T^1 in Figure 2.1). Even in the absence of production effects, the tariff makes the community worse off by distorting the prices faced by consumers.

vi. The welfare loss (from u_F to u_T^1) identified in effect v is referred to as the *consumption loss* from the tariff. The remainder of the welfare loss (from u_T^1 to u_T when resources are mobile between sectors) can be interpreted as the loss in real income arising from the change in production induced by the distortion in producers' prices. This is usually termed the *production loss* from the tariff. An alternative way of viewing the decomposition of the total welfare loss into consumption and production effects is obtained by assuming that initially production shifts to P_T but that consumers continue to face world prices. This would put consumption at C_S with a community-indifference curve tangent to p_1^*. The production loss is the resulting shift from u_F to u_S. Now let consumers also face the tariff-distorted price. Consumption then moves from C_S to C_T, the consumption loss being the associated fall in utility (from u_S to u_T).

vii. Even though income equals expenditure at world prices, it is clear from Figure 2.1 that expenditure exceeds the value of output at domestic prices (C_T is on a higher domestic price line than p_T). The reason for this is that we have implicitly assumed that the government recycles the tariff revenue back to the community. The expenditure of this recycled revenue by the community accounts for consumption being at C_T rather than C_R. In addition, the drawing of Figure 2.1 reflects the assumption that the tariff is redistributed in a non-distortionary way (the domestic price line through C_T is parallel to p_T).

The foregoing analysis illustrates the welfare loss incurred by a small open economy imposing a tariff. However, the welfare comparison of the free trade and tariff-distorted equilibria is qualitative only. Because utility is assumed to be ordinal, the indices attached to the various indifference curves cannot be used to measure the welfare gain or loss from a particular policy. Nevertheless,

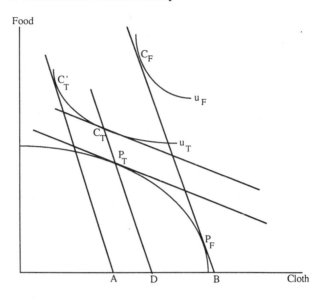

Figure 2.2

it is possible to define measures of welfare change which are expressed in the same units as income. The best known such measures are the *compensating variation* (CV) and the *equivalent variation* (EV) defined by Hicks (1946, pp. 330–3) as well as the much discussed (and misused) *Marshallian consumer surplus.* [1] Where possible, we confine our attention to the equivalent variation, which is the measure most commonly encountered in the tariff literature. The concept is illustrated with the aid of Figure 2.2 in which C_T and C_F again represent the respective tariff-distorted and free-trade consumption points.

Consider the following question: Starting in free-trade equilibrium C_F, what is the maximum income (valued at free-trade prices) which consumers would give up to avoid imposition of the tariff (i.e. to be on indifference curve u_T)? This hypothetical sacrifice of income which is seen by consumers as "equivalent" to the tariff is the *equivalent variation measure of loss from the tariff*. In terms of Figure 2.2, it is the parallel shift of the income line C_FB required to yield a consumption equilibrium on indifference curve u_T. The income line would, in fact, have to shift to position $C_T'A$ where it is tangent to u_T. If we measure this loss of income in units of the exportable, it amounts to AB units of cloth. It consists of a production cost *DB* (which equals the difference in GNP between P_F and P_T valued at world prices) and a consumption cost *AD*.

This EV measure of the *deadweight loss* (DWL) of a tariff can be alternatively illustrated using a more familiar demand–supply framework. Figure 2.3a is a general equilibrium demand–supply representation in which the rela-

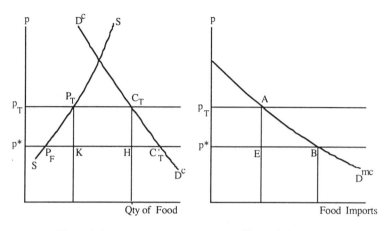

Figure 2.3a   Figure 2.3b

tive price of food (p) is graphed against the quantity of food. SS is the "general equilibrium" supply curve which graphs the equilibrium output of food for each relative price as determined by tangencies of price lines and the production frontier. D^c is the compensated demand curve giving the equilibrium food consumption for different relative prices if income were to adjust to maintain utility at u_T. p^* and p_T are the relative prices of food under free trade and the tariff, respectively. Points C_T, C'_T, P_T and P_F in Figure 2.3a correspond to the similarly labelled points in Figure 2.2. Area $p_TC_TC'_Tp^*$ in Figure 2.3a then measures the gross loss of income to consumers arising from the tariff. Of this, $p_TP_TP_Fp^*$ is transferred to specific factors in the protected sector, and P_TC_THK is recycled tariff revenue. The deadweight loss is then given by the residual "triangles" P_TKP_F (which equals DB in Figure 2.2) and $C_TC'_TH$ (which equals AD in Figure 2.2). An alternative representation which we shall use from time to time is given in Figure 2.3b. Curve D^{mc} is the economy's compensated demand for imports; it is obtained by subtracting SS in Figure 2.3a horizontally from D^c. The area p_TABp^* is the total loss of consumer surplus under the tariff net of the transfer to rents in the protected sector (it equals $P_TC_TC'_TP_F$ in Figure 2.3a), and p_TAEp^* is clearly the tariff revenue. The triangular area AEB is the sum of the two triangles P_TKP_F and $C_TC'_TH$ in Figure 2.3a and is therefore an alternative representation of the EV measure of the deadweight loss of the tariff.

The triangular deadweight loss areas identified in Figure 2.3 are often referred to as "Harberger triangles", a reflection of the role of Harberger in developing and popularizing such measures of the deadweight loss of tax policies (see e.g. Harberger, 1964). The task of estimating them and the question of whether they are of an empirically important magnitude are matters which have occupied the attention of many economists. It is a question we shall return to in Section 2.8.

Before proceeding, we again emphasize that the EV measure is based on the *compensated* demand curve associated with the tariff-distorted utility level u_T. However, in many cases (e.g. partial equilibrium analysis of monopolistic markets), we shall be forced to work with the ordinary (constant income) demand curve, with the relevant areas reflecting Marshallian consumer surplus. Unfortunately, Marshallian consumer surplus is, in general, an unsatisfactory measure of welfare change: in particular, when more than one price is changing, it is not uniquely defined. On the other hand, when only one price is changing, it is well defined and can be shown to lie between the EV and CV measures. To the extent that many of the problems we shall be considering involve a change in only one price, this should be reassuring, but the reader should be aware of the shortcomings of consumer surplus as a welfare measure and regard analysis which uses it as illustrative only. A more complete discussion of these issues and a comparison of the different welfare measures can be found in most modern texts on welfare economics (e.g. Broadway and Bruce, 1984; see also Auerbach, 1985).

2.2.   Tariffs and non-economic objectives

A clear result that emerges from the preceding analysis is that for a small country (in the absence of other distortions) restricted trade under a tariff is inferior to free trade. However, casual observation suggests that governments do not always pursue such a socially optimal course. In particular, governments are in the business of trading off the competing demands of various political lobbies, a process which does not necessarily guarantee efficient outcomes. At this stage we do not wish to pursue the question of how pressure groups determine government policy (see Chapter 8). However, such underlying political pressures may often be manifested in a simple form: a government decides to use a policy such as a tariff to achieve a target level for some well-defined variable (e.g. a minimum level of output for an import-competing sector, a target level of revenue, or a balance of trade objective). Where such a "non-economic" objective is pursued, tariffs (or other equivalent forms of trade taxes) are often used. For example, various types of trade policies were contemplated as a means of protecting jobs in the U.S. automobile industry from a perceived threat from Japanese auto imports. Eventually, voluntary export restraints (another type of trade restriction; see Chapter 4) were introduced by Japanese car exporters. More generally, the *escape clause* in the U.S. Trade Agreements Act permits U.S. industries to petition the U.S. International Trade Commission to reverse negotiated tariff reductions where such tariff reductions can be shown to be causing serious injury to the domestic industry. Thus, there

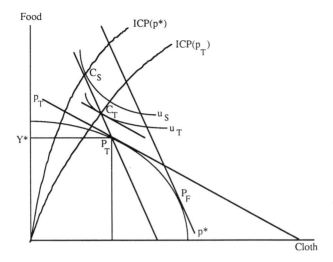

Figure 2.4

appears to be a widespread presumption that certain non-economic objectives should be achieved via tariffs or similar import restrictions. The question to be asked here is whether restrictions on international trade, specifically tariffs, represent the most efficient means of achieving the stated objective or whether there is a superior instrument. This problem has been analysed by a number of authors, in particular Bhagwati and Srinivasan (1969) and Vandendorpe (1974), and the answer turns out to be very simple: the best instrument for achieving a particular target is a policy which directly affects the target variable – for example, an output subsidy to an industry is the best means of achieving a target level of output in that sector and a tariff on imports is the best means of restricting imports to a desired level. We illustrate this proposition for two objectives.

(a)   Output objective

Suppose the government wishes to achieve an assured level Y^* of output of the importable (Figure 2.4). To realize this outcome under a tariff, the tariff has to be set at a rate which rotates the domestic price line from its free-trade position p^* to position p_T, tangent to the production frontier at food output Y^* (production point P_T). Consumption and welfare under the tariff are C_T and u_T, respectively.

Suppose now that, instead of a tariff, the output objective has been realized by a production subsidy to producers of food. Like the tariff, the subsidy has to be set to yield a domestic producers' price p_T. However, the production subsidy

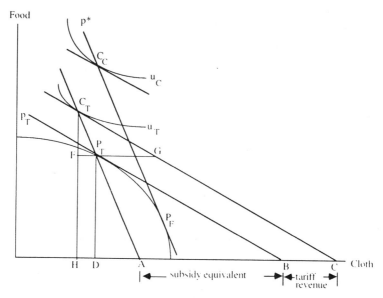

Figure 2.5

does not distort the consumer price away from the free-trade level. Accordingly, consumption is located where the ICP for $p*$ cuts the world price line through P_T, at C_S in Figure 2.4. Welfare is at u_S, higher than under the tariff. From our discussion of the consumption and production effects of tariffs in the previous section (effect vi), it is clear that the production subsidy incurs the production loss of the tariff but avoids the consumption loss (the difference between u_S and u_T in Figures 2.1 and 2.4) because it does not distort the price facing consumers. Thus, if a target output of the importable is the objective, a production subsidy appears to be a preferable instrument to a tariff.

At this stage, we should remind ourselves that any subsidy has to be financed. In the case of the output subsidy just considered, it has been assumed that financing is effected in a non-distortionary way. Nevertheless, the cost to the taxpayer of such a subsidy is still of interest to policy makers (and taxpayers!). This cost is referred to as the *subsidy equivalent* (SE) of the tariff and equals the tariff per unit multiplied by output under the tariff. In Figure 2.5 it is shown, in units of cloth, as distance AB on the horizontal axis; it is the difference between the value of food output at domestic producers' price (measured in cloth units) and food output valued at world price (measured in cloth units) (i.e. $DB - DA = AB$). Because it is so easy to estimate and because it gives both politicians and the public a simple measure of the total cost to taxpayers of using an output subsidy to replicate the protective effect of a tariff, it is not surprising to find subsidy equivalents cited frequently in empirical studies of protection.

Figure 2.5 can also be used to illustrate the tariff revenue measured in units of cloth. Imports of food are FC_T, and the tariff revenue is the difference between the value of these imports at tariff distorted prices (FG units of cloth) and their value at world prices (FP_T units of cloth). Thus, the tariff revenue is P_TG units of cloth (BC on the horizontal axis). This verifies our earlier claim that, under a tariff, expenditure exceeds the value of output at domestic prices because of the recycled tariff revenue BC.

Now suppose that lump-sum taxation is not available as a means of financing the subsidy. Does the subsidy retain its superiority over the tariff in such situations? To answer this question we use Figure 2.5 to consider the combination of a production subsidy to food and a consumption tax on food, each at the same rate as the tariff. Under the production subsidy by itself, production is at P_T, and the cost of financing the subsidy (the subsidy equivalent) is AB units of cloth. If the consumption tax is also imposed, consumers and producers face the same prices as under the tariff, so production and consumption are the same as under the tariff. The revenue from the consumption tax is the difference between the value of food consumption at distorted prices and the value of that consumption at domestic prices. Measured in units of cloth, this is given by AC ($HC - HA$ in Figure 2.5), which is clearly just sufficient to finance the subsidy (AB) and have the same residual revenue (BC) as the tariff. It is therefore clear that *the tariff is equivalent to an output subsidy to the importable financed by a consumption tax on the importable, both at the same rate as the tariff.* The gross revenue from the consumption tax in this situation is generally referred to as the *consumer tax equivalent* (CTE) of the tariff. Obviously, the CTE equals the sum of the SE and the tariff revenue. The CTE of a tariff is, like the SE, an easily estimated quantity, which is cited in many applied studies.

Returning now to our earlier question of how a subsidy might be ranked vis-à-vis a tariff when it has to be financed by distortionary taxes, we can conclude the following: If the subsidy is financed by a consumption tax at the same rate on the same good, then it is the same as the tariff, no better, no worse.[2] On the other hand, if we have the option of taxing a good with a less elastic demand than the importable, then we should be able to finance the subsidy with a lower distortion than under the tariff.[3] Given this option, the subsidy still seems to possess considerable appeal.

Another result is implicit in the foregoing analysis. You will have noticed that the consumption tax which was imposed in conjuction with the production subsidy at the same rate as the tariff yielded more revenue than the tariff (enough extra revenue in fact to finance the production subsidy). It is therefore clear that a consumption tax is a more efficient tool for raising revenue than

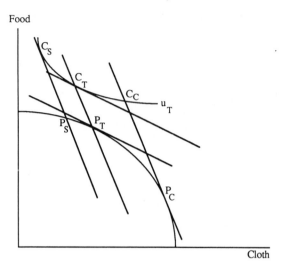

Figure 2.6

tariffs. Indeed this should be obvious, given that a consumption tax applies to more units than a tariff (all units consumed rather than just imports). However, given that a consumption tax by itself only distorts the price faced by consumers, with no distortion to production, it is even more attractive. Under a consumption tax at the same rate as the tariff, production is at the free-trade point P_F in Figure 2.5, while consumption is at C_C with welfare u_C being higher than under the tariff, a reflection of the absence of the tariff's production distortion. This clear superiority of consumption taxes as revenue-raising devices should be carefully noted, particularly given the widespread use of tariffs apparently for this purpose.

(b)   Import restriction objective

Suppose now that it is desired (possibly for balance-of-payments reasons) to limit the volume of imports to some target level. (This is easy in the present case because there is only one importable good; we consider the case of several importables later.) Here we compare a tariff with a consumption tax and a production subsidy and show that it is superior to both as a means of import restriction. Naturally, this type of argument is somewhat inconclusive because there may be some other policy we have not thought of which is superior to the tariff. Proof that the tariff is indeed the best policy for pursuing import restriction can be found in Appendix 2, together with formal proofs of other optimality results for the achievement of non-economic objectives.

Figure 2.6 shows equilibrium under a given tariff with production at P_T, consumption at C_T and welfare u_T. Let us now consider (i) a production subsidy to food producers and (ii) a consumption tax on food, each of which is designed to leave the community as well off as it is under the tariff (i.e. on indifference curve u_T).

Under a production subsidy, consumers face the world price ratio while producers face a distorted price. Consumers are thus indifferent between the tariff and the subsidy at point C_S, where a world price line is tangent to indifference curve u_T. Because the production point must lie on the same world price line as the consumption point, the relevant subsidy must be such that production occurs at P_S, where the world price line through C_S cuts the production frontier. Because of the concavity of the production frontier and the convexity of the indifference surface, imports are higher under this subsidy than under the tariff.

In contrast, under a consumption tax, producers face the world price while consumers face a distorted price. Thus, under a consumption tax, output is at P_C whatever the tax. For the tax to yield the same utility (u_T) as the tariff, consumers must be at point C_C, where the world price line through P_C cuts u_T. Again, given the curvature of the relevant surfaces, imports are higher than under the tariff.

Thus the community is indifferent between the tariff and a production subsidy or consumption tax, either of which yields higher imports than the tariff. To restrict imports to the same extent as the tariff, both of these instruments would have to be set at an even higher rate, thus reducing community welfare below u_T. It follows that the tariff is a more efficient instrument for restricting imports than either of these alternatives.

These illustrations lend support to the quite general proposition stated at the beginning of this section: The most efficient means of achieving a particular target is by a policy which directly affects the target variable. Of course, the target variable may not always be defined as simply as the output or the imports of a single homogeneous good. Quite often, the government will intervene to protect the output of an industry which comprises several distinct commodities. It may wish to limit the overall level of imports or the imports of a particular type of product (e.g. automobiles). In all of these cases, the target variable is an aggregate comprising a number of heterogeneous commodities. What is the optimal policy in such situations? Not surprisingly, the broad conclusions obtained for the one-good case also apply here: use tariffs for controlling imports, production subsidies for achieving a target composite output, and so forth. However, the form that the tariff or subsidy should take will vary depending on whether the government's objective is expressed in value or volume terms. Examples exist of both types of objective. It is quite common for limits to be placed on the total volume of automobile imports. The voluntary export restraints imposed by the Japanese government on automobile exports to the

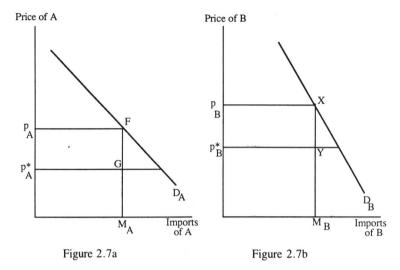

Price of A   Price of B

Figure 2.7a   Figure 2.7b

United States are restrictions on the number of vehicles exported. Similarly, the market-sharing arrangement which protects Australian car manufacturers is enforced by restrictions on the total volume of car imports. Although neither of these objectives is enforced by means of a tariff, the point is that the underlying objective is a restriction on the total volume of imports in a particular category. On the other hand, general balance-of-trade objectives and target output levels in a multi-product industry are of necessity expressed in value terms.

We begin by noting that for a small country facing fixed relative prices of its traded goods, the various goods in the category may be safely aggregated into a single commodity (regardless of whether a volume or a value objective is used), so the analysis and conclusions of the two-good model must apply here (if output is your objective, subsidize output, and so on). To derive the additional implications of product heterogeneity within a category, we shall consider volume and value objectives in turn. Before doing so, we note that tariffs (or indeed any tax or subsidy) can be defined in two ways: specific and ad valorem. A *specific tariff* is expressed as t dollars per unit of the good while an *ad valorem tariff* is expressed as t per cent of the c.i.f. import price. Although in most circumstances the form in which a tariff is expressed does not make any difference, the distinction is important in the present problem.

Suppose that the government wishes to use a tariff (or a set of tariffs) to limit the *volume* of imports of a class of good (e.g. automobiles) of which there are two product types (e.g. big cars and small cars) denoted A and B. Figure 2.7 illustrates the import demand curve for each of these product types (A in Figure 2.7a, B in Figure 2.7b). D_A and D_B are the respective import demand curves for A and B, with p_A^* and p_B^* denoting their world prices, p_A and p_B their tariff-inclusive domestic prices and M_A and M_B the quantities imported in the tariff-distorted situation. It is now straightforward to show that a uniform specific tariff (i.e. one which is the same for both A and B) minimizes the total deadweight loss for the product group.

Given that the total volume of imports is fixed ($M_A + M_B = \bar{M}$, say), then total deadweight loss for the two product types is minimized by equating marginal deadweight loss for A and B. To see this, consider the effect on total DWL of reallocating one unit of total imports from good B to good A. If the reduction in deadweight loss associated with an extra unit of imports of A exceeds the increase in DWL associated with the foregone unit of imports of B, then the reallocation would decrease total DWL. Reallocations of imports away from B towards A should clearly continue until the deadweight losses for the marginal units of each good are equalized. Of course, the marginal deadweight loss for each product type (FG for A and XY for B) is simply the tariff per unit, so the optimum outcome involves equating the tariff per unit across products within the constrained category (i.e. a *uniform specific tariff*).

Now suppose instead that the objective is to constrain the *value* of imports (valued at world prices) to some level $\bar{V}$ (i.e. $p_A^* M_A + p_B^* M_B = \bar{V}$). Because the constraint is now in terms of, say, dollars of imports, an optimal allocation between A and B involves the marginal DWL of a dollar's worth of A being equated to the marginal DWL of a dollar's worth of B. In other words, the DWL associated with the marginal unit (the specific tariff) divided by the world price of the good should be the same for both A and B (i.e. a *uniform ad valorem tariff* across product types).

By similar reasoning, we can show that the optimal instrument to achieve a target volume of output of a group of goods (e.g. a given number of automobiles) is a uniform specific output subsidy, whereas a uniform ad valorem output subsidy is the best means of achieving a target value of output of a heterogeneous class of goods. Applications to other situations are left to the reader.

It is easy to see how departures from the preceding optimal rules bias the quantity composition of a particular restricted class. For example, if a uniform specific tariff is used when the objective is restriction of the value of imports, the marginal deadweight loss associated with a foregone dollar amount of imports (the specific tariff divided by the world price of the good) is lower for more expensive goods than for cheaper goods. In such a case (ignoring income effects), the uniform specific tariff leads to an excessive bias towards expensive goods in the import mix; total deadweight loss would be lower if more of the good(s) with the lower marginal deadweight loss (the cheaper goods) were imported. We shall return to this question when we consider volume and value import quotas in the next chapter and also in relation to voluntary export restraints in Chapter 4.

Although the analysis of trade policy in this chapter has so far been couched entirely in terms of tariffs, it would be quite misleading to suggest that tariffs are the most pervasive form of distortion affecting international trade. The reality is quite the reverse. The two major rounds of multilateral trade negotiations conducted under the auspices of the General Agreement on Tariffs and Trade (GATT) have seen major reductions in tariff levels, with average tariff cuts of about 35 per cent being achieved in the Kennedy Round of negotiations (1967) and further cuts of about 33 per cent being agreed to in the subsequent Tokyo Round (1979). The accumulated effect of these and previous tariff reductions has been to reduce average tariff rates for the industrial countries to about 6 per cent at the time of writing. However, as tariff levels have been reduced, governments have increasingly resorted to a range of other policies to protect their domestic industries. We now consider some of these policies.

2.3.   Quantitative restrictions

Probably the most widespread form of non-tariff distortion to trade is direct quantitative restriction. This may take many forms: explicit import quotas, market sharing schemes, local content schemes and voluntary export restraints (VERs). All of these except VERs are imposed by the importing country. It may be surprising that quantitative trade restrictions are so widely used, given that they violate fundamental GATT prohibitions on the use of non-tariff barriers to trade. However, these rules do permit countries to use instruments such as quotas to protect domestic agriculture, as anti-dumping measures and as temporary "safeguard" actions where imports threaten serious injury to a domestic industry. In addition, voluntary export restraints, being "voluntary", are readily negotiated on a bilateral basis outside the GATT framework and have therefore thrived. Despite their obvious similarity to import quotas, VERs raise some separate issues, and we shall defer consideration of them until Chapter 4. Local content schemes also have some distinctive properties and are treated separately in the next section. We begin with the simplest case of an explicit import quota.

An import quota imposes an upper limit on the home country's imports of a particular commodity or group of commodities. The quota can be expressed in volume or value terms. As we shall see in the next chapter, there are good reasons why a value quota may entail a lower level of distortion than a volume quota; but it is more difficult to administer, not least because of the opportunities for manipulation of import value by transfer pricing. Consequently, volume quotas are the most commonly encountered form of quantitative import restriction. The effects of such a quota are illustrated by adapting Figure 2.3a as shown in Figure 2.8a.

DD represents the (compensated) total demand by residents for the importable good, food (defined at the quota-distorted utility level). Suppose that an

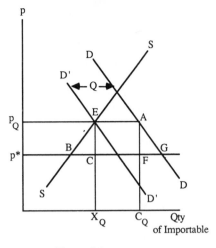

Figure 2.8a

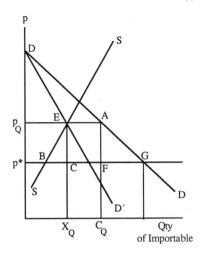

Figure 2.8b

import quota restricts imports to Q (assume the quota is fully utilized). Beyond this quota, all demand must be met from domestic production. We are thus able to derive a demand curve for domestically produced food by subtracting Q horizontally from DD. The resulting curve is represented by $D'D'$ in Figure 2.8a. The equilibrium domestic price of food is then such as to equate the demand for domestically produced food $(D'D')$ to domestic food output (SS). This occurs at point E in Figure 2.8a and results in a domestic relative food price of p_Q. Domestic food output is X_Q, and the economy's consumption of food is C_Q. The deadweight loss under the quota is given by the area $EBC + AFG$. This is the net outcome of a loss to consumers of $p_Q AGp^*$, of which $p_Q EBp^*$ is transferred to rents in the protected sector, and $EAFC$ is transferred from consumers to the ultimate recipients of quota rents. These latter rents arise because the quantitative restriction on imports pushes the equilibrium domestic price of imports (p_Q) above the world price p^*, thus conferring rents of p^*p_Q per unit on the holders of import licences. Whether the import licence holders are the ultimate recipients of these quota rents depends on the manner in which the licences are allocated: if they are given to the importers free of charge, then the importers capture the entire rents. On the other hand, licences may be auctioned by the government and the proceeds distributed in a non-distortionary fashion, in which case the wider community receives some or all of the rents. If the import licences are given to foreign firms who send the profits home, the quota rents accrue to the foreign country and must then be counted as a loss to the economy imposing the quota. Even in this case, however, it is possible for the home economy to capture the rents by imposing a tariff of p^*p_Q per unit on the good in question. Indeed, this may be done anyway as a means of tranferring the quota rents to the taxpayer. Note that such a tariff has no further effect on the domestic price of the importable.

Regardless of the distribution of the quota rents, it is clear that an import quota is equivalent in all important respects to a tariff of p^*p_Q per unit. Such a tariff would yield the same output, consumption and imports of food, the same transfer of rents to the protected industry, the same domestic price and the same deadweight loss triangles as the tariff. In other words, for any given quota, there exists a tariff (termed the *implicit tariff*) which is equivalent to the quota (in all respects except the distribution of the quota rents or tariff revenue). It is thus tempting to conclude that it does not matter whether tariffs or quotas are used to restrict imports, and indeed it is common practice in empirical work to use the tariff-equivalent of any quota (i.e. the implicit tariff) as a convenient measure of the protection afforded by that quota. Nevertheless, it is now well known that this simple equivalence of tariffs and quotas breaks down once we leave the simple static competitive framework of the present chapter. Fundamental differences exist between the two instruments which make use of tariff-equivalents a rather dubious practice. These differences are explored in detail in later chapters.

Not all types of quantitative restriction are of the simple kind just analysed. One common variant is the type of variable import quota implicit in market-sharing schemes. In such schemes, a specified proportion of total domestic demand is to be satisfied by domestic producers. An extreme example of this is the Australian Car Plan, in which vehicle manufacturers are guaranteed 80 per cent of the domestic market. This market share is enforced by a system of variable quotas. Such a scheme is illustrated in Figure 2.8b for the case in which a proportion k of total quantity demanded is to be supplied by domestic producers [equivalently, imports are restricted to proportion $(1 - k)$ of domestic demand]. Figure 2.8b is the same as Figure 2.8a in every respect except the position of the net-demand curve for domestically produced food DD'. This is obtained by taking proportion k of the total amount demanded (as given by DD) at each price [i.e. subtracting proportion $(1 - k)$ of DD horizontally]. Thus the import quota implied by this scheme (the horizontal distance between DD and DD') varies depending on the domestic price. Nevertheless, the effects of this scheme are qualitatively identical to a fixed import quota; domestic price p_Q is determined by the intersection of DD' and SS, deadweight loss from the policy is $(EBC + AFG)$ and so forth.

2.4.   Local content schemes

Another type of quantitative restriction which has been analysed extensively (see Corden, 1971; Grossman, 1981; McCulloch and Johnson, 1973; Mussa, 1984; Vousden, 1987) is the *content protection* or *local content* scheme. As noted by McCulloch and Johnson, this is a type of proportionally distributed quota in which duty-free imports are permitted in some specified proportion to purchases from domestic producers. This type of scheme requires that domestic final good producers purchase a specified minimum proportion of their intermediate goods from domestic firms. Producers satisfying the requirement are given a concessional rate of duty (usually a zero tariff) on their imported intermediate goods or components and may have to pay a penalty tariff on their imports if they violate the local content requirement. As was the case for simple import quotas, content protection requirements may be specified in volume or value terms, with the nature of the specification depending largely on the nature of the goods involved. If the final and intermediate goods are reasonably homogeneous, a volume-based scheme is most likely to be used (e.g. the scheme used in the Australian tobacco industry). On the other hand, if heterogeneous products are involved, a value-based formula is unavoidable (e.g. the local content schemes applying to automobile manufacture in Australia and various Latin American countries and in Canada before the Canada–United States Auto Pact). Although schemes of this type are not as widespread as some other forms of protection, they warrant detailed consideration because (a) they have frequently been applied in a very restrictive manner and (b) they are analytically different from tariffs and quotas because the buyer (in this case the final good manufacturer) pays a two-part price. One of the better documented examples of content protection is the scheme applied to the Australian motor-vehicle industry, which requires that domestically produced components constitute at least 85 per cent of the value of Australian-manufactured cars (calculated on a company basis). This extremely stringent local content requirement affords a very high level of protection to Australian manufacturers of car components and imposes correspondingly high costs on Australian producers of finished motor vehicles. This resulted in a predictable plea for "compensating" protection to be afforded to final good producers in the industry, the result being the guaranteed 80 per cent market share referred to in Section 2.3.

Although many actual content protection schemes are necessarily defined in value terms, for purposes of illustration, we shall analyse the simpler volume-based type of scheme.[4] Consider the following very simple scenario. A final good (autos) is produced using a single intermediate good (engines). In addition, assume a fixed input–output ratio of unity (i.e. one engine per car). Output of the final good is denoted by C, and the intermediate good may be purchased from domestic component producers (in quantity X at a price p) or imported (in quantity X^* at price p^*). Imported and domestically produced components are assumed to be perfect substitutes for each other. All relevant markets are competitive. Because of the fixed input–output ratio, we have

$$C = X + X^*. \tag{1}$$

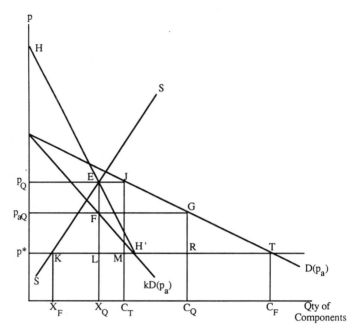

Figure 2.9

Now suppose the government imposes a local content requirement on final good producers which specifies that a proportion k of total components must be purchased domestically, that is,

$$X = k(X + X^*) = kC. \tag{2}$$

Thus, auto producers purchase proportion k of their engines domestically at price p and proportion $(1 - k)$ at the c.i.f. import price p^*, implying that the "average" price of an engine is given by

$$p_a = kp + (1 - k)p^*. \tag{3}$$

Final good producers' total demand for components $(X + X^*)$ is a function $D(p_a)$ of this average price, as illustrated in Figure 2.9. Under the local content rule (2), the demand for domestically produced components as a function of p_a is $kD(p_a)$, which is derived in the same way as curve DD' in Figure 2.8b.

To determine the equilibrium price and output in the domestic components sector, it is necessary to derive the demand for domestically produced components in terms of the domestic price p, which is, after all, the price faced by domestic component producers. This is given by the schedule HH' in Figure 2.9. For any given demand for domestically produced engines, HH' shows the domestic price which car producers are willing to pay [knowing that the remaining proportion $(1 - k)$ of imported engines will cost them only p^* per unit]. Because, by definition, the average price lies between p and p^*, p necessarily lies above p_a, and so HH' lies above the curve $kD(p_a)$ for all average prices above p^*. At point H', $p_a = p = p^*$; so HH' and $kD(p_a)$ coincide at H'.

In Figure 2.9, the equilibrium in the domestic components market is determined by the intersection (point E) of HH' and the supply curve for components (SS). Equilibrium domestic price is p_Q and output of components is X_Q. The average price associated with this domestic output of the intermediate good is p_{aQ} and is read off $kD(p_a)$ at F. At this average price, total demand for components (C_Q) can be read off the total demand curve at G. Compared with free trade, the deadweight loss under the content scheme is given by the area ($EKL + GRT$).[5]

Figure 2.9 can also be used to explore the difference between content protection and a tariff (or, indeed, a quota). The fundamental difference is that under a tariff, the purchaser pays the same price for all units consumed (imported or otherwise), whereas under a local content scheme, the purchaser pays a lower price for imported units than for domestically produced units. This unique property of content protection schemes distinguishes them clearly from tariffs and quotas and gives them one clear advantage: if the aim of the policy is to achieve a target level of output of the intermediate good, then a content protection scheme achieves that objective at a lower welfare cost than a tariff. In terms of Figure 2.9, the tariff per unit which would yield the same output X_Q of components as the content scheme is p^*p_Q. This would result in the same DWL on the production side (EKL) as the content scheme but a higher DWL on the consumption side (JMT compared with GRT for the content scheme) because the price to the user is p_Q under the tariff (the user paying the same price for all units) compared with the lower price of p_{aQ} under the content scheme. This reflects the ability of the content scheme to offer the same price as a tariff (p_Q) to the domestic intermediate goods producer while offering imports to the user at a lower (duty-free) price. It is for this reason that local content schemes are sometimes seen as a relatively desirable form of protection. Unfortunately, however, they share the various other deficiencies of simpler forms of quantitative restrictions. These will become apparent in later chapters.

2.5. Export subsidies

Like quantitative trade restrictions, export subsidies are strictly forbidden under the GATT rules. Nevertheless, like quotas, such subsidies are widespread, particularly in markets for agricultural products and capital goods, and exist in many less transparent guises (e.g. tax concessions to export-related R&D and subsidized export financing). It is worth noting that subsidies to domestic

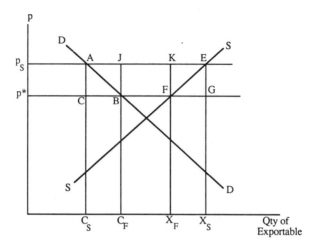

Figure 2.10

producers are permitted under GATT rules provided that the GATT is notified if the subsidies affect international trade. On the other hand, other countries are permitted to impose countervailing duties or import controls when subsidies by foreign governments are deemed to be injurious to domestic industry.

The basic export subsidy is illustrated for an exportable good (cloth) in Figure 2.10, where p^* denotes the f.o.b. export price of cloth (which lies below the c.i.f. import price). This is greater than the price which would clear the domestic market; so under free trade, the excess of domestic production (X_F) over domestic consumption (C_F) would be exported. Now suppose the government decides to subsidize exports of cloth at a rate of p^*p_S per unit and that p_S is less than the c.i.f. import price (not shown). This means that domestic firms can now receive price p_S for each unit exported; so unless domestic consumers also pay p_S, it would pay producers to export all units. The final outcome is that domestic producers receive p_S for all units (so that from their point of view the export subsidy is equivalent to a production subsidy) and expand their output to X_S. Domestic consumers have to pay p_s per unit, leading them to reduce their demand to C_S with exports expanding to ($X_S - C_S$). Although the export subsidy yields the same output as a production subsidy set at the same rate, it differs from a production subsidy in two important respects: (i) it raises the price faced by consumers (recall that this is undistorted by an output subsidy), and (ii) it involves a smaller cost to the taxpayer because it applies to fewer units.

In Figure 2.10, the cost of the subsidy to the taxpayer is $AEGC$ and the cost to consumers is p_SABp^*. Against these costs, there is a transfer to rents in the cloth sector of $p_S EFp^*$. The net outcome is a deadweight loss equal to $(ABC + EFG)$.

An interesting variant of the simple export subsidy is the *incremental export subsidy*. This is a subsidy paid only on the increment in exports over some specified base, and it is largely motivated by a desire to reduce the size of the transfer from taxpayers to producers. The cost to the taxpayer of the subsidy illustrated in Figure 2.10 is $AEGC$; however, only the area $(AJBC + KEGF)$ is needed to yield the same export stimulus, the area $JKFB$ being pure rent to the exporters. An incremental subsidy using, say, the free-trade level of exports as its base would avoid the need to pay this infra-marginal component of the subsidy. This type of subsidy has been employed in a number of countries, the best documented case being the Australian Export Expansion Grants Scheme which was in operation from 1978 to 1983; see Kleiman and Pincus (K&P) (1981, 1982). This scheme was notable for several other features, in particular its use of a moving base determined by particular firms' past exporting performance. As K&P (1981) have noted, use of a moving base leads to cyclical fluctuations in exports and output and also yields export revenue below that achieved using a fixed base. To see this, suppose that in the first period of operation of the scheme the firms increase their exports to the same level as under an ordinary export subsidy (as illustrated in Figure 2.10). Now suppose that this higher level of exports becomes the base for the second period, that is, the subsidy is only payable on any increment in exports above the first period level. Because exports greater than $(X_S - C_S)$ are not profit-maximizing at price p_S (see Figure 2.10), firms do not expand their exports in the second period and so do not qualify for the subsidy in that period. Instead, they face price p^* in the second period and revert to exporting at the free-trade level. In the next period, the whole cycle starts again. Note that, although the subsidy applies only to incremental export units, domestic consumers must still pay the higher price p_S in the period in which exports are increased; otherwise those units could more profitably be sold as incremental exports.

Of course, the cyclical movement of exports will be smoothed (or may disappear entirely; see K&P, 1981, p. 149) if at any time different firms are at different stages of the cycle. However, the cycle is reinstated if the domestic industry consists of a monopolist (K&P, 1981), in which case exports may be shown to fall below the free-trade level in the down-swing of the cycle (see Richardson and Wilkie, 1986).

2.6.   Export taxes and the Lerner symmetry theorem

Export taxes are less widely used by developed countries than export subsidies, but they are often used by third-world countries, primarily as a revenue-raising device. They may also be used by larger countries as a means of favourably influencing their terms of trade (see Chapter 4). Clearly, an export tax has the opposite effect to an export subsidy on domestic price, output and exports. Less obvious is the fact that, given our assumption of a zero balance of trade, an ad valorem export tax has the same effects as an ad valorem tariff at the same rate on the importable. This result, known as *Lerner's symmetry theorem* (Lerner, 1936), is readily established by noting that the two instruments have the same effect on relative prices. Let p_F and p_F^* denote the domestic and world prices of food and p_C and p_C^* be the corresponding prices for cloth, then an ad valorem tax at rate t on cloth exports implies that

$$p_C^* = (1 + t)p_C.$$

Thus, if there is free trade in the importable, the relative domestic price of food in the presence of the export tax is

$$\frac{p_F}{p_C} = \frac{p_F^*(1 + t)}{p_C^*}$$

which is the same as if the export tax were removed and replaced by an ad valorem tariff on imports at rate t [which would imply $p_F = p_F^*(1 + t)$]. The only difference is that the absolute price level under the export tax is lower than under the tariff, by a factor of $1/(1 + t)$. Thus the domestic price line p_T in Figure 2.1 is the same whether the tax at rate t applies to imports or exports. The equilibrium is the same in both cases and yields the same welfare costs. This symmetry between import and export taxes is really not surprising. Given that the country's international trade must balance, it is immaterial at what point in the circular flow of goods a tax is imposed, at the export stage or at the import stage. If exports are taxed, they will fall, and to maintain trade balance, imports must also contract (and vice versa). Of course, the two policies differ in their effects whenever the balance of trade is non-zero,[6] with an export tax tending temporarily to worsen the trade balance and a tariff leading to a temporary balance of trade surplus. However, in the long run, the trade balance equilibrates, and the policies are equivalent.

The Lerner symmetry result may be readily generalized to the case of many goods and is unaffected by the presence of some goods which are not traded internationally at all. In the case of many importables and exportables, a uniform ad valorem tariff at rate t on all imports is equivalent to a uniform ad valorem tax at rate t on all exports. Given that such policies do not alter the relative prices within the respective groups of (export and import) commodities, the above two-good analysis serves to establish this result. Now suppose there are some non-traded goods (e.g. houses) in the economy, goods which for some reason (e.g. high transport costs) are not traded internationally by the country in question. Then, the domestic market for each such good must clear, and the resulting market-clearing prices of these goods are functions of the prices of the traded goods in the economy (exportables and importables). In particular, given that changing all prices in the same proportion does not affect excess demand for a good (i.e. the excess demand functions are homogeneous of degree zero in prices), an equi-proportional change in all traded goods prices will require the prices of non-traded goods to change in the same proportion if their excess demands are to remain zero. Because replacing a tariff at rate t by an export tax at rate t reduces all traded good prices by the same factor of $1/(1 + t)$, equilibrium non-traded goods prices will also fall by this same proportion. Thus, no relative prices have changed, imports and exports are the same under both policies and the symmetry of import and export taxes is preserved (see Woodland, 1982, for a mathematical treatment). Finally, it should also be noted that (i) the foregoing analysis does not depend on the country in question being small in world markets, and (ii) although we have assumed competitive markets, the Lerner Symmetry Theorem continues to hold in the presence of imperfect competition (see Kaempfer and Tower, 1982).

The preceding symmetry result is of interest for several reasons. First, from a purely expository point of view, it means that we do not have to spend any time considering export taxes as a distinct instrument of policy – it is sufficient to analyse tariffs. Second, the result implies that nothing would be changed if a reduction in tariff rates were accompanied by an equivalent increase in export taxes (so that relative traded goods prices are unchanged) and thirdly, the result serves to emphasise the dual role of tariffs as a tax on a nation's exporters, something which is usually overlooked in political debates.

2.7. Preferential government procurement policies

Another type of protection which is employed in most, if not all, countries is the favouring of domestic firms in the granting of government contracts, particularly military contracts. Such schemes closely resemble production subsidies. However, unlike explicit production subsidies, in some cases they create no greater distortion than is present in any government spending. These points are illustrated in Figure 2.11.

Suppose D_G represents the government's demand curve for a particular product (to be met entirely by domestic producers) and D_{G+P} is the horizontal sum of the government and private demand curves for the good (private demand not shown). As usual, SS is the domestic industry's supply curve. As the diagram is drawn, the government's demand for the good exceeds domestic supply at free-trade prices. Thus, to satisfy its demand for the good, the government must pay the price which clears its part of the market, namely, p_G (determined by the intersection of SS and D_G). On the other hand, private

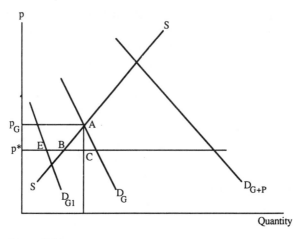

Figure 2.11

consumers of the good can continue to purchase it at the undistorted price p^*. In such a case, the preferential procurement is identical to a production subsidy to the domestic industry of p^*p_G per unit, costing the taxpayer an amount p_GACp^* in excess of a non-preferential procurement with a deadweight loss equal to area ABC and no distortion to private consumers. Of course, it may be that the government demand is less than the domestic industry chooses to produce in free trade (as is the case when the government demand curve is D_{G1} in Figure 2.11). Such relatively small procurements, although nominally preferential, involve no additional distortion; the government satisfies its demand at price p^* (at point E), with the remaining domestic supply of EB going to private buyers. Thus, we expect favourable treatment of domestic firms to make little or no difference unless the government purchase is large relative to the domestic industry.

This completes our initial cataloguing and analysis of the various protection measures. We shall have more to say about most of them (particularly tariffs and import quotas) in later chapters. In addition, there are many minor variants on the above policies which are too numerous to mention here. There are also some important variants, notably variable import levies or export subsidies and voluntary export restraints, which are more appropriately dealt with in a large-country framework. These are considered in detail in Chapter 4. We now return to an important empirical question which was foreshadowed in Section 2.1, the measurement of the deadweight loss in a protected economy.

2.8.   Measuring the costs of a tariff

In Section 2.1 we illustrated the welfare loss associated with a tariff and defined the equivalent variation measure of this loss. In this section, we consider two related questions: (i) how can the EV measure of the DWL of protection be estimated and (ii) is this DWL empirically significant? Obviously the details will vary depending on the particular type of policy we are considering. Nevertheless, it should be clear from the preceding analysis that many of these policies are very similar. In particular, we have seen that, in a static competitive framework, a tariff, an import quota and an export tax are equivalent. Moreover, an export (import) subsidy is just a negative export tax (tariff). In dealing with production subsidies or consumption taxes, we must allow for the fact that the former does not distort consumer prices whereas the latter does not distort producer prices. However, it is clear that all taxes on international trade can be treated in the same framework. We shall therefore frame our discussion in terms of the costs of a tariff as defined in Section 2.1 and given by the Harberger triangle *AEB* in Figure 2.3b; it is this area which we wish to estimate. Numerous studies have estimated such DWL triangles for various protected economies, and as we shall see, the results suggest that these costs are quite small as a percentage of GNP.

The techniques for estimating deadweight loss have advanced considerably in recent years. In particular, developments in modern duality theory and general equilibrium simulation methods have made it possible to derive "exact" estimates of the equivalent variation (and the compensating variation), and such methods are used in many of the empirical works we shall discuss. Although these developments are beyond the scope of the present chapter, interested readers can find a useful survey and discussion of the issues in Auerbach (1985). Here we shall be content to derive an approximate measure of the DWL of a tariff. Such approximations are commonplace in the literature, and although they have been subjected to some criticism in recent years, they remain popular and useful as a relatively quick and easy means of gauging the magnitude of the losses imposed by various distortions. However, it should always be remembered that they are only approximations, the accuracy of which is often difficult to judge.

To derive a simple approximation of the DWL of a tariff as a percentage of GNP (Y), assume that the compensated demand curve for imports derived in Figure 2.3b (reproduced here in Figure 2.12) is a straight line. Then the DWL triangle *AEB* in Figure 2.12 as a percentage of Y is

$$\frac{\text{DWL}}{Y} = \frac{1}{2}(p_T - p^*)\Delta M = \frac{1}{2}r^2\left[\frac{\Delta M}{M} \cdot \frac{p_T}{p_T - p^*}\right]\frac{p_T M}{Y} = \frac{1}{2}r^2\alpha\eta_M \quad (4)$$

where

η_M is the compensated (own) price elasticity of demand for imports,
$\alpha \equiv (p_T M)/Y$ is the fraction of GNP spent on imports and
$r \equiv (p_T - p^*)/p_T$ is the proportion by which free trade will reduce the domestic price.[7]

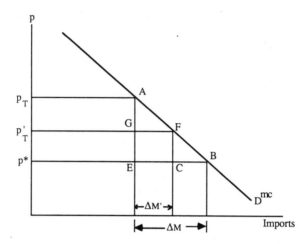

Figure 2.12

Equation (4) corresponds to the formula obtained by Johnson (1960) for the case of two goods and is adequate for our purposes here. Johnson also considers the case of many goods as have many authors since (see e.g. Diewert, 1984). We shall defer consideration of the general case until Chapter 9.

It is also possible to derive a slightly more general form of Equation (4) for the case of a percentage reduction in tariffs. This is illustrated in Figure 2.12 by supposing that a small tariff reduction (say a $100k$ per cent fall in r) lowers the domestic price from p_T to p'_T. This causes the DWL relative to free trade to fall from AEB to FCB, implying a net gain of $AECF$. It can then be easily shown[8] that the gain as a percentage of GNP is

$$-\frac{\Delta DWL}{Y} = \frac{1}{2} \frac{k\eta_M \alpha r_0 (r_0 + r_1)}{1 - r_1} \tag{5}$$

where r_0 is the initial (higher) value of r and r_1 is the value of r after tariff reduction. Note that when $k = 1$ (complete removal of tariffs), $r_1 = 0$; and Equation (5) reduces to Equation (4).

Let us now consider the likely magnitude of $(\Delta DWL)/Y$ under, say, a complete removal of tariffs as in Equation (4).

If we suppose that the short-run values of η_M[9] lie between -0.5 and -2 and assume an import share of 0.25[10] and an average tariff rate of $\frac{1}{3}$[11] (so that $r = 0.25$), then the formula in (4) would suggest a DWL of about 1.5 per cent of GNP. As noted by Johnson (1960), this is because the expression on the right-hand side of Equation (4) is necessarily the product of four fractions and one other low number. In the longer run, we might expect η_M to be somewhat higher. If we follow Magee (1972) and posit a figure of 8, we obtain a DWL of just over 6 per cent of GNP.

Bearing in mind that the above calculations (i) measure the DWL associated with complete elimination of tariffs, (ii) assume that all imports are protected by tariffs and (iii) assume, in any case, a rather high value for the import share α (see note 9), one would expect more careful analysis to yield somewhat lower estimates for these "static" gains from tariff reduction. This does turn out to be the case. Magee (1972) considers a disaggregated model in which he considers three categories of imports: (i) imports which are close substitutes for U.S. production and are restricted by tariffs; (ii) imports which are poor substitutes for U.S. production, may or may not be subject to tariffs, but are not subject to import quotas; and (iii) imports subject to import quotas or government-to-government agreements. For category (i), Magee estimates static DWL of $97 million per year (short run) and $291 million per year (long run). These are, respectively, 0.01 and 0.03 per cent of GDP in the base year (1971). The equivalent long-run loss from quota restrictions is $2.4 billion per year,[12] or 0.2 per cent of 1971 GDP.

Similarly low estimates emerge from the studies by Cline et al. (1977) and Brown and Whalley (1980). The first of these yields estimates of static short-run welfare gains for the United States, Canada, Japan and the European Economic Community (E.E.C.) under a range of tariff-cutting formulae which were considered in the Tokyo Round of Multilateral Trade Negotiations. For the case of complete elimination of tariffs, the relevant DWL was $1.179 billion for the United States and $0.292 billion for Canada.[13] These figures amount to 0.08 and 0.19 per cent of the respective countries' base year (1974) GNP.

Brown and Whalley (1980) also analyse the effects of some of the proposed Tokyo Round tariff-cutting formulae, but in the context of a general equilibrium model which permits, among other things, terms of trade effects (see Chapter 4). Their estimates of the EV imply maximum gains[14] of $1.35 billion for the United States[15], approximately 0.1 per cent of base year (1973) GDP.

On the basis of these results, it would be tempting to conclude that the conventional static welfare costs of tariffs, as illustrated in Figure 2.3 and approximated in Equation (4), are quite insignificant in relative terms.[16] However, there are good reasons to believe that the true costs of protection are much higher than the above estimates if certain key assumptions are relaxed.

A particularly crucial assumption relates to the degree of inter-sectoral mobility of factors. Most of the studies employ a specific-factors model with labour as the only mobile factor (see Section 1.4). Although such a framework is ideal for analysing the short-run income-distributional effects of a tariff, it does not capture the full welfare effects of the tariff in the longer run when there is greater inter-sectoral mobility of factors and thus a higher production gain from tariff removal. Hartigan and Tower (1982) ran a number of simula-

tions using a specific-factors model in which the "specific" factors have varying degrees of mobility between sectors and varying degrees of heterogeneity.
In the "Stolper–Samuelson" case with two perfectly mobile homogeneous
factors (capital and labour), Hartigan and Tower show that a move to unilateral free trade by the United States (i.e. foreign tariffs unchanged) would
raise United States real income 8.5 per cent above its base level.[17] In contrast,
when labour is perfectly mobile and there are two other factors, land and
capital, which are 99 per cent immobile to other industries, the gain from
unilateral removal of trade barriers is only 0.19 per cent of base year real
income.[18] If capital and land are both perfectly mobile between sectors and
the United States removal of tariffs (and tariff equivalents) is matched by a
complete removal of foreign tariffs (multilateral free trade), then the United
States gain from the move to free trade is as high as 18.89 per cent of base
year real income![19] It would thus appear that when longer run inter-sectoral
factor movements are taken into account, the gains from trade liberalization
are relatively high.

Another cause of the low estimates in some of the models may have been
their extensive use of the so-called Armington assumption. This is a convenient
modelling device under which the goods produced in each country are assumed
to be imperfect substitutes for goods produced in other countries (even if a domestic and a foreign good are physically identical). In particular, this means
that the home country is the only country producing its home-produced goods.
The implications of this are twofold. First, the home country's (and any country's) trade policy affects its terms of trade (because the prices of its exportable
goods are determined so as to clear a world market in which it is, by definition,
the only supplier). In particular, any trade restriction leads to a terms-of-trade
improvement which reduces the cost of the restriction (see Section 4.1 for a
proper analysis of this case). The magnitude of the terms-of-trade effects arising
from the Armington assumption is thought to be quite large (see Brown, 1987),
suggesting that models using this assumption can seriously underestimate the
gains from trade liberalization. Second, the assumption of imperfect substitutes
limits the gains from import substitution when a tariff is removed. In a model
with constant returns to scale (a horizontal supply curve) and domestic and
foreign goods which are perfect substitutes, removal of a tariff can result in
imports completely displacing domestic production, with a correspondingly
higher production gain from trade liberalization.[20] The reader may like to
check this point using a simple supply–demand diagram.

Yet another group of criticisms relates to the degree of aggregation used in
some of the models. Corden (1975, p. 57) notes that use of an average tariff rate
does not take account of the additional costs arising from the variance (or non-
uniformity) of tariff rates across goods (the same point is implicit in Johnson,
1960). We have already seen (Section 2.2) that a given restriction in the value of
imports is most efficiently achieved by an ad valorem tariff which is uniform

across all imported goods. Any non-uniformity of the tariff rates would therefore impose additional costs on the community. Allowance for this "aggregation bias" by Magee (1972) results in his uncorrected DWL estimates for tariffs (as previously given) being multiplied by a factor of 2.87.

A related issue is raised by Dixon (1978), who observes that use of highly aggregated data may obscure the gains from tariff reduction when tariff rates differ markedly across groups of close substitutes. Using the example of woollen and synthetic sweaters with a 33 per cent tariff applying to synthetic sweaters but no tariff on woollen sweaters and other goods (food), Dixon shows that the consumption gain resulting from elimination of the tariff on synthetics increases dramatically (ranging from a two-fold to a fourteen-fold increase, depending on the free-trade share of woollens in sweater consumption) as the elasticity of substitution between woollens and synthetics rises from 2 to, say, 10. This is exactly what we would expect, and it highlights the need for estimates based on finer commodity classifications.

Finally, we note that in addition to the static "triangle" costs which were the subject of this section, many other costs are associated with protection, many of which are thought to be empirically more significant than those just discussed. Particularly important are (i) rent-seeking costs associated with the distribution of the tariff revenue or the quota rents, (ii) costs of monopoly power conferred on domestic producers by particular policies, (iii) reduced economies of scale and resulting higher unit cost and (iv) reduced product variety. On the other hand, certain benefits are claimed for protection in situations where "smallness" is not the norm, in particular, gains from improved terms of trade (for large countries) and capturing of foreign rents (in non-competitive industries with restricted entry). These various costs and benefits will be examined in some detail in later chapters.

In addition, it is important not to ignore the presence of other taxes and distortions in the system (although we have done so for convenience in the preceding simple analysis). Such distortions can sometimes provide a second-best argument for protection, an issue we take up in more detail in Chapter 9. Such considerations should be properly accounted for in any complete analysis, as indeed they are in the array of modern general equilibrium models of tariff-cutting which incorporate the full structure of taxation (see e.g. Boadway and Treddenick, 1978, Dixon et al., 1981).

2.9. Effective protection

In the preceding sections we have largely confined our attention to the production of net outputs – that is, outputs produced for final consumption. With the exception of our brief analysis of content protection, we have subsumed the role of intermediate goods in the production process. To the extent that we were concerned with the welfare effects of protection, net outputs were indeed the appropriate objects of interest. After all, it is these outputs which are consumed and which enter into the consumers' utility functions. If we are only interested in net outputs, then, as we have seen, ordinary tax and tariff rates (nominal tariffs) together with world prices determine those outputs and thence the economy's set of attainable consumption bundles and its welfare.[21]

On the other hand, a range of separate questions arises when the presence of intermediate goods is acknowledged. For example, we may be interested in the total value of primary factors employed in a particular sector of the economy. In the presence of intermediate goods, this depends not just on the sector's production for final demand but also its production of goods for use as intermediate inputs. Thus, if we are interested in a sector's total use of primary resources, *gross output* (net output + production for intermediate use) appears to be a more appropriate concept to work with. It may be, for example, that the government wishes to increase the income to a factor which is specific to a particular industry (possibly an industry which is located in a politically marginal constituency). The income of that factor will, in some way, be related to the overall level of activity in the industry (i.e. gross output) rather than to production for final use. We are therefore confronted with the question of how to measure protection of gross output, so-called effective protection.

In devising such a measure, a useful starting point is to consider how nominal tariffs and subsidies measure protection to net outputs. We can then attempt to define protection of gross output in an analogous way. The ad valorem nominal tariff or subsidy for a particular good is the proportional increase in the producer price of net output of the good relative to free trade [i.e. $(p - p^*)/p^*$]. It is therefore consistent to define a measure of effective protection of a "sector" as the proportional increase in the price of the sector's gross output relative to free trade. An appropriate price for gross output is the *value-added per unit*. This has the necessary property that the economy's total value of gross output (priced at value-added per unit) equals the total value of net output (valued at equilibrium prices) – because the total value of net outputs also equals the sum of the values added in each activity (GNP at factor cost) which, in turn, equals the sum of the gross outputs each multiplied by its value-added per unit.[22] Accordingly, we define the *effective rate of protection* (ERP) to be the proportional increase in the value-added per unit relative to free trade. This leads us to Corden's (1966b) definition of the ERP. For an industry producing a single good (j) by combining primary factors of production with n intermediate goods, the ERP is given by

$$e_j \equiv \frac{v_j - v_j^*}{v_j^*} = \frac{\left[p_j - \sum_i p_i a_{ij} \right] - \left[p_j^* - \sum_i p_i^* a_{ij} \right]}{p_j^* - \sum_i p_i^* a_{ij}}$$

$$= \frac{p_j^* t_j - \sum\limits_{i} p_i^* t_i a_{ij}}{p_j^* - \sum\limits_{i} p_i^* a_{ij}} \tag{6}$$

where

$a_{ij} \equiv$ the amount of good i required to produce one unit of good j,

$p_i^* \equiv$ the world price of good i,

$t_i \equiv$ the nominal ad valorem tariff rate on good i,

$p_i \equiv$ the domestic price of good i faced by final-good producers $=$
$p_i^*(1 + t_i)$,

$v_j \equiv$ value-added per unit of good j in the tariff-distorted situation $= p_j$
$- \Sigma_i p_i a_{ij}$ and

$v_j^* \equiv$ value-added per unit of good j under free trade $= p_j^* - \Sigma_i p_i^* a_{ij}$.

The nominal tariff rate on good i, t_i, is the ordinary tariff rate expressed as a percentage of a good's c.i.f. import price. Although we shall, for simplicity, refer to it as a tariff, it may include various taxes, subsidies and other distortions. For example, if good i is an intermediate good, a tax on its use would increase its price to final-good producers and so would appear in the same way as a tariff, whereas a production subsidy to producers of i would not affect its price to final-good producers (assuming some of it is imported and the country is small) and so should not be included in t_i. On the other hand, at the final-product stage, a production subsidy to final-good producers increases the price they receive and so should be treated in the same way as a tariff, whereas a consumption tax does not affect them at all (again assuming some of the good is imported). Thus, the tariffs t_i can (indeed should) be interpreted in a quite general way to encompass all distortions which affect the relevant price and to exclude other distortions.

A clear advantage of Equation (6) as a measure of effective protection is that it appears to capture certain general equilibrium phenomena in a simple way, avoiding the informational requirements of full general equilibrium computations. This economy of information appears to be the main argument for calculating effective rates of protection rather than undertaking a general equilibrium analysis using nominal rates.

Among other things, Equation (6) shows how the effective tariff rate e_j is related to the nominal tariff rates of the final and intermediate goods. As an exercise, the reader may care to check that (a) when there are no intermediate goods (i.e. the a_{ij} are zero), the effective rate reduces to the nominal rate, and (b) when all the nominal rates are equal, the effective rate has the same value; thus uniform nominal protection in an economy implies uniform effective protection. More importantly, Equation (6) shows how tariffs and taxes applied to a sector's intermediate inputs reduce the effective protection afforded to the sector. Clearly, a sector may be protected by positive tariffs at the final-good stage and yet receive negative effective protection ($e_j < 0$) if the tariffs and taxes applied to its intermediate inputs are sufficiently high. In such cases, the sector in question is seen to be bearing the burden of protection afforded to other sectors of the economy even though a cursory glance at nominal tariffs and subsidies may suggest that it is a beneficiary of protection. Such information is obviously of interest to industry lobbies or industry-specific factors engaged in a contest for their share of government-conferred rents. Other results relating effective rates to the structure of the nominal rates in an industry can be found in Corden (1971).

Despite these interesting implications of a formula such as Equation (6), an important question remains to be answered. Although we have identified value-added per unit as a price of gross output and have defined the effective rate of protection as the proportional divergence of this price from its free-trade level, it is not yet clear that the effective rate works as a measure of protection of gross output in the same way that the nominal rate works as a measure of net output protection. The role of nominal rates is clear. If a nominal tariff on a good causes that good's price to rise relative to other final-good prices, then the economy will produce more of the good, moving around its production frontier (as illustrated for the two-good case in Figure 2.1). Put simply, if you know the nominal tariff rates, then you know the final-goods prices and that enables you to determine the net outputs. Of course, this simple link between nominal rates and net outputs is using the fact that final-good prices support the equilibrium outputs; that is, the total value of net output, valued at the prevailing final-good prices, cannot be increased by reallocating net output among the sectors. In the two-good case, this is illustrated by the tangency between the relative price line and the production frontier [see part (b), Section 1.1]. If a vector of prices supports a vector of outputs, then the effect of a change in the prices on the sectoral outputs can be readily deduced (in the two-good case, it is simply a matter of seeing how a rotation of the producer price line changes the tangency with the production frontier).

Clearly, effective rates of protection (as defined here) can fulfil this same function as predictors of gross outputs if the vector of values-added per unit supports the vector of actual gross outputs. Unfortunately, this is the case only if there is limited substitution among the intermediate inputs. To understand the intuition, we first consider the case in which there is no substitution among inputs – that is, fixed input–output coefficients. As a starting point, we know that, for a given vector of final-good prices p, the value of net output valued at those prices is at a maximum. Furthermore, at given prices p and fixed input–output coefficients a_{ij}, the values-added are also fixed (see definition). In addition, we have observed that the total value of gross output "priced" at value-added per unit equals the total value of net output. Thus, if the latter is maximized at the given p_i, the former is also maximized at the given v_i; it follows that the vector of the v_i supports the vector of gross outputs. It would then be straightforward to use this property to deduce the gross outputs from the values-added per unit (which are in turn implied by the effective rates). The difficulty arises when the a_{ij} can vary. Then, although the value of net output is maximized at given p, reallocations of net outputs around this maximum may involve changes in the mix of intermediate goods (i.e. changes in the a_{ij}). If this implies an increase in the value of intermediate-goods production which more than offsets the fall in the value of net output, it will imply an increase in the value of gross output. In such cases, the actual vector of gross outputs is not supported by the vector of the v_i because the total value of gross output can be increased by a small reallocation of outputs away from the equilibrium value. The connection between values-added per unit and the gross outputs then becomes rather more complicated.

The foregoing argument can be made more precise with the aid of some simple algebra. The condition that the p_i support the vector Y of net outputs may be written as

$$\sum_i p_i \, dY_i \leq 0 \tag{7}$$

where dY_i represents a small change in the ith net output (Y_i).

The identity expressing the two alternative formulations of national output is written as

$$\sum_i v_i X_i = \sum_i p_i Y_i \tag{8}$$

where X_i is the gross output of good i.

Taking total differentials of Equation (8), we see that for the given p_i, changes in the X_i along the economy's production frontier must satisfy

$$\sum_i v_i \, dX_i - \sum_i \sum_j p_j X_j (da_{ji}) = \sum_i p_i \, dY_i \leq 0. \tag{9}$$

Now, the values-added per unit will support the gross outputs if and only if $\sum_i v_i \, dX_i \leq 0$, and from Equation (9) we see that this will hold if

$$\sum_i \sum_j p_j X_j (da_{ji}) \leq 0. \tag{10}$$

Equation (10) defines overall limits on substitutability in the economy's technology. In particular, it is satisfied if the a_{ij} are constant (see Ethier, 1977, for discussion of other cases). It is worth noting that Equation (10) is merely a sufficient condition for the values-added per unit to support the gross output vector (i.e. weaker restrictions on substitutability might also be sufficient). On the other hand, for those cases in which the above inequalities hold with equality, it will clearly be both necessary and sufficient. Finally, it is worth stressing Ethier's point that if the coefficients are not constant but Equation (10) is still satisfied, then e_j must be defined as the proportional change in the actual value added (i.e. allowing for changes in the input coefficients).

From this discussion, we can conclude that the effective rate of protection, defined as the proportional divergence of value-added per unit from its free-trade level, is a valid measure of protection of gross output if substitutability among inputs is limited in the manner implied by condition (10). However, if information on factor substitution is required, the principal advantage of ERPs (economy of information) is lost, and the researcher may prefer to use a full general equilibrium model and nominal tariff rates rather than bothering to calculate effective rates at all.[23] Of course, ERPs in their simplest form (i.e. with constant a_{ij}) still provide a useful means of obtaining rough initial estimates of the effects of a tariff structure on the pattern of sectoral outputs. In this respect, they fulfil a similar role to the linear approximations of deadweight loss considered in the previous section.

2.10.   Summary

This chapter has attempted to cover a wide range of protection issues relevant to a small competitive economy. Tariffs, it was noted, are costly to an economy because they divert resources away from more productive uses and because they distort the prices paid by consumers. Indeed, in the absence of other distortions, a small competitive economy would maximize its welfare by having no tariffs at all. However, it is unarguable that governments do employ instruments such as tariffs to achieve various income-distributional and non-economic objectives. The relevant question then is which policy is the most efficient means of achieving a stated objective. The answer, as it turns out, is simple: Use the policy which directly affects the variable being targeted; for example, use an output subsidy to achieve a target level of output.

Although tariffs are a convenient starting point for any analysis of protection, they are but one of an increasingly diverse and complicated array of protective instruments. We considered a number of these in the latter part of the chapter. The following properties of some of these non-tariff barriers to trade are worth noting:

i.   In the static, competitive framework of this chapter, an import quota is equivalent to a tariff (the so-called implicit tariff) which yields the same domestic price as the quota. The same equivalence exists between a tariff and a market-sharing scheme, which is just a particular type of variable quota.

ii.   A tariff (or its quota-equivalent) is equivalent to an export tax at the same rate; this is the so-called Lerner symmetry theorem.

iii. Content protection schemes are a means of protecting domestic intermediate-good producers by requiring final-good producers to purchase a specified percentage of their components from domestic producers, whereas the remaining proportion may be imported duty free. As a means of protecting intermediate-good or component producers, these schemes differ from both tariffs and quotas because they allow final-good producers to obtain imported units of components at a lower price than domestically produced units; for this reason, they are often seen as a more efficient means of protecting output of an intermediate-goods sector.

iv. Preferential government procurement policies are equivalent to a production subsidy if the government's demand for the good exceeds the industry's free-trade output; if the government's demand is smaller than this, they do not distort domestic producer prices at all.

Finally, we considered the problem of measuring protection to sectors where some goods are produced for intermediate use. It was found that, if factor substitutability is limited, then the percentage change in a commodity's value-added per unit is an appropriate measure of protection of that commodity's gross output (= output for final demand + output for intermediate use). It is then possible to use standard well-known formulae for effective rates of protection to measure the protection afforded to a sector's total level of activity. On the other hand, if there is excessive substitutability among inputs or if the object of protection is something other than gross output, then these simple formulae may be unreliable measures of a sector's level of protection.

CHAPTER 3

Import quotas and tariffs: Some other issues

In the previous chapter we established the result that in a static competitive economy, a tariff and an import quota are equivalent in the sense that a tariff yielding the same domestic price as the quota also yields the same level of imports and output and the same deadweight loss to the community. Given such apparent equivalence, it is reasonable to conclude that it does not matter whether tariffs or quotas are used to protect output or restrict imports.

Certainly there are situations in which the equivalence of the two policies can be used to deduce interesting and relevant results. One such case is the use of trade restrictions to constrain the imports of a class of heterogeneous commodities (e.g. automobiles). This problem was considered in the previous chapter for the case of tariffs. In Section 3.1, we shall exploit the equivalence of tariffs and quotas to consider the effects of an import quota applied to such a class of commodities. Of particular interest is the way in which quotas on the volume of imports shift the composition of imports towards more expensive items.

Despite the usefulness of equivalence in deriving such results, it is now well known that tariffs and quotas are generally not equivalent in most situations beyond the static competitive model. In particular, if there is monopoly in the protected sector or if the policies are imposed by larger countries involved in a trade war, it will matter very much which policy is used. These cases are taken up in Chapters 5 and 4, respectively. Even in the simple case of a small competitive economy, equivalence breaks down in a number of important cases. In Sections 3.2–3.4, we consider these cases and explore a number of issues which relate to the comparison of tariffs and quotas.

In identifying situations where tariffs and quotas are not equivalent, we start with the simplest departure from the basic model: allowing the parameters of the economy to shift over time. Once the demand or supply curves for a good, or its world price, are subject to change, quotas and tariffs affect the market for the good in quite different ways (this case is often referred to as *dynamic non-equivalence* and is considered in Section 3.2). This, in turn, suggests that the two policies must also differ in the presence of uncertainty (where the parameters exhibit fluctuations which are unknown *ex ante*). Indeed, the case of uncertainty raises other interesting issues, in particular the so-called insurance argument for protection. The case of uncertainty is dealt with in Section 3.3.

Finally, in Section 3.4, we incorporate rent seeking and its costs into the basic model. Like most government policies, tariffs and quotas create rents which are the subject of competition among economic agents. Rent seekers use economic resources to lobby for a share of the revenue from a tariff or for the rents embodied in the scarce import licences under a quota. Such use of resources is largely wasteful in the sense that it merely redistributes existing wealth without changing aggregate welfare. It is thus possible to identify and estimate rent-seeking costs of a tariff or quota, which may be added to the Harberger deadweight loss triangles of the previous chapter. These costs are thought to be empirically quite large and are therefore of considerable interest to the policy maker. However, it is again notable that the outcome under rent–revenue seeking differs depending on whether a tariff or a quota is used, yet another example of the non-equivalence of the two policies.

3.1.   Quotas and heterogeneous product categories

We now consider the implications of applying an import quota to a class of heterogeneous or differentiated commodities. For ease of exposition, we shall work in terms of the following example. Suppose a country wishes to restrict imports of cars and that there are only two types of car, cheap cars (A) and expensive cars (B). Assume that type A and B cars are gross substitutes and that equiproportionate increases in the prices of both types of cars reduce total excess demand (=import demand) for cars but do not change the ratio of excess demands for the two types. In other words, we are assuming that both car types have similar income effects and similar cross-substitution effects with other commodities. Such an assumption is reasonable if the two car types are close substitutes for each other. Its role here is to make the composition of car imports depend only on the relative prices of the two car types. If one type becomes relatively more expensive, the proportion of that type of car in total car imports will fall (see Falvey, 1979). Finally, we assume that the market for import quota licences is competitive; thus, in equilibrium, there are no unexploited profit opportunities.

Now consider the effects of a volume quota, that is, a limit on the total number of cars imported, so that imports of A and B type cars (M_A and M_B, respectively) satisfy the constraint

$$M_A + M_B = \bar{M}.$$

Let p_A and p_B be the domestic prices of cheap and expensive cars, and let p_A^* and p_B^* be their respective world prices. Given that the market for quota licences is competitive, importers allocate their imports between cheap and expensive cars so that the premium per car (the excess of the quota-distorted domestic price over the world price) is the same for both types of car. If this is not the case (say, $p_A - p_A^*$ is greater than $p_B - p_B^*$), then the profit per car will be greater from importing additional cheap cars and fewer expensive cars. Such reallocation will continue until either only one type of car is imported or until the premia for both types of car are driven to equality; that is, until

$$p_A - p_A^* = p_B - p_B^* = T. \tag{1}$$

Thus (assuming both types of car are imported in equilibrium), a volume quota is equivalent to a uniform specific tariff of T per unit applied to the goods subject to import restriction. In the previous chapter we saw that a uniform specific tariff is an optimal instrument for restricting the volume of imports of a class of goods. It is not surprising that a volume quota (which achieves such a noneconomic objective directly) should be equivalent to such a policy. The interesting question here is how a volume quota affects the composition of imports within the restricted category relative to free trade. To answer this question, given our earlier assumptions, we merely have to check how the volume quota affects relative prices. Under the quota, the difference between domestic relative prices and free-trade relative prices is

$$\frac{p_A}{p_B} - \frac{p_A^*}{p_B^*} = \frac{p_A^* + T}{p_B^* + T} - \frac{p_A^*}{p_B^*} = \frac{T(p_B^* - p_A^*)}{p_B^*(p_B^* + T)} > 0 \tag{2}$$

since A is, by definition, the cheaper type of car ($p_A^* < p_B^*$). Thus a volume quota increases the relative price of cheaper cars, leading to a shift towards more expensive cars in the composition of imports. This tendency for volume quotas to bias the import mix towards more expensive items has been noted in relation to a number of markets to which quantitative import restrictions have been applied. Falvey (1979) cites the cases of textiles and steel imports into the United States, where restrictions expressed in volume terms have led to upgrading of the quality of goods imported. Similar effects have also been noted in relation to the voluntary export restraints imposed in 1981 on Japanese auto exporters to the United States (Collyns and Dunaway, 1987; Feenstra, 1984) and the orderly marketing agreements that protect the United States footwear industry (Aw and Roberts, 1986). All of these examples relate to voluntary export restraints (VERs) or orderly marketing agreements (OMAs) rather than explicit import quotas, but the basic restriction is of the same general kind. It is therefore not surprising that an upgrading effect should apply (for a discussion of some different features of the VER case, see Chapter 4). The same type of effect has also been observed in the composition of Australian car imports which were restricted by a volume import quota until 1988.

In contrast to a volume quota, a value quota does not distort the import mix at all. If the government wishes to restrict the value of car imports (at world prices) to some value (say, V dollars), we have

$$p_A^* M_A + p_B^* M_B^* = V.$$

Importers facing a limit on the dollar value of car imports will now import type A and B cars up to the point at which the premium from a dollar's worth of additional imports is the same for both car types (any divergence between these premia for types A and B implies higher profits from importing more of the car type with the higher premium per dollar). Thus, in an equilibrium where both types of car are imported,

$$\frac{p_A - p_A^*}{p_A^*} = \frac{p_B - p_B^*}{p_B^*} = t. \tag{3}$$

The value quota is seen to be equivalent to a *uniform ad valorem tariff* at rate t applied to all goods in the category. Again, this is not surprising, because such a tariff was seen in Chapter 2 to be an optimal means of restricting the total value of a class of imports. Given this equivalence, it is immediately clear that the relative price of type A and B cars is the same under the value quota as under free trade since

$$\frac{p_A}{p_B} = \frac{(1 + t)p_A^*}{(1 + t)p_B^*} = \frac{p_A^*}{p_B^*}. \tag{4}$$

Given the assumptions which make import composition depend only on relative price, the import mix under a value quota is the same as under free trade. The implication is that if a country wishes to restrict imports of a class of closely substitutable goods, then it can minimize the distortion associated with such a policy by restricting the value rather than the volume of imports of goods in the class.

The difficulty is that value quotas are difficult to implement, primarily because they are subject to manipulation. If, for example, foreign exporters can use transfer pricing to artificially reduce the c.i.f. import price (p_A^* or p_B^*) of some or all of the restricted goods, they can recoup their profits via rents from the import licences (they may either hold the licences themselves or they may collude in some way with domestic importers). Uniform ad valorem tariffs are an acceptable alternative but may be unavailable if their use runs counter to GATT-negotiated tariff reductions. In any case, political factors also seem to favour the use of quotas rather than tariffs (see Chapter 8).

Thus it may be that a government (for political and administrative reasons) chooses volume quotas as its instrument of import restriction. We must then pose the question: is there a way of allocating these quotas which makes them less distortionary? One proposal which has been canvassed is the allocation of some or all of the quota for a particular class of goods by means of ad valorem tender bids; that is, importing firms submit bids for import licences expressed in ad valorem terms, and the bidders above the quota-clearing bid receive licences. Such an allocation scheme (which has been tried in the Australian car industry; see Industries Assistance Commission, 1980) is seen as replicating a uniform ad valorem tariff (or, equivalently, a value quota) and thus avoiding the distortions in the import mix associated with a volume quota. Unfortunately, unless such an allocation mechanism can somehow remove the underlying constraint on the volume of imports which is implicit in the use of a volume quota, it will make matters worse. We know that a uniform specific tariff is the optimal means of restricting the volume of a class of imports. It follows that using the equivalent of a uniform ad valorem tariff to achieve that same volume of imports involves a higher distortion. In particular, under the system of ad valorem tender bids, the marginal deadweight loss on foregone units of imports is higher for expensive items than for cheaper items, implying that the proportion of cheaper goods in total imports is too high under such a policy. Of course, allocation by ad valorem tender bids would be optimal if somehow the volume constraint could be (surreptitiously) replaced by a value constraint, but it is not clear how this could be implemented in practice. In short, there does not appear to be any way of making a volume quota "change its spots". These issues and other aspects of the Australian experiment are analysed in detail in Gibbs and Konovalov (1984).

We now turn to a range of cases in which tariffs and quotas are not equivalent.

3.2.   Dynamic non-equivalence of tariffs and quotas

The simplest case of non-equivalence arises when the parameters of the economy are shifting over time. Here we consider one example of this so-called *dynamic non-equivalence,* the case of a shift in an industry's supply curve (Figure 3.1). As in the previous chapter, DD represents the total demand by residents for the importable good (food), and $D'D'$ is the demand curve for domestically produced food. p^* is the c.i.f. import price and p_Q the domestic price under the quota Q. In the initial quota equilibrium (at E), the quota is equivalent to the implicit tariff of p^*p_Q per unit. Output under both policies is X_1, consumption is C_1 and imports are equal to the quota.

Now let the supply curve SS shift upwards to $S'S'$. It is straightforward to show that the two policies are no longer equivalent. Under the quota, a new domestic equilibrium is established at T, where $D'D'$ intersects the new supply curve; with imports fixed, equilibrium domestic price must rise to induce higher domestic output to meet domestic demand. Output falls to X_2, consumption falls to C_2 and domestic consumers pay a higher price than before (p'_Q). In contrast, under the tariff which is equivalent to the quota in the initial equilibrium (p^*p_Q per unit), domestic price cannot rise above p_Q (because there is a perfectly elastic supply of imports at the world price plus the tariff); hence output under the tariff falls further than under the quota (to X_3, where p_Q intersects $S'S'$). Thus, from the point of view of the protected sector, the quota

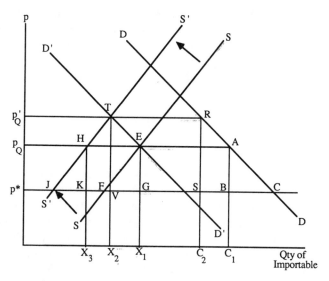

Figure 3.1

is the preferred policy because it results in a smaller reduction in output and a higher price than under the tariff. Rents in the sector are higher under the quota by the area $p'_Q THp_Q$. On the other hand, the quota imposes a higher deadweight loss on the community than the tariff, and the excess cost of the quota is given by the area $(HTVK + RABS)$.

Clearly two policies which were equivalent before the shift in the supply curve are no longer equivalent after the shift. One aspect of this non-equivalence which is particularly worth noting is the manner in which protection under the quota adjusts upwards (from p^*p_Q per unit to $p^*p'_Q$ per unit) in response to an increase in the industry's costs of production, whereas protection under the tariff remains fixed at p^*p_Q per unit. It is in this sense that quota protection is often described as "open ended". Such open endedness is often perceived as a particular disadvantage of quotas; in particular, policy makers have the concern that an industry protected by quotas may, in the presence of other pressures (e.g. powerful unions), have less incentive to resist cost increases because part of the burden of higher costs can be passed on to domestic consumers. A tariff, on the other hand, imposes a discipline on firms because the firm must bear the full burden of any upwards shift in its cost curve.

We have now seen one example of dynamic non-equivalence of tariffs and quotas. A similar analysis could have been carried out for shifts in the demand curve or the c.i.f. import price. In each case, it is easy to verify that tariffs and quotas imply very different responses to such shifts.

There is a further important implication of the preceding analysis: If the effects of tariffs and quotas differ in response to shifts in parameters, then we might expect them also to differ in the presence of uncertainty (when parameters are shifting in a random way). In the next section we present a simple uncertainty model in which the two policies are clearly seen to differ in the presence of random fluctuations in world price and the demand curve for imports.

3.3.   Tariffs and quotas under uncertainty

(a)   Uncertain world price

Suppose the small country we have been considering faces a randomly fluctuating world price for its importable good. Such price uncertainty is common in the real world, particularly with respect to raw materials. If, as the analysis of the previous section suggests, a tariff and a quota cannot be fully equivalent in this situation, then on what basis should they be compared? A popular basis of comparison (or non-economic objective) is the achievement of a common expected level of imports (see Pelcovits, 1976; Young and Anderson, 1980). Before we proceed, it is important to distinguish between the effects of specific and ad valorem tariffs when the world price is fluctuating. Under an ad valorem tariff, the world price movements are reflected in magnified movements in the domestic price; for example, a rise of ε in world price implies a rise of $(1 + t)\varepsilon$ in the domestic price, where t is the ad valorem tariff rate. However, under a specific tariff, the movements in the domestic price exactly match the movements in the world price. We shall begin by showing that a specific tariff yields a higher value of expected consumer surplus than a quota when the world price is fluctuating randomly.

In Figure 3.2, D_m is the economy's demand curve for imports of the good, and p^* is the mean value of its c.i.f. import price. Suppose that this price can take on values of $p^* + \varepsilon$ and $p^* - \varepsilon$, each with probability $\frac{1}{2}$.

We now compare the expected losses of consumer surplus (relative to free trade) under the two policies for a given expected quantity of imports. In Figure 3.2, Q denotes both the level of the quota and the expected level of imports under the tariff. p_Q is the domestic price under the quota regardless of the level of world price. In other words, the quota acts as a price-stabilizing tool, insulating the domestic economy completely from foreign price fluctuations. In this particular case (where the only disturbance is a fluctuating world price), the quota is formally identical to a variable import levy of the kind employed by the European Economic Community (EEC) to support the domestic prices of its agricultural products (variable import levies are discussed in detail in the next chapter). Under a specific tariff of T dollars per unit, the domestic price is always T dollars above the world price, with imports adjusting accordingly. In Figure 3.2, when the world price is $p^* - \varepsilon$, imports under the tariff are Q_1, and

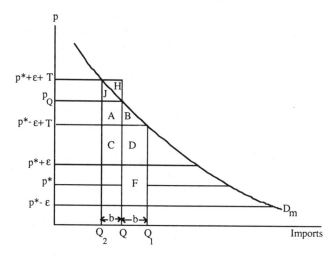

Figure 3.2

when the world price is $p^* + \varepsilon$, imports under the tariff are Q_2. Because Q is, by definition, the mean of Q_1 and Q_2, the distances Q_1Q and QQ_2 are equal. We call their common value b.

Now, using consumer surplus measures, consider the excess deadweight loss of the quota relative to the tariff for the two alternative values of the world price. When the world price is $p^* + \varepsilon$ the tariff has an excess DWL, which may be written in terms of the areas marked in Figure 3.2 as $(J + A + C)$. This is clearly less than the rectangular area $(J + H + A + C)$, which equals bT. When the world price is $p^* - \varepsilon$, an excess DWL is associated with the quota of $(B + D + F)$, which is greater than the rectangular area $(D + F)$, which also equals bT. Thus the expected excess DWL of the quota relative to the specific tariff is greater than

$$\frac{1}{2}(-bT) + \frac{1}{2}bT = 0.$$

In other words, the specific tariff is superior to the quota. It can also be shown to be superior to an ad valorem tariff. As explained earlier, an ad valorem tariff results in the world price fluctuations being magnified in the domestic price. In terms of Figure 3.2, under an ad valorem tariff when world price is high, the domestic price is above $(p^* + \varepsilon + T)$; and when world price is low, the domestic price is *below* $(p^* - \varepsilon + T)$. This means that if a specific tariff is replaced by one expressed in ad valorem terms, $(J + A + C)$ is widened to the left while area $(B + D + F)$ is widened by an equal amount to the right (since Q is still the arithmetic mean of the two alternative import levels under the tariff). However, the height of the addition to $(J + A + C)$ exceeds the height of the addition to the area $(B + D + F)$. It follows that the excess DWL of the tariff when the price is high is increased relative to the excess DWL of the quota when the price is low, implying that the expected excess DWL of a quota over a tariff is lower when the tariff is ad valorem rather than specific. We conclude that the specific tariff dominates both policies.

Whether an ad valorem tariff can also be superior to a quota in this case is unclear from the preceding analysis. However, Pelcovits (1976) was able to show that if the demand curve for imports is linear, then an ad valorem tariff is superior to a quota provided the tariff rate (and the associated magnification of world price movements) is not too high.

The result that a specific tariff dominates an ad valorem tariff and an import quota as a means of attaining a given expected level of imports, should not be at all surprising to the reader who followed our earlier analysis of import restriction for heterogeneous product categories. The constraint on imports is just like a volume quota on a heterogeneous class of goods with the two "types" of goods subject to restriction being the importable in the two states of the world (high price and low price). This parallel can be seen immediately if we write the constraint on expected imports as

$$\frac{1}{2} M_A + \frac{1}{2} M_B = Q, \quad \text{that is,} \quad M_A + M_B = 2Q$$

where M_A and M_B are imports in the two states of the world. We know that a uniform specific tariff is the optimal means of achieving such an objective. A specific tariff which is uniform across states of the world is just an ordinary specific tariff. On the other hand, a fixed import quota (Q) implies a fixed domestic price in both states of the world and thus a higher implicit tariff per unit in the low-price state of the world, $[p_Q - (p^* - \varepsilon)]$ per unit, than in the high-price state, $[p_Q - (p^* + \varepsilon)]$ per unit. This means that under a quota, the consumer surplus foregone on the marginal unit is higher in the low-price state of the world than in the high-price state, implying that expected consumer surplus can be increased by importing less when world price is high (since the cost of foregoing a unit is lower in this state) and importing more when it is low. Under an ad valorem tariff (which implies the same percentage loss of surplus on the marginal unit in both states), the marginal loss per unit is higher in the high-price state, implying gains to society from reallocating some units of the fixed quantity of imports from the low-price state to the high-price state (i.e. a narrowing of the domestic price dispersion back towards the specific tariff).

In the preceding analysis, we were comparing a tariff and a quota which yielded the same expected quantity of imports. An alternative common objective would be a given *value* of imports (i.e. a given foreign exchange expendi-

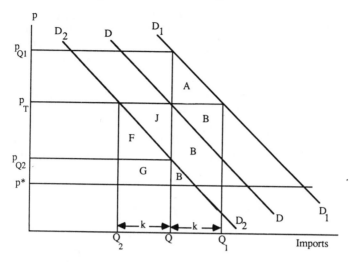

Figure 3.3

ture). The optimal outcome in this case would be one which equates the loss of consumer surplus on the marginal unit of foreign exchange (rather than the marginal physical unit) across states of the world. This outcome is achieved by having the excess of domestic over world price the same percentage of world price in both states (i.e. an ad valorem tariff). See Young and Anderson (1980) for a formal proof that an ad valorem tariff is indeed the most efficient policy for import restriction in this case.

(b)   Uncertain demand for imports

It is also straightforward to compare a tariff and a quota which yield the same expected level of exports when there are random fluctuations in the demand curve for imports (arising from fluctuations in the demand and/or the supply schedules for importables). Without fluctuations in the world price, the ad valorem and specific tariffs are equivalent. Moreover, when the demand curve shifts, the price changes under a quota but not under a tariff; under a tariff, imports bear the full burden of adjustment (as in the case analysed in Section 3.2). This is illustrated in Figure 3.3.

The (assumed fixed) world price of the importable is p^*, and Q is the expected level of imports under both policies. DD is the mean of the two possible demand curves D_1D_1 and D_2D_2, each of which is equally probable; thus, at any given price, the horizontal distance between DD and D_1D_1 equals the horizontal distance between DD and D_2D_2. Under the quota Q, in the high-demand state of the world (D_1D_1) the domestic price is p_{Q1}, whereas in the low-demand state of the world (D_2D_2) the domestic price is p_{Q2}. The tariff which yields the same expected quantity of imports as the quota is $p*p_T$ per unit. This involves a domestic price p_T in both high- and low-demand states with imports Q_1 in the high-demand state and Q_2 in the low-demand state. Clearly, $Q_2Q = QQ_1$; let this common value be denoted by k.

When the demand curve is in position D_1D_1, there is an excess DWL of the quota over the tariff given by the area $(A + B)$ in Figure 3.3. When the demand curve is D_2D_2, there is an excess DWL of the tariff over the quota equal to the area $(F + G)$. Clearly, $(A + B) > B = k(p_T - p*)$. It is also clear from the diagram that $(F + G) < (F + G + J) = k(p_T - p*)$. It follows that the expected DWL of the quota over the tariff is

$$\frac{1}{2}\{A + B - (F + G)\} > \frac{1}{2}[B - (F + G + J)]$$
$$= \frac{1}{2}[k(p_T - p*) - k(p_T - p*)] = 0.$$

Thus the quota involves a higher expected DWL than the tariff and is therefore the inferior instrument in this case.

(c)   Risk aversion

The foregoing analysis suggests that in the presence of uncertainty a tariff is a better tool for restricting imports than a quota. This reinforces the common view among economists favouring tariffs over quotas. On the other hand, this conclusion has been reached by choosing the policy which (subject to the constraint on imports) maximizes expected consumer surplus. It is well known however that consumer surplus is a valid measure of welfare only under special conditions. In particular, for the case in which only one commodity price is changing, as in sub-section (a), changes in utility are correctly measured by consumer surplus methods only if the coefficient of relative risk aversion equals the income elasticity of demand for the good in question (see Turnovsky, Shalit and Schmitz, 1980). In other words, the analysis of the previous section was placing implicit limits on the degree of risk aversion of producers and consumers.

For the reader who is unfamiliar with the concept of risk aversion, we offer the following brief explanation. Consider an individual who is faced with a gamble in which the prize is x dollars with probability π and y dollars with probability $(1 - \pi)$. The expected payoff for such a gamble is $\pi x + (1 - \pi)y$ dollars. If the individual would rather receive this expected payoff with certainty than participate in the gamble, he is said to be risk averse. For an expected utility function u, risk aversion amounts to assuming that

$$u(\pi x + (1 - \pi)y) > \pi u(x) + (1 - \pi)u(y) \tag{5}$$

that is, the utility of the expected payoff from the gamble exceeds the expected utility of the gamble itself. Because Equation (5) is the same as the condition for the expected utility function u to be concave, risk aversion is synonymous with concavity of the expected utility function. The coefficient of relative risk aversion is just a measure of this concavity and is defined as

$$\rho \equiv -\frac{Yu''(Y)}{u'(Y)}$$

where Y denotes income. Note that ρ is defined so as to be independent of the units in which expected utility is measured.

If agents are risk averse, then any fluctuations in real income associated with a particular policy tend to render the policy less attractive. For example, in the case of a randomly fluctuating world price, as in sub-section (a), a tariff yields greater fluctuations in real income than the quota. This is because it restricts imports in the state of the world when the world price is high, thus imposing a cost on the economy additional to the real income loss associated with the higher world price. Similarly, when the world price is low, the country benefits from both the expanded trade under the tariff and the positive income effect of a lower world price. Although the income effects of the changes in world price are present under both policies, the point is that the changes in imports under the tariff reinforce these income effects, increasing rather than reducing the magnitude of fluctuations in real income. If individuals are risk averse, these fluctuations reduce the attractiveness of the tariff, and if the degree of risk aversion is sufficiently high, the quota is the preferred policy (see Young and Anderson, 1982, for proof). One possible implication of this result is that the prevalence of quantitative import restrictions in the real world is evidence of high degrees of risk aversion on the part of economic agents. However, given the range of other explanations for the spread of quotas and similar policies (see Deardorff, 1987), it is perhaps unwise to put too much weight on this particular interpretation of events. Finally, we emphasise that the preceding results single out a particular policy (e.g. a quota) as preferable to other policies, assuming that import restriction is the government's objective. The results should in no way be construed as offering an argument for trade restriction or protection per se.

(d)   Protection as insurance

So far we have considered the use of tariffs or quotas to achieve a non-economic objective such as a targeted expected value of imports. We now consider an argument that an economy may benefit from protection in the presence of uncertainty even if there is no underlying non-economic objective. Not surprisingly, the argument is based on second-best considerations, specifically the imperfect operation of insurance markets; but like all second-best arguments, interest centres on the details of the distortion or market failure which the proposed policy is to correct and the manner in which it is corrected.

Newbery and Stiglitz (1984) consider the following example of "Pareto-inferior trade". Suppose there are two crops produced in the world, one risky (e.g. because of the possibilities of drought or frosts) and one safe. If there is no international trade, the fall of the output of the risky crop in a bad season drives up its market-clearing price, reducing the fall in producer incomes. Similarly, a fall in the price when there is a good crop reduces the rise in incomes in a good season. For the special case in which the demand curve for the good has unitary price elasticity, the price changes just offset the crop variations, keeping income the same from season to season. In any case, changes in the market-clearing price work to reduce the variance of producer incomes. Essentially, the risk is borne by consumers who face highly variable prices. When the economy is opened up to trade with the rest of the world, it is possible that fluctuations in producer incomes will replace fluctuations in price. This would be the case if, for example, the rest of the world has a good season while the country in question has a bad season or vice versa. For the special case in which the country's output is perfectly negatively correlated with that of the rest of the world, the world output of the crop is constant at any given world price; thus, for a given world demand curve for the crop, the equilibrium world price is constant regardless of the season in each country. This means that the income of producers in a particular country varies in proportion to their output, being high in a good season and low in a bad season. International trade has made income from the risky crop more risky but, by stabilizing world price, has reduced the risk borne by consumers. If producers are risk averse, some resources will shift out of production of the risky crop into the safe crop, pushing up the world market-clearing price of the risky crop. If consumers are not too risk averse, they will lose more because of the higher average price than they gain from reduced price variability. On the other hand, if producers are sufficiently risk averse, they lose more from the increased variance of their income than they gain from a higher average price. It is possible that all are made worse off by opening the economy up to international trade.

If insurance markets were perfect, agents could completely insure against risk. Then the riskiness of particular activities would not matter, and international trade would necessarily be welfare-improving in the usual sense. However, it is well known that agents' ability to cover risk by means of insurance is constrained. Insurance markets for some contingencies may not exist at all, whereas for others, only incomplete insurance may be offered. This "incompleteness" of insurance markets is explained in part by the phenomena of moral hazard and/or adverse selection (see Arrow, 1970). *Moral hazard* exists when insurers cannot observe the level of effort expended by the insured to prevent an undesirable risky event from taking place, and when the presence of insurance reduces such effort by the individual; for example, individuals who have insured the contents of their home against theft may be careless in securing their home against break-ins. *Adverse selection* arises because the insured may have better information about the riskiness of the events against which they are insuring than the insurer; for instance, chronically ill people are more likely to purchase medical insurance. The presence of either of these factors in a particular insurance market may imply that either the market is inoperative or the insurance it offers against risk is only partial. Given such constraints on agents' ability to insure against risk, risk will matter, and the Pareto-inferior trade we have just described would appear to be a distinct possibility. The implication is that individual economies can gain from restricting trade and that protection has a role in offering "insurance" which would not otherwise be provided. The role of trade policy in this context has been explicitly modelled by Eaton and Grossman (1985).

The main problem with this "tariffs as insurance" argument is that there is no reason to suppose that such government-provided insurance is immune from the problems of moral hazard and adverse selection which led to incompleteness of private insurance markets. This point has been made cogently by Dixit (1987a, 1989), who argues that the sources of a "failure" of the market should be explicitly modelled when considering government policies which are designed to correct the market failure. Consider, for example, how moral hazard and adverse selection might enter the Newbery and Stiglitz scenario. Producers insure against the contingency of a bad harvest; and if they think that the insurer cannot monitor their effort, they may reduce their own productive efforts, safe in the knowledge that their income in the low-crop state of the world is assured[1] (moral hazard). In addition, farmers who are less adept at coping with or preparing for bad seasons, whose land is unsuitably located, who are growing varieties of crops which are more susceptible to bad seasons, and so forth, will be the most likely purchasers of any form of crop or income insurance (adverse selection). The private insurance industry responds to these problems by offering incomplete coverage of risks. Under free trade, output of the risky activity is accordingly less than it would otherwise be. Now suppose the government in one country protects producers of its risky crop by imposing a tariff on imports of that crop. More factors then move into that sector, implicitly taking up the tariff insurance offered by the government. However, these factors tend to be the ones which the private insurance sector was attempting to discourage: the producers and land for whom the downside risk is higher and the producers and workers who are more likely to respond to insurance of their income by reducing their effort. Thus the tariff has merely imposed costs on the community which the private insurance sector sought to avoid. Such considerations cast considerable doubt on the validity of the insurance argument for protection.

This completes our analysis of tariffs and quotas under uncertainty. We now move to an entirely different extension of the basic model, inclusion of the rent-seeking costs associated with tariffs and quotas. Allowing for these costs is the first step in the process of identifying costs of protection beyond the "Harberger triangles" used in this and the previous chapter for evaluating different policies. Introducing rent seeking into the model also provides a further instance of the non-equivalence of tariffs and quotas.

3.4.   The rent-seeking costs of tariffs and quotas

The term *rent seeking* was used by Anne Krueger (Krueger, 1974) to describe the competition for the rents that accompany most forms of pre-existing government intervention or regulation. The real resources used up in such activity are generally regarded as being wasted because their use does not create wealth but merely transfers existing wealth between groups or individuals[2] (see Tullock, 1967). In this section we consider how measures of the social cost of protection should be modified to allow for additional waste arising from rent seeking. Before we consider the different forms that this rent seeking can take, it is worth noting that we are not considering the lobbying for or against a particular policy which precedes the introduction of that policy. Such lobbying (which is also frequently called rent seeking) can be viewed as something which would have occurred anyway (whether or not the policy was adopted) and so should not be counted as a cost of the policy.[3] For the remainder of this section we turn our attention to the rent seeking which is induced by pre-existing tariffs and import quotas. Lobbying aimed at persuading government to introduce a distortion will be analysed in Chapter 8 in which we consider why a particular protective instrument is adopted and what determines its level.

In her original (1974) article, Krueger considers the particular case in which the rents being contested arise from quantitative trade restrictions (e.g. import quotas). In the case of an import quota, these rents occur if import licences are handed out free of charge. The rent seeking which ensues is a contest to capture a share of the scarce import licences, and it may take various forms, the most obvious of which are direct lobbying of politicians (involving such costs as trips to the capital city and establishing premises there), overinvestment in physical plant (to quality for licences allocated in proportion to firms' capacities), bribery[4] and other forms of corruption. There is reason to believe that in many countries these quota rents (and the associated rent-seeking costs) can be very large indeed. For example, Krueger calculates that in India in 1964, total rents amounted to 7.3 per cent of GNP. Of this figure, rents associated with import licences represented over two-thirds. In 1968 in Turkey, quota rents were calculated to be about 15 per cent of GNP (Krueger, 1974 p. 294). Moreover, there is reason to suppose that the rent seeking associated with quota licences is just the tip of the iceberg. For example, by including other distortions such as price controls and rationing, Mohammed and Whalley (1984) estimate total contestable rents associated with pre-existing government policies in India to be somewhere between 30 and 45 per cent of GNP.

When the instrument of import restriction is a tariff, we would similarly expect to find some resources directed at capturing a share of the recycled tariff revenue; the frequent, highly visible campaigns by interest groups for government funding of particular projects constitute an obvious example of such revenue seeking (Bhagwati and Srinivasan, 1980). The contest for the tariff revenue may however be less clearly defined than the contest for the import quota rents, with the latter usually being conducted among a small number of participants, each facing a clearly defined expected return (a certain number of quota licences). In contrast, the expected return from the tariff revenue (which is traditionally spread over a large number of people) may be so small that it is not profitable for any individual to incur the cost of entering the contest. It seems more likely that the revenue-seeking contest takes place in a broader sphere, the object being a share of total government revenue. If this is the case, then we are faced with the problem that the lobbying for revenue may occur whether the tariff is there or not and so cannot be counted as a specific cost of the tariff. For this reason, quota rent seeking appeals as a more interesting and relevant notion than tariff revenue seeking. Nevertheless, there are many instances, particularly in developing countries, in which import duties generate a sizable proportion of total revenue, and the notion of tariff revenue seeking does seem appropriate in such cases.

We now consider both the effects and the social costs of rent seeking. In evaluating the latter, the economist must consider two distinct questions:

i.   What is the value of resources dissipated by the rent seekers in their quest for the rent or revenue? In particular, what relationship does this resource dissipation bear to the value of the rent contested? A standard working assumption here is that the value of resources dissipated equals the value of the rent or revenue contested. A partial equilibrium view (partial because the rent-seeking sector itself is excluded) combined with the assumption that rent seekers compete for the entire tariff revenue or quota rents implies that the social cost of a quota or its tariff-equivalent is equal to the sum of areas A and B (the Harberger triangles) in Figure 3.4 and the rectangle of quota rents or tariff revenue, R (referred to as the *Krueger rectangle* for obvious reasons). This would certainly be a convenient way of evaluating the costs of protec-

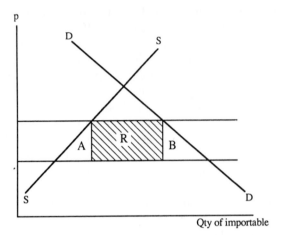

Figure 3.4

tion; in the absence of a theory of the rent-seeking sector, the usual practice has been to use R as an estimate of rent-seeking costs.

ii. Accepting for the moment that rent seekers waste resources equal in value to the rent–revenue rectangle, does that rectangle represent the cost of rent seeking to society when general equilibrium considerations are taken into account?

Question (i) has been the subject of much research for the case in which a single rent seeker captures all of an indivisible rent, such as the granting of a government contract or the securing of a monopoly position as a result of government regulation (see Corcoran, 1984; Hillman and Katz, 1984; Tullock, 1980). The relevant case here, in which rents are shared among the rent seekers (as is usually true for tariff revenue or quota licences) has been analysed by Long and Vousden (1987). They show that the Krueger rectangle is a good *long-run* measure of the resources dissipated by the rent seekers if (i) there is free entry (exit) into (out of) the rent-seeking activity; and if either (ii) individuals are risk-neutral or (iii) individuals are risk-averse and the rent contested is a small proportion of the rent seekers' total wealth. Certainly, risk aversion (together with the riskiness of the rent-seeking activity) does reduce the proportion of rents dissipated below unity. However, this effect is negligible if the rent in question is a small proportion of the individuals' total wealth.

We now turn to question (ii). Assuming that the value of rents sought *is* a good measure of the value of resources dissipated in seeking those rents, does that resource cost equal the actual social cost

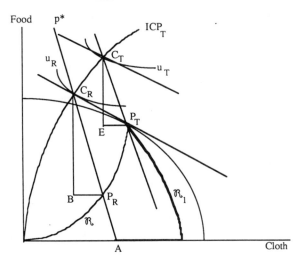

Figure 3.5

of the rent-seeking activity when general equilibrium effects are taken into account? To make the main points in the simplest possible way, we start with the case in which all of the tariff revenue or quota rents are sought. We shall then proceed to the more realistic case in which only part of the revenue or rents is sought.

(a)   *Entire rent sought*

We begin by considering the case of a tariff, illustrated in Figure 3.5. In the absence of revenue seeking or lobbying, tariff-distorted equilibrium involves production at P_T, consumption at C_T and utility u_T. Now suppose that all of the tariff revenue is sought by competitive rent seekers. Given our assumption that the value of resources dissipated in this process equals the revenue sought, the tariff revenue effectively "disappears", and domestic factor income equals expenditure valued at domestic prices; that is, the economy's consumption point is moved down the income consumption path (ICP) for the tariff-distorted price (ICP$_T$) to position C_R. Because of the balance-of-trade constraint, the economy can only consume a bundle equal in value to what it produces, so the new production point must lie on the world price line p^* through C_R.

The production point P_R lies inside the production frontier, reflecting the loss of productive resources to revenue seeking. To fix P_R, we construct the so-called Rybczynski curve ($\mathfrak{R}$) through P_T. This represents the locus of outputs of food and cloth as capital and labour are withdrawn in the ratio required by revenue- or rent-seeking activity at the given (tariff- or quota-distorted) domestic price ratio. Whereas the Rybczynski theorem and its extensions relate to the effects of various patterns of factor growth on sectoral outputs, this Rybczynski curve illustrates that process in reverse. Because the economy's production point must be on both the Rybczynski curve $\mathfrak{R}$ and the world price line p^*, it will be at their intersection point P_R, as shown in Figure 3.5.

A number of features of the equilibrium in Figure 3.5 are worth noting:

i.   Imports (BC_R) probably differ from their value (EC_T) in the absence of revenue seeking. Clearly, the level of food imports depends on the form of the curve $\mathfrak{R}$, which in turn depends on the lobbying technology. If the quantity of imports is changed by revenue seeking, then the equilibrium tariff revenue also changes as does the value of resources dissipated in revenue seeking.

ii. The equilibrium consumption point and utility are independent of the lobbying technology (they are always C_R and u_R, respectively).

iii. Although the Rybczynski curve is drawn with a positive slope in Figure 3.5, let us note that it could easily be negatively sloped depending on the relationship between the capital intensities in food, cloth and lobbying. To take a simple case, suppose lobbying uses only labour and that food is the labour-intensive good. Then the lobbying activity amounts to a contraction of the economy's labour supply. Rybczynski's theorem applies (in reverse), and the capital-intensive sector expands while the labour-intensive sector contracts, giving a negatively sloped Rybczynski curve like $\mathfrak{R}_1$ in Figure 3.5. This is an interesting case (discussed in detail by Bhagwati and Srinivasan, 1980),[5] which opens up the possibility that the economy's production point might move back towards the free-trade point (along $\mathfrak{R}_1$), a potentially welfare-improving change. However, in the present case with full revenue seeking, consumption is anchored at C_R, and p^* cannot intersect $\mathfrak{R}_1$ in its negatively sloped region. Equilibrium production must be on the price line p^*. In the case illustrated, it is attained at point A: The lobbying activity expands, moving the economy down $\mathfrak{R}_1$ until it hits the cloth axis; then, as further resources are drawn into the lobbying effort, the economy's only remaining output (cloth) contracts further along the horizontal axis until point A on price line p^* is reached. Consumption is then at point C_R, and there are no remaining uncaptured rents to attract further revenue seekers into the activity. As noted in (ii), equilibrium consumption and utility were not affected by the particular form of the Rybczynski curve.

iv. For full revenue seeking, the social cost of the rent seeking valued at tariff-distorted prices is exactly equal to the value of the tariff revenue in the absence of revenue seeking (the horizontal distance between the domestic price lines through C_T and C_R). In general, this differs from the actual tariff revenue in the presence of revenue seeking, which is the horizontal distance between the domestic price line through C_R and a parallel line through P_R. Whether the actual tariff revenue overstates or understates the true cost of the revenue seeking depends on where the Rybczynski curve cuts the price line p^* (in Figure 3.5, imports and tariff revenue are higher after rent seeking than before), which in turn reflects how the withdrawal of resources associated with revenue seeking changes relative outputs of food and cloth. Thus the Krueger rectangle is not an exact measure of the cost, but it may still be a reasonable approximation.

These remarks apply to the case of a tariff. Let us now reinterpret Figure 3.5 as applying to an import quota for which all of the quota licences are sought. As for the tariff, let the equilibrium without rent seeking involve production at P_T, consumption at C_T and utility u_T. Then, when all of the quota rents are sought, the consumption point moves down onto the domestic price line tangent to the economy's production point. It is here that we encounter a nonequivalence between tariffs and quotas. You will recall that imports in the revenue-seeking equilibrium do not, in general, equal imports in the absence of revenue seeking. Indeed, in the diagram as drawn, they tend to be larger with revenue seeking than without it ($BC_R > EC_T$). However, under a binding quota, imports must necessarily be EC_T with or without rent seeking. Thus, with rent seeking, the quota is violated unless the relative price of food rises to clear the excess demand for food. The economy's consumption point is still a point of tangency between a community indifference curve and the domestic price line tangent to the economy's production point, but the slope of that domestic price line has changed (so as to clear the domestic market for food), and the production point has rotated around the production frontier (with more food being produced). The quota is clearly not equivalent to its implicit tariff in this case. In fact, it is inferior to the tariff because it involves a higher equilibrium domestic relative price of food.[6] Furthermore, the equilibrium price under the quota depends on the lobbying technology as embodied in the Rybczynski curve (the position of which determines the level of imports BC_R before the price adjusts to clear the market). This non-equivalence of tariffs and quotas in the presence of rent or revenue seeking can be reinforced if the rent-seeking technology differs from the revenue-seeking technology (different Rybczynski curves).

In general, the entire tariff revenue or quota rents are not sought by the lobbyists. Prior expenditure commitments by governments tie up considerable amounts of revenue, which lobbyists realize is not worth competing for. Similarly, import licences may sometimes be allocated (at least partially) by mechanisms which are immune from rent seeking (e.g. by lottery), and such licences

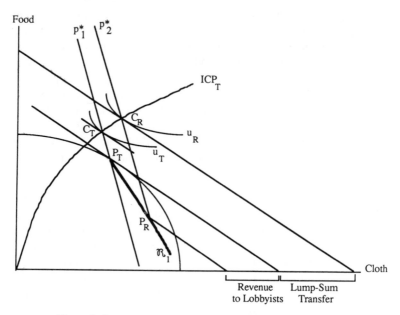

Figure 3.6

obviously do not give rise to any lobbying. The following sub-section considers what happens in such cases.

(b)   Partial rent seeking

Once again, we consider tariffs first. Suppose lobbyists seek only part of the tariff revenue, while the remainder is distributed to the community as a lump-sum transfer. Suppose also that the Rybczynski line is of the negatively sloped form $\mathcal{R}_1$ and lies to the right of the world price line p^* through P_T. Then it can be seen from Figure 3.6 that a tariff-ridden economy may be better off with revenue seeking than without it.

As before, the tariff-distorted equilibrium without revenue seeking is at P_T, C_T. With partial revenue seeking, production is at P_R on $\mathcal{R}_1$ and the consumption point is at C_R on the world price line p_2^* through P_R. Utility is u_R, a welfare improvement over the no-lobbying, tariff-distorted equilibrium (u_T) so that, as suggested, revenue seeking actually benefits the community. This result is made possible by the recycling of part of the revenue to the community, which allows a positive income effect to work with the negatively sloped Rybczynski curve to move the economy's consumption point out along the income consumption path ICP_T. The details of the process are as follows. Lobbying withdraws resources in a way which causes production of the exportable to expand at the expense of the importable, thereby moving the world price line out from p_1^* to p_2^*. Imports rise, increasing the tariff revenue, including the lump-sum transfer component of that revenue (and also, presumably, the revenue captured by lobbyists).[7] The resulting increase in income (at domestic prices) provides the means of sustaining the higher consumption point C_R. Although this result may seem counter-intuitive, it has to be remembered that lobbying (which is equivalent to contraction of factor supplies) is being introduced into a system which is already characterized by a distortion (the tariff). The economy is thus in a second-best situation, and the introduction of lobbying may lead to a welfare improvement. The loss due to dissipation of resources in lobbying activity is more than offset by the benefits of a pattern of production which is closer to free trade.

We now turn our attention to quotas, assuming that only part of the quota licences are actively sought. Once again, the crucial difference between a tariff and a quota is that imports can change under a tariff but are fixed under a quota. This constancy of imports under the quota prevents any welfare-improving income effects through increased recycled quota rents. Thus the gains from increased trade which were potentially attainable under a tariff with partial revenue seeking are unattainable under an import quota (i.e. u_R necessarily lies below u_T). We conclude that rent seeking cannot increase welfare in the presence of an import quota (see Anam, 1982). Nevertheless, if quota rents are only partially sought, there is no reason why P_R should not lie on the negatively sloped portion of $\mathcal{R}_1$, implying some reduction of the cost of rent seeking below the value of rents sought because of an improved allocation of resources between food and cloth.

This completes our analysis of tariffs and quotas in the presence of distortion-triggered lobbying. We now return to the question of how to measure the cost of protection when resources are dissipated through rent seeking.

(c)   The cost of rent seeking

As explained earlier, there may be some justification for assuming that the Krueger rectangle is an accurate measure of the resources used by rent seekers. The question remains: does the value of resources dissipated necessarily equal the social cost of rent seeking in a general equilibrium context? On the basis of the foregoing analysis, the answer to this question is clearly no. We have seen, for example, that the withdrawal of factors for lobbying may take the economy to a more efficient production point and thereby reduce the cost of rent seeking below the rent rectangle (the case of quotas) or even make the cost negative (the welfare improvement in the case of partial tariff revenue seeking). It is obviously safer to work with a full general equilibrium model.

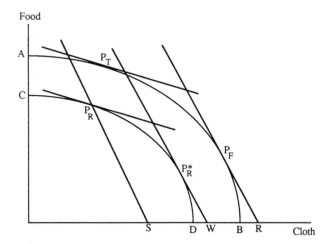

Figure 3.7

Bhagwati (1980) considers the possibilities that may arise if the two-sector general equilibrium model is used to estimate the deadweight loss of a tariff or quota. Because the consumption cost is largely unaffected by the presence of rent seeking, we consider only the estimation of the production cost. In Figure 3.7, AB represents the economy's production frontier with P_F the free-trade production point and P_T the production point under a tariff in the absence of lobbying. P_R denotes the actual production point of the economy with the tariff and the revenue seeking that accompanies it. It may be thought of as a point of tangency of a tariff-distorted price line and a "shrunk" production frontier (CD), which represents the locus of efficient outputs of food and cloth when the capital and labour required for lobbying have been removed from productive use. If those same resources were being used for lobbying at *free-trade* prices, the economy would produce at P_R^*. Of the four production points we have identified, only one (P_R) is observable. Presumably, in estimating the standard production cost of protection, we would choose a procedure which minimizes the number of hypothetical production points we have to calculate. We can observe P_R and estimate either P_F or P_R^*.[8] If we estimate P_F, then we conclude that the production cost of the tariff is SR. This will in fact be the entire production cost including any costs or benefits arising from rent seeking. It would therefore be unnecessary in this case to derive a separate estimate of the cost of rent seeking per se. On the other hand, we may form our estimate of the free-trade production point on the assumption that the economy's supplies of capital and labour are the same as at P_R (i.e. we are not aware of the leakage of resources to distortion-triggered lobbying). This would lead us to point P_R^* on the inner production frontier CD, and we would estimate the production cost of the tariff as SW, omitting the component WR of the total production cost. WR

would then have to be estimated separately as a cost of rent seeking. It is possible that the Krueger rectangle (revalued in terms of world prices) may be a suitable approximation for *WR*, but that remains an open question.

3.5.   Summary

In this chapter we have explored further issues relating to tariffs and import quotas in competitive markets. One of these, the quality upgrading that accompanies volume quota restriction of imports of a group of goods, was explained by noting the equivalence between a volume quota and a uniform specific tariff on the one hand and a value quota and a uniform ad valorem tariff on the other. Because a uniform specific tariff makes the more expensive items in a restricted group relatively cheaper, it encourages a shift towards imports of these items (upgrading). The same is true of a volume quota. On the other hand, a value quota does not significantly affect relative prices within the restricted group and so does not induce a shift in the composition of imports.

Although tariffs and quotas have been seen to be equivalent in the simple static competitive model, one of the main points of this chapter is that this equivalence breaks down when other elements are added to the problem. In particular, the shifting of parameters over time (in either a deterministic or a stochastic sense) was seen to imply very different outcomes under the two policies. In the case of an uncertain world price, it was found that a government wishing to constrain the expected volume of its imports achieves a higher level of expected consumer surplus by using a specific tariff than by using either an ad valorem tariff or an import quota. On the other hand, if it wishes to constrain the expected value of imports, expected consumer surplus is highest under an ad valorem tariff. These results are changed if economic agents are sufficiently risk averse, in which case expected consumer surplus is not a valid criterion for policy comparison; with sufficient risk aversion, the price (and income) stabilizing properties of an import quota make it the preferred policy. Finally, it should be emphasised that even if a particular policy is found to be the most efficient means of restricting trade, it remains a *second-best* policy for a small country. The first-best policy is not to restrict trade at all.

If rent- or revenue-seeking costs are incorporated into the model, further evidence is provided of the non-equivalence of tariffs and quotas. In addition, the costs of activity directed at capturing a share of the quota rents or tariff revenue is thought to be an empirically significant component of the overall cost of protection. The value of resources used in this non-productive activity may be reasonably approximated by the value of the rents or revenue contested, the so-called Krueger rectangle. However, general equilibrium effects associated with the waste of productive resources by the rent-seeking sector may, in certain cases, reduce the welfare cost of the rent seeking below the area of the rectangle.

CHAPTER 4

Protection for a large country

The analysis of Chapters 2 and 3 was conducted in terms of an economy which was too small to affect the prices at which it bought and sold goods in world markets. Such an approach offers both a simple means of obtaining insights into the workings of various policies and a reasonably accurate representation of most real world economies. However, it is an inadequate tool for analysing the trade relations among such major trading countries or blocs as the United States, Japan and the EEC. In this chapter we temporarily leave the small-country case and consider economies which are large enough to use their buying and selling power to influence world prices. For the time being, we retain the assumption that producers are atomistic price takers. The logical starting point for any analysis of protection in a large-country context is the observation that a country which can, by its own actions, affect the price at which it buys or sells a traded good may gain by using a tariff or an export tax to restrict trade. The resulting gains from an improved terms of trade must be balanced at the margin against the increased domestic deadweight losses from a higher trade tax. The outcome of this exercise is the so-called optimal tariff. In the first section we consider how the optimum tariff is derived. We then employ a two-country model to consider the outcome when one country's optimal tariff induces the other country to impose a retaliatory tariff. The equilibrium of such a trade war is seen to depend crucially on whether trade is restricted by a price-related tool such as a tariff or a quantitative device such as a quota. An alternative policy tool which has become increasingly popular in recent years is the voluntary export restraint (VER). VERs are analysed in some detail in Section 4.4. In the final section of the chapter we consider variable import levies and export subsidies, policies which are a central part of the EEC's Common Agricultural Policy.

4.1. The optimal tariff

Consider a two-good economy which is a large buyer in the world market for its importable good. In Figure 4.1, *DD* is the country's demand curve for imports, and because the country is large, it faces an upward-sloping foreign supply curve of imports, *SS*. Although *SS* represents the marginal cost curve for foreign exporters, from the home economy's point of view it is the *average cost of imports;* it tells us what the home economy must pay for each unit it imports.

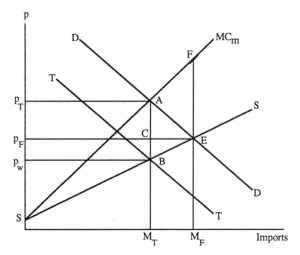

Figure 4.1

Because this curve is upward-sloping (i.e. foreign producers export more only if a higher price is offered), the *marginal cost of imports* to the home economy is also upward-sloping and lies above SS. This is because the cost to the economy of an extra unit of imports includes not only the price of the marginal unit (as given by SS) but also the added cost of paying for the inframarginal units (because their price rises with the price of the marginal unit). This marginal cost-of-imports curve is shown as MC_m in Figure 4.1.

In a free-trade situation, world equilibrium is at the point E, where the domestic demand curve and the foreign supply curve intersect, giving price p_F and quantity imported M_F. However at this point, the value to the home country of an extra unit of imports is less than the marginal cost of that unit (by an amount EF). The home country can therefore increase its welfare by reducing imports to level M_T, determined by the point of intersection (A) of the demand curve and MC_m; the resulting gain is equal to the area FAE. This gain has come about because the home country's restriction of import demand has reduced the equilibrium relative price at which it buys imports – that is, its terms of trade have improved, p_w denotes the new world relative price of imports. So far the story should be a familiar one: a country which is a monopsonist gains by reducing its demand for a good, thereby forcing down its price, in much the same way as a firm which is a monopsonistic buyer of labour can obtain its labour more cheaply by employing fewer workers. The difference in the present case is that import restriction is not realized without government intervention because the agents of the economy are too small to exercise any monopsony power. On the other hand, the government can move the economy from the suboptimal free-trade point E to the optimal point A by imposing a trade-restricting policy such as a tariff. A tariff of AB per unit will shift the demand curve for imports down to TT in Figure 4.1, and equilibrium in the world market will be realized at B with world price p_w and domestic price p_T. The tariff of $p_w p_T$ per unit is termed the *optimal tariff*.

The foregoing amounts to the so-called *terms of trade argument for protection*: if an economy in a freely trading world is large enough to use trade restrictions to improve its terms of trade then it gains by doing so. If it also wishes to achieve some domestic non-economic objective, then it should use the instrument appropriate to that objective (e.g. a production subsidy), using the tariff separately to improve its terms of trade. This principle (which is a straightforward extension of the principle of targeting instruments to objectives, enunciated in Chapter 2) is established formally in Appendix 2, where we also derive the standard formula for the optimal tariff in a two-good world.

Although a large country can secure improved terms of trade by imposing a tariff, it does so at the cost of increased domestic deadweight losses (the Harberger triangles of Chapter 2). Because of this trade-off, it does not pay a country to increase its tariff indefinitely. The two effects are illustrated in Figure 4.1. Relative to free trade, domestic consumers lose the area $p_T A E p_F$ (this is net of transfers to domestic producers because we are using the demand curve for imports, not importables). Against this, we must count the recycled tariff revenue, $p_T A B p_w$. Of this, $p_T A C P_F$ is transferred from domestic consumers to domestic taxpayers and $p_F C B p_w$ is transferred from foreign producers to domestic taxpayers. The net gain (AFE) from the tariff is thus seen to equal the excess of area $p_F C P p_w$ (the terms of trade gain) over area AEC (the domestic deadweight loss). The optimal tariff is such that the marginal gain from the terms of trade improvement associated with a small tariff increase equals the marginal loss via domestic distortion costs. In particular, the optimal tariff must be less than the prohibitive tariff (the tariff which eliminates imports) because a small reduction of the tariff below the prohibitive level involves no terms-of-trade loss (because imports are zero) but yields a gain by reducing the domestic distortion cost of the tariff: accordingly, the economy must gain by reducing the tariff below the prohibitive level.

Note that there are several implicit assumptions in this model which ensure that the optimal tariff is positive. In particular, the monotonic forms we have assumed for SS and DD (positively sloped and negatively sloped, respectively) effectively exclude the possibility that the export supply of the foreign country (for example) may be non-unique for some prices. If this possibility is admitted, then a negative optimal tariff (i.e. an import subsidy) may be the outcome (for further discussion of this possibility, see Riley, 1970). In addition, we have confined our attention to impact effects. A tariff imposed by the home country may have significant effects on income distribution in the foreign country. If

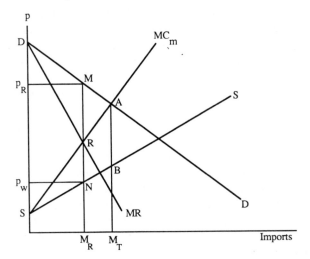

Figure 4.2

such redistributions reduce the foreign supply of exports, shifting SS to the left, then the home country's marginal cost of imports will be increased. If such an effect outweighs the other gains from a positive tariff, then the home country would have done better by imposing an import subsidy (see Kemp, 1967).

Finally, we note that although an individual large country can make itself better off by imposing its optimal tariff, the welfare of the world as a whole will be reduced by such an action. This is readily illustrated with the aid of Figure 4.1 in which total world welfare can be measured as the sum of domestic net "consumer surplus" from imports plus foreign net producer surplus from exports, that is, the area below the demand curve DD and above the foreign supply curve SS up to the quantity of goods traded. When the home country imposes its optimal tariff, this area is reduced by the triangle ABE (the tariff revenue being merely an inter-country transfer), indicating a fall in total world welfare.

This presentation of the optimal tariff argument is helpful because it presents the argument in terms of the simple textbook model of monopsony, and because it illustrates the trade-off between gains and losses in arriving at the optimal tariff.[1] It can also be used to compare the optimal tariff with the tariff which yields the government the highest revenue, the so-called *maximum revenue tariff*. This comparison is made with the aid of Figure 4.2.

The government, as collector of the tariff revenue, is equivalent to a monopolistic firm which buys imports from abroad at an average cost given by curve SS and sells them at a price given by the demand curve, the profits being the tariff revenue. For the case illustrated in Figure 4.2, there is a unique tariff level at which tariff revenue is maximized. This maximum is attained at point R where the marginal revenue curve derived from D (MR in Figure 4.2) intersects MC_m. Such an equilibrium clearly involves a lower level of imports than under the optimal tariff (M_R as opposed to M_T) and therefore requires a higher tariff per unit (MN as opposed to AB). We have thus shown, for the case in which tariff revenue is a single-peaked function of the tariff level (as it is in Figure 4.2), that the maximum revenue tariff exceeds the optimal tariff.[2] In other words, if governments are using tariffs primarily as a revenue-raising device, then it is likely that they will restrict trade more than is optimal from their country's point of view.

The export tax equivalent of this result is also of interest, not least because it has implications (perhaps surprisingly) for government tax policy towards monopolistic exporting bodies such as grain-marketing firms. Recall that the Lerner symmetry theorem tells us that an export tax is equivalent to a tariff at the same rate. This implies the following analogue of the previous tariff result: the maximum revenue export tax exceeds the optimal export tax. Now consider the case of a monopolistic domestic marketing firm which buys, say, wheat from domestic producers (at their marginal cost of production) and exports it to foreign consumers. It uses its monopoly power to maximize profits from exporting but is constrained to charge domestic consumers the price paid to domestic producers (i.e. a zero profit constraint on its domestic sales). The profit maximization problem of such a firm is the same as the problem faced by a government using an export tax to maximize revenue (both wish to maximize the profits that accrue from the excess of the export price over the domestic supply price). Both restrict exports below the optimal level. Accordingly, a government pursuing welfare (rather than revenue) optimization would have to subsidize exports by the firm. This case and other types of export monopolies (e.g. producer cartels and marketing boards) are analysed in detail in Just, Schmitz and Zilberman (1979). The optimal government tax or subsidy policy towards such monopolies varies from case to case, the particular example given here being intended merely as an illustration of how simple techniques can be applied to this type of problem.

We now digress briefly and reconsider the basic optimal tariff problem of Figure 4.1, using the alternative representation of offer curves and trade indifference curves (see Chapter 1). This provides us with a more convenient framework for use in the next two sections in which we consider tariffs and quotas in the presence of retaliation. It is also the standard treatment of the subject in most trade textbooks. Figure 4.3 illustrates this approach.

In a two-country world, OR denotes the home country's offer curve, and OR^* is the foreign country's offer curve under free trade. The equilibrium terms of trade are given by the ray OE. At the world equilibrium point E, the terms-of-trade line is tangent to trade indifference curves u and u^* for the home and foreign countries, respectively. It is clear from Figure 4.3 that, if the foreign country pursues free trade, the home country can attain a higher trade indif-

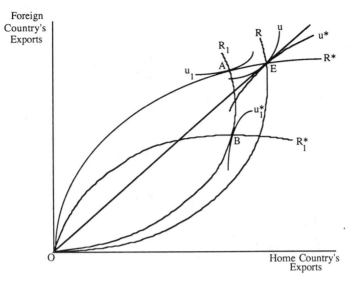

Figure 4.3

ference curve by imposing a tariff. A tariff has the effect of shifting the home country's offer curve inward along any price ray through the origin (because the tariff reduces the volume of trade at any terms of trade). The offer curve OR_1 is the tariff-distorted offer curve that puts the home country on its highest possible trade indifference curve consistent with the foreign country's offer curve – this is the indifference curve u_1 which is tangent to $OR*$ at A. The domestic price ratio at A is given by the slope of u_1 at A, and the associated tariff is the home country's optimal tariff. We thus see again that if the foreign country has a zero tariff, the home country gains by imposing a positive tariff.

It seems unlikely that the foreign country will react passively to this tariff. After all, it stands to gain by imposing its own retaliatory tariff. A tariff which shifts its offer curve down to position OR_1^* will maximize its utility subject to the home country's offer curve OR_1 (at point B on indifference curve u_1^*). In the presence of such retaliation, two questions must be asked: what equilibrium is likely to emerge from such non-cooperative behaviour and can the home country still be better off than under free trade? To answer these questions, we now turn to a more thorough analysis of tariffs and retaliation.

4.2. Tariffs and retaliation

Let us assume that each country chooses its tariff to maximize its welfare, taking the tariff of the other country as given – so-called non-cooperative Nash behaviour. The outcome of this behaviour is a *non-cooperative Nash equi-*

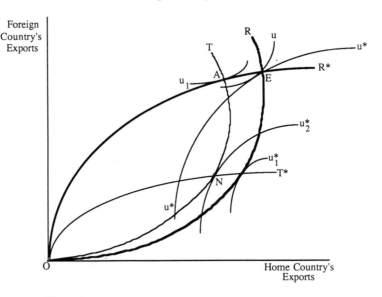

Figure 4.4

librium, a term used to describe an equilibrium of a contest between a number of agents in which each agent is at an optimum, given the actions of all other agents in the contest. It is to be distinguished from a cooperative Nash equilibrium in which the agents collude to maximize their joint welfare. Unless stated otherwise, the term *Nash equilibrium* will be taken to mean a non-cooperative equilibrium.

To derive the Nash equilibrium in the present problem we shall use the standard device of deriving reaction curves showing how each country's optimal behaviour depends on the other country's tariff. The point of intersection of these reaction curves then determines the Nash equilibrium volume of trade and the two countries' tariff levels. In Figure 4.4, curve *OT* represents the locus of tangencies of home country trade indifference curves and foreign offer curves; in other words, it represents the locus of the home country's optimal responses to various levels of the foreign tariff. Similarly, *OT** is the foreign country's reaction curve, being the locus of tangencies between foreign trade indifference curves and home country offer curves. As one country increases its tariff towards the level which would eliminate trade, the optimal tariff for the other country approaches zero (there can be no terms-of-trade gain when there is zero trade). This occurs at the origin on both reaction curves. Furthermore, at the origin, *OT* has the same slope as the home country's free-trade offer curve *OR*, and *OT** has the same slope as the foreign free-trade offer curve *OR**. However, when positive quantities are traded, each country gains by imposing a positive tariff for any given non-prohibitive tariff of the other country. Thus OT lies to the left of OR, and OT^* lies below OR^* as shown in Figure 4.4.

Point N represents the Nash equilibrium. The origin is not an equilibrium (although it looks like one in Figure 4.4) because it requires one country to impose a prohibitive tariff while the other responds with free trade. In such a situation, the country imposing the tariff would clearly do better by moving to its optimal tariff, which we know to be below the prohibitive rate (Section 4.1). This would then allow positive trade to take place, and the other country would gain by imposing a retaliatory tariff: the system moves away from O towards N. Thus, one conclusion of this model is that tariff retaliation which yields a Nash equilibrium does not eliminate trade. Of course, it is still possible that trade may be eliminated asymptotically with successive retaliations taking the world economy closer to O (but never actually reaching O). However, Tower (1976b) shows that this possibility can also be ruled out, provided neither country would be completely specialized under autarky. In other words, in a world in which incomplete specialization is the rule, a tariff war would allow trade to continue at a strictly positive level. As we shall see in the next section, this is in marked contrast to the outcome when a trade war is conducted using quantitative trade restrictions.

Figure 4.4 can also be used to illustrate the possibility (originally noted by Johnson, 1953) that one of the two countries may be better off at N than under free trade at E. In the diagram as drawn, the foreign country is on trade indifference curve u_2^*, which is superior to the free-trade indifference curve u^*. In other words, even in the presence of retaliation, one country may gain by imposing a tariff.

The determination of the Nash equilibrium tariff levels can also be illustrated by drawing the reaction curves in the tariff plane (Figure 4.5). This representation gives us another way of looking at the problem and will also be useful when we analyse negotiated tariff reductions in Chapter 10. In Figure 4.5, we confine our attention to the simple case in which each country's reaction curve is downward sloping and there is a unique Nash equilibrium. The tariff levels for the home and foreign countries are denoted by t and t^*, respectively. The reaction curve $t(t^*)$ shows the home country's welfare-maximizing tariff for given values of t^*. The foreign country's tariff reaction curve $t^*(t)$ is similarly defined. The intersection point of the two reaction curves at N yields the Nash equilibrium tariff levels for the two countries. Each country's tariff reaction curve (i) is single valued (i.e. there is a unique best tariff response to any tariff set by the other country), (ii) has a positive intercept on its own axis at its optimal tariff rate ($\hat{t}$ and $\hat{t}^*$ for the home and foreign countries, respectively), (iii) involves a positive tariff when the other country is imposing its optimal tariff (e.g. the foreign country's retaliatory move to u_1^* in Figure 4.3 corresponds to a tariff of t_1^* in Figure 4.5a), and (iv) intercepts the other country's

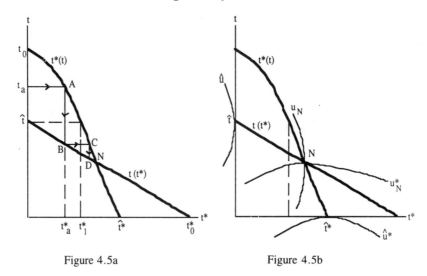

Figure 4.5a   Figure 4.5b

tariff axis at that country's prohibitive tariff (t_0^* and t_0, respectively, on the horizontal and vertical axes of Figure 4.5a) which is greater than its optimal tariff (we argued in Section 4.1 that the optimal tariff is not prohibitive). These properties are sufficient to ensure that the Nash equilibrium N is not associated with the elimination of trade.

It is also possible to use Figure 4.5 to analyse the welfare consequences of a tariff war. To do this, we first ascertain the form of each country's indifference curves in the (t^*,t)-plane. For the home country, we begin by noting that, below its reaction curve, its tariff is below the Nash optimal level (the optimum being on the reaction curve) so that, at a given level of t^*, an increase in t would increase the home country's welfare. For its welfare to remain constant, the other country's tariff t^* would also have to rise. Thus, in the region below $t(t^*)$, the home country's indifference curves are upward sloping. Above $t(t^*)$ a rise in t would reduce home country welfare (by moving the tariff further away from its optimum) unless there were a compensating fall in the other country's tariff. This implies a negative slope for the home country's indifference curves in the region above $t(t^*)$ with the curves crossing $t(t^*)$ vertically. Curves further to the left correspond to higher levels of home country welfare (because of the lower level of the foreign tariff). Thus the indifference curve through $\hat{t}$, labelled $\hat{u}$ in Figure 4.5b, corresponds to a higher level of welfare than the curve u_N passing through the Nash equilibrium. By similar reasoning, the foreign country's indifference curves are positively sloped to the left of its reaction curve $t^*(t)$ and negatively sloped to the right of $t^*(t)$, crossing the reaction curve with a zero slope. Lower curves correspond to higher levels of foreign welfare because of the lower home country tariff. Thus u_N^*, the foreign indifference curve through

N in Figure 4.5b, represents a lower level of foreign welfare than the curve $\hat{u}^*$ passing through the foreign optimal tariff point $\hat{t}^*$. In fact, it is easy to see that a country's welfare falls as it moves along its reaction curve away from its optimal tariff towards a zero tariff (i.e. as trade is increasingly restricted by higher tariffs imposed by the other country).

In the case illustrated in Figure 4.5, the Nash equilibrium at N is unique and is also stable in the sense that Nash behaviour by the two countries moves the system towards point N. The reader can easily use Figure 4.5a to verify that N is stable by assuming some arbitrary initial tariff for, say, the home country. Suppose it is t_a. Then the foreign country will maximize its welfare, given t_a, by choosing its tariff at level t_a^* to put it on its reaction curve at point A. Given t_a^*, the home country will move to point B on its reaction curve, and so on, with the system in Figure 4.5a adjusting towards N along the path $ABCD$. Although this type of sequential adjustment is an idealized version of what might actually take place, it is a useful way of illustrating stability without resorting to mathematics. In fact, N can be seen to be stable within a "neighborhood" of equilibrium whenever the home country's reaction curve is flatter than the foreign country's reaction curve (the case illustrated). The reader may also like to use a diagram to verify that the equilibrium is unstable when the home country reaction curve is steeper than the foreign curve.

Finally, it is important to note that Figure 4.5 illustrates only one of many possible outcomes. It is also theoretically possible to have multiple equilibria (some stable, some unstable) or a tariff cycle (in which a particular sequence of tariff responses is repeated ad infinitum) (see Johnson, 1953, for details of these cases). Despite this range of possibilities, one result is quite firm: in the absence of complete specialization, trade is not eliminated. In addition, one country may gain from imposing a tariff, even in the presence of retaliation.[3] Both of these results stand in marked contrast to the outcome when the two countries employ trade quotas as their means of protection. This is the subject of the next section.

4.3.   Quotas and retaliation

Rodriguez (1974) and Tower (1975) have independently established that when two countries exhibiting non-cooperative Nash behaviour employ import or export quotas as their means of trade restriction, (i) trade is asymptotically reduced to zero, and (ii) neither country can gain relative to free trade by initiating quota warfare. These results are illustrated using Figure 4.6.

As before, OR and OR^* are, respectively, the home and foreign country undistorted offer curves. Free-trade equilibrium is at E. If the home country is the first to restrict trade, it moves to point A where its trade indifference curve u_1 is tangent to OR^*. In the present case we assume that this is achieved by the

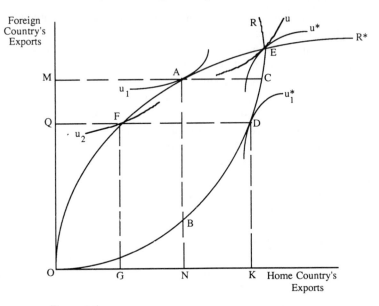

Figure 4.6

home country imposing an import quota of OM, in which case the home country's offer curve becomes $OCAM$[4] with the home country on indifference curve u_1.

How will the foreign country retaliate? The answer depends, in part, on which segment of the home country's quota-distorted offer curve the foreign country's optimum point is located. If it is in the segment BC (say at point D where foreign indifference curve u_1^* is tangent to $OCAM$), then retaliation by means of an import quota does not work because foreign imports under the required quota (OK) would be greater than their level at A (ON); that is, the foreign country's quota would not be binding. In such a case, point D can only be realized by means of an export quota of OQ. On the other hand, if the foreign country's optimum is in the segment OB of the home country's offer curve, then it is immaterial whether it uses an export or an import quota (because segment OB coincides with the undistorted segment of OR, the foreign country's optimizing choice in such a case is the same as if the home country had not restricted trade at all).

A difficulty arises if the foreign country's optimum occurs at C. An export quota designed to place it at C (with an associated offer curve OAC) cannot be relied on to achieve that result because foreign country imports are indeterminate; any point in the interval AC (the intersection of home country offer curve

OCAM and foreign country offer curve *OAC*) is an equilibrium. Accordingly, to enforce its retaliatory quota, the foreign country must impose an export quota slightly less than *OM*, say *OQ*, with the foreign offer curve becoming *OFD* and equilibrium occurring at *D*. The home country's new optimum is now at the corner point *F* on indifference curve u_2 (the closest it can get to its preferred point *A*), which it can attain by imposing an export quota of *OG*. It can also respond by imposing an import quota strictly less than *OQ* (a quota on imports of exactly *OQ* would be unenforceable because equilibrium may lie anywhere in the interval *FD*). If the reader is left a little confused by the analysis of this case, the following intuition may be helpful. The basic point is that a country cannot enforce a favourable terms-of-trade shift (e.g. from the ray *OA* to the ray *OC* for the foreign country) by imposing an export quota which coincides with the other country's import quota. Although both wish to achieve the same level of trade restriction of this particular good, they have different preferred levels of trade in the other good. To enforce the desired level of trade in the other good (and hence the desired terms-of-trade shift), the retaliating country must impose a marginally tighter trade restriction than currently prevails (e.g. *OQ* rather than *OM*).

It should now be clear that in all possible cases, each stage of the retaliatory process necessarily involves further reduction of one country's imports with no subsequent increase in those imports at a later stage. In the long run, the volume of trade asyptotically approaches zero. Although trade is never actually eliminated, under quotas there is no Nash equilibrium associated with a non-zero level of trade as was the case with tariffs. Furthermore, it is possible to show that this result (asymptotic elimination of trade) holds so long as one country uses a quota (even if the other country uses a tariff) (see Tower, 1975). Clearly both countries must be worse off in a situation of no trade than they are under free trade; that is, in the presence of retaliation, neither country stands to gain by imposing a quota. Recall that when tariffs were the sole instrument, it was possible to construct cases in which one country gained at the expense of the other by initiating a round of retaliatory tariffs. This is clearly not possible here.

Thus, in contrast to the case in which tariffs are the sole retaliatory device, use of quotas in a trade war is likely to cause severe contraction in the volume of international trade and be very damaging to the participants. Despite this clear disadvantage of quota protection (to which can be added several other disadvantages – see Chapters 3 and 5), quantitative trade restrictions of all kinds have been favoured in the last two decades both by governments and trade negotiations.[5] One of the more notable features of the spread of this type of trade barrier has been the pervasiveness of *voluntary export restraints* (VERs). We now consider in detail the properties of this particular variant of the simple import quota.

4.4.   Voluntary export restraints

A VER is a quota imposed by an exporting country on its exports to another country in response to pressure by the importing country (in the form of threats of various types of import restriction). Although not strictly "voluntary" (being imposed under an implicit or explicit threat), VERs are the outcome of negotiations between the two governments involved and, therefore, may reflect some preferences of the exporting country. Because they implicitly remove any threat of retaliation, they are sometimes viewed as a cooperative alternative to the asymptotic elimination of trade which may occur when non-cooperative strategies are pursued by means of quotas.

A VER has several features which differentiate it from other forms of trade restriction such as tariffs and import quotas. Firstly, it is a policy designed to protect producers in the importing country which is administered by the exporting country. Secondly, it is "source specific" in the sense that it applies to a small number of specified exporters (possibly only one) unlike tariffs and import quotas which usually apply to imports from most of a country's suppliers. An interesting implication of this property is that exporters which are not covered by a particular VER may increase their exports to the importing country when the VER is imposed. These "nonrestraining exporters" (Takacs, 1978) tend to be primarily countries which are too small to warrant the costs of negotiating an agreement. Thirdly, VERs are typically implemented for a specified period in contrast to other types of trade barrier which are imposed for an indefinite period (although this may make little difference in practice).

As noted in Chapter 2, VERs are a convenient means for countries to restrict trade outside the framework of GATT and have therefore become quite widespread. They have become most pervasive in the textiles and clothing area, applying to 80 per cent of the world trade in these industries through the various bilateral agreements which constitute the Multifibre Arrangement (MFA). The MFA is the culmination of several decades of growing protectionism in textiles and clothing trade, having its humble origins in a temporary agreement between the United States and Japan in the 1930s. VERs are also particularly in evidence in the steel industry, in which they limit steel exports from Japan and the EEC to the United States, and the automobile industry, in which they restrict exports from Japan to the United States, Germany, France, the United Kingdom and Italy. More recently they have begun to be applied to a range of electronic consumer goods.

We begin by considering the properties of VERs in a simple two-country framework. Figure 4.7 illustrates the effects of a VER for a large country (country H) which imports from one other country (A). In Figure 4.7a, D represents country H's demand curve for imports and S_A is country A's supply curve of exports in free trade. All markets are assumed to be competitive[6] (except for

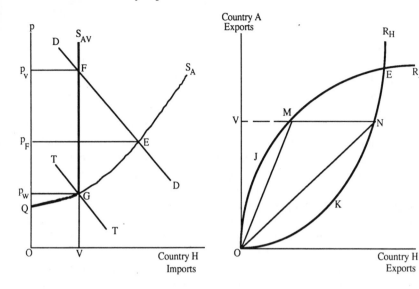

Figure 4.7a   Figure 4.7b

market power at the national level). Under free trade, equilibrium is at E, and the price in both countries is p_F. A VER restricting exports to OV units restricts A's supply curve to QGS_{AV} and equilibrium moves to F with the world price of the commodity rising to p_v. This is also the domestic price in country H.

Compare this outcome with a tariff (or its import quota equivalent) which yields the same level of imports (OV) for country H. This would be achieved by a tariff which shifted H's demand curve for imports down to position T, intersecting S_A at point G. In this case, the world price is p_w while the domestic price in country H is p_v, the same as under the VER. Relative to a tariff or quota, the VER implies a worsened terms of trade for the importing country. Under the tariff, country H captures the tariff-revenue–quota-rents rectangle p_vFGp_w whereas under the VER the rectangle goes to the exporting country. Note, however, that, in general, the domestic price in H is not the same under the two policies because of income effects associated with changes in the terms of trade. These are not captured in the partial equilibrium analysis of Figure 4.7a, but the same general point can be made in a general equilibrium framework using offer curves as in Figure 4.7b. OR_H and OR_A represent country H's and country A's offer curves, respectively. Free trade is at E. A VER which restricts A's exports to OV changes A's offer curve to $OJMN$. Equilibrium is at N with the world relative price (and A's domestic price) given by the slope of the ray ON. The domestic price is determined by preferences, and other factors in H.[7] On the other hand, a tariff or import quota yielding the same level of imports for

H as the VER would distort H's offer curve to $OKNV$. Equilibrium would be at M with terms of trade given by OM. Clearly country H is on a lower trade-indifference curve at N than at M, whereas country A is better off at N. Thus, in this simple case of import equivalence with only two countries, the country imposing the VER gains relative to a tariff or import quota, and the importing country loses. The result is entirely due to the worsened terms of trade for the importing country under the VER. Note that domestic relative prices in H would normally be different at M and N because the slopes of the country H trade-indifference curves through M and N will usually be different. Thus, a VER and a tariff which are import-equivalent are not, as a rule, equivalent with respect to domestic price. The case in which the two policies are price-equivalent is considered by Brecher and Bhagwati (1987).

The foregoing analysis presents one aspect of what can be regarded as the conventional wisdom on VERs. One reason VERs are seen as being acceptable to exporting countries is that the country administering the restriction captures the premium on the scarce imports. In particular, if an exporting country knows that its exports are about to be restricted by a foreign country imposing an import quota, it is clearly in its interests to pre-empt such a quota by introducing a VER and thus ensure that the rents from the restricted exports accrue to it rather than the foreign country. Moreover, the importing country may view this transfer of rents as an acceptable price to pay for being able to appear less protectionist. For cases in which the threat of import restrictions by an importing country is credible (i.e. they are not ruled out absolutely by GATT rules), these considerations would appear to offer another reason for the popularity of VERs.

Despite the spread of VERs, there remain markets in which the more traditional tools of import restriction continue to be used. It is therefore interesting to identify situations in which an exporting country does better by passively accepting the import restrictions of foreign countries (or possibly retaliating with similar restrictions of its own) than by implementing a VER. An obvious case in which VERs have little or no role is if the importing country is small. However, even if the importing country is large, an exporting country may prefer foreign import restrictions to a VER.

One such case involves the presence of a second exporting country (country B) which is not subject to a VER. This is illustrated in Figure 4.8, in which S_B is country B's export supply curve. S_{A+B} is the horizontal sum of S_A and S_B. As before, free trade is at E and p_F is the free trade price. The imposition of a VER restricting A's exports to H to OV units restricts A's supply curve to QNS_{AV}. The aggregate supply curve becomes S_V, the horizontal sum of QNS_{AV} and S_B (i.e. $QNAJF$). The new equilibrium is at F where S_V intersects D. The world price of the commodity (and its domestic price in country H) rises to p_V.

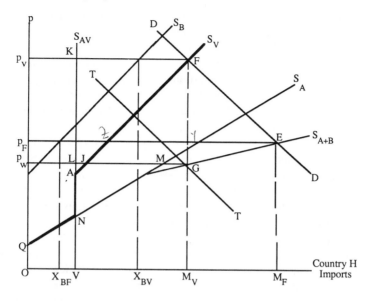

Figure 4.8

The nonrestraining exporter, country B, responds to the VER by increasing its exports from X_{BF} to X_{BV}. The volume of trade is reduced from M_F to M_V. This same level of imports into H can be achieved by a tariff which shifts H's demand curve for imports down to position T intersecting S_{A+B} at G. Under the tariff, the rectangle $p_v FGp_w$ goes to H whereas under the VER, only part of the rectangle, the area $p_v FJp_w$, goes to the two exporting countries. The remainder, area FJG, is an excess deadweight loss (for the world as a whole) of the VER relative to a tariff or quota; it reflects the inefficiency associated with the resources attracted into exporting in the nonrestraining country. Clearly the importing country is worse off under the VER than under the import-equivalent tariff while the nonrestraining exporter is better off.

However, country A may also be worse off than under a tariff if its additional rents (relative to the tariff) on the OV units sold under the VER (area $p_v KLp_w$) are less than the rents it may lose on units produced up to price p_w (area LMN). Of course, this outcome is unlikely if country B is a small part of the market. However, it is a distinct possibility if country A shares the world market with another large exporter (country B) who refuses to enter an agreement to limit exports. In such a case, it would not pay country A to use a VER to preempt imposition of a tariff or quota by H because the VER would cause substantial rents to be shifted from A to the unrestraining exporter.[8]

Another aspect of VERs which deserves mention is their tendency to increase the average quality of restricted exports. Given that VERs are expressed in volume terms, they are no different in this regard from a volume import quota. In the previous chapter, we found that volume quotas applied to a heterogeneous class of close substitutes (e.g. different grades of steel and textiles) increased the proportion of higher-grade expensive items in the total class of restricted imports. Clearly the same effect is at work in the case of VERs: restriction of the volume exported leads to a uniform premium per unit for export licences across all goods in the restricted class. As we saw in Chapter 3, this makes more expensive items relatively cheaper compared with free trade, thus favouring a shift in the composition of exports towards those items. Contrary to what is often suggested, no collusive behaviour is required on the part of foreign exporters to produce this result. However, as shown by Falvey (1979), the same effects are observed when the exporter is a monopolist, the case people probably have in mind when they speak of exporting countries "getting around" VERs by exporting higher-quality goods. Certainly, the possibility of upgrading makes a volume constraint on exports less binding on the exporter than an "equivalent" value constraint (in which the relative prices of the different grades are much the same as under free trade and hence there are no gains from upgrading). Finally, it is worth noting that some of the observed shift to higher-quality, more expensive imports can be explained by a switch in imports towards non-restraining exporting countries which specialize in higher-quality varieties. However, most empirical research on the subject has recognized this possibility and made explicit allowance for it.

This completes our analysis of VERs for the time being. Further insights can be obtained by considering the case of oligopolistic industries in which firms in both countries can gain from a VER. This case will be considered in Chapter 6. The interested reader can find a useful discussion of other aspects of VERs in Hamilton (1985).

4.5.   Variable import levies and export subsidies

Another type of policy which is of particular interest in the large country case is the variable import levy or export subsidy. These are policies in which the rate of duty or subsidy is varied according to movements in world price of a particular good, the objective being to stabilize the good's domestic price (i.e. world price + the tariff or subsidy) so that the rate of duty (subsidy) rises (falls) when the world price falls (rises). The most widely documented instance of variable levies in the modern world is the EEC's Common Agricultural Policy (CAP). The policy employs a variable levy on imports to support prices at an artificially high level in the EEC. In the event that these high internal prices bring about an excess supply of particular goods, those goods will be exported

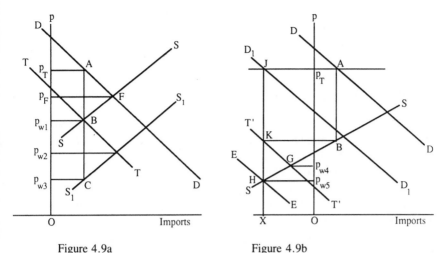

Figure 4.9a   Figure 4.9b

at a price supported by variable export subsidies (*restitution payments*). The ad valorem rates of these levies and subsidies tend to be very high by any standard. For example, for the years 1978–80, the average rate of implicit producer subsidy for wheat was approximately 110 per cent, for coarse grains 83 per cent and for ruminant meats 94 per cent (see Chisholm and Tyers, 1985).

Aside from the obvious distortions created by the CAP in the European Community, the policy (with a similar use of direct quantitative trade restrictions by China, the Soviet Union and Japan) has had significant effects on world markets. In particular, it is seen as being an important contributing factor towards the increased volatility of world prices of agricultural commodities in the past two decades (see Johnson, 1975). Chisholm and Tyers (1985) have estimated that complete liberalization of OECD and NIC[9] trade in wheat would almost halve the coefficient of variation of world wheat prices, while similar trade liberalization for coarse grains and ruminant meats is estimated to reduce the coefficient of variation of world prices for these products by more than 25 per cent (see Chisholm and Tyers, 1985, p. 198, table 3).

The way in which a variable levy can contribute to world price volatility is illustrated in Figure 4.9. *DD* represents the (undistorted) demand curve for imports by the country imposing the levy (to the left of the vertical axis it represents that country's supply curve of exports) and *SS* is the rest of the world's supply curve of exports to the country in question (to the left of the vertical axis it becomes the rest of the world's demand curve for imports). In the absence of any intervention, equilibrium will be at the free-trade point *F* where *SS* and *DD* intersect, with an associated world (domestic) price of p_F (Figure 4.9a). Now suppose that the country in question wishes to support the domestic price of the good at the constant level p_T. Given the initial values of the parameters, this can be accomplished by a tariff or levy on imports of AB per unit (which causes the tariff-distorted domestic import demand curve TT to intersect SS at point B). The world price of the good is driven down to p_{w1}, the usual terms-of-trade improvement for a large country imposing a tariff on its imports. So far, everything is much the same as in Figure 4.1, with the exception that the tariff per unit is not necessarily the country's optimal tariff.

Now consider the effect of various parametric changes. First, suppose that the foreign export supply curve shifts to the right from SS to S_1S_1 (either because of a good harvest or because a foreign government subsidizes production or exports of the good). This case is illustrated in Figure 4.9a. At the initial tariff of AB per unit, this drives down the market-clearing world price to p_{w2}, determined by the intersection of TT and S_1S_1. The domestic price in the levy-imposing country would also fall. However, because the government of that country is committed to a domestic price of p_T, it increases the levy per unit to AC, driving the world price down below p_{w2} to p_{w3}. Thus the use of the variable levy is seen to magnify world price fluctuations caused by exogenous factors. Moreover, if the fall of the foreign supply curve from SS to S_1S_1 is entirely the result of a foreign export or output subsidy (equal to the vertical distance between the supply curves), then the foreign government's subsidy payments on the exported units ($p_{w1}BCp_{w3}$) will be fully captured as revenue by the levy-imposing country (whose revenue from the levy increases from p_TABp_{w1} to p_TACp_{w3}). Clearly (as Sampson and Snape, 1980, have noted), the exporting countries, faced with a variable levy which renders their total exports inelastic, should collude to impose an export tax; this would have the opposite effect to a subsidy, shifting revenue from the government imposing the variable levy to the governments of the exporting countries. However, in the absence of such collusion among exporters, an individual exporting country may lose by imposing a tax on its exports if the levy-imposing country shifts its demand to other countries which are not imposing such a tax. Indeed, there may be gains to individual countries from subsidizing their exports if this enables them to shift rents away from other exporting countries. This possibility is explored further in an oligopoly framework in Chapter 6.

Regardless of the relative merits of various policy responses for other countries, it is clear that the response of world price to an exogenous shift in the foreign export supply curve is larger than it would have been in the absence of the variable levy. This point can be further illustrated by considering the effect of an exogenous shift in the DD curve. Suppose DD shifts down to D_1D_1 in Figure 4.9b, perhaps because of a seasonal increase in the domestic supply of the "importable". In the case illustrated, the levy-imposing country becomes an exporter of the good at price p_T (exporting amount OX), so that, to maintain the domestic price at p_T, the variable levy becomes a variable export subsidy of

JH per unit (the subsidy-distorted demand-for-imports–supply-of-exports curve *EE* intersecting *SS* at point *H*), which drives the world price down to p_{w5}. This involves "restitution payments" funded by the taxpayer of an amount given by the area $Jp_{T}p_{w5}H$. As well as illustrating how the variable import levy can become a variable export subsidy when parameters change (e.g. during different parts of the season), this case offers further evidence of the role of variable levies in destabilizing world price. In the absence of the variable subsidy, the fall in world price caused by, say, a higher than usual harvest in the EEC would be markedly less. At a subsidy–tariff at the original rate of $JK = AB$ per unit, the distorted demand curve would be $T'T'$, which would intersect *SS* at point G, implying an equilibrium world price of p_{w4}, which is seen to be higher than the price p_{w5} prevailing under the variable subsidy.

In summary, we have seen that use of a variable levy–subsidy to insulate a large economy from exogenous shocks magnifies the effects of those shocks in the rest of the world. The implication appears to be that the considerable volatility exhibited by commodity prices throughout the 1970s and 1980s may be as much due to government policies as to natural forces. In addition, such policies exhibit the usual feature of any tariff or export subsidy imposed by a large country: they depress the world price (in this case the mean world price) of the good to which the policy is applied.

4.6. Summary

When a country is large enough to affect the prices of the goods it buys or sells in world markets, it can usually gain by restricting trade below the free-trade level even though this reduces welfare for the world as a whole. As is clear from the Lerner symmetry theorem, it does not matter if this trade restriction is effected by imposing a tariff on imports or a tax on exports (or, indeed, the quota-equivalent of either). We chose to deal in terms of tariffs. A tariff serves to improve the country's terms of trade by restricting demand for imports, thereby driving down their market-clearing world price. The optimal tariff for a large country is arrived at by trading off this terms-of-trade gain against the domestic distortion cost of the tariff. It is never optimal for a country to set a tariff which eliminates trade.

The optimal tariff is derived on the assumption that foreign countries react passively. If a foreign country retaliates by levying its own tariff, the gain to the country imposing the first tariff is reduced. Although the outcome of such a tariff war may make both countries worse off than they are under free trade, it is possible to construct cases in which one country can gain relative to free trade. One important result is that a tariff war never completely eliminates trade and, in the absence of complete specialization, it results in a strictly positive volume of trade. This is in contrast to the case in which import or export quotas are the instruments used for trade restriction – a trade war conducted using quotas reduces trade asymptotically to zero. This offers yet another instance of the non-equivalence of tariffs and quotas and provides further evidence of the superiority of tariffs.

One of the most pervasive of quota-type trade restrictions is the voluntary export restraint (VER). Exporting countries may introduce VERs to pre-empt the likely imposition of import quotas or tariffs by a foreign country; in this way they capture the rents arising from the restricted volume of goods sold. However, there are situations in which it may pay an exporting country to accept a foreign import restriction rather than impose its own VER, most notably the case in which there is a large exporting country not subject to a VER. When applied to classes of heterogeneous products, VERs (like volume-based import quotas) induce a shift towards more expensive items in the class of restricted exports – the so-called "upgrading" effect.

Variable import levies (export subsidies) are another type of policy which has become widespread. These policies, which are used to maintain a stable domestic price in the face of fluctuating demand and supply, shift the burden of adjustment onto world prices. They are thought to be responsible for much of the increased volatility exhibited by world commodity prices in the 1970s and 1980s.

PART II

Protection and imperfect competition

CHAPTER 5

Monopoly

To this point we have assumed that all of the relevant markets are competitive. In this and the following two chapters we shall relax this assumption and turn our attention to cases in which firms possess some market power. Such cases should be of considerable interest to any student of protectionist regimes, many of the more notable examples of protection being industries such as steel, automobiles and electronic goods, in which a small number of firms produce under conditions of economies of scale. Even agricultural trade, apparently closest to the competitive model, is frequently conducted through government marketing boards and international trading companies and is therefore likely to involve some elements of imperfect competition. A further aspect of trade which has received increasing attention in recent years is intra-industry trade associated with product differentiation – such trade is frequently non-competitive. Given the range of cases to be considered, the extent of the recent literature in this area and the undeniable empirical importance of trade and protection in imperfectly competitive industries, we shall spend some time developing and exploring the models. In this chapter we shall deal with the simplest non-competitive market structure: monopoly. This leads naturally into the treatment of oligopoly in Chapter 6. The case of trade in differentiated products is considered in some detail in Chapter 7.

Throughout much of these three chapters we shall be analysing industries which are characterized by significant economies of scale. It can be argued that these are the most likely industries to exhibit non-competitive market structures. Nevertheless, certain insights are obtained by looking at the (frequently simpler) case in which unit costs of production are an increasing function of output. Among other things, this case offers a particularly convenient framework for demonstrating the non-equivalence of tariffs and import quotas (and highlighting the shortcomings of the latter) when the protected sector is non-competitive. In addition, the increasing-costs case may correspond to the actual situation in industries in which the firms form a cartel or when the government superimposes a marketing board on otherwise competitive producers. We shall therefore start with the case of increasing average costs and then move on to consider potentially more interesting situations involving economies of scale. For the bulk of the chapter, we shall be considering an industry in which there is a single domestic producer; however, in Section 5.3 we shift our attention to the case in which there is no domestic production of the good, and the domestic market is supplied entirely by a foreign monopolist. Throughout the chapter we shall maintain the small-country assumption so as to abstract from terms-of-trade effects of the kind considered in the previous chapter.

5.1.   Increasing costs

In this section we consider the case of an industry in which there is a single domestic firm producing under conditions of increasing cost. We begin by considering the effects of tariffs in such an industry and then examine import quotas in the same framework. An important result to emerge from this analysis is that tariffs and quotas differ markedly in their effects in the presence of domestic monopoly. This non-equivalence is a consequence of the greater monopoly power conferred on the producer by a quota.

(a)   Tariffs and monopoly

As we shall see later, it is quite possible that an import-competing monopolist may become an exporter if given sufficient tariff protection in the home market. However, because this case is rather more complicated, we rule it out for the time being by assuming that the f.o.b. export price is too low for exporting of the good to be profitable.[1] Both cases are considered in detail by Fishelson and Hillman (1979), and we follow their approach here. The effect of a tariff on the behavior of a monopolist supplying the domestic market in a small country is illustrated in Figure 5.1.

The existence of a domestic monopoly in the good means that for prices between the c.i.f. import price (p_M) and that price plus the tariff ($p_T \equiv p_M + T$ where the tariff is T per unit) the firm faces a downward-sloping demand curve for its product. Thus, in Figure 5.1, the average revenue curve facing the monopolist is $p_T ABD$. DD is the underlying demand curve for the product. If the marginal revenue curve derived from DD is mm, then the marginal revenue curve facing the monopolist is $p_T ACm$. MC is the (assumed upward sloping) marginal cost curve for the good.

Clearly this case differs from the competitive case solely because there is a range of prices (p_M to p_T) in which the monopolist faces the downward-sloping demand curve DD (and the associated marginal revenue curve mm). If there were no tariff, this would collapse to the competitive case with the producer being forced to charge p_M. It is the protection afforded by the tariff which gives the monopoly the prospect of regaining some of the market power it would have in the absence of imports.

Let us now consider what happens as the tariff-inclusive price ($p_M + T$) is gradually increased above p_M by raising the tariff.

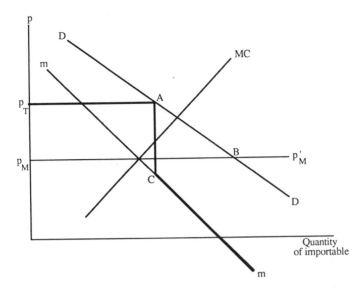

Figure 5.1

In Figure 5.2a, a tariff of $p_M p_T^1$ per unit is imposed. The firm maximizes profits where its MR curve ($p_T^1 A C m$) cuts MC at B. It produces Q_1 and charges p_T^1, consumers demand C_1 and $Q_1 C_1$ is satisfied by imports. This is the same outcome which would occur if the industry were competitive. The tariff-inclusive price is sufficiently low to prevent the producer having any usable monopoly power. This is the case so long as a tariff does not completely prohibit imports (i.e. tariffs up to $p_M p_C$ per unit, where p_C is the competitive autarky price).

When the tariff-inclusive price is increased above p_C (to, say, p_T^2 in Figure 5.2b), the monopoly supplies the whole market, producing at F in Figure 5.2b where the MC curve passes through the vertical discontinuity in its MR curve.[2] It produces Q_2 and charges p_T^2, using all of the protection afforded. In this case the tariff is high enough to prohibit imports (and thus give the producer some market power), but not high enough to remove the threat of imports (which forces the monopoly to produce Q_2 rather than its unconstrained preferred output $\hat{Q}_2$).

Figure 5.2c illustrates the case in which the tariff-inclusive price is p_T^3, above the producer's unconstrained profit-maximizing price $\hat{p}_T$. In this case the MC curve cuts the downward-sloping segment of the MR curve at G, resulting in production of Q_3 and a price of $\hat{p}_T$. $\hat{p}_T p_T^3$ of the tariff is unused or redundant protection (or *water-in-the-tariff*). Since $\hat{p}_T$ is the producer's absolute optimum, it does not pay him to charge a higher price, even if a high tariff offers

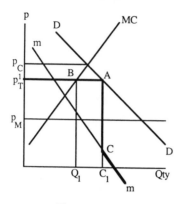

Figure 5.2a

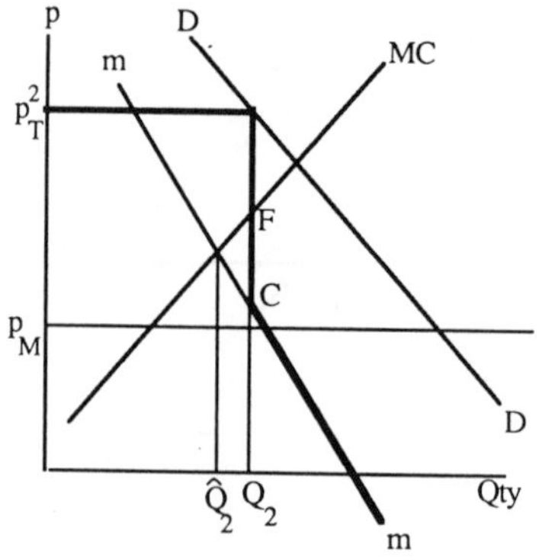

Figure 5.2b

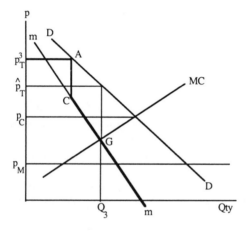

Figure 5.2c

him that possibility. In this case the tariff is sufficiently high to effectively remove any threat from imports so that the monopolist can act as if unconstrained.

We conclude that any tariff above $p_M\hat{p}_T$ per unit is redundant. This contrasts with the case of a competitive industry in which any tariff above $p_M p_C$ is redundant (because any price above p_C involves an excess supply which could only be disposed of at the f.o.b. export price; accordingly, the price would be driven down to the equilibrium price p_C). The fact that a monopolist is able to use more protection than an equivalent competitive industry is hardly surprising, given a monopolist's natural tendency to restrict output and raise price relative to their competitive levels.

Let us now introduce the possibility of exporting into the model. Let p_E

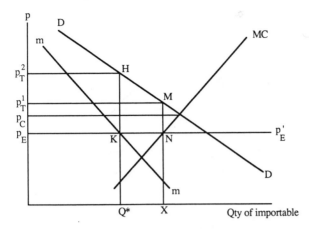

Figure 5.3

denote the f.o.b. export price and assume that it lies above the intersection of
the MC curve and mm in Figure 5.3 (to keep the diagram simple, p_M is not
shown in Figure 5.3, though we shall refer to it in defining the various tariff
levels). Given the possibility of earning additional revenue by exporting marginal units at price p_E, the MR curve facing the monopolist will not fall below
p_E. He will produce where MR = MC and then act as a two-market monopolist,
allocating sales between the markets by equating MR from exporting (p_E) to
MR from domestic sales (a curve like $p_T ACm$ in Figure 5.1). Tariff-inclusive
prices up to p_C (Figure 5.3) yield the competitive outcome with positive imports. For prices between p_C and p_T^1 (MR curve for p_T^1 is $p_T^1 MN p_E'$), the monopolist supplies the whole domestic market (producing where the MC curve passes
through the vertical discontinuity in the MR curve) and makes full use of the
tariff.

For prices between p_T^1 and p_T^2 (MR curve for p_T^2 is $p_T^2 HK p_E'$), the MR curve
cuts the MC curve on the horizontal p_E segment, so that X is produced. The
domestic market is supplied at the tariff-inclusive price (p_E passes through the
vertical discontinuity in the domestic MR schedule), the remainder being exported. If the domestic firm were not faced with import competition (but could
still export), it would still choose to produce X (where MC = MR = p_E) but
would equate p_E to mm (at K) to determine domestic sales of Q^* sold at price
p_T^2, Q^*X being exported. This is its absolute profit maximum, and it follows
that the part of any tariff above $p_M p_T^2$ is redundant. Note that the maximum
usable protection in this case ($p_M p_T^2$) exceeds the maximum usable protection
when exports were excluded. Given the presence of a profitable export market
separated from the domestic market by the tariff (and transport costs), the
monopolist price-discriminates between markets, with increased opportunity to

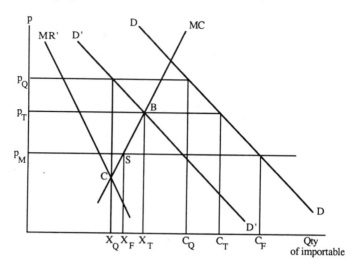

Figure 5.4

restrict sales and raise price in the domestic market (when compared with the no-exports case).

This type of price discrimination has traditionally been described as *dumping* (Viner, 1923); however, there are various other definitions of dumping which do not involve international price discrimination (see, in particular, Ethier, 1982).

(b)   *Tariffs versus quotas under monopoly*

In the previous chapter, we saw how tariffs and import quotas would differ in their effects in the presence of changing parameters and rent or revenue seeking. We now consider a different source of non-equivalence of these two policies: monopoly in the protected sector. We begin by considering quotas on their own and then proceed to compare them with tariffs. For simplicity, we assume no exports of the good in question (sufficiently low p_E), though this assumption is in no way crucial to the results.

The basic difference between tariffs and quotas in the presence of monopoly is that a tariff permits a perfectly elastic supply of imports at the world price plus the tariff, whereas a quota renders the supply of imports inelastic at the level prescribed by the quota. Thus monopoly power is limited for all tariffs (except those which are high enough to be redundant), whereas a quota allows the monopolist unrestricted movement along his demand curve (the market demand curve net of imports) so that he is free to set price and output much as he would in a closed economy (Figure 5.4). *DD* is the total demand for the importable, $D'D'$ is demand net of the quota, and MR' is the marginal revenue

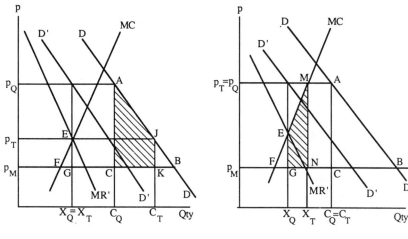

Figure 5.5a   Figure 5.5b

curve derived from $D'D'$. The monopolist maximizes profits where MR' inter-sects MC at C with output X_Q, price p_Q and consumption C_Q. As drawn, this involves a lower output than free trade $(X_Q < X_F)$, so the quota has been anti-protective. This is because the monopoly power conferred by the quota creates a tendency towards output contraction. In the case drawn in Figure 5.4 this tendency is dominant. On the other hand, MR' could have intersected MC to the right of the free-trade point (S), in which case the quota would have offered some protection to domestic output. The anti-protective effect is more likely to dominate, the less elastic is the demand curve $D'D'$ faced by the monopolist.

Figure 5.4 also shows the effects of a tariff $(p_M p_T$ per unit) which allows the same level of imports as the quota. The tariff, being non-prohibitive, forces the monopolist to act in the same manner as a competitive industry with a lower price $(p_T < p_Q)$ and higher output $(X_T > X_F > X_Q)$ than under the quota. We should also note that this "import-equivalent" tariff is less than the implicit tariff (the tariff which yields the same price as the quota, $p_M p_Q$ per unit), and it can be shown to involve a lower deadweight loss than the quota (see Mc-Culloch, 1973). In addition, unlike the quota, the tariff never causes output to fall below the free-trade level. It is thus clear that when the import-competing sector consists of a single producer there is no full equivalence of tariffs and quotas; if we wish to compare the two policies, we must specify the basis for comparison. The simplest such basis is the achievement of some common non-economic objective.

In Figure 5.5a, we compare a tariff and a quota which yield the same output $(X_Q = X_T)$ of the monopolist's good. p_T denotes the tariff-inclusive price. The quota involves a higher price (p_Q) and lower consumption of the good $(C_Q < C_T)$ than the tariff; this is no more than a reflection of the firm's increased monopoly power under the quota. The deadweight loss areas under the two policies are as follows:

DWL of tariff relative to free trade $= EFG + JKB$.
DWL of quota relative to free trade $= EFG + ABC$.
Excess DWL of quota over tariff $= ABC - JKB = AJKC$ (shaded).

In other words, because both policies yield the same output (by assumption), they both have the same production DWL, but the higher price under the quota implies a higher consumption DWL. Thus the quota is inferior to the tariff as a means of protecting output.

Although the attainment of a target output is a plausible objective, a protectionist government may also be persuaded to maintain the price of the protected good at some target level. Accordingly, in Figure 5.5b we compare a tariff and a quota which yield a common price ($p_T = p_Q$). Because both policies involve the same price, their consumption-side deadweight losses are the same. On the other hand, because the domestic firm is a price-taker under the tariff, it will produce more at the given price under the tariff (X_T) than under the quota (where it uses its monopoly power to restrict output to X_Q). The deadweight loss from the production distortion is therefore smaller under the quota. Thus the quota is superior to the tariff as a means of achieving the target price. This may be readily verified in terms of the areas of Figure 5.5b as follows:

DWL of tariff relative to free trade $= MNF + ABC$.
DWL of quota relative to free trade $= EFG + ABC$.
Excess DWL of tariff over quota $= MNF - EFG = MNGE$ (shaded).

The implication of this analysis seems to be that, in the context of domestic monopoly, a quota may be superior to a tariff or vice versa depending on the policy maker's underlying objective. Nevertheless, it is common to regard the monopoly case as further evidence of the shortcomings of quotas as instruments of trade policy. They confer monopoly power on a producer who would otherwise have to compete with imports at a fixed price (give or take a tariff) and for this reason are seen as undesirable. Certainly, they entail higher deadweight losses than tariffs if the underlying objective is either domestic output or import restriction [see McCulloch (1973) for the further case of profit equivalence].

In this analysis we have implicitly assumed that the policy maker knows the monopolist's responses to changes in the level of each instrument; that is, we have assumed the government to be a *Stackelberg leader,* using its knowledge of the monopolist's reaction function to set the relevant instrument at the level necessary to achieve its objective. If, on the other hand, the monopolist knows the government's policy objective (e.g. price or market share), the firm becomes the Stackelberg leader, and the government is the follower. The firm then maximizes profits subject to the government policy objective (however

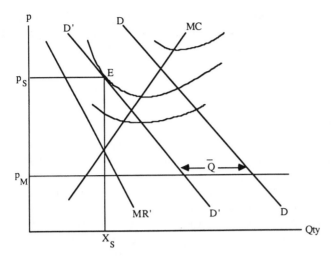

Figure 5.6

achieved). Clearly, in this case it is immaterial to the outcome whether a tariff or a quota is used, because the firm views the tariff or quota as a variable, the value of which will be determined by the firm's behaviour subject to the overriding government policy target. *It follows that, when the monopolist knows the government's objective, the equivalence of tariffs and quotas is restored.* This quite general result is illustrated for the case of an import objective in Figure 5.6.

As before, DD is the total demand for the good, whereas $D'D'$ is demand net of $\bar{Q}$, the government's target level of imports. $D'D'$ is both the demand curve facing the firm and the reaction curve of the policy maker. MR' is the marginal curve derived from $D'D'$. In addition, we can draw iso-profit curves for the firm. These are downward sloping to the left of the MC curve (to the left of the MC curve, price exceeds marginal cost so that an increase in output means higher profits; to keep the firm on the same iso-profit contour, higher output would have to be accompanied by a lower price). They are upward sloping to the right of the MC curve (by a symmetrical argument) and horizontal where they cross the MC curve. Higher iso-profit contours are associated with higher profits (higher price at the same output). The firm, acting as a Stackelberg leader, wishes to attain the highest iso-profit curve subject to the government's reaction function $D'D'$. This is at the point of tangency E in Figure 5.6. Output and price are X_S and p_S, respectively, regardless of whether a tariff or a quota is used to achieve the import target.[3] X_S can also be derived as the intersection of MC and MR'. This is no coincidence: the firm knows that the government wishes to restrict imports to a certain level, so that it is essentially facing a quota, even though a tariff may be the means used to enforce the objective.[4] The quota and the tariff are equivalent instruments in this case. The case of a target market share can be treated similarly to this and was the context in which Sweeney, Tower and Willett (1977) advanced the preceding equivalence proposition.

5.2.   Economies of scale

Although the increasing-costs case provides a simple framework in which to consider certain aspects of protection of monopolistic industries (e.g. comparison of tariffs and quotas), many of the more interesting questions involve industries in which there are significant economies of scale. Indeed, the presence of fixed costs which are large relative to the size of the market is an important reason why some industries only support a small number of firms. The case of natural monopoly, in which only one firm can earn positive profits, is a special case of this phenomenon. Of course, competition from imports also affects the viability of domestic production in such an industry. In the case of a small economy, a firm which would be a natural monopolist in the absence of international trade may be unable to make a profit at the price determined by a perfectly elastic supply of imports. However, a sufficiently high tariff enables the domestic firm to enter the industry.[5] Here, we shall begin our analysis of the economies-of-scale case by considering the implications of using a tariff in this way.

We suppose that there is a domestic firm which would be the single domestic producer of a particular good if there were no import competition (i.e. a natural monopolist). The firm faces a U-shaped average cost curve for producing a good which is a perfect substitute for the imported good. Although the assumption that domestic and imported goods are perfect substitutes has been made throughout the book to this point, it is worthy of emphasis here because it has special implications in the presence of decreasing-costs or economies-of-scale. In particular, it implies that the domestic market is supplied either entirely by imports or entirely by the domestic producer. This can be seen as follows. If the firm makes a profit by producing some units of the good, then its average costs are reduced and its profits increased by producing all units of the good. In such a case, imports are completely displaced by the domestic firm's product.[6] The only other possibility is that the firm cannot produce any units at a profit, in which case domestic output is zero, and the market is supplied entirely by imports. While this all-or-nothing outcome may seem at odds with a world in which many importables are sourced both domestically and abroad, it is a logical consequence of the perfect-substitutes assumption. If we depart from the case of a single homogeneous good and allow domestic and foreign firms to produce goods which are imperfect substitutes for each other, then a more

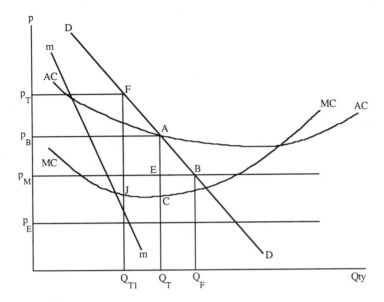

Figure 5.7

"usual" outcome can be observed. If one of the goods is supplied to the home market entirely by the domestic industry while the other is supplied entirely by imports, it will appear as though the "good" is simultaneously produced domestically and imported. The case in which a large number of differentiates of a particular product are available (each produced under economies of scale) is a well-documented example of this sort of thing. For our present purposes, the case of a single homogeneous good is quite adequate. However, in the next chapter, the case of two imperfect substitutes is analysed in an oligopoly framework; product differentiation is considered in detail in Chapter 7. We now examine the effects of various protection policies in the presence of scale economies. As before, it is convenient to start with tariffs.

(a)   Tariffs

Suppose that the c.i.f. import price p_M lies below the price at which the domestic firm would earn zero profits (the *break-even price, p_B*). For the time being, we also assume that both the average and marginal cost curves (AC and MC) are everywhere above the f.o.b. export price p_E, so it will never pay the producer to export (see sub-section d for a case with exporting). Thus, in the absence of protection, the domestic industry will not produce at all (Figure 5.7). The domestic market is satisfied by Q_F units of imports supplied at price p_M.

Now suppose the government imposes a tariff on imports of $t_B = p_M p_B$ per unit, enabling the domestic producer to produce Q_T at zero profit. This tariff, which is just sufficient to ensure viability of the domestic industry, is frequently referred to as the *made-to-measure tariff* (see Corden, 1966a). Any tariff above t_B results in the entire market being supplied by the monopolist. For tariff t_B, consumers pay p_B for quantity Q_T, and the cost to the community relative to free trade is the area $p_B A B p_M$ (Figure 5.7). Note that unlike the increasing-costs case, there is no offsetting tariff revenue (since imports are zero) and no transfer to rents in the protected sector (since p_B = average cost). For a given marginal cost curve, the deadweight loss is greater the larger the fixed cost associated with domestic production (implying a higher average cost curve). For example, for the special case in which the marginal cost of domestic production is constant and equal to p_M, fixed costs would equal the area $p_B A E p_M$, a simple illustration of how the protective effect of a tariff may be dissipated by the firm's costs of entry. We shall return to this theme when we consider inefficient entry of oligopolistic firms in the next chapter.

Insofar as comparisons with the increasing costs model are meaningful, it would appear, on the basis of this case, that tariff protection is rather more costly in the presence of economies of scale. Certainly, on the basis of the static model used here, there is no case for using a made-to-measure tariff to establish an otherwise non-existent domestic industry. Moreover, tariffs above the made-to-measure tariff simply lead to increased monopoly power for the domestic firm reflected in reduced output (and consumption), a higher unit cost of production and a higher price to the domestic consumer. For example, a tariff of $p_M p_T$ would induce the monopolist (who supplies the whole domestic market) to move up his demand curve to point F, reduce output to Q_{T1} (with an associated rise in his average cost) and charge the full tariff-inclusive price p_T. The reader may wish to check that there would be a rise in the deadweight loss (relative to that under the made-to-measure tariff) equal to the area $FACJ$. These results do not sit well with the claims of some politicians and pressure groups that tariff protection enables decreasing-cost industries to achieve longer production runs and pass on the resulting lower unit costs to the domestic consumer. Whether such claims have more substance under slightly different market structures (e.g. oligopoly) is a matter for consideration in subsequent chapters.

(b)   Subsidies

Although the previous analysis shows that the economy is worse off under a tariff, Corden (1967) raises the interesting possibility that the economy may gain by using a production subsidy to establish the industry in question so that it produces where price equals marginal cost. His argument is illustrated in Figure 5.8 in which we compare the free-trade point M with the economy's production

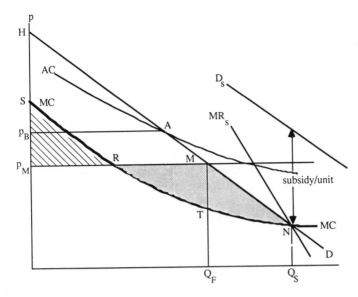

Figure 5.8

point if a subsidy is used to achieve marginal cost pricing (i.e. point N, the intersection of the demand and marginal cost curves).

In each situation, the consumer surplus measure of the net benefit to the economy is the area under the demand curve and above the relevant marginal cost curve (i.e. total benefit of the quantity consumed minus the cost of producing that quantity). When all of the good is supplied by imports, the marginal cost is the price of a unit of imports (p_M); so if the economy is at M,

$$\text{net benefit} = HMp_M.$$

On the other hand, if all of the good is produced domestically at N, then the relevant marginal cost is the producer's MC curve. In this case,

$$\text{net benefit} = HNS = HMp_M + RMN - SRp_M.$$

Therefore, the excess gain from producing at N relative to free trade at M is $RMN - SRp_M$. The two areas in question are shaded in Figure 5.8. Clearly, for some values of p_M, $RMN > SRp_M$, and it is then optimal to induce domestic production at N. Moreover, the values of p_M in question are less than p_B since, for $p_M = p_B$, profits are zero at output Q_F; so $RMT = SRp_M$ and N is better than M by area MTN.

It follows that there is a range of values of the c.i.f. import price below p_B for which it is socially desirable to have this industry producing at N, even though the industry is not viable under free trade. This outcome can be induced by means of a production subsidy (financed by a lump-sum tax) which shifts the demand curve up (to D_s) so that its associated MR curve (MR_s) intersects MC at N. The minimum value of p_M (say p^*) for which such intervention is desirable is that which yields

$$RMN = SRp_M.$$

This analysis suggests that there may be a case (when $p^* < p_M < p_B$) for using a subsidy to establish an otherwise non-existent industry, but that use of a tariff for the same purpose always makes the community worse off. Of course, other difficulties are associated with use of a subsidy. In particular, a made-to-measure subsidy of this kind offers the monopolist little incentive to produce output at minimum cost – indeed, there would appear to be considerable scope for the firm to mislead the policy maker about its true costs and to "cost-pad" at the taxpayer's expense. For this reason, we should be wary about recommending subsidized establishment of industries.

(c)   Quotas

The role of quotas in the present case is much the same as it was in the increasing-costs case; that is, a quota confers monopoly power on the domestic firm by rendering its demand curve less elastic. In addition, in the presence of decreasing costs, quotas are a means of offering some protection to the domestic industry without eliminating imports entirely. Beyond these simple observations, it is difficult to say much of interest. In particular, it is not possible to provide the clear ranking of quotas vis-à-vis tariffs that was offered in part (b) of Section 5.1. This is partly because, with economies of scale, it is difficult to find a common basis for comparing the two policies. For example, there can be no import equivalence between a tariff and a non-zero import quota because imports are zero for all tariffs above the made-to-measure tariff, whereas under the quota they equal the (non-zero) amount of the quota. Furthermore, it is often true that a tariff which appears to be output-equivalent to a given quota has water in it [see Section 5.1, part (a)], so that it actually results in a higher output than that prevailing under the quota. Apart from these problems, the ranking of policies in this case all too often depends on the values of key parameters (e.g. cost and demand curves). For these reasons, we shall not consider quotas further in this section.

(d)   Tariff-induced exporting

So far in this section we have assumed that the protected industry supplies the domestic market only. However, if the f.o.b. export price p_E is not too low, it is possible that the tariff can also make exporting profitable. This possibility,

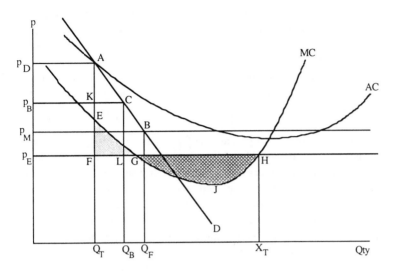

Figure 5.9

often promoted in various guises by protectionist lobbies ("import protection is export promotion"), has been analysed by several academic economists, in particular Wonnacott and Wonnacott (1967) and Pursell and Snape (1973). It relies on the export price lying below the AC curve but intersecting the MC curve (Figure 5.9).

In free trade, the economy imports Q_F at price p_M. Now suppose a tariff of $p_M p_D$ per unit (just sufficient for the producer to break even on domestic sales) is imposed on imports. It is then possible that the producer may find it optimal to produce X_T (at H where MC intersects p_E), selling Q_T to the domestic market at price p_D and exporting $Q_T X_T$ at price p_E. This outcome occurs if shaded area $GHJ >$ shaded area EFG (i.e. if there are marginal profits in exporting). If such exporting turns out to be profitable, it is because the tariff provides a "protected base", enabling the firm to price-discriminate between domestic and foreign consumers and to cover its overheads in the domestic market. In the case illustrated in Figure 5.9, the DWL measure for the tariff must be modified by allowing for the profits from exporting; the cost is now

$$p_D A B p_M + EFG - GHJ.$$

If a tariff (say $p_M p_B$ per unit in Figure 5.9) is applied which is just sufficient for the producer to earn zero profits taking the net profits from exporting into account, then the deadweight loss will be, as in Section 5.2, part (a), the loss to domestic consumers, area $p_B C B p_M$ in Figure 5.9 (output X_T, domestic sales Q_B). This is the best the economy can do using a tariff to establish its industry. A higher tariff would occasion further distortion. For example, the tariff $p_M p_D$ per unit would involve an additional deadweight loss (over that of the tariff $p_M p_B$ per unit) equal to the area $ACLF$.[7] It is therefore clear that, even if a tariff induces exporting, it still imposes a net cost of at least $p_B CB p_M$ on the community, so it cannot be justified as a means of promoting entry of a domestic firm or of offering further assistance to an existing firm. On the other hand, a case for a production subsidy can be made along the lines of the argument in Section 5.2, part (b) (see Pursell and Snape, 1973).

This completes our analysis of protection of domestic monopoly. To be sure, many other issues could be considered here, but most of these are better dealt with in a framework in which there is more than one firm and/or a domestic firm with international market power, cases which are the concern of the next two chapters. In the final section of this chapter we consider a quite different aspect of monopoly in the domestic market: the case in which the entire domestic market is supplied by a foreign multinational firm. This case, analysed in an elegant and influential paper by Katrak (1977), provides an argument for protection which is both interesting and novel. It also anticipates the more recent developments of the rent-shifting argument for protection which is discussed at length in the next chapter.

5.3.   The optimal tariff for extracting foreign rents

Suppose that the domestic market for a good is supplied entirely by a foreign monopolist which sends the profits back to its own country. In such a situation, the home country may gain by using a tariff as a means of extracting these foreign rents. Although we continue to assume that the home country is small in world markets, the argument for a tariff in this case closely resembles the optimal tariff argument for a large country. In essence, the country is using a tariff to influence the price at which the monopolist supplies the good, in the same way as a tariff is used to improve a large country's terms of trade. Indeed, the only formal difference between the two problems is that the price response of a foreign monopoly to a fall in demand for its good may differ from the price response of a competitive world market in the standard optimal tariff problem.

The argument is presented in Figure 5.10, in which p^* is the (constant) c.i.f. cost to the monopolist of bringing a unit of the good into the home country, DD the domestic demand curve for the good as a function of the good's domestic price p and MR the marginal revenue curve derived from DD. Under free trade, the monopolist's marginal cost of providing a unit of the good to the domestic market is p^*. Thus, in the absence of tariffs and other taxes or subsidies, the foreign firm supplies Q_F units of the good (determined by the intersection of p^* and MR at A). Domestic consumers pay price p_F with the resulting profits (area $p_F P A p^*$) being remitted to the foreign country. This represents an additional

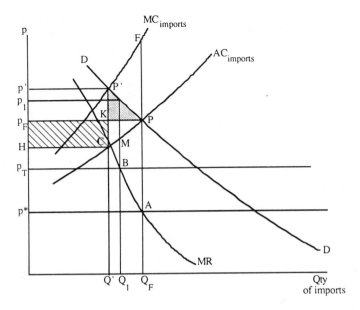

Figure 5.10

cost per unit of imports of p^*p_F to the home country. The average cost of imports to the home country (its effective terms of trade) under free trade is therefore p_F.

Now suppose that the home country imposes an arbitrary tariff of p^*p_T on imports of the good. The monopolist's marginal cost curve is shifted up from p^* to p_T, with equilibrium moving to the intersection of p_T and MR at B; imports fall to Q_1 and domestic price rises to p_1. The average cost of imports to the economy is now equal to the sum of p^* and the monopolist's repatriated profits per unit. This is

$$p_F + (p_Fp_1 - p^*p_T)$$

which is less than p_F if the expression in parentheses is negative (i.e. if the increase in the domestic price is less than the tariff per unit). It is possible to show (see Brander and Spencer, 1984) that this condition is satisfied if the demand curve DD is not too convex. If this is the case, then the foreign firm is responding to the tariff by reducing its supply price, and the economy's average cost of imports (its effective terms of trade) has accordingly been reduced (to Q_1M) by the imposition of the tariff. This appears to be not significantly different from the use of a tariff by a large country to improve its terms of trade. The different element here is that a tariff-induced fall in demand for the good does not necessarily reduce the average cost of imports. The movement up the

DD curve implies a leftward shift of the monopolist's demand curve when it is expressed as a function of her supply price. Whether the monopolist responds to this leftward shift by reducing her supply price (the case illustrated) or raising it depends on how the elasticity of demand changes as the curve shifts in. If the curve becomes sufficiently less elastic as it moves inwards, the monopolist increases her supply price (see Jones, 1987). The Brander and Spencer condition that the *DD* curve be "not too convex" is equivalent to the requirement that the elasticity of the monopolist's supply-price demand curve not fall too much as the curve shifts leftward. Here we shall assume this requirement to be satisfied. The average cost-of-imports curve would then be upward sloping like $AC_{imports}$ in Figure 5.10, with point P corresponding to a zero tariff, points below P on the curve (e.g. M) corresponding to positive tariffs (higher tariffs as we move down the curve) and points beyond P to the right being associated with an import subsidy.

From this point, the analysis follows the large-country optimal tariff derivation exactly. $MC_{imports}$ is the marginal cost-of-imports curve for the economy, and it is derived from $AC_{imports}$ in the usual way (see Chapter 4). In particular, recall that $MC_{imports}$ must lie above $AC_{imports}$ because that curve is upward sloping. We then see that at the free-trade point p, the economy's valuation of a marginal unit of imports (as read off *DD*) is less than their marginal cost (at F). The economy can gain (the area $FP'P$) by using a tariff to restrict imports to the point (P') where their marginal cost to the economy equals their marginal value. The gain is realized by trading off a higher domestic price against the foreign rents captured from the monopolist by means of the tariff. The optimal tariff for this purpose is $P'C$, the difference between the good's domestic price and its supply price (the vertical difference between the demand curve and the $AC_{imports}$ curve) at optimal imports Q'. Relative to free trade, consumers lose $p'P'Pp_F$ against which the economy gains tariff revenue equal to $p'P'CH$, yielding a net gain equal to the rents shifted from the foreign firm to the domestic taxpayer ($p_F KCH$) minus the domestic distortion cost of the tariff ($P'PK$). The former can also be interpreted as the gain from an improved effective terms of trade.

Having drawn the full parallel between this problem and the standard optimal tariff problem, we note the following points:

i.   If the demand curve is "too convex", a tariff will *increase* the monopolist's supply price to the home country. This would imply a downward-sloping $AC_{imports}$ curve with the $MC_{imports}$ curve lying below it; the optimal point would then be located further down *DD* to the right of P, implying that in such a case the optimal trade policy is an import subsidy rather than a tariff. This possibility is absent in the normal optimal tariff problem where it is assumed that the world market is competitive. With competitive foreign markets, any fall in demand must, ceteris paribus, reduce the foreign supply price.[8]

ii. Although we have referred to an optimal tariff (mainly to emphasise the parallel with the standard optimal tariff problem), in fact a tariff is not the first-best policy here. Given that the primary objective is to capture foreign profits, the first-best policy would be a profits tax (see Katrak, 1977). However, governments are often severely constrained in their use of such taxes because of the need to keep their rates roughly in line with those of similar countries (otherwise they risk being impoverished by international tax arbitrage). For this reason, a tariff may not be a bad policy, not least because it can be precisely applied to specific goods or industries.

iii. The argument for a tariff as a means of capturing foreign rents for the domestic taxpayer is interesting because it is a rare instance of a small country being able to gain by using a tariff. On the other hand, it can be readily generalized to the case of a large country. It is also possible to broaden the model to accommodate domestic production of the good, the role of the tariff in such a model being to shift foreign rents from the foreign firm to both domestic taxpayers and domestic firms (see Brander and Spencer, 1984). This possibility will be explored further in the next chapter.

5.4. Summary

It is well known that in a small open economy, a firm which has a domestic monopoly in production has no real monopoly power unless its costs are particularly low relative to world price. Competition from a perfectly elastic supply of imports tends to make the domestic monopolist into a price-taker. However, protection of such an industry by means of tariffs or import quotas may confer some monopoly power on the firm. This tendency is particularly marked in the case of quota protection: import quotas make the supply of imports inelastic, enabling the monopoly to set price by moving along its domestic demand curve net of the quota. Tariffs can also give the monopolist some ability to raise price and restrict output, but unless the tariff is very high, this ability is limited by competition from a perfectly elastic supply of imports (at the world price + the tariff). Moreover, if the tariff is below the prohibitive level, the monopolist has no monopoly power at all. These considerations high-light another important area of non-equivalence between tariffs and quotas. Given such non-equivalence, the two policies can be ranked on the basis of how efficiently they achieve whatever non-economic distributional goal the government has in mind. The ranking of policies to emerge from such a comparison tends to vary depending on the underlying objective. Nevertheless, it is generally felt that in the presence of domestic monopoly, tariffs are to be preferred because they represent more of a constraint on monopoly power.

An important element of most monopolistic industries is the presence of substantial economies of scale. When a monopolistic industry exhibits decreasing average costs of production, use of tariffs to render the industry viable implies a substantial deadweight loss to the community, not least because of the higher cost of the inframarginal units which displace imports. Moreover, increased tariff protection to an established industry confers further monopoly power on the producer, making it possible to increase price to the home market and move further up the average cost curve, sacrificing economies of scale. A production subsidy would appear to be a preferable instrument to a tariff for establishing a domestic "natural monopoly".

It may be that a particular good is not produced domestically at all but is supplied from abroad by a foreign monopolist who repatriates any profits earned. Then, if the domestic government is constrained in its use of a profits tax, there may be an argument for using a tariff to transfer some of the foreign firm's rents from domestic sales to government revenue. Under reasonable assumptions about the form of the demand curve, there is a positive (and non-prohibitive) optimal tariff which trades off the gains in captured foreign rents against the domestic distortion cost. Because the gains from such a tariff are the result of a fall in the foreign firm's supply price of imports, this argument is formally identical to the standard large-country terms-of-trade argument for a tariff. However, the suggestion that a small country can gain by imposing a tariff on a foreign monopolist is quite novel.

CHAPTER 6

Oligopoly

Although the model of monopoly in the previous chapter is a useful starting point, many of the more interesting questions in the protection debate are better addressed using a model with more than one firm. Accordingly, we now consider the case of oligopoly. Oligopoly is a difficult industrial structure to analyse, primarily because the number of firms is small enough for strategic interactions between them to matter, and it is incumbent upon the theorist to make some assumption (which may be quite arbitrary) about the nature of these interactions. Such difficulties do not arise when an industry consists of a single firm because there are no interactions to consider (with the possible exception of behavior to deter entry), whereas under perfect competition and monopolistic competition (see Chapter 7), the number of firms is sufficiently large for the interactions among them to be insignificant. Nevertheless, many protected industries (e.g. steel and automobiles) do consist of a small number of firms, and the issues raised by the possibility of strategic behaviour are important. Indeed, many of the recent developments in the theory of protection have focused on the strategic interactions between large domestic and foreign firms. In this chapter we consider some of these issues and their implications for policy.

The literature on trade and oligopoly has been something of a growth area in recent years, and many aspects of it will not be satisfactorily resolved for some time. Here, we shall be content to focus on some of the main themes and issues which have emerged so far; in particular, the idea that, in the presence of oligopoly, an economy can benefit by using trade policy to give its producers an advantage in domestic and/or world markets. We also attempt to give the reader some feel for the role of alternative assumptions in models of oligopoly and trade. Results vary considerably, depending on whether or not the world market is "integrated" or "segmented" and on whether firms can freely enter and leave an industry. A particularly interesting possibility that arises in industries whose world markets are integrated and free entry competes away any rents, is the "inefficient entry" of new firms in response to increased protection. Such entry is characterized by shorter production runs, higher unit costs and an empirically large welfare cost to the community.

6.1.   Tariffs and rent shifting

The idea that even a small country can gain by using a tariff to shift rents from foreign firms to domestic taxpayers (Katrak, 1977) was introduced in Chapter 5 and is our starting point for the models of strategic trade policy to be considered in this section. Katrak's original model is easily modified to allow for a domestic firm (or firms) producing the same good as the foreign firm for sale in the domestic market only. The tariff then serves to shift rents from foreign producers to domestic taxpayers and firms. To illustrate this, we assume that (i) the domestic market is supplied by a foreign firm and a domestic firm, (ii) the domestic and foreign markets are segmented (i.e. there are separate demand functions for the two markets) and (iii) the industry's product is produced in both countries with a constant marginal cost. Assumptions ii and iii enable us to consider the home market in isolation without the added complication of the foreign firm's behaviour with respect to its own market. In particular, iii implies that the cost of producing an extra unit of the good is independent of the market in which it is sold and the amount sold to the other market. When marginal cost is, say, a decreasing function of a firm's total output, the marginal cost in one market depends on the amount the firm produces for sale to the other market. The implications of such interdependence are considered in Section 6.2. The interested reader will find the constant-cost version of the model set out in full in Appendix 3.

If we let x and y denote, respectively, the domestic and foreign firms' sales to the home market, the profits of the home firm are given by

$$\pi = xp(x + y) - cx - F \tag{1}$$

where $p(x + y)$ is the demand curve in the home market, c the home firm's constant marginal cost and F the fixed cost. The foreign firm's variable profits from sales to the home market are

$$\pi^* = yp(x + y) - c^*y \tag{2}$$

where c^* is the foreign firm's marginal cost.

Now suppose that each firm chooses its sales to the home market to maximize its profits taking the other firm's sales as given; that is, we are assuming *Cournot–Nash behaviour* on the part of firms. The assumption that each firm forms its conjectures about its opponent's behavior in this way is rather arbitrary and, as we shall see later, other types of conjecture can produce different results. We also make the usual assumptions that (i) each firm's profit function has a unique maximum for any value of its opponent's sales, (ii) the Cournot equilibrium exists and is unique and (iii) an increase in either firm's sales reduces both the revenue and the marginal revenue of its opponents. These

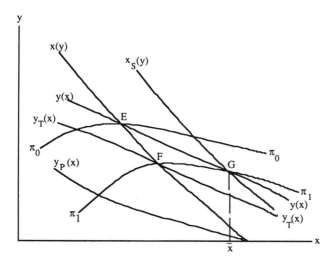

Figure 6.1

assumptions yield reaction (or "best response") curves as shown in Figure 6.1; $x(y)$ denotes the home firm's optimal sales as a function of the foreign firm's sales and $y(x)$ is the foreign firm's reaction function. Both curves are easily seen to be negatively sloped. For example, higher sales by the foreign firm reduce the home firm's marginal revenue and drive its marginal profits below zero; the home firm responds by reducing its sales. Stability of the Nash–Cournot equilibrium at E requires that $y(x)$ be flatter than $x(y)$. These properties of the reaction curves are derived algebraically in Appendix 3.

Figure 6.1 also shows the iso-profit contours for the home firm. To the left of the home firm's reaction curve, these are upward sloping because a higher value of x increases profits (since x is below the value which maximizes π), and an increase in foreign firm sales y is required to reduce profits to their original level. Similarly, to the right of $x(y)$, higher x reduces π and must therefore be accompanied by lower y, hence the iso-profit contours are downward sloping to the right of $x(y)$. Furthermore, lower contours correspond to higher profits for the home firm because lower foreign firm sales (smaller y) result in increased home firm profits for any value of x. By similar reasoning, we can construct the foreign firm's iso-profit contours. (Although these are not illustrated in Figure 6.1, we shall have cause to use them later.) These are negatively sloped above $y(x)$ and positively sloped below $y(x)$, crossing $y(x)$ vertically. Curves further to the left correspond to higher foreign firm profits.

Now consider the effect of a specific tariff of t per unit imposed by the home country on imports of the good. The foreign firm's profits are now given by

$$\pi^* = yp(x + y) - c^*y - ty = yp(x + y) - (c^* + t)y. \tag{2a}$$

The tariff has the same effect on the foreign firm as an increase in its marginal cost of production: at any x, the foreign firm moves up along its marginal revenue curve and supplies less to the home market. The foreign reaction curve moves down from $y(x)$ to a position such as $y_T(x)$, with the new equilibrium at F. The domestic firm is now earning higher profits as indicated by the move from iso-profit curve π_0 to curve π_1 (see Appendix 3 for a formal derivation of these comparative static effects). Note that the home firm could have realized the same profit outcome itself if it had been able to credibly precommit its output to $\bar{x}$, where iso-profit curve π_1 cuts $y(x)$. The presumption is that with Cournot behaviour on the part of firms, such a commitment would not be credible because the home firm is not on its reaction curve $x(y)$. The government's prior announcement of the tariff is seen as making credible the home firm's output expansion to point F, thus shifting rents from the foreign firm to the home firm. This gain from a tariff is additional to the rents transferred from the foreign producer to the domestic taxpayer, which was the source of gain in the Katrak model considered in Chapter 5. Offsetting these gains is the usual domestic distortion cost of the tariff. Domestic welfare is maximized by setting the tariff to equate the marginal gain to the marginal loss.[1] Certainly the conditions for a positive tariff to be optimal are less stringent in this case than when the domestic market is supplied entirely by a foreign monopolist (see Brander and Spencer, 1984).

It is also possible to use Figure 6.1 to compare the tariff which yielded domestic firm profits of π_1 (at F) with a production subsidy yielding the same level of profits. A subsidy of s per unit leads to domestic firm profits of

$$\pi = xp(x + y) - cx + sx - F. \tag{1a}$$

Such a subsidy has the same effect as a fall in the home firm's marginal cost: profit-maximizing x is higher for any value of y, with the home firm's reaction curve shifting to the right. The subsidy which increases home firm profits to π_1 involves the $x(y)$ curve shifting to position $x_S(y)$ [i.e. passing through point G where $y(x)$ intersects π_1 – for purposes of illustration we assume that such an intersection exists]. Thus the subsidy involves higher domestic output than the profit-equivalent tariff. This fact can be used to show that domestic price is lower under the subsidy. Since profits are the same (and positive) under both policies, but output is higher under the subsidy, per unit variable profits must be lower under the subsidy. Unit variable costs are the same (iii) under both policies and so do not affect the comparison; however, variable profits under the subsidy are boosted by the subsidy payment to the producer. It follows that price under the subsidy must be lower (and domestic consumption higher) than

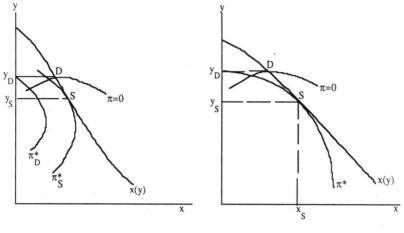

Figure 6.2a   Figure 6.2b

under the profit-equivalent tariff.[2] Thus, as in the competitive case, the subsidy achieves the same assistance to the domestic producer at a lower cost to domestic consumers. However, unlike the competitive case, it is not possible to conclude that the subsidy is superior to the tariff; the rents shifted from the foreign firm to domestic taxpayers under the tariff may be large enough to make the tariff the superior instrument.

The foregoing analysis has assumed the existence of a domestic firm engaged in positive production. However, in many instances tariff protection may be contemplated when a domestic firm is a potential entrant into the industry; indeed, a tariff may be sought by the domestic producer as a means of securing entry. Use of a tariff for this purpose was considered in the context of monopoly in the previous chapter. Here, we consider the possibility that a large foreign firm may act to deter entry of the domestic firm and analyse the effects of a tariff in the presence of such entry-deterring behaviour.

Following Brander and Spencer (1981), suppose that the foreign firm (by virtue of its incumbency in the market) acts as a Stackelberg leader with the knowledge that if the domestic firm enters the market, it will follow Cournot behaviour [i.e. will be on reaction curve $x(y)$ as previously defined]. Thus, if the domestic firm enters, the foreign firm maximizes its profits at point S in Figure 6.2a where its iso-profit contour π^*_S is tangent to the domestic firm's reaction curve. However, it is possible that the foreign firm can earn higher profits than π^*_S by setting its sales to the home market at a level which would deter entry by the domestic firm. This entry-deterring level of y (denoted y_D) is illustrated in Figure 6.2a. It is the value of y which drives domestic firm profits to zero and is thus determined by the intersection of the home firm reaction curve $x(y)$ and the zero-profits domestic iso-profit contour at D. For the Stackelberg equilibrium S to be associated with positive production by the home firm, it must lie to the south-east of D. We assume this to be the case.

In the case illustrated in Figure 6.2a, it is more profitable for the foreign firm to deter entry (iso-profit contour π_D^* associated with entry deterrence is to the left of the contour π_S^* passing through the Stackelberg equilibrium S). If this is the case and domestic entry is deterred, then a domestic tariff does not change the foreign firm's sales to the home market which are held at the entry-deterring level y_D [recall that the tariff does not shift the domestic reaction curve $x(y)$]. Thus, with potential (but not actual) entry, domestic consumption (and production) of the good in question is not affected by a tariff, so there is no domestic distortion. In the absence of such a cost, a tariff is unambiguously beneficial to the home country; the tariff revenue represents a transfer from the foreign monopolist to the domestic taxpayer with no offsetting costs. The optimal course for the domestic economy would therefore appear to be to set the tariff at the level which extracts all of the foreign monopoly rents. The difficulty with this course of action is that the tariff affects the relative profitability of entry deterrence for the foreign firm. Because y_S (the Stackelberg level of y) is less than y_D, a higher tariff will cause a greater fall in profits at the entry-deterring equilibrium D than at the post-entry Stackelberg equilibrium S because at S the tariff applies to a lower level of imports.[3] It is thus possible that a tariff exists (call it t^*) at which the foreign firm is indifferent between equilibria S and D. This is illustrated in Figure 6.2b where S and $(0, y_D)$ are both on the same iso-profit curve π^*.

As already explained, there are clear gains to the home country from increasing the tariff up to t^*. However, an infinitesimal increment of the tariff above t^* (which results in entry of the domestic firm) is likely to reduce welfare. This is because, for foreign profits to remain constant in the jump from D to S, when $t = t^*$, $p(x + y)$ must rise (since the foreign firm is selling a smaller quantity at S than at D, unit profits must increase, and since unit cost and the tariff per unit are both constant, average revenue must rise). Thus domestic consumers are hurt by a small increment in the tariff above t^*. Also, since imports jump down from y_D to y_S, there is a downward jump in tariff revenue. Foreign rents are the same in both situations, but there is a further loss to the economy if it is more costly to produce output x_S at home than abroad (i.e. if $cx_S + F > x_S$)[4] as would be the case if there are significant fixed costs F. Thus, unless domestic marginal cost is considerably less than foreign marginal cost, a small increment in the tariff above t^* will probably make the home economy worse off. To determine whether the economy can benefit by using a tariff to promote entry of a domestic firm, it is necessary to compare the gain from increasing the tariff up to t^* with any losses from increasing t above t^*.[5]

In this section we have seen that the existence of a domestic firm competing with a foreign firm in the domestic market strengthens the Katrak rent-shifting argument for a tariff because the tariff shifts rents to the home firm as well as to the domestic taxpayer. On the other hand, if there is no domestic firm in the industry, it is unclear whether anything is to be gained by using a tariff to help establish a domestic producer.

6.2. Exporting by the domestic firm

In the previous section we examined the use of a tariff to give a domestic firm a competitive advantage in the home market. The associated rent shifting from the foreign firm to the domestic firm was seen as a source of gain, though clearly such gains must be weighed against other effects of a tariff (e.g. the cost it imposes on domestic consumers) in deciding whether a tariff is warranted. Now suppose that the domestic firm can also export to the foreign market. What is the role of trade policy in this situation? For the time being, we shall continue to assume that the domestic and foreign markets are segmented and that the marginal cost of production is constant for both firms. With the same notation as before and with asterisks to denote variables in the foreign market (i.e. x^* denotes the home firm's sales to the foreign market and y^* denotes the foreign firm's sales to its own market), the profits of the domestic and foreign firms are, respectively,

$$\pi = xp(x + y) + x^*p^*(x^* + y^*) - c(x + x^*) - F$$
$$= [xp(x + y) - cx] + [x^*p^*(x^* + y^*) - cx^*] - F \qquad (3)$$

$$\pi^* = yp(x + y) + y^*p^*(x^* + y^*) - c^*(y + y^*) - F^*$$
$$= [yp(x + y) - c^*y] + [y^*p^*(x^* + y^*) - c^*y^*] - F^* \qquad (4)$$

where F^* is the foreign firm's fixed cost.

Once again, assume Cournot–Nash behavior on the part of firms (i.e. each firm chooses its sales in the two markets to maximize its profits, taking its opponent's sales in each market as given). As is clear from Equations (3) and (4), one implication of the assumption of constant marginal costs is that each firm, having made the decision to enter the industry, maximizes its total profits by maximizing its variable profits separately for each market. Thus it is possible to solve the profit-maximizing problem for each market in isolation. In what follows we shall concentrate on the quantities sold in the foreign market. The reaction curves are illustrated in Figure 6.3, and they (and the iso-profit contours) have the same form as in the previous section. Given the assumption of Cournot behaviour, equilibrium is at C. The most interesting feature of this equilibrium is that it may be as drawn with positive values of both x^* and y^* and that the corresponding equilibrium for the home country may similarly involve positive x and y. In other words, it would appear that two-way trade in identical

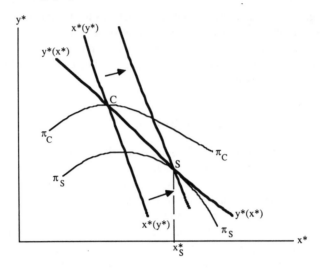

Figure 6.3

products may take place. Let us first check that this is a reasonable outcome and then seek an intuitive explanation. Consider the case in which marginal costs are the same in both countries ($c = c^*$). Then the optimizing conditions for both firms in the foreign market are

$$x^*p^{*\prime} + p^* = c \tag{5}$$

$$y^*p^{*\prime} + p^* = c \tag{6}$$

It is clear from Equations (5) and (6) that $x^* = y^*$. By symmetry, $x = y$ in the home country. Thus, if marginal costs are the same in both countries, each firm supplies half the market in each country. It is straightforward to show that if marginal costs differ, the firm with the higher marginal cost has its market share reduced accordingly. Similarly, the analysis of the previous section can be used to show how a tariff imposed by one country increases its own firm's market share. Transport costs have a similar effect, with each firm having, ceteris paribus, a larger share of its own market (see Brander and Krugman, 1983).

It is not difficult to see why the kind of two-way trade we have just identified ("cross-hauling") should occur. Under autarky, the firm operating in each country is earning monopoly rents. With the opening of international trade, a firm's marginal revenue from the first unit exported equals the price in the export market. Because this exceeds marginal cost, positive exports are profitable for both firms when marginal costs are the same in both countries. This process is pro-competitive in the sense that it forces price down closer to marginal cost.[6] This aspect of cross-hauling is welfare improving for both countries. Of course, given that international trade involves transport costs, the welfare outcome depends on whether the gains from reduced monopoly power in each country exceed the waste associated with costly transportation. Nevertheless, it is possible that cross-hauling may increase welfare in both countries (see Brander and Krugman, 1983).[7] On the other hand, if transport costs are sufficiently large, trade is welfare reducing but may nevertheless take place because it yields positive marginal profits for both firms. In such a case, trade-restricting policies such as tariffs would be beneficial.

Interestingly enough, it is possible to show that trade is necessarily welfare improving if the industry in question is characterized by free entry (unlike the case just considered in which the number of firms is fixed). This is because in the free-entry case, profits are zero and cross-hauling does not occur if transport costs are too high. Price equals average cost (including transport costs), and a lower price means higher welfare. Insofar as cross-hauling reduces the price in both markets, it must be welfare improving (see Venables, 1985, for details).

Note also that the foregoing analysis is based on the assumption of market segmentation. If the world market is integrated, with a single price prevailing internationally, cross-hauling is not profitable (though, of course, a firm in one country may export to the other country for reasons of comparative advantage which are absent from the Brander and Krugman model). The implications of both free entry and integrated markets will be considered further in Section 6.4.

We now turn to the question of whether a country exporting to a segmented market can gain by protecting its own firm. Obviously, it can secure an advantage for its own firm in its domestic market by means of a tariff or production subsidy as in Section 6.1. Of these two policies, only a production subsidy has any effect in its export market. To simplify matters, assume that the good in question is not consumed in the domestic country, so that there are no domestic consumption effects to consider, and an export subsidy is the same as a production subsidy. Figure 6.3 can then be used to illustrate how the home country can gain by subsidizing its exports. With the Cournot–Nash equilibrium at C, the domestic firm is on iso-profit contour π_C. If it could credibly threaten to increase its sales to x_S^*, it would be able to maximize its profits [on iso-profit curve π_S tangent to $y^*(x^*)$ at S, the Stackelberg solution]. However, as we observed in the previous section, with Cournot conjectures such a threat would not be credible, and government policy, in this case an export subsidy, is required to move the equilibrium to S. Such a subsidy would increase exports (x^*) at any level of foreign firm sales (y^*) and thus shift the domestic firm's reaction curve to the right (see Appendix 3 for a derivation of the comparative static effects of an export subsidy). The optimal export subsidy is that which causes $x^*(y^*)$ to pass through the Stackelberg equilibrium S. The implication is that an export subsidy is justified as a means of increasing the market share of the home firm, thus capturing some foreign rents for the domestic economy.

This result, attributable to Brander and Spencer (1985), runs counter to the traditional view that an export subsidy is bad because it drives down the world price of the home country's exports; the usual terms-of-trade argument (as presented in Chapter 4) would indicate an export tax as the appropriate policy. However, in the present model, there is no terms-of-trade reason for government intervention because there is only one domestic firm (which will take full account of terms-of-trade effects in its own decisions) and no domestic consumption (so that terms-of-trade effects arising from decisions by atomistic consumers are absent).

Before proceeding, let us say something briefly about the case in which each firm's marginal cost is a decreasing function of its output. In this case, which has been analysed by Krugman (1984), the two markets are linked through the cost function; for example, higher output by the home firm in the home market reduces its marginal cost so that additional units supplied to the export market are cheaper to produce. This situation was encountered in Chapter 5, where a tariff on imports made it possible for a monopolist to cover fixed costs in the home market and thus be able to earn profits from (otherwise unprofitable) exporting. In the present framework, the implication is that a domestic tariff enables the home firm to increase its share in its own market (by shifting the foreign reaction curve down as in Figure 6.1). However, the increased domestic output reduces the home firm's marginal cost (and the reduced foreign output increases the foreign firm's marginal cost) so that the domestic firm also has an advantage in the foreign market. In fact, a fall in its marginal cost works in the same way as a production subsidy, shifting its reaction curve in Figure 6.3 to the right. Thus, with decreasing marginal costs and the interdependence between markets that this implies, the rent-shifting effect of a domestic tariff is amplified: it exhibits both the domestic market share effect discussed in Section 6.1 and the foreign market share effect of an export subsidy discussed in this section. In this sense, "import protection is export promotion". The argument for using protection to secure an advantage for a domestic firm(s) in the domestic and/or foreign markets appears to be strengthened when marginal costs are decreasing.

Arguments and examples of the kind we have been considering have been an implicit part of the protectionist debate for years. The idea that trade policy has a role to play in capturing foreign rents has long been popular with protectionist groups though it has never been precisely formulated. The new theory in this area serves a most useful purpose in formalizing this body of thought and exposing it to careful scrutiny. As it turns out, the rent-shifting arguments for protection appear to have a number of shortcomings.

A fundamental problem is that the nature and degree of government intervention is highly sensitive to the way in which each firm forms its conjectures about its opponent's response. For example, as Eaton and Grossman (1986) have

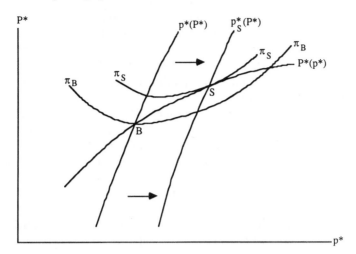

Figure 6.4

noted, if the two firms engage in *Bertrand price competition* (in which each firm is assumed to choose its own price to maximize its profits, taking the other firm's price as given), the optimal policy is an export tax. This case is illustrated in Figure 6.4.

Let p^* denote the price of the home firm's good in the foreign market, and let P^* denote the foreign firm's price in that market. Assume that the domestic and foreign goods are imperfect substitutes. Then domestic and foreign firm variable profits from the foreign market are, respectively,

$$\pi_F = (p^* - c)x^*(p^*, P^*) \qquad \pi_F^* = (P^* - c^*)y^*(p^*, P^*) \tag{7}$$

where

$$x_{p^*}^* < 0 \qquad x_{P^*}^* > 0 \qquad y_{p^*}^* > 0 \qquad y_{P^*}^* < 0.$$

If we assume that a rise in one firm's price increases its opponent's profits and also makes a rise in its opponent's price marginally more profitable (or less costly), then the reaction curves are positively sloped in the (p^*, P^*) plane. For example, a rise in P^* will, by assumption, increase the marginal return (or reduce the marginal loss) from increasing p^*, leading the home firm to increase p^*. For stability of the Bertrand equilibrium at B, we assume that the foreign firm's reaction curve $P^*(p^*)$ is flatter than the home firm's curve $p^*(P^*)$. Finally, we note that the iso-profit contours are downward sloping to the left of the home firm's reaction curve and upward sloping to the right of the reaction curve, crossing the curve horizontally. This is because to the left of $p^*(P^*)$, p^* is below its profit-maximizing value (which it attains on the reaction curve); an increase in p^* in that region therefore increases profits, and a fall in the price of the substitute good P^* is needed to reduce profits back to their original level. Similarly, to the right of $p^*(P^*)$, higher p^* reduces profits, and a higher price of the substitute is needed to hold profits constant. Because lower P^* reduces domestic firm profits, higher iso-profit contours correspond to higher profit levels for the home firm.

At the Bertrand equilibrium B, the domestic firm is on iso-profit contour π_B. Given the foreign firm's reaction curve, it could maximize its profits at the Stackelberg equilibrium at S where iso-profit contour π_S is tangent to the reaction curve $P^*(p^*)$. Under Bertrand price competition, the domestic firm is unable to force the foreign firm along its reaction curve to S. However, S may be attained as a Bertrand equilibrium if the government intervenes to shift the domestic firm's reaction curve to the right [to $p_S^*(P^*)$ in Figure 6.4] so that it intersects the foreign reaction curve at S. However, such a shift involves a higher export price p^* than in free trade and therefore would require an export tax, not an export subsidy.

Of course, it may be argued that *both* Cournot and Bertrand conjectures are unlikely descriptions of actual firm behaviour because they implicitly assume that firms do not learn from their mistakes. Under Cournot (Bertrand), a firm consistently underestimates (overestimates) the quantity response of its rival but apparently does not spot the systematic error. It may therefore be better to employ a conjectural hypothesis under which firms make full use of the information available to them, so-called *consistent conjectures* in which each firm's conjecture about the slope of its opponent's reaction curve is proved correct. This amounts to rational expectations applied to game theory (see Bresnahan, 1981). Unfortunately, it is difficult to reach any general conclusions about the nature of the optimal policy in this case. It was originally thought (Eaton and Grossman, 1986) that under consistent conjectures the optimum would be attained by the firms without any government intervention at all (i.e. free trade), but several authors have now constructed cases with consistent conjectures in which the optimal trade tax is non-zero (see Csaplar and Tower, 1988; Turnovsky, 1986). The difficulty is that each firm's reaction function embodies its conjecture of the slope of its rival's reaction function, which in turn depends on the levels of some of the available taxes and subsidies. It is then possible that a country may do better by distorting its own reaction function by a tax or subsidy, knowing that this distortion then feeds into the other country's conjectures. Of course, determination of the nature and level of the optimal policy is quite complicated, and the scope for empirical error is large indeed.

We conclude that the type of intervention required to effect optimal capture of rents for the home firm in a foreign market varies considerably depending on the type of conjectures employed by the two firms and on the parameters of the system. Given the obvious informational demands of a clear policy prescription, it would be dangerous to promote any particular form of protection.

Another difficulty with the rent-shifting argument for protection is identified by Dixit and Grossman (1986). If the industry which is a candidate for protection is actually one of a group of industries (e.g. the high-tech industries) which compete among themselves for a common specific factor (e.g. scientists) which is in fixed supply, then protection accorded to one may harm the others in the group in a way which reduces national welfare. Suppose exports of one industry are subsidized (in order to shift that industry's reaction curve to pass through the Stackelberg equilibrium as in Figure 6.3). The increased output of this industry drives up the price of the specific factor to all industries in the group, thus reducing the output and rents of those which are not subsidized (and, perhaps some which are subsidized, depending on their technology, rate of subsidy, etc.). If the positive rent shifting associated with a particular subsidized industry is more than offset by adverse rent shifting in the rest of the group, the subsidy is welfare reducing (the reaction curve for the group shifts to the left in Figure 6.3). Clearly, the targeting of certain industries for export assistance is more likely to be welfare improving if the targeted industries are those in which the rent-shifting effect is higher than the average for the group (so that more is gained from the subsidized industries than is lost from the rest). Unfortunately, the process of identifying these industries is likely to prove both costly and unreliable. Nor is a uniform (ad valorem) rate of subsidy to the whole group a solution because with a fixed pool of the specific factor some industries must contract,[8] and there is no guarantee that they will be the correct ones from a rent-shifting point of view. Thus, in addition to the danger of choosing the incorrect policy because of an invalid hypothesis about firms' conjectures, there is the strong likelihood that the government will impose a burden on some industries in a group and on the economy as a whole by "picking the winners" incorrectly.

Finally, we come to what is perhaps the most obvious objection to the rent-shifting argument for protection: that it is empirically insignificant. In the long run, most industries are characterized by free entry and large rents only remain in industries exhibiting substantial economies of scale (e.g. a high fixed cost relative to the size of the market). If profits are zero, there are no rents to be shifted between countries, and the whole argument evaporates. Nevertheless, there are industries in which the number of firms remains relatively small over time (e.g. steel and automobiles), and it is these which must be examined to assess the magnitude of rent-shifting gains from protection. To this end, Dixit (1987b) has used an oligopoly model along the Brander and Spencer lines (but using conjectural variations rather than simply Cournot behaviour) to analyse data relating to Japanese–U.S. trade in automobiles. Despite the tentative nature of the study, the results are revealing. For example, for 1979 data, he is able to show that if tariffs are the only policy used to protect U.S. auto manufacturers, a move from the MFN (most favoured nation) tariff on Japanese auto imports of 2.9 per cent to an optimal tariff (allowing for domestic consumption costs, rent shifting and terms of trade effects) of 16.8 per cent yields welfare gains of only $78 million, a fall in Japanese profits of $406 million with U.S. profits increasing by only $89 million and U.S. tariff revenue going up by $569 million. U.S. consumers lose $580 million. A slightly better welfare outcome is obtained by using a combination of optimal tariff and production subsidy. However, even this would only yield a modest welfare gain (relative to the MFN tariff) of $307 million, about $1.50 per U.S. resident. These results certainly suggest that any rent-shifting gains from protection are rather meagre.

It thus appears that the rent-shifting arguments for protection are difficult to sustain on both theoretical and empirical grounds. Nevertheless, the theory has fulfilled a most useful function by formalizing a popular strain of protectionist thinking which had previously escaped rigorous appraisal. Now that the argument has been made more precise, it is relatively easy to identify its shortcomings.[9]

6.3.   Trade restrictions as facilitating practices

Even if the normative results of the preceding models do not amount to a convincing case for protection, there is no reason why the models themselves should not be used to help us understand actual behaviour in protected oligopolies. In this section we consider one aspect of the positive theory of oligopoly and trade: the effect of quantitative trade restrictions in facilitating collusion between domestic and foreign firms. The basic idea is a simple one: in a Bertrand duopoly of the kind considered in the previous section, the imposition of an import quota or VER in the domestic market conveys clear information to the domestic firm about the foreign firm's reaction curve; it knows the foreign firm's price must always adjust to satisfy the quantitative restriction on its exports. This changes the strategic relationship between the domestic and foreign firm with the domestic firm adopting a price leadership role. The result is that the home firm's price of the good is increased. If the quantitative restriction is not too much below the free-trade level of domestic imports, the foreign firm will be selling much the same quantity as before at a higher price. Accordingly, both firms earn higher profits. Mutual gains of this kind could also be achieved if the firms were to collude explicitly. The trade restriction thus facilitates tacit collusion between domestic and foreign firms.

The idea that protection changes the strategic relationships between the firms in an industry appears to originate with Eastman and Stykolt (1960). However, the Eastman and Stykolt analysis was not presented in terms of a formal model,

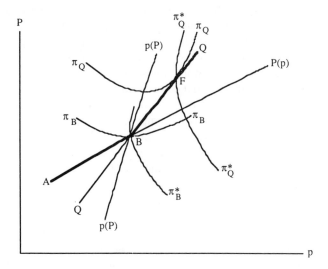

Figure 6.5

and their emphasis was on tariffs rather than quantitative restrictions. After Eastman and Stykolt, the subject was neglected until Itoh and Ono (1982) showed that an import quota could change the strategic relationship between a domestic and foreign firm in a way which was beneficial to both firms, whereas no such clear dominance is associated with a tariff (since a tariff does not offer the domestic firm the same opportunity to raise prices). Ono (1984) extends the analysis to encompass VERs. Harris (1985) and Krishna (1989) have independently developed these ideas in the context of a Bertrand duopoly. The following treatment uses the approach of Harris.

Let us suppose, as in Section 6.1, that the domestic market is supplied by a foreign firm and a domestic firm, the latter producing only for its home market. The two firms produce goods which are close (but not perfect) substitutes. Retaining the assumption of constant marginal costs for both firms, their variable profits are given by

$$\pi = (p - c)x(p, P) \qquad \pi^* = (P - c^*)y(p, P) \qquad (8)$$

where, as before, each firm's demand is a decreasing function of its own price and an increasing function of its opponent's price. Figure 6.5 shows the reaction curves of the foreign and domestic firms in the home market $[P(p)$ and $p(P)$, respectively]. The curves (including the iso-profit contours) are derived in the same way as those in Figure 6.4.

Under free trade, Bertrand–Nash equilibrium is at point B in Figure 6.5. Now suppose either an import quota imposed by the home country or a VER imposed by the foreign country constrains the foreign firm's exports to their free-trade level. A reader schooled in standard competitive theory might expect such a quota to have no effect. However, we have already seen (Chapter 5) that in the presence of monopoly power, a quota set at the free-trade level does lead to a domestic price different from that prevailing under free trade because it reduces the elasticity of the demand curve facing the domestic firm and thus confers more monopoly power on that firm. In the present case a related effect is at work which changes the nature of competition between the domestic and foreign firms. The domestic firm now knows that the foreign firm's price response to any given domestic price p must be such as to keep its exports to the home country at the free-trade level. In other words, the domestic firm knows the foreign firm's policy-distorted reaction curve (ABQ in Figure 6.5) and can use this information to act as a price leader.

The locus QQ represents the locus of values of (p, P) satisfying the quantitative trade restriction. It is upward sloping because higher p increases the demand for the foreign firm's good; to hold that demand at the level prescribed by the policy, the foreign price P would also have to rise. Moreover, the curve must pass through the free-trade point because the free-trade outcome satisfies the policy by definition. The interesting case has QQ positioned between $P(p)$ and $p(P)$ to the north-east of B as illustrated; that is, the policy is binding on the foreign firm for prices above the free-trade level. For the case of linear demand, it is straightforward to check that QQ has this form and is steeper than $P(p)$.

The home firm can now maximize its profits by setting its price where its iso-profit locus π_Q is tangent to ABQ at F in Figure 6.5. This involves a higher level of profits than under free trade (where the iso-profit curve is π_B). Moreover, the foreign firm is also better off, its profits having risen from π_B^* to π_Q^*. This rise in foreign firm profits is a consequence of the fact that the foreign firm is selling the same quantity as in free trade but at a higher price. The move from B to F is a clear illustration of how quantitative trade restrictions facilitate tacit collusion between oligopolistic firms. In the absence of a binding agreement between the firms, neither firm will trust a promise by the other to raise its price above the free-trade level at B, even though both would like higher prices. However, an import quota or a VER precommits the quantity sold by one of the players (the foreign firm) so that higher prices for both firms are sustainable.

It is clear that, provided a quantitative trade restriction does not depart too much from the free-trade level of imports or exports, we would expect it to be supported by both foreign and domestic firms. This is in contrast to the case of competitive markets considered in Chapter 4. In the competitive case, firms whose exports are restricted by a VER are (in the absence of compensation) unambiguously worse off than under free trade, their government's motivation for implementing the VER being to capture the rents associated with what is perceived as inevitable trade restriction. However, when the industry is an oligopoly, foreign exporting firms stand to gain from a modest VER, and the likelihood that the foreign country will support such measures is greatly increased. This helps explain why voluntary export restraints are "voluntary".

6.4. Free entry and integrated markets

The analysis of trade policies in the previous sections was largely confined to the case of a fixed number of firms (two) with segmented markets. In this section we briefly consider some of the implications of alternative assumptions, specifically allowing free entry and exit of firms and an integrated world market for the non-competitive good.

The model with segmented markets and a fixed number of firms has the convenient property that each market can be solved for separately, and any given trade policy only affects prices in one market (e.g. a tariff only changes prices in the domestic market of the country imposing it, an export subsidy only affects prices in the country's export market). Of course, as we have seen, this neat separation also depends on the assumption of constant marginal costs. However, even with constant marginal costs, prices in the two markets become interdependent after we allow free entry and exit of firms. This interdependence is implied by the long-run zero profit condition which is associated with free entry and exit when the number of firms is relatively large.

To see how changing the entry assumption can alter things, we retain the assumption of segmented markets (with positive transport costs) for the time being and consider the case of a tariff imposed by a country which also exports the good in question. With a fixed number of firms, the tariff has the effects described in the first section of this chapter, namely sales of the home firm in the domestic market are increased at the expense of sales of the foreign firm. Domestic price is higher and consumption is reduced while the price paid to foreign firms for imports falls (the usual terms-of-trade gain). However, because each firm maximizes its profits for the home market in isolation, prices and other variables in the foreign market are unaffected. The tariff simply reduces foreign firm profits in the home market (its export market) and increases home firm profits.

With free entry and exit, profits for both home and foreign firms are zero in the long run. At initial free-trade prices, a tariff on the foreign firm's exports to the home country drives foreign firm profits below zero. Foreign firms leave the industry, and their producer price must rise in one of the two markets to restore profits to their long-run zero level. However, a higher price in one market leads to positive profits for home firms inducing new entrants into the domestic industry. Clearly, the final outcome must involve a fall in producer price in one market if domestic firm profits are to remain zero. To determine which price rises and which price falls, we note that with positive transport costs each group of firms has a larger market share in its home market. If the home price p were to rise and the foreign price p^* were to fall, that would adversely affect foreign firm profits in the market in which their share is higher. To restore foreign firm profits to zero, the rise in the home market price would have to exceed the fall in the foreign market price. However, this would have the effect of increasing home firm profits more in their own market than they would be reduced in their export market, leading to positive home firm profits. This outcome is incompatible with long-run zero profits. It follows that the price must rise in the foreign market (providing foreign firms with sufficient extra profits to offset the cost of the tariff and the profits foregone in their export market) and that domestic producer price (=consumer price) must fall (by more than foreign price rises to offset the effect of the larger domestic market share of home firms); see Venables (1985) for a proof of this result. We conclude that in this case (free entry, perfect substitutes and positive transport costs), the outcome is a lower domestic consumer price and an improved terms of trade, so there are unambiguous gains to the home country from imposing a tariff up to the prohibitive level. A similar argument can be used to demonstrate how the home country can gain from a small export subsidy. These are very strong results indeed, and they hinge on the assumption that the two goods are perfect substitutes. If the two goods are not perfect substitutes, then their relative prices can change in each market. For the special case in which transport costs are zero, it can be shown that a tariff leads to an increase in domestic consumer prices (but a fall in the relative price of the home good) and a fall in the price which the home economy pays for its imports, in other words the usual trade-off between a terms-of-trade gain and a domestic distortion cost.[10]

Further possibilities arise if, instead of national markets being segmented, there is a single integrated world market for each good (and hence a single producer price). This case has been analysed by Horstmann and Markusen (1986), who demonstrate the possibility that the entry of domestic firms induced by a tariff or an export subsidy may lead to no change or possibly a contraction of firm output.

To obtain this "inefficient entry" result, Horstmann and Markusen work with a model in which the imperfectly competitive sector in each country produces a single product (X for the home country, Y for the foreign country) but the products of the two countries are imperfect substitutes.[11] With integrated markets, each firm faces a single world-demand curve for its good, unlike the segmented markets model in which there are two country-specific demand curves for each good. As well as making the usual assumptions to ensure the existence of an equilibrium, Horstmann and Markusen also require that (i) changes in the quantity sold of one good, say Y, shift the demand curve for the other good, X, in a horizontally parallel fashion; and (ii) the demand curves for the two goods are not too convex (in particular, they are assumed to be less convex than a

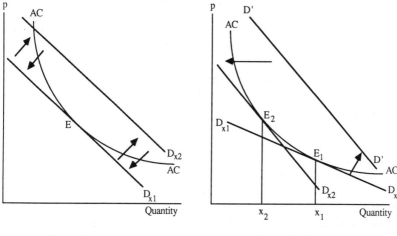

Figure 6.6a   Figure 6.6b

constant elasticity demand curve). The case of linear demand is the simplest to analyse and is illustrated in Figures 6.6a,b.

Figure 6.6a illustrates the case of a tariff (specific or ad valorem) imposed by the home country on imports of good Y. The tariff on Y does not change the slope of the demand curve faced by the representative X-producer but merely shifts it upwards from D_{x1} to D_{x2}, yielding positive profits to X-producers and inducing entry of domestic firms. As these new firms enter, the demand curve shifts back down to its original position of D_{x1}, and firm equilibrium returns to the original zero-profits point E. Thus, the tariff has led to entry of firms into the domestic industry with no change in firm scale or unit cost. The domestic "expansionary" effect of the tariff has been dissipated in fixed entry costs incurred by new firms. The domestic consumer price of Y is increased by the tariff while the foreign producer price is reduced. With no expansion of firm scale, a tariff increases welfare if and only if it yields a terms-of-trade gain greater than the distortion it induces in the domestic consumption of Y, that is, the standard optimum tariff calculation (see Chapter 4). A specific subsidy applied to exports of X would also lead to unchanged firm scale but would have an adverse effect on the terms of trade and so would be unambiguously bad.

An even less favourable outcome arises when an export subsidy is ad valorem rather than specific. For any given consumer price, an ad valorem subsidy to exports of X leads to a greater increase in producer price the higher the consumer price. Such a subsidy causes the firm demand curve for X (in terms of producer price) to become steeper, moving from D_{x1} to, say, D' as shown in Figure 7.6b. Starting at initial zero-profits equilibrium at E_1, the upward shift in the demand curve for X means positive profits to firms in the industry, attracting new entrants. Production by the new firms causes the firm demand curve to shift to the left in a parallel fashion (to D_{x2}) until a new long-run equilibrium is attained at the tangency point E_2. In this case, the entry of new firms induced by the export subsidy has forced all firms in the industry to contract output (from x_1 to x_2) and move up their average cost curve. Thus, in contrast to the model of Venables, an export subsidy is unambiguously bad (and worse than a specific export subsidy) because it worsens the terms of trade and increases average cost at the firm level.

The results of Horstmann and Markusen are interesting for a number of reasons, not least because they accord with and formalize a long-held perception of many economists that protection may induce excessive entry in industries exhibiting economies of scale.[12] It is also worth noting the contrast between the conclusions of Horstmann and Markusen and those of somewhat similar models. For example, Venables (1985) finds a strong case for unilateral imposition of tariffs and export subsidies whereas Horstmann and Markusen find no compelling reason for use of either of these instruments (apart from the standard terms of trade argument for a tariff). This highlights just how sensitive many of these models are to assumptions about entry of firms, the type of market (segmented or integrated), the properties assumed for demand curves and so forth. The protectionist debate will presumably lead to closer scrutiny of these assumptions, and hopefully the outcome will be a less bewildering array of models and results. At this stage the debate seems to be moving away from the arguments of proponents of the "new protectionism" back towards a more critical view of all forms of protection. In particular, as we have seen, the rent-shifting argument for protection is now thought to be neither theoretically robust nor empirically significant. In addition, the role of protectionism in restricting firm scale is now being examined more seriously.

6.5.   Empirical studies

The theory surveyed in the first four sections of this chapter raises a multitude of empirical questions which applied economists have only recently begun to tackle. This is perhaps ironic, given that much of the theory has itself been motivated by earlier empirical work, notably studies of protection in Canada by Eastman and Stykolt (1967) and Wonnacott and Wonnacott (1967). The more recent applied literature has been able to build on the important contributions of these earlier authors by employing the techniques of numerical general equilibrium modelling. Although many questions remain to be answered, the literature appears to have reached a consensus that the gains from trade liberalization are dramatically increased when economies of scale and imperfect competition are incorporated into the model.

The first study to explicitly introduce these elements into a full general equilibrium model appears to be that of Harris and Cox (1984) and Harris (1984). Harris and Cox (H&C) employ a model with both competitive and non-competitive sectors, free entry and exit in all sectors and allowance for economies of scale in the non-competitive sectors. The economy is assumed to be small in its import market but large in its export market. World markets are integrated and domestic firms are assumed to produce goods which are imperfect substitutes for foreign goods. In the non-competitive sectors, the domestic price of a protected good is assumed to be an average of the zero-profits equilibrium price (determined by the tangency of a firm's demand curve and its average cost curve as in Figure 6.6) and a collusive price equal to the world price of the competing import plus the tariff: what H&C term an "Eastman–Stykolt price" (ESP). By changing the weighting of these two prices, one can consider the sensitivity of trade liberalization results to the degree of monopoly power in non-competitive sectors, a higher weighting for the ESP corresponding to more collusive behaviour.

Harris and Cox then use the model in conjunction with Canadian data to simulate the respective effects of unilateral and multilateral removal of all trade restrictions affecting Canadian trade. Note that the latter is not the same as full multilateral removal of trade restrictions because it assumes that trade barriers between countries other than Canada (e.g. the United States and Japan) are unchanged. It is therefore more appropriate to refer to H&C's "multilateral" trade liberalization experiment as "multiple-bilateral" trade liberalization (between Canada and each of its trading partners). The numerical results of the H&C simulations are striking. For the case in which all industries are perfectly competitive, and production exhibits constant returns to scale (the standard case in which the gains are simply the Harberger triangles), unilateral free trade yields a zero welfare gain to Canada whereas multiple-bilateral free trade results in a Canadian welfare gain of about 2.4 per cent of (base year) GNP. These figures are much in line with those of the studies surveyed in Chapter 2.[13] On the other hand, in the case with non-competitive firms and economies of scale, the welfare gains are increased dramatically: to 4.1 per cent of GNP for unilateral free trade and 8.6 per cent of GNP for multiple-bilateral free trade (assuming the product price to be an arithmetic average of the ESP and the "zero-profits price"). These welfare gains are associated with very large increases in scale, average production runs increasing by 37.2 per cent under unilateral free trade and 67.7 per cent under multiple-bilateral free trade. Thus, it seems fair to surmise that much of the additional welfare gain in this case can be attributed to exit of firms from protected industries. Given the similarities between the Harris and Cox model and the Horstmann and Markusen model considered in the previous section (integrated markets, free entry, etc.), we would expect results of this type as the inefficient entry caused by protection is reversed.

Further large increases in the welfare gains result if the Eastman–Stykolt price is given a higher weighting in the determination of product prices in non-competitive industries (i.e. assuming more collusive behaviour on the part of domestic firms). For example, when the weight of the ESP is raised from 0.5 to 0.8, the gain from multiple-bilateral free trade increases from 8.6 per cent to 16.2 per cent of GNE. In other words, the gains from trade liberalization are much larger the greater the degree of monopoly power in the protected economy; trade provides more competition and thus reduces the divergence between domestic price and marginal cost. This pro-competitive aspect of trade (equivalently the pro-monopoly aspect of protection) was stressed in the previous chapter and was also a feature of the models surveyed in this chapter.

Whether the gains from trade liberalization are as large as the Harris and Cox study suggests remains a question for further analysis. It seems unlikely that actual multilateral trade liberalization exercises are going to yield as large a welfare gain to Canada as that attained under H&C's multiple-bilateral free-trade simulation. This is because with other countries' trade barriers intact, Canada can expect to make substantial gains from having increased access to foreign markets, access which is denied to other countries in the H&C simulation. In the absence of such preferential access, this source of welfare gain would disappear, and the overall gain to Canada would be reduced accordingly. This point is given some emphasis by Wigle (1988) who uses a variant of the Whalley (1986) general equilibrium model of global trade to simulate a number of alternative trade liberalization experiments involving the Canadian economy. After recalibrating his model to incorporate the H&C model's assumptions about pricing behaviour, trade elasticities and capital mobility, Wigle estimates that while multiple-bilateral free trade would yield a Canadian welfare gain equal to approximately 4.8 per cent of GNP, true multilateral free trade would yield a gain of only 0.7 per cent of GNP. This difference presumably reflects the loss of preferential access to foreign markets in the move to multilateral free trade. However, it is interesting to note that Wigle's estimate of the gain from multiple-bilateral free trade (4.8 per cent) is little more than half the Harris and Cox figure (8.6 per cent). Wigle's estimates of the gains from other liberalization exercises are similarly quite low.[14] This is obviously a source of some concern because it underlines the sensitivity of the results to the specifications of the model. One important difference between the Wigle and H&C models is the degree of aggregation, with the Whalley–Wigle model having only two manufacturing sectors compared with twenty sectors in the H&C model. It would thus seem that the Wigle model may not be picking up a lot of the inter- and intra-industry rationalization that is captured by Harris and Cox, and this would help account for the difference in results. The role of aggregation in yielding reduced estimates of the cost of protection was briefly discussed in Section 2.8, and the contrast in results between these two models appears to provide a useful illustration of the point.

It is also possible to use applied general equilibrium models of the Whalley, Harris and Cox and Wigle variety to explore some other issues of trade policy. One of the more interesting such issues to be analysed in this context is the estimation of possible outcome of a trade war, something which we discussed in a theoretical context in Chapter 4. Using a variant of the Wigle model (described earlier), Markusen and Wigle (1989) compute Nash equilibrium (average) tariff rates (including tariff-equivalents of other forms of protection) for the United States and Canada. These Nash equilibrium tariffs, which would be the outcome of a tariff war in which the participants exhibit non-cooperative Nash behaviour, are essentially as defined in Chapter 4 and illustrated in Figures 4.4. and 4.5; however, like the models just surveyed, Markusen and Wigle allow for non-competitive firms (with free entry), international factor mobility and economies of scale. Interestingly, they are able to generate a unique, stable Nash equilibrium involving average tariff rates of 5.8 per cent and 18.1 per cent for Canada and the United States, respectively, the higher rate for the United States presumably reflecting the greater potential of a larger country for terms-of-trade gains. These contrast with the actual tariff rates in the 1976 benchmark data of 13.2 per cent and 4.6 per cent for Canada and the United States, respectively. Relative to free trade, the Nash equilibrium is found to imply a welfare loss of $4 billion for Canada and $380 million for the United States (both in 1977 U.S. dollars). The latter figure is only .02 per cent of U.S. GNP and so comes close to the Johnson case in which one country (in this case the United States) may gain from a tariff war (see Chapter 4). Certainly, the possible terms-of-trade losses associated with U.S. tariff reduction may be one reason why the U.S. gain from liberalization is so small. However, another contributing factor may be the lesser importance of scale effects in the larger (and hence more competitive) U.S. market. In fact, Markusen and Wigle judge U.S. scale effects to be relatively unimportant and choose to omit them from the model.

Although the estimates emerging from these various simulations vary considerably from model to model, there is a rough consensus among the models that the presence of economies of scale (and imperfect competition) adds significantly to the gains from trade liberalization. Further refinement and development of modelling techniques will enable us to be more precise about the actual size of this gain.

6.6.   Summary

In oligopolistic markets, protection can be seen to have a role in giving domestic firms a strategic advantage relative to their foreign rivals. For example, a country can use a tariff to shift rents from a foreign exporter to its own domestic firm. The rents thus shifted are additional to those captured by the tariff as government revenue. When there is no domestic production of a particular good but a domestic firm is a potential entrant into the market, a foreign firm can set its output at an entry-deterring level. In such cases, the domestic economy unambiguously gains by levying a tariff up to the point at which the domestic firm is on the margin of not being deterred from entry. However, increases of the tariff above this level may reduce welfare.

Similarly, in a Cournot oligopoly, export subsidies can be employed to increase the market share of a domestic firm in a foreign market. The subsidy has the effect of pre-committing the firm's sales to the foreign market, giving it a strategic advantage relative to foreign firms. However, this result is sensitive to the nature of the firms' conjectures with respect to their rival(s). For example, in a Bertrand duopoly, the optimal policy for the domestic government is an export tax rather than a subsidy. The argument for use of protection as a rent-shifting device is further undermined in industries in which free entry can compete away any rents in the long run. Furthermore, for industries in which entry is limited (by, say, high fixed costs), there is some evidence that the rent-shifting gains from protection are empirically small.

The case of oligopolistic markets offers some insight into the popularity of quantitative trade restrictions, particularly voluntary export restraints. In a Bertrand duopoly, quantitative restrictions on imports to the home country convey information to the domestic firm about the foreign firm's reaction function; that is, price must always adjust to keep the quantity traded constant. This enables the domestic firm to act as a price leader, the outcome being an equilibrium in which both the home and the foreign firm are charging higher prices (and earning higher profits) than under free trade. The quota or VER serves to facilitate tacit collusion between the two firms at the expense of consumers in the importing country.

The effects of protection in oligopolistic markets are very sensitive to the particular assumptions made about the structure of the market(s). In particular, it makes a difference (i) whether the domestic and foreign markets are segmented (allowing firms to price discriminate) or whether there is a single integrated world market (with a single price), and (ii) whether the number of firms in the industry is fixed or whether free entry–exit of firms competes away rents. A particularly interesting case which seems to reflect the properties of many oligopolistic markets is the free-entry, integrated markets combination. In such a case, the stimulus provided by protection is dissipated in fixed costs incurred by new firms attracted into the industry (so-called inefficient entry), with no increase in firm scale. Empirical studies of this case suggest that the gains from the increased firm scale (and firm exit) that accompanies trade liberalization are potentially quite large.

CHAPTER 7

Monopolistic competition and product differentiation

In this chapter, we explore the effects of trade restrictions in industries producing differentiated products. Such industries are not, in general, characterized by perfect competition, particularly if there are economies of scale, but, unless fixed costs are very high, we usually expect more than one producer, probably a large number of producers in the industry. The most suitable model appears to be one in which there is a large number of firms in the industry, each possessing some market power with respect to its own product (which is imperfectly substitutable for those produced by other firms in the industry), but not perceiving any strategic interaction between itself and its competitors. Presumably, the industry would also be characterized by free entry–exit of firms with long-run zero profits. This type of market structure, termed *monopolistic competition,* combines some elements of perfect competition (no strategic interactions between firms, free entry) with some elements of the oligopoly models of the previous chapter. Monopolistic competition differs from oligopoly precisely because the number of firms is large enough for strategic interactions among them to be negligible.

Allowing explicitly for product differentiation serves to emphasize some aspects of protection policy which we have previously ignored. In particular, consumers may derive additional benefits from product variety; consumer welfare is affected to the extent that trade restrictions change the number of product varieties available. In addition, in industries producing differentiated products, intra-industry trade (previously encountered in the Brander and Krugman model of Chapter 6) assumes greater importance, with trading economies simultaneously importing some product-differentiates and exporting others in the same industry. Intra-industry trade is known to be an important component of international trade, particularly between developed countries.[1] In particular, there is ample evidence of two-way trade in commodities such as automobiles, automobile components and consumer durables, and the effects of trade policy on this type of trade should be taken into account.

For most of this chapter we shall be concerned with models of monopolistic competition. However, there is also an interesting case in which product differentiation and intra-industry trade are consistent with perfect competition and a constant-returns-to-scale technology. This will be explored in Section 7.5.

7.1   Types of product differentiation

Most manufactured commodities are available in a range of varieties (or product-differentiates). These varieties may differ only in respect of brand-names or packaging (as for many detergents, toothpastes, etc.) or they may differ in more substantial ways (e.g. houses with different floor-plans, books by different authors, styles of clothing). In addition, the product differentiation may be horizontal or vertical. Horizontal product differentiation refers to product types which differ in specifications but are of the same "quality" in the sense that they embody the same value of resources (e.g. recordings by different performers, identical houses at different locations, brands of pasta). Vertical product differentiation exists when the product varieties differ in quality, a good embodying a higher value of resources being ranked above a shoddy good. The literature has tended to emphasize horizontal differentiation and, with the exception of Section 7.5, the treatment in this chapter will reflect this emphasis.

There are various reasons for the existence of a range of varieties of any one product. Obviously, variation in income across consumers explains much vertical product differentiation, with higher-income individuals tending to buy higher-quality varieties. In the absence of income differences, individuals may nevertheless have different preferences for "characteristics" which commodities in a group possess in varying proportions. In some cases it may be possible to combine some of the commodities in the group to obtain a more preferred bundle of characteristics (e.g. dining at a Vietnamese restaurant one night and an Italian restaurant the next, buying summer and winter clothes at the same time, buying a number of books or records). In other cases (buying a car, a stereo or a washing machine) the consumption technology or consumers' preferences and/or budget constraints do not favour such combinations, with the result that the consumer only purchases a single preferred good. Although these two cases can, in principle, be dealt with in the same framework (see Lancaster, 1979), two distinct approaches have evolved. The case in which consumers derive utility from "simultaneously" consuming a number of differentiates of a given product was developed by Spence (1976) and Dixit and Stiglitz (1977). Their approach (hereafter called SDS product differentiation) is sometimes termed the "love of variety" model and treats the product-differentiates in a commodity group as symmetric substitutes with consumption of more varieties yielding higher utility to consumers. This is akin to the benefits derived by residents in a large city from its greater diversity of shopping, restaurants and nightlife (the "city lights" effect). On the other hand, Lancaster (1979, 1980) has tended to emphasize the case in which each consumer has a preferred product specification and consumes the available product which comes closest to her ideal. In the next two sections we shall examine these two approaches and see what they imply about the effects of restrictions on trade between two economies producing differentiated products. In both cases, the innate complexity of the problem makes it necessary to resort to special assumptions, but it is reassuring that the two approaches yield broadly similar results.

7.2. International trade with SDS product differentiation

A number of authors have adapted the SDS model to explore the effects of international trade in the presence of product differentiation (see Dixit and Norman, 1980; Krugman, 1979, 1980, 1982; Lawrence and Spiller, 1983). Here we follow the approach of Krugman (1979, 1980) and assume that each country has only one industry which produces a range of differentiated products. This enables us to focus on intra-industry trade and identify the gains associated with such trade, as distinct from the gains from inter-industry trade considered in previous chapters. One important implication of this type of model is that international trade can occur between countries with identical costs (i.e. trade is not driven by comparative advantage). In Section 7.4, we consider the implications of adding another sector so that questions such as the composition of trade and comparative advantage can be addressed.

Consider an economy in which many identical consumers derive utility by consuming n varieties of a differentiated product. Utility of each consumer is assumed to be given by the special form

$$U = \sum_{i=1}^{n} v(c_i), \qquad v' > 0, \qquad v'' < 0, \qquad v(0) \geq 0 \qquad (1)$$

where c_i is the individual's consumption of variety i. Before proceeding, it is worth noting the following implications of assuming this form for the utility function.

i. Because the subutility function (v) for each variety is the same across varieties (i.e. there is no innate preference for any one variety), and because v is concave (diminishing marginal utility from any one variety), the representative consumer on a given income is better off the larger the number of varieties – that is, she is better off consuming smaller amounts of a larger number of goods.[2] This is what is meant when the SDS representation of product differentiation is described as the "love of variety" approach. It is analogous to the preference of a risk-averse investor for a diversified portfolio of securities.

ii. The demand elasticities associated with a utility function of the form Equation (1) have special properties. Note that if the number of varieties is very large, then the effect of a change in the price of one variety on the consumer's marginal utility of income can be safely neglected.

The own-price elasticity of demand for each variety can then be approximated by[3]

$$\varepsilon = -\frac{v'(c)}{cv''(c)} \tag{2}$$

For the special case in which the function v is given by

$$v(c_i) = c_i^{\theta}, \tag{3}$$

the elasticity of demand is constant, and as $n \to \infty$, it can be shown that[4]

$$\varepsilon \to \frac{1}{1 - \theta}.$$

Thus, for this particular form of utility function the own-price elasticity of demand of each variety tends to a finite value as the number of varieties becomes infinite. Moreover, for any utility function of the form given by Equation (1), the cross-price elasticity of demand for each variety approaches zero as the number of varieties becomes infinite. These properties are a little disturbing. After all, when there are a large number of substitutes for a particular good, we expect both the own-price and cross-price elasticities of demand for the good in question to become very large; we certainly do not expect the cross-price elasticity to approach zero! These observations have caused some economists to cast doubt on usefulness of the SDS approach. However, it should be remembered that the approach applies to a particular type of product differentiation. When v is given by Equation (3), the elasticity of substitution between any pair of goods is a constant $[1/(1 - \theta)]$ which is the same for all pairs of product varieties and does not depend on the number of varieties. Thus, for example, an avid reader who buys a lot of books may regard a large number of books as equally good substitutes for each other, and a sudden doubling of the range of choice may not affect the elasticity of substitution between any available pair. In such a case, it is quite plausible that the cross-price elasticities of demand for different books are low, given that over time the individual buys them all anyway. Viewed in this way, perhaps the SDS approach is not a bad approximation when the number of available varieties of certain products is sufficiently large for no variety to represent a significant portion of the consumer's budget.

iii. Precisely because cross-price effects are negligible when preferences are given by Equation (1), there is no significant strategic interaction between firms; hence monopolistic competition is an appropriate market structure in this case.

iv. Notwithstanding the discussion in (ii), it is still possible that each variety's own price elasticity of demand as approximated by Equation (2) may be a decreasing function of c_i. This would seem at least roughly to capture the idea that as more varieties become available (with less of each being consumed), the demand curve for each becomes more elastic. Krugman makes this assumption in his 1979 paper, and we shall allow it as a possibility in what follows. Because the elasticity in Equation (2) is essentially the reciprocal of the coefficient of relative risk aversion associated with v (as defined in Chapter 3) and because relative risk aversion is generally thought to increase with wealth or income, the assumption may not be too unreasonable.

We now turn to a specification of the production side of the model. Because one purpose of the model is to show how international trade can occur in the absence of any differences in comparative costs between countries, we assume that all goods have the same cost curve. Moreover, each good is produced with the economy's only factor of production, call it labour. There is a fixed labour requirement of α units for producing any variety. In addition, each unit of output requires β units of labour. Arriving at or changing a product's specification is assumed to be a costless process. Thus, the labour required to produce x_i units of good i is given by

$$l_i = \alpha + \beta x_i \qquad \alpha, \beta \text{ positive constants.} \tag{4}$$

The assumption that there is a fixed cost associated with the production of each variety is important for two reasons: it is a simple way of incorporating economies of scale into the model, and it limits the number of varieties which can be produced at a profit – thus consumers cannot be offered infinite variety. Furthermore, because there are economies of scale, each variety is produced by at most one firm.[5] There are no economies of scope[6] in the industry, so there is no reason for one firm to produce more than one variety. We thus have a situation in which each product-differentiate is produced by exactly one firm.

Let each firm choose its output to maximize its profits, taking the outputs of the other firms as given. This involves equating its marginal cost to its marginal revenue. For the firm producing product variety i, we have

$$\text{MR}_i \equiv p_i + x_i p_i' = p_i \left(1 - \frac{1}{\varepsilon_i} \right) = w\beta \equiv \text{MC}_i. \tag{5}$$

This can be rewritten

$$\frac{p_i}{w} = \beta \left(\frac{\varepsilon_i}{\varepsilon_i - 1} \right) \equiv \beta f(c_i). \tag{5a}$$

Assume that the economy's labour force equals the number of individuals L. Then

$$x_i = Lc_i. \tag{6}$$

Finally, it is assumed that the number of firms is sufficiently large (i.e. the market is sufficiently large relative to the fixed cost α) for free entry–exit of firms to and from the industry to equate profits to zero in the long run[7]; that is,

$$p_i x_i = (\alpha + \beta x_i)w. \tag{7}$$

Using Equation (6), this can be written as

$$\frac{p_i}{w} = \beta + \frac{\alpha}{Lc_i}. \tag{7a}$$

Equations (5a) and (7a) jointly determine c_i and (p_i/w). Because these equations are the same for all varieties, the solution (assuming it is unique) is the same for all i. In other words $c_i = c$, $p_i/w = p/w$ for $i = 1, 2, \ldots, n$. Because price, output and quantity consumed do not differ across varieties, we shall omit subscripts in what follows.

The determination of equilibrium c and (p/w) is illustrated in Figure 7.1. Figure 7.1a represents the case in which ε is a decreasing function of c. PP represents the profit-maximizing combinations of (p/w) and c which satisfy Equation (5a). It is upward sloping because higher c reduces the elasticity of demand for a typical variety (by assumption), thus increasing the monopoly power of firms which respond by charging a higher price (measured in wage units). If the elasticity of demand is constant, profit-maximizing price is unaffected by the value of c – in such a case (illustrated in Figure 7.1b) the PP curve is horizontal. ZZ represents the locus of values of (p/w) and c associated with zero profits [Equation (7a)]. It is downward sloping in both diagrams of Figure 7.1 because higher c implies higher output (for a given number of consumers, L), lower unit costs and hence a lower break-even price. Point E_0 in both diagrams represents equilibrium for the industry and the economy.

It remains to determine the equilibrium number of firms in the industry (and thus the number of varieties of the product). This will be determined so as to clear the market for labour, that is,

$$\sum_i l_i = n(\alpha + \beta cL) = L \tag{8}$$

so that n is given by

$$n = \frac{L}{\alpha + \beta cL}. \tag{8a}$$

Having determined the equilibrium price, output, consumption and product variety for the economy in question, we now consider how this equilibrium is likely to be affected by trade with another economy with population L^*. To

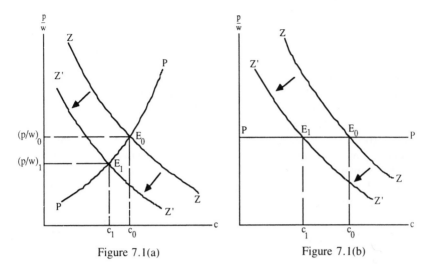

Figure 7.1(a)   Figure 7.1(b)

keep matters simple (and to highlight the determinants of intra-industry trade), we assume that utility and cost functions in both economies are the same. The foreign country's equilibrium is given by Equations (5a), (7a) and (8a) with L replaced by L^* (as is usual, asterisks are used to denote the variables of the other country). The opening up of trade between the two countries simply means that the number of consumers purchasing any one variety of the product increases from the population of the country where it is produced (L or L^*) to the combined population of the two countries ($L + L^*$). Hence, the effects of trade can be determined by considering the effects of an increase in L in Figure 7.1. PP is unaffected by such a change in the size of the market, whereas ZZ shifts down to the left, the larger market (L) implying increased output (cL) at any given value of c and, hence, lower unit costs and a lower break-even price. Equilibrium shifts from E_0 to E_1 in both diagrams of Figure 7.1 with consumption of each variety falling from c_0 to c_1, and the price of a typical variety, measured in wage units, falling from $(p/w)_0$ to $(p/w)_1$ in Figure 7.1a and remaining unchanged in Figure 7.1b. From the zero-profit condition, we have that

$$x = \frac{\alpha}{(p/w) - \beta}. \tag{9}$$

Clearly, the output of each variety increases in the case where (p/w) falls (Figure 7.1a) but is unaffected if a constant elasticity of demand holds (p/w) fixed (Figure 7.1b). Because output x now equals $c(L + L^*)$, the number of varieties produced in each country is given by

$$n = \frac{L}{\alpha + \beta x} = \frac{L}{\alpha + \beta c(L + L^*)} \qquad n^* = \frac{L^*}{\alpha + \beta x} = \frac{L^*}{\alpha + \beta c(L + L^*)}.$$

(8b)

Equation (8b) tells us that under free trade: (i) the number of varieties produced in each country is proportional to the country's population (i.e. the larger country produces more varieties); (ii) in the variable elasticity case of Figure 7.1a, fewer varieties are produced in each country under free trade than under autarky (because x is higher under free trade); and (iii) when the elasticity of demand is constant (as in Figure 7.1b), the number of varieties produced in each country is unaffected by trade (since x is unchanged). On the other hand, the total number of varieties available to consumers $(n + n^*)$ is higher than under autarky in both cases. This is because

$$n + n^* = \frac{L}{\alpha + \beta c(L + L^*)} + \frac{L^*}{\alpha + \beta c(L + L^*)} = \frac{L + L^*}{\alpha + \beta c(L + L^*)}.$$

(10)

In other words, the total number of products produced in the world economy is the same as the number which would be produced by a single economy comprising $(L + L^*)$ individuals. Thus, to see what happens to product variety (the total number of varieties available to any consumer) when the two economies trade, we need only consider the effect of an increase in the population of one economy on the number of varieties it produces – that is, differentiate Equation (8a) with respect to L. Because dn/dL is positive,[8] product variety increases even if the number of varieties produced in each country falls (as it does if ε is a decreasing function of c). Note also that in the constant elasticity case, the smaller of the two countries realizes the larger gains from trade because it experiences a larger increase in the number of available varieties (and increased product variety is the only source of gain).

Let us reflect on the conclusions of the Krugman model. First, it provides an explanation for international trade which is not based on differences in factor endowments. Two economies producing differentiated products trade to take advantage of the wider market represented by the integrated world economy. The outcome of this may not be any increase in output by any one firm; more consumers may simply each consume less of a larger number of varieties with output of each variety unaffected (as is the case when each variety's own-price elasticity of demand is a constant). On the other hand, it is possible that longer production runs may result from sales to the larger market with each country producing fewer varieties (as occurs when the elasticity of demand for each variety is a decreasing function of the amount consumed). Whatever the implications for firm output, it is clear that international trade in the differentiated product occurs with different varieties being produced in each country. This trade is "intra-industry" in the sense that each country both imports and exports products in the same commodity classification. Second, as a result of such trade, consumers in both countries benefit by being able to purchase an increased number of varieties of the good in question. They may derive an additional benefit if the increased number of varieties renders demand for each variety more elastic, reducing the monopoly power of both firms and leading to a lower equilibrium price. The model therefore identifies potential gains from trade associated with increased product variety and reduced unit costs (the latter achieved by longer production runs and passed on to the consumer as lower prices).[9]

It is tempting to infer from the foregoing analysis that trade restrictions such as tariffs simply reverse these effects, increasing prices and reducing product variety and outputs, but it is not quite so simple. For example, in the constant elasticity case, tariffs do not change the elasticity of demand; so the producer price (measured in wage units) and output of each variety are also unchanged [from Equations (5a) and (7a) with L replaced by $L + L^*$]. It follows from Equation (10) that the number of varieties available is similarly unaffected. Thus the only effect of a tariff in this case is to shift consumption from imported varieties to domestic varieties (see Gros, 1987, for details). Of course, as the tariff is increased up to the prohibitive level, the consumption of imported varieties approaches zero and, in the limit, we are back at the autarky solution with reduced product variety in each country. However, non-prohibitive tariffs have no effect on product variety or outputs; existing varieties are simply consumed in smaller quantities in their export market (and correspondingly larger quantities in their home market). Despite this limited menu of effects, the model does suggest additional costs arising from protection in industries characterized by product differentiation and economies of scale, particularly when the protection is at a level which eliminates trade.

Harris (1984) attempts to estimate the contribution of product differentiation effects to the overall cost of protection by incorporating some industries producing product-differentiates in his general equilibrium model of the Canadian economy (see Section 6.5). His model, which assumes constant elasticity SDS-type preferences, differs from the Krugman model in assuming that the home economy is small in its import markets but large in its export markets and that the price in non-competitive markets is an average of the Eastman-Stykolt price (see Chapter 6) and the zero-profits price (as already derived) – that is, he is assuming a higher price (and a greater degree of monopoly power) than Krugman. His approach is interesting because it highlights many of the difficulties which empirical researchers must confront when dealing with product differentiation. For example, his use of the Eastman-Stykolt price (= world price + tariff) to determine an average price serves the function of making producer prices and outputs depend on protection levels, in contrast to the constant elasticity version of the Krugman model in which non-prohibitive tariffs do not affect these variables.

On the other hand, the way in which the model determines the level of product variety is less satisfactory. Because of the small open economy assumption and the difficulties of modelling the product selection process in foreign industries, Harris assumes that the number of imported varieties of a product is in a constant ratio to the number of domestically produced varieties ("competitive foreign product differentiation"). Although this assumption is quite consistent with the Krugman model (and the Lancaster model considered in the next section), it prevents the displacement of domestic varieties by foreign varieties when trade is liberalized. Instead, when reduced protection renders some domestic product varieties unviable, the number of competing foreign varieties is reduced also. This reduction in product variety (combined with SDS preferences, which attach a high cost to reduced variety) appears to be a primary cause of Harris's relatively low estimates for welfare gains in the presence of product differentiation. Inclusion of product-differentiated industries in the non-competitive model discussed in Chapter 6 leads to Canadian welfare gains of only 2.7 per cent of GNP for unilateral free trade and 6.2 per cent of GNP for multiple-bilateral free trade. These figures are considerably below those which were cited in Chapter 6 for the case of homogeneous products (4.1 per cent of GNP for unilateral free trade and 8.6 per cent of GNP for multiple-bilateral free trade) and run counter to the Krugman predictions of additional gains from trade liberalization due to increased product variety. As Harris acknowledges, it seems unlikely that removal of trade restrictions would not induce some foreign varieties to enter the Canadian market where domestic varieties have become unprofitable. If this response occurs, product variety would fall less and might even increase. It is something of a challenge for empirical researchers using the SDS framework to incorporate this type of foreign response into their models.

It should be clear from the analysis of this section that models which employ the SDS specification of preferences have a number of limitations. Apart from their unrealistic assumptions about demand elasticities, they do not appear suitable for capturing fully the effects of non-prohibitive trade restrictions – in particular, product variety and the proportion of domestic to imported varieties are unaffected by non-prohibitive tariffs. There is a further shortcoming which applies equally to the Lancaster model of the next section. The set (as distinct from the number) of product varieties produced in each country is indeterminate. These deficiencies of the SDS-Krugman set of models should be kept in mind when using them in empirical and other applications. Nevertheless, the approach remains a useful one, not least for its simplicity, which may yet make it a suitable framework for empirical research.

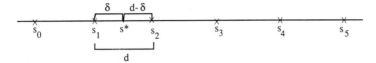

Figure 7.2

7.3   The Lancaster model

In this section we consider Lancaster's approach to product differentiation. It is more satisfactory than the SDS approach in a number of respects, particularly in its implications for demand elasticities. However, analytical simplicity dictates that it too requires some special assumptions.

The basic idea is as follows. Consumers each possess a preferred specification (or bundle of attributes or characteristics) for a good, but, as in the model of the previous section, only a finite number of goods are actually produced. Thus, in general, most consumers are unable to obtain a good which offers their exact preferred specification, and they are forced to consume the available good which comes closest to their ideal. Suppose product specification can be represented as a scalar along a line[10] as in Figure 7.2 and assume that consumers are identical in all respects (income, etc.) except for their preferred product specification. Consider a consumer whose ideal specification is s^*. Suppose the closest available commodities have specifications s_1 and s_2, which are distance d apart and distances δ and $(d - \delta)$, respectively, from s^*. Given the prices of s_1 and s_2, the individual demands less of either good the greater the distance between her ideal s^* and the good in question; there also exists a critical s^* (and associated δ) such that all consumers whose ideal lies to the right of that s^* consume s_2, and all those to the left will consume s_1. This point on the line represents the division between the market for s_1 and the market for s_2 at the existing prices and implies a "market width" for each good which depends on the prices of the goods.

It is thus possible to define market demand curves for each product on the line. Each individual has a demand curve for the product and this depends on the prices of the goods on either side of the consumer's ideal specification and the distance between the ideal and the two goods. These individual demand curves are then summed across all consumers in the half-market on either side of the product in question. For simplicity, assume that consumers are uniformly distributed along the line – that is, at any point s on the line, there are the same number of individuals (say N) for whom s is the ideal variety. The market demand curve for the product is then simply N times the integral of the individual demand curves over the interval of the product's two half-markets. The demand for a good with price p, for which the adjoining goods on the product spectrum each have price p', is then given by $D(p, p', d)$ where D has the following properties:

i. D is a decreasing function of its own price p. In this case, a higher value of p reduces demand by reducing the demand by each individual in the market and also by reducing the number of individuals in the market (the market width).

ii. D is an increasing function of p', reflecting the fact that adjacent goods are substitutes (the substitution being effected via the individual demand curves and changes in the market widths).

iii. D is an increasing function of d because a greater distance between available products implies, ceteris paribus, a greater market width, hence, a greater number of consumers purchasing the good and an accordingly higher demand.

Note that even this simple version of the Lancaster framework highlights the fundamental differences between his approach and that of SDS–Krugman. In this model, not all goods are equally good substitutes for each other. Other things being equal, varieties which are further apart on the product line are poorer substitutes. Moreover, as the number of varieties increases, the distance between goods decreases. This has two important implications: (i) the larger the number of varieties, the higher the own-price and cross-price elasticities of demand for each good, with both elasticities becoming infinite as the distance between adjacent goods approaches zero (perfect substitutes); (ii) a greater range of goods implies that the distance between a consumer's ideal variety and the closest available variety is reduced. Implication (i) is in marked contrast to the SDS version of product differentiation in which proliferation of varieties did not make different varieties significantly closer substitutes. On the other hand, (ii) shows that, as in the SDS model, consumers in the Lancaster model benefit from greater product variety but for a different reason. Preferences of the SDS kind explicitly incorporate a love of variety, with each individual consuming all available varieties and convex preferences favouring a more diverse menu. In the Lancaster model, variety is beneficial because it enables consumers to obtain goods closer to their ideal specifications.

As in the model of the previous section, all goods are assumed to have the same cost function, with the cost of producing x_i units of the ith variety of the good given by

$$C_i = \alpha + \beta x_i, \qquad \alpha, \beta = \text{positive constants.} \tag{11}$$

Suppose that each producer chooses his price and product specification, taking other firms' values of these variables as given. Given that all goods in the product spectrum are produced with the same technology [Equation (11)], and

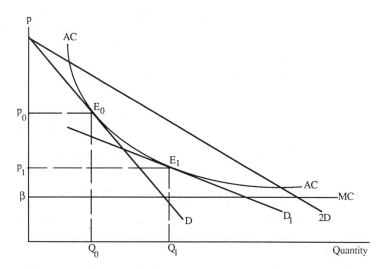

Figure 7.3

the distribution of consumers' ideal specifications is uniform along the spectrum, it can be shown (see Lancaster, 1979) that the resulting Nash equilibrium involves product varieties equally spaced along the line, each selling at the same price (so that output and consumption of all varieties are also identical).

We now consider the effects of free trade between two identical such economies. We will then explore the effects of tariffs on the pattern of trade and production in the two countries. As in the SDS–Krugman model, trade between two identical economies results in half of the available varieties being produced in each country. The Lancaster model shares one inadequacy of the SDS approach in being unable to predict which varieties will be produced in which country after trade. However, because product variety does have some structure in the Lancaster case, it is at least possible to explore the implications of different patterns of specialization. In the Lancaster approach, tariffs generally have some effect on variables such as producer price and output, whereas in SDS–Krugman, non-prohibitive trade policies have little effect on the equilibrium, apart from the switch in consumption from imported to home varieties.

The move from autarky to free trade is illustrated in Figure 7.3. The diagram illustrates the average and marginal cost curves for a typical product-differentiate. D is the demand curve for the good under autarky. Initial equilibrium is at E_0, where the firm is maximizing profits (by equating marginal cost to marginal revenue), and free entry and exit of firms have equated long-run profits to zero. Output is Q_0 and domestic price is p_0.

With the opening of the two economies to free trade, if the number of available products is unchanged (remember, the same products were produced in both countries under autarky), the demand for the typical variety is doubled (because the number of consumers is doubled). This is because only one firm produces any given variety, a firm in one of the two countries ceasing to produce this variety. The remaining firm then faces the demand curve 2D, the horizontal sum of its new export market and its original domestic market. Given that the initial equilibrium at E_0 involved zero profits, the firm in question now earns positive profits. This encourages entry by "new" firms which produce additional product lines (these may simply be "old" firms which have wisely changed the specification of their product), thus narrowing the distance d between products, thereby increasing the elasticity of demand for the good and moving its demand curve downwards.

Final equilibrium is at a point such as E_1 in Figure 7.3 where a demand curve (D_1, the horizontal sum of the equal demands in the home and export markets) is tangent to the firm's average cost curve. Notice that the firm is producing a higher output (Q_1) at a lower price (p_1) than under autarky. This is because the proliferation of varieties has placed other goods closer to this good on the product line, increasing its price-elasticity of demand and reducing the firm's monopoly power. It is also clear from the foregoing that the number of available varieties is greater than under autarky. On the other hand, fewer varieties are produced in each economy (i.e. the total number of goods produced is less than twice the original number) precisely because the greater product variety has reduced monopoly power for all firms. These results are broadly similar to those of the Krugman model for the case in which the elasticity of demand of a typical variety was a decreasing function of quantity consumed. Trade makes more products available to the consumers of both countries and also reduces price because the increased product variety reduces the monopoly power of producers forcing them down their average cost curves. Consumers gain from both of these effects.

As explained already, the model as it stands does not tell us which country produces which varieties. There are clearly many possible patterns of specialization consistent with the equilibrium we have just described. However, in analysing the effects of tariffs, the essential aspect of the pattern of production is whether domestic and foreign varieties are in proximity on the product line or are far removed from one another. To capture these alternative possibilities, it is convenient to consider two polar cases, one in which there is an imported variety that lies between any two domestically produced varieties, the so-called *interleaved* case, and an alternative situation in which the product spectrum is partitioned, with domestic varieties on one side of the partition and imported varieties on the other – this is referred to as the "split" case. In the interleaved case, domestic and imported varieties are close substitutes whereas, in the split case, they are very poor substitutes (with the trivial exception of the two varieties at the boundary of the partition). Although either of these polar cases is

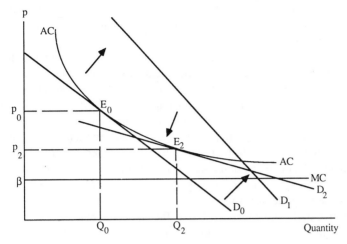

Figure 7.4

a possible configuration, there are reasons for supposing the interleaved case to more closely approximate the likely outcome.[11] In any event, we shall assume in what follows that the pattern of specialization, whether split or interleaved, is the same before and after tariffs are imposed.

It is also helpful to depart from our initial assumption that the two economies are identical in all respects (an assumption which was made for expository convenience only). Maintaining the assumption that both economies share the same tastes and technology, we suppose that one of them (the "home" country) is small relative to the other and that it produces varieties of the differentiated product for home consumption but does not export them. Initial equilibrium for a typical domestic variety is at the tangency point E_0 in Figure 7.4. Free-trade output is Q_0 and price is p_0. Now suppose the home country unilaterally imposes a tariff on all imported varieties of the good. This increases foreign firms' marginal cost of selling to the home country and so the home consumer pays a higher price for imported varieties. The effects of this on domestic producers and consumers then depends on the pattern of specialization in production of the differentiated good. In the split case, the higher price of imported varieties causes no substitution towards domestically produced varieties (because they are at the other end of the product spectrum).[12] Consequently, the demand curve for the home variety does not move from its initial position D_0, and equilibrium remains at E_0. Domestic consumers who buy imported varieties are worse off because of the higher domestic price of those varieties, but there are no other effects.

On the other hand if home and imported varieties are interleaved, a tariff induces substitution away from imported varieties to the adjacent domestic ones. In this case the demand curve for a home variety shifts upwards to, say, D_1 in Figure 7.4 and also becomes less elastic because of the increased monopoly power (greater market width) bestowed on domestic producers. The resulting positive profits for domestic firms induce new firms to enter, reducing the distance d between varieties, shifting the demand curve for a typical domestic variety down and making it more elastic (because closer substitutes are now available). Whether the new long-run equilibrium lies to the right or the left of E_0 depends on whether the initial fall in the elasticity of demand (due to the increase in the price p' of imported varieties) is more than offset by the subsequent increase in that elasticity when new firms enter. It is quite conceivable that the latter effect may dominate, leading to the outcome illustrated in Figure 7.4. Under the tariff, long-run output of a typical domestic variety increases to Q_2, while its price falls to p_2 – that is, a higher output and a lower price than under free trade. Note that in this case the price of domestic varieties falls even though imported varieties are more expensive because of the tariff.[13]

This opens up the interesting possibility that there may be sufficient gains from a tariff (in the form of tariff revenue and lower prices of domestic varieties) to more than compensate those consumers who are hurt by higher prices of imported varieties. If such a Pareto improvement were to occur, it would be because the tariff, in encouraging new entrants and a greater range of products, reduces the monopoly power of existing producers. However, it must be stressed that this is only a possibility, and perhaps a quite remote one; it depends very much on the parameters of the model. Moreover, there are many other factors which would stand in the way of such a welfare improvement. For example, foreign firms may withdraw from the domestic market when their market-width shrinks (the model actually requires new foreign firms to enter so as to preserve the interleaving), in which case product variety may actually fall, with the demand for the remaining products being less elastic and equilibrium price higher than under free trade. These are similar to the issues which were raised in our earlier discussion of the Harris welfare estimations. It is also important to note that the model ignores the costs to the domestic economy of introducing new varieties. If these costs are included, it is possible that they may outweigh any welfare gains, in which case free trade would be superior, even if a tariff does lead to greater product variety.

This analysis applies to the case of unilateral imposition of a tariff by a small country. We now consider briefly how the results would be affected if the world consisted of two large countries, each exporting varieties of the differentiated good to the other and each imposing tariffs of equal height on imported varieties. The new element is that tariffs imposed by one country reduce the profits of the other country in its export market. Suppose that domestic and foreign markets for any given variety are segmented (i.e. there is not a single integrated world market for any variety). Then, in the split case, imposition of a tariff by the foreign country causes losses by domestic firms (who were originally just breaking even and whose position in the domestic market was unaffected by the tariff). Some firms will leave the industry, leading to a reduced number of varieties, greater market width and increased monopoly power for the producers of the remaining varieties. This implies a higher price for domestic varieties than under free trade so that consumers, who must also pay more for imported varieties, are unambiguously worse off. In the interleaved case, the loss of profits in the export market at least partly offsets the gain in the domestic market. Profits may be negative, in which case product variety falls and the price of domestic varieties increases. If the gain in the home market is the dominant effect, there will still be entry of new domestic firms and the outcome resembles the case of a unilateral tariff considered earlier. However, the losses in the export market reduce the number of new varieties that can be produced at a profit, so that price does not fall as much (or rises more than) in the unilateral case. The interested reader can find a more detailed discussion of this bilateral tariff case in Lancaster (1984).

It should be clear from the analysis of this and the preceding section that both the Lancaster and SDS–Krugman models are in substantial agreement that trade of an intra-industry kind can arise between identical economies (i.e. there exists trade which is not explained by differences in country size, comparative advantage or factor endowments) and that any welfare gains from such trade arise because consumers have access to a greater variety of goods, possibly at a lower price. However, the two models differ considerably in their treatment of non-prohibitive tariffs: in the Lancaster model, we saw that both domestic output and product variety are usually changed by such a tariff whereas in the SDS–Krugman model, they are not. The choice between the two types of model depends very much on the type of problem to be analysed and on how much complexity the researcher is prepared to deal with.

7.4 The composition of trade

In the previous sections we considered trade between two economies producing only the differentiated product. The value of this approach was that it provided a simple means of considering intra-industry trade and the effects of restrictions on such trade. However, in the real world, intra-industry trade coexists with inter-industry trade, and to accommodate both it is necessary to have another sector in the model (which may be either another differentiated product or a perfectly competitive industry producing a homogeneous good). A number of authors have now attempted this exercise using both the Lancaster and SDS–Krugman approaches.[14] A particular concern of much of this literature has been to see whether the standard Heckscher–Ohlin propositions for a world in which two countries produce two homogeneous goods under competitive conditions carry over to the case in which one of the goods is a differentiated product exhibiting economies of scale and an imperfectly competitive market structure. As it turns out, monopolistic competition fits remarkably well into the Heckscher–Ohlin world, with factor price equalization, the Rybczynski theorem and other results being largely unaffected. Moreover, the pattern of *net* trade is exactly what Heckscher–Ohlin would predict: the capital-abundant country is a net exporter of the capital intensive good and a net importer of the labour-intensive good. The important difference is that though a country may be a net exporter of manufactured goods (the differentiated products sector), it usually still imports some varieties. In other words, a particular inter-industry pattern of trade (e.g. net exports of manufactures in return for net imports of, say, food) may be consistent with various levels of intra-industry trade. One of the more worthwhile contributions of this branch of the literature has been to offer insights into how the composition of trade (as between inter- and intra-industry) is determined. The broad consensus is that intra-industry trade is likely to represent a larger share of total trade between countries with similar factor endowments. An interesting polar case is the situation of identical factor endowments: as the original Heckscher–Ohlin model predicts, no inter-industry trade will occur between such countries, and accordingly, all trade is intra-industry. On the other hand, as countries' capital–labour ratios move further apart, the proportion of trade which is inter-industry will grow. If the difference in factor endowments is large enough, each country will completely specialize in producing the product(s) of one industry, in which case there will be no intra-industry trade at all.

It follows that the gains from trade liberalization in such a model are of both an inter-industry and intra-industry kind. There is some reason to suppose that removal of trade restrictions are easier when trade is of the intra-industry kind. This is because producers in both countries can gain from access to a larger market; if such mutual gains are present, we can expect producers in both countries to support freer trade. On the other hand, when trade is inter-industry, reduction in trade barriers on a particular good harms producers in the country which has a comparative disadvantage in the production of that good. These producers will oppose any move towards freer trade. Thus, the political economy of the exercise favours trade liberalization between similar countries for which the trade is primarily intra-industry (see Krugman, 1982).

7.5   Falvey model of product differentiation

So far, we have taken it for granted that product differentiation necessarily involves economies of scale and imperfect competition. However, Falvey (1981) has developed a simple model in which product differentiation is based on factor content in a way that is consistent with constant returns to scale and perfect competition. Moreover, the pattern of intra-industry trade is driven by relative factor endowments.

Consider an industry which uses labour and sector-specific capital to produce a continuum of qualities of a vertically differentiated product. Units of factors are chosen so that each unit of the good requires one unit of labour, and a unit of quality α requires α units of capital – in other words, higher-quality products are more capital-intensive than lower-quality products. The model is partial equilibrium insofar as it suppresses the demand side of the economy (the implicit assumption being that higher-income individuals demand higher-quality versions of the good), and it assumes that the industry in question faces a perfectly elastic supply of labour at the going wage.[15] The good is produced in two countries using the same constant-returns-to-scale technology. Quality is assumed to be defined over a closed interval $[\bar{a}, \underline{a}]$. Within that interval, the cost of producing a unit of a product of quality α is

$$c(\alpha) = w + \alpha r$$

and

$$c^*(\alpha) = w^* + \alpha r^*$$

for the home and foreign countries, respectively, where w and w^* are, respectively, the home and the foreign wage and r and r^* the domestic and foreign returns to capital. Given the assumption of perfect competition, this unit cost equals the price of a unit of quality α. Now, suppose that $w > w^*$ and $r < r^*$. Then, in the case in which some qualities are produced in both countries (the only interesting case), the lowest-quality good $(\underline{a})$ is produced more cheaply in the foreign country because it embodies less capital than any other quality, and the highest-quality good $(\bar{a})$ is produced in the home country because it is the most capital-intensive.

In other words, the pattern of specialization in production is determined by relative factor prices with the home country having relatively cheaper industry-specific capital and producing the capital-intensive range of qualities. In particular, all qualities above a level α_1 are supplied by the home country and those below α_1 are supplied by the foreign country, where α_1 is the quality level at which unit costs are the same for both countries[16]; that is,

$$c(\alpha_1) = c^*(\alpha_1) \Rightarrow \alpha_1 = \frac{w - w^*}{r^* - r}.$$

The determination of α_1 is illustrated in Figure 7.5.

The returns to sector-specific capital in each country adjust to equate the demand for the respective factors to their (assumed fixed) supplies. Demand for sector-specific capital in one country is a decreasing function of its own return

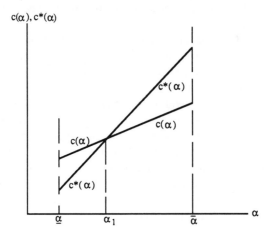

Figure 7.5

[e.g. higher r increases $c(\alpha)$, thus reducing demand for the home country's good at any quality level, and also reducing the range of qualities produced by the home country by increasing α_1], and an increasing function of the return to the other country's capital (e.g. higher r^* reduces α_1, thereby increasing the range of qualities supplied by the home country and increasing the derived demand for its capital). Figure 7.6 illustrates the determination of the equilibrium values of r and r^*.

EE represents the locus of equilibrium values of r and r^*, yielding equilibrium for the home country's sector-specific capital. E^*E^* is the corresponding equilibrium locus for the foreign country. Both are upward sloping because, starting from a position of equilibrium, an increase in the rate of return for a country's own capital reduces demand and thus opens up an excess supply of that capital. To restore equilibrium, the rate of return for the other country's capital must rise. E^*E^* is drawn flatter than EE, reflecting the assumption that the equilibrium at P is stable.[17] This completes the description of the free-trade equilibrium. Like the models of the previous sections, the equilibrium is characterized by two-way trade in differentiated products of the industry in question (i.e. intra-industry trade), however, the nature of the gains from trade is quite different. There is no gain via economies of scale from selling to a larger market (because production exhibits constant returns to scale). Nor is there necessarily any gain in terms of increased product variety. The benefits arise mainly for the usual reasons of comparative advantage; with free trade, consumers are able to buy the quality of good they desire from the cheaper source. In this sense, the Falvey model is a natural extension of the standard Heckscher–Ohlin framework to encompass product differentiation without abandoning such features as perfect competition and constant returns to scale.

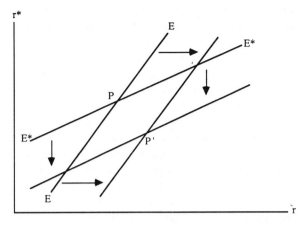

Figure 7.6

What is the effect of a tariff imposed by the home country on imports of those qualities produced by the foreign country? Other things being equal, the tariff reduces α_1, expanding the range of qualities which home producers can sell to the home market. This increases the domestic demand for the sector-specific capital, increasing its equilibrium return at any given r^* – that is, EE shifts to the right in Figure 7.6. The associated fall in the home country's demand for imports of varieties near α_1 reduces the foreign country's demand for its capital and thus shifts E^*E^* down. The equilibrium therefore moves from P to P', with the direction of change of r and r^* ambiguous – in the case illustrated, r rises and r^* falls. It can be shown that under reasonable assumptions r^* will fall,[18] so that the tariff forces down foreign costs and, hence, improves the home country's terms of trade. On the other hand, it seems likely that the tariff will create a range of untraded qualities in a neighbourhood of the original market division, α_1. The home country imports qualities below α_F and exports those above α_H, where α_F and α_H are the solutions of

$$c(\alpha_F) = (1 + t)c^*(\alpha_F) \qquad c(\alpha_H) = c^*(\alpha_H) .$$

that is,

$$\alpha_F = \frac{w - w^*(1 + t)}{r^*(1 + t) - r} \qquad \alpha_H = \frac{w - w^*}{r^* - r}$$

where t is the ad valorem tariff rate imposed by the home country. Certainly, if the direct effect of the tariff in reducing α_F dominates any potentially offsetting effects associated with a fall in r^* (and a rise in r), a lower value of α_F will result. On the other hand, a fall in $(r^* - r)$ will increase α_H. Thus under reasonable assumptions, a tariff imposed by the home country opens up an interval (α_F, α_H) of non-traded qualities while expanding the range of qualities produced domestically from $(\alpha_1, \bar{\alpha})$ to $(\alpha_F, \bar{\alpha})$. This captures an aspect of protection in product-differentiated industries which is absent from the Krugman model (in which a non-prohibitive tariff leaves the number of varieties produced and traded by both countries unchanged) and obscured in the Lancaster model (in Lancaster's interleaved case, the number of domestic varieties necessarily equals the number of imported varieties, with a tariff possibly changing the number of varieties but preserving this equality).

The Falvey model is therefore a useful tool for analysing the way in which countries can use protection to limit trade in some vertically differentiated product varieties and increase the range of varieties produced by domestic firms. Although the model is often criticized for leaving out many of the salient features of product-differentiated markets (in particular, imperfect competition and economies of scale), it captures one feature (the pattern of intra-industry trade) which most other models are unable to address.

7.6   Summary

In this chapter we have considered the likely effects of trade restriction in markets producing differentiated products. An important role of trade in the presence of product differentiation is the increased product variety it offers to consumers. This product variety may be valued for its own sake, as in the Spence–Dixit–Stiglitz (SDS) framework used by Krugman, or it may benefit consumers by making goods available which are closer to their preferred product specification as in the Lancaster model. In both the SDS and Lancaster models, trade opens up a larger market to firms in both countries, and this tends to encourage longer production runs and lower unit costs. In addition, competition from varieties produced in the other country drives some firms (and varieties) out of the market. Thus, the most likely outcome under free trade is a greater product variety than under autarky, with fewer varieties produced in larger quantities in each country. The main exception to this result is the constant-elasticity version of the Krugman model in which trade merely serves to expand the number of varieties in the market with no firm rationalization. Although there are more consumers in the wider world market, each consumes less of every variety than under autarky, leaving total demand for each variety unchanged. Unfortunately, this is the version of the model most easily adapted for empirical work.

What can we say about the effects of trade-restricting policies such as tariffs in this sort of framework? Although the changes which occur in the move from free trade to autarky should give us an indication of the likely effects of tariffs, it is not quite so simple. For example, in the constant-elasticity version of the Krugman model, non-prohibitive tariffs do not affect domestic producer prices, firm outputs or the number of varieties produced. They merely serve to shift consumption from imported varieties to domestic varieties with producers reallocating their fixed output between markets. Only the case of a prohibitive tariff is able to generate the sort of effects we might like. On the other hand, the Lancaster model offers a diverse array of possible outcomes, depending on the substitution relationships between domestic and foreign varieties. If domestic and imported varieties are very poor substitutes, domestic firms do not benefit greatly from a tariff, but they can lose if a foreign tariff reduces their foreign sales. The likely outcome is the exit of some firms and a reduced number of varieties, each sold at a higher price than before the tariff. Domestic consumers face higher import prices and reduced product variety and are unambiguously worse off. In the opposite polar case in which domestic and foreign varieties are close substitutes, a tariff shifts demand to domestic varieties, benefiting domestic firms. Whether domestic consumers are better off depends very much on the response of foreign firms. If the tariff drives enough of these firms out of the domestic market, product variety may be reduced, and the remaining firms (domestic and foreign) will use their increased monopoly power to raise price and restrict quantity sold. Consumers then lose via the higher price *and* the reduced product variety.

One important conclusion to emerge from all of the product differentiation models is that international trade can occur between economies with identical factor endowments and technologies. In a two-country model with economies of scale, it pays firms in both countries to sell their own product-differentiate to the larger world market. We thus observe countries simultaneously exporting some product-differentiates and importing others in the same industry – so-called intra-industry trade. Although the standard explanation for such trade involves imperfect competition and economies of scale, it can also be generated by a competitive constant-returns-to-scale model. If products are vertically differentiated with higher-quality products embodying a higher ratio of an industry-specific factor (capital) to the mobile factor (labour), then a capital-abundant country exports the higher-quality varieties while the labour-abundant country exports products at the lower end of the spectrum. Here, both the volume and the pattern of intra-industry trade is the outcome of differences in factor endowments between the countries. In such a model, the likely effect of a tariff is a reduction in the range of varieties traded.

PART III

The political economy of protection

CHAPTER 8

Endogenous protection

In the previous chapters of this book we have been largely content to treat protection policies as something which are exogenously determined. Admittedly, we have frequently considered how a government might choose a policy to achieve a given non-economic (or income-distributional) objective, and we have ranked policies on the basis of their efficiency in achieving such an objective. However, the manner in which the objective is determined has remained unclear. Indeed (terms-of-trade arguments aside), we have not even begun to explain why tariffs and other impediments to trade exist in the first place. For example, if free trade is the optimal situation for a small country, why do we not observe groups or individuals who stand to lose from a tariff using lump-sum transfers to bribe tariff proponents to support free trade? Relative to a tariff, no-one would be worse off, and many would be better off. In a system of majority voting with perfect information, costless lump-sum transfers and zero voting costs, the transfers could be adjusted so that those who are better off under free trade always constitute a majority – free trade would win every time. The reality is that redistributions are costly, and political markets are not perfect. There are clear gainers and losers associated with any form of protection, and it would be unusual in practice for the former to compensate the latter to any great degree. Indeed, the standard theories of the income-distributional effects of tariffs, the Stolper–Samuelson theorem and the specific factors model (see Chapter 1), implicitly assume that no such compensation occurs.

In a way, the modern so-called political economy of protection starts with the Stolper–Samuelson theorem and its clear result that one factor gains from protection at the expense of another. Similarly, in the specific-factors model, factors specific to the protected sector gain at the expense of factors specific to other sectors. What these income-distribution models do not tell us is how the conflict of interest inherent in any government policy decision is resolved and what policy is likely to be the outcome. To answer such questions, it is necessary to have a model of the political process itself.

In the late 1950s, a number of political scientists and economists began to develop models describing how government economic policies such as taxes and subsidies are determined so as to equilibrate "political markets" (see Becker, 1983; Buchanan and Tullock, 1962; Downs, 1957; Olson, 1965; Peltzman, 1976; Stigler, 1971). In such markets, votes take on the role assumed by

177

dollars in conventional economic markets. Policies can be supported or op-posed directly at the ballot box, or indirectly by public campaigns aimed at influencing votes or by donating campaign funds (which can be used to buy votes) to political parties. There are many aspects of the process which can be modelled: the voting process itself, the manner in which parties (in, say, a standard two-party system) compete for votes on an issue and the behaviour of pressure groups (and why they are formed). Obviously, any model which attempted to include all of these features would be too unwieldy to yield interesting results. Consequently, researchers have tended to concentrate on at most two groups of players at a time, and some have resorted to a convenient reduced-form version of the political process. The outcome is a reasonably unified (if incomplete) picture of the way in which protection levels are deter-mined by self-interested political forces.[1] Recent research has also begun to cast some light on the political choice among different forms of protection and goes some way towards explaining the shift away from tariffs towards quan-titative forms of trade restriction (such as import quotas, voluntary export restraints, content protection schemes). In the first three sections of this chapter we survey the main theories of tariff level determination, and in Section 8.4 we present some of the recent discussion on the choice of the form of protective instrument.

8.1   Direct majority voting

Suppose for the time being that there are no political parties and that the citizens of an economy vote directly on every issue, in particular on the level of a proposed tariff. Although this is clearly unrealistic, it does give an insight into the forces which are at work when voting is expressed indirectly through elected representatives. Mayer (1984) models tariff determination under majority vot-ing for both the Heckscher–Ohlin–Samuelson (HOS) model and the multisec-tor specific-factors model.

Mayer's results for the HOS model are, with a few modifications, a transla-tion of the Stolper-Samuelson conclusions to a majority voting framework. Consider a two-sector economy with capital and labour which are mobile between sectors. Suppose each individual in this economy owns one unit of labour and a non-negative amount of capital – individual i's capital–labour ratio then equals her stock of capital k^i. Each individual's income consists of income derived from her ownership of the two factors plus her share of total tariff revenues. So that the redistribution of the tariff revenue does not lead to undue complications, Mayer assumes that it is allocated in a "neutral" fashion with individual i's share of this revenue equal to her income share from factor ownership which is, in turn, equal to her overall share of total national income.

Now consider the effects of a tariff. Suppose, for purposes of illustration that the importable good is capital-intensive. Then we know that the real wage falls, and the real return to capital rises. Thus, individuals who own a higher ratio of capital to labour are more likely to gain. In fact, as Mayer shows, individuals gain from a tariff if their capital–labour ratio k^i exceeds the economy's capital–labour ratio k, and individuals with k^i less than k benefit from an import subsidy. Moreover, under standard assumptions, there is a tariff level (negative for a subsidy) which maximizes the utility of individual i and this tariff level can be shown to be an increasing function of k^i (i.e. individuals owning relatively more of the factor whose return has risen will favour higher protection). Under a system of direct majority voting, the tariff level adopted will be that which maximizes the utility of the median voter. All voters with capital–labour ratios higher (lower) than that of the median voter prefer higher (lower) tariff levels, and the economy opts for a positive tariff level if the median voter has a higher capital–labour ratio than the economy as a whole. Clearly, the outcome depends on (i) the factor endowments of the economy, (ii) the distribution of factor ownership among the voters and (iii) which good is capital-intensive.

As noted in Chapter 1, although the Stolper–Samuelson approach may be useful for comparing long-run equilibria, it is an inadequate tool for analysing attitudes of factor owners to protection in real economies in which support for protection is seen to be largely unanimous across different factors in the one industry. Moreover, as noted by Mayer, the HOS model fails to explain how an industry whose factor owners constitute a small number of voters can be successful in securing tariff protection. To cope with both of these problems he turns to a multi-sector version of the specific-factors model.

It is assumed that each potential voter owns one unit of labour (the mobile factor) and some of at most one industry-specific factor (some individuals may only own labour). Starting from a free-trade situation, it is proposed that a tariff be introduced for one sector – call it sector g. The question posed is: assuming costs of voting which are uniform across individuals, are there circumstances in which a majority will support the tariff? The answer depends on three things: (i) the magnitude of the stakes for the various voters relative to voting costs; (ii) the way in which the tariff changes the wage rate relative to average factor returns and (iii) the size of any fall in aggregate real income arising from the tariff (i.e. the deadweight loss of the tariff, which in the Mayer model is distributed among individuals in the same proportions as factor incomes). Mayer considers the case of a "small" tariff for which (iii) is effectively zero. To see the relevance of (ii), suppose that the tariff increases the wage relative to the average of all factor prices (the average being obtained by weighting each factor price change by the share of that factor in national income), a situation described as sector g being "biased towards labour". Then, it is more likely that a large number of voters who do not own sector g's specific factor will gain from the tariff (through their ownership of labour) and support it at the ballot box. On the other hand, if a tariff in sector g merely changes the wage in the same proportion as the average of all factor prices (sector g is "unbiased towards labour"), then owners of specific factors other than g lose, owners of g's sector-specific factor gain and those who own labour only are unaffected. Given that those tied to specific factors in other sectors normally outnumber those in sector g, we would expect a majority to vote against a tariff in g in this case.

However, for a small tariff, the gains to the protected specific factor in sector g are approximately equal to the total losses of the unprotected specific factors (the deadweight loss of the tariff is approximately zero so the only effects are distributional). It then follows that if there is more than one unprotected sector, the loss imposed on any one of the unprotected specific factors by a small tariff is less than the gain to the specific factor in sector g. It follows that the gains to an owner of a given share of sector g's specific factor are larger than the losses to an owner of the same share of a specific factor outside sector g when the number of sectors exceeds two (see Mayer, 1984, pp. 980 and 981 for a formal proof). Thus, the gains from voting against the tariff are smaller than the gains from supporting the tariff for individuals holding an identical share of their respective sectors. If individuals all face the same (positive) cost of participating in the voting process, those individuals for whom the stakes are small may choose not to vote because the net return from doing so is negative. This tends to remove the smaller owners of specific factors in the unprotected part of the economy from the voting process and makes it more likely that a majority of those remaining will vote for the tariff. In other words, voting costs, combined with the asymmetry between gains to a small sector and losses to factor owners in the rest of the economy, can conceivably lead to adoption of a tariff in a majority voting system.

Although this is an ingenious explanation of how a small minority of the population can be successful in gaining acceptance of a policy which favours them at the expense of the rest of the community, it applies to a political system which is seldom observed in the real world; direct majority voting is usually only observed in special situations such as votes to change constitutions. Furthermore, even if we view direct voting as a reasonable approximation of the common system of voting by elected representatives, it would be unusual for a single issue such as tariff protection to figure prominently in the outcome.

Having stated these reservations, it should be said that the basic point of Mayer's model is that "minority" sectoral interests prevail because the gains exceed the losses for similar individuals and a fixed cost of participating in the political process removes the smaller losers from the contest before it removes comparable members of the beneficiary group. Stated in this way, his conclusion remains plausible, particularly if the political process is conducted through pressure groups rather than directly by means of the ballot box. Bearing this in mind, we now turn to some other theories of tariff determination in which the main players are political parties and pressure groups.

8.2 Pressure groups

As we know, actual policies are rarely decided by direct majority voting. Instead, in most democracies, policy issues are resolved by the voting of elected representatives along party lines. Moreover, many policy matters are decided among a fairly small subset of these elected representatives – for example senior government ministers decide on an approach to a problem and convince the rest of their party to support them. In this environment, individual voters have insignificant power, and it may be in their interests to form a coalition with others who share their interest to exert pressure on the policy makers. Much has been written about the factors influencing the formation and functions of pressure groups (see, in particular, Olson, 1965; Pincus, 1975; Stigler, 1974), and it is beyond the scope of this book to go into the subject in great detail. We do, however, note the following aspects of the operation of pressure groups.

i. There is a region of increasing returns to pressure group activity. Usually this also implies increasing returns to group membership because the activity level of the group is higher the larger the number of contributing members. On the other hand, a small number of wealthy and vocal members can yield the same political effectiveness as a larger group of atomistic contributors. Certainly, a small group of ordinary individuals is unlikely to exert much political pressure.

ii. As the membership of a pressure group becomes larger, cost per contributor tends to increase because of the free-rider problem that accompanies size: because the benefit (e.g. a tariff) obtained by a pressure group is available to all beneficiaries whether they contribute or not, there is an incentive for some members to free-ride. This incentive is generally stronger in larger groups because the costs of enforcing contributions are larger and the marginal effect of the last member's contribution on the probability of the group's success and/or the value of the rent captured is likely to be smaller. Other organization costs that increase with size also tend to increase the cost per contributor as the pressure group takes in more members. These organization costs are further increased if the members of the group are spread over a large geographical area.

iii. When a group is large, it is likely that the benefits from a particular policy are spread more thinly across the members. If there is a fixed cost (which may merely be an information cost) for each member to participate in the group, the perceived benefit for some individuals may well fall short of this cost; in such a case, the individual will choose not to contribute to the group (the analogue of not voting in the Mayer model).

These observations help explain why consumer interests, for example, have been notably unsuccessful in forming a coalition to oppose tariffs and other distortions. The size of the group and its geographical dispersion tend to reduce the per capita benefits and increase the per capita costs associated with group membership, discouraging individuals from joining or forming such a group. The same reasons can be offered to explain why specific factors in non-protected sectors have had limited success in preventing the introduction of tariffs in other sectors. On the other hand, producer groups seeking protection typically involve a smaller number of (relatively homogeneous) agents with benefits shared less widely at a lower cost per producer, favouring the formation of coalitions of producers within an industry. In other words, it is apparently the asymmetry between the two groups of interests (e.g. consumers and producers) which leads to the adoption of a socially suboptimal policy such as a tariff.

Assuming that both the pro-tariff and anti-tariff interests are represented by pressure groups, the next question to be asked is how these two groups interact to determine an equilibrium tariff level. There are various possible identities for the main gainers and losers from a tariff, and the choice of two particular groups as opponents is a little arbitrary. Findlay and Wellisz (1982) consider a contest between the specific factor in the protected sector and the specific factor in the other sector of the (two-sector) economy. Here, for purposes of illustration, we adhere to the traditional textbook dichotomy between "producers" (i.e. factors which are specific to the industry seeking protection) and "consumers", though the analysis is unaffected if the lobbies are defined in terms of factor ownership as in the Findlay and Wellisz model.[2] The following model is set out in full in Appendix 4 together with proofs of the main results of this section.

Producers are assumed to expend resources lobbying for an increase in the tariff on their good whereas consumers exert pressure to have the tariff level reduced. We write the tariff of T dollars per unit as an increasing function of producer pressure (x_F) and a decreasing function of consumer pressure (x_C):

$$T = T(x_F, x_C), \qquad T_F \equiv \frac{\partial T}{\partial x_F} > 0; \qquad T_C \equiv \frac{\partial T}{\partial x_C} < 0;$$

$$T_{FF} \equiv \frac{\partial^2 T}{\partial x_F^2} < 0; \qquad T_{CC} \equiv \frac{\partial^2 T}{\partial x_C^2} > 0. \tag{1}$$

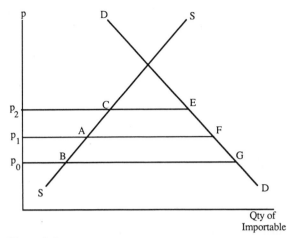

Figure 8.1

The signs on the partial derivatives T_{FF} and T_{CC} indicate that pressure by each group is subject to diminishing marginal effectiveness. At this stage we have assumed nothing about the cross-partial derivatives $T_{FC} = T_{CF}$ ($\partial^2 T / \partial x_C \, \partial x_F$). These capture the effect of increased effort by one group on the marginal effectiveness of the other group. Thus, when $T_{CF} = T_{FC} < 0$, higher producer pressure increases the marginal effectiveness of consumer pressure whereas higher consumer pressure reduces the marginal effectiveness of producer pressure, a situation we might describe as *consumer-biased political influence*. Similarly, when $T_{CF} = T_{FC} > 0$, higher producer pressure reduces the marginal effectiveness of consumer pressure whereas increased consumer pressure raises the marginal effectiveness of producer pressure (*producer-biased political influence*). Because there is no good reason for supposing either of these cases to be more likely than the other,[3] we shall, for purposes of illustration, confine our attention to the case in which the cross-effects are zero ($T_{CF} = T_{FC} = 0$) – that is, neither group can use additional effort to affect the marginal effectiveness of its opponents.

Now, suppose consumers choose their pressure level x_C to maximize consumer surplus minus the cost (or disutility) of applying pressure, taking the pressure of producers (x_F) as given. Similarly, let producers choose x_F to maximize their rents minus the cost of lobbying, taking x_C as given. Further, assume that the marginal cost of lobbying is positive and increasing in the level of pressure for each group. As seen in Figure 8.1, producer rents (R) are an increasing, convex function of producer price. For example, the increase in rents when price rises from p_0 to p_1 is the area $p_1 A B p_0$, which is less than the increase in rents (area $p_2 C A p_1$) resulting from an equal rise in price from p_1 to

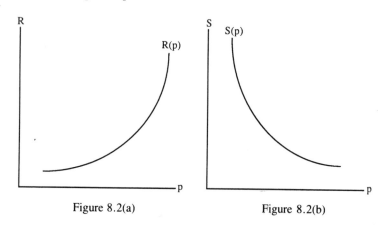

Figure 8.2(a)   Figure 8.2(b)

p_2. In particular, this implies that the marginal gain to producers from a given tariff increase is larger at higher prices ($R''(p) > 0$). Similarly, when price rises from p_0 to p_1, consumer surplus falls by $p_1 F G p_0$ whereas a further equal price rise from p_1 to p_2 reduces consumer surplus by the smaller area $p_2 E F p_1$. Thus consumer surplus (S) is a decreasing, convex function of price. The marginal gain to consumers from a given tariff reduction is larger at lower prices ($S''(p) > 0$). R and S are illustrated as functions of price in Figures 8.2a and 8.2b, respectively.

Let us now derive the reaction curves of the two groups. First, consider the reaction of consumers to an increase in x_F. Higher x_F increases domestic price by means of a higher tariff and so reduces the marginal gain to consumers from tariff reduction [a move down along $S(p)$ in Figure 8.2b] inducing them to reduce their pressure x_C. Thus, the reaction curve for consumers $x_C^*(x_F)$ is downward sloping. Now, consider the reaction of the producer group to an increase in x_C. Higher x_C means a lower domestic price and, hence, a lower marginal increment in rents from a given tariff increase [a move down the $R(p)$ function in Figure 8.2a]. Producers respond to this fall in the marginal return to producer pressure by reducing x_F, so the producer group's reaction curve $x_F^*(x_C)$ is also downward sloping. The two curves are illustrated in Figure 8.3 with stability considerations dictating that $x_C^*(x_F)$ be steeper than $x_F^*(x_C)$. The Nash equilibrium is at E_0, implying equilibrium pressure levels of x_{C0} and x_{F0} which can be substituted into Equation (1) to give the equilibrium tariff level.

Figure 8.3 can be used to analyse the effects of changes in various parameters on the equilibrium tariff level. Suppose for example that the industry in question experiences a sudden unanticipated fall in the world price of its good (due perhaps to aggressive export expansion by another country). This means that at any given level of x_F, consumers now face a lower price than before, implying an increased marginal return to them [a move down $S(p)$ in Figure 8.2b] from

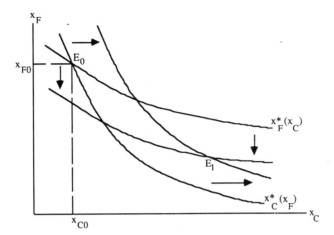

Figure 8.3

resisting protectionist pressures. Accordingly, at any x_F, consumer pressure is increased: the consumer reaction curve $x_C^*(x_F)$ shifts to the right in Figure 8.3. On the other hand, for producers facing a reduced price, the marginal return to lobbying is smaller than before the price fall [a move down the $R(p)$ curve], and they will be induced to exert less pressure, implying a downward shift in $x_F^*(x_C)$. The new Nash equilibrium is E_1.

Note that there is a clear antiprotectionist bias to these results, with protectionist pressure falling relative to antiprotectionist pressure (i.e. the ratio x_F/x_C decreases). If the tariff simply depends on relative pressures (i.e. the function T is homogeneous of degree zero), this would imply a fall in the tariff level.[4] This result runs counter to the popular view (and empirical fact) that protectionist pressures are usually relatively stronger when industries are experiencing falling world prices for their commodities. Note, however, that we have used consumer surplus analysis to obtain our results [with the implied forms for $R(p)$ and $S(p)$ illustrated in Figure 8.2]. As we noted in Chapter 3, use of consumer surplus to analyse the effects of a change in a single commodity price is only valid if the consumers' coefficient of relative risk aversion equals the income elasticity of demand for the good in question (see Turnovsky, Shalit and Schmitz, 1980). In the present case there is no uncertainty, so it is probably less confusing to the reader if we restate this condition as one of equality between the income elasticity of demand and the income elasticity of marginal utility (which is formally the same as the coefficient of relative risk aversion). The basic point remains the same: use of consumer surplus implicitly places restrictions on the curvature of the utility function.

Similarly, our assumption that producers simply maximize producer rents

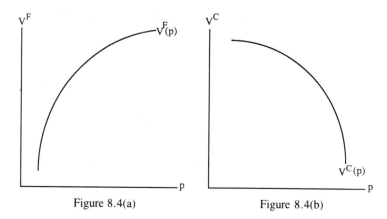

Figure 8.4(a)   Figure 8.4(b)

assumes that producers' marginal utility of income is constant (i.e. they are risk-neutral). If, instead, the marginal utility of income of producers were to fall as income increased, then, though lower price reduces the marginal rent losses from further price falls, it also increases the marginal disutility of a unit of foregone rents (because of the lower level of producers' real incomes). If the latter effect is sufficiently strong, the marginal disutility of a price fall would become larger as price falls and producer utility would be a concave function of price [$V^F(p)$ as illustrated in Figure 8.4b]. The same argument can be applied to consumer utilities: if the marginal utility of income is sufficiently strongly diminishing in income, then consumers' marginal utility of a fall in price decreases as price falls, making consumer utility a concave function of price [$V^C(p)$ in Figure 8.4b].

It should be apparent from the foregoing discussion that the results of the model will depend on the curvature of the respective group utility functions. This should not be surprising because individuals' exertion of effort for or against a particular policy is clearly greater the larger their marginal gain from such effort, and the curvature of the utility function tells us precisely how that marginal gain is related to the parameters of the economy (e.g. the prevailing world price of the good). To see how the outcome is affected, let us now repeat our analysis of the effects of a fall in world price, assuming that each group chooses its pressure level to maximize its utility net of the cost of applying pressure and that producers' and consumers' marginal utilities of income are sufficiently diminishing functions of income (i.e. both groups are sufficiently risk-averse) to make their respective utilities [$V^F(p)$, $V^C(p)$] concave functions of price as illustrated in Figure 8.4. This means that the marginal return to producers from a given increment in the tariff is lower at higher prices, and the marginal gain to consumers from a given tariff reduction is smaller at lower prices.

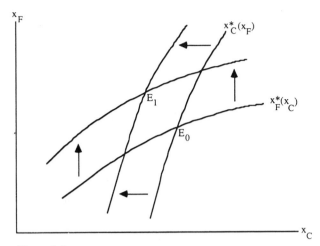

Figure 8.5

The derivation of the reaction curves proceeds along the same lines as before. Now, when consumers are confronted with higher x_F and an associated higher domestic price, the marginal benefit of tariff reduction is increased [concave $V^C(p)$], and they will increase their pressure. When producers are confronted with higher x_C, the associated lower domestic price implies an increased marginal benefit from protection (see Figure 8.4a), and they also will respond by exerting more pressure. Thus, both reaction curves are positively sloped, with stability requiring that $x_C^*(x_F)$ be steeper than $x_F^*(x_C)$. Initial equilibrium is at E_0 in Figure 8.5. A sudden fall in world price increases the marginal benefit of protection to producers [since $V^F(p)$ is concave] causing them to increase x_F, thus shifting $x_F^*(x_C)$ up. Similarly, at the lower price, the marginal gain to consumers from tariff reduction is reduced and consumers exert less pressure against the tariff – $x_C^*(x_F)$ shifts to the left. Equilibrium moves from E_0 to E_1 with relative protectionist pressure (x_F/x_C) increasing. Thus, provided consumers and producers have a strongly diminishing marginal utility of income, the tendency is for relative protectionist pressure to increase when world price falls and (symmetrically) for relative anti-protectionist pressure to increase when world price rises. In other words, if consumers and producers are sufficiently risk-averse, the protectionist lobby is more aggressive and its opponents more compliant when world price is falling than when it is rising. Many reasons have been offered for this frequently observed asymmetry of protectionist responses. For example, Cheh (1974) suggests that governments respond in a way which minimizes short-run labour adjustment costs. To the extent that these costs are higher for industries whose product price is falling, we might expect such industries to be more favoured by protectionist decisions. Another popular explanation appeals to Corden's *conservative social welfare function*, which embodies the objective that "any significant absolute reductions in real incomes of any significant section of the community should be avoided" (Corden, 1974, p. 107).[5] A discussion of these and other reasons for the relative strength of protectionism in bad times can be found in Baldwin (1984). One shortcoming of many of these explanations is that they attribute government policy responses to particular government objectives without explaining how the objectives are formed. The model of this section generates the commonly observed asymmetric response as the outcome of competition between risk-averse pressure groups.

It is also possible to use the pressure groups model to establish a result due to Hillman (1982): *a declining industry will continue to decline*. Hillman uses a Stigler–Peltzman political support model in which he assumes political support and blame is aimed at the component of price for which the government is directly responsible, in this case the tariff. This same approach is implicit in the tariff function of Equation (1), with lobbies expending resources to affect the tariff level (rather than the price level). Suppose an industry is faced with a fall in the world price of its good. The preceding analysis showed us that the equilibrium tariff level could rise or fall depending on the degree of risk aversion of the lobbyists. However, it is possible to show that the domestic price of the good must fall. Although a formal proof of this result is presented in Appendix 4, non-mathematical readers should find the following intuitive explanation adequate. Consider the position of the lobbies if the tariff were to rise so as to leave the domestic price unchanged when the world price falls. At an unchanged domestic price, the utilities (and the marginal utilities with respect to price) of both groups (not counting lobbying costs) are also unchanged. However, to achieve the higher tariff level needed for this outcome, the relative lobbying effort of the producer group would have to rise, thus increasing marginal lobbying costs of producers relative to consumers. The resulting relative increase in the marginal return to consumer pressure would induce a shift in relative lobbying effort towards the consumer group and a reduced domestic price. Thus, despite the presence of a protectionist lobby, domestic price falls when world price falls, and the declining industry continues to decline (even though the tariff on the good may increase). To the extent that protectionist lobbies attempt to resist the changes wrought by shifting comparative advantage, this is an encouraging result because it suggests that structural change will proceed in the right direction (albeit at a reduced pace) primarily because of diminishing marginal returns to political pressure.

Further encouragement along these lines is offered by Cassing and Hillman (1986) who model the dynamics of industry decline, allowing the industry's size to feed back into its political support and, hence, its level of protection. Anderson (1980), among others, has identified industry size as a significant explanatory variable for the level of protection afforded to an industry. Accordingly, Cassing and Hillman assume that the tariff level is an increasing function of the (intersectorally mobile) labour employed in the industry. In particular there is a range of values of labour input over which the tariff is assumed to decline at an increasing rate as the number of jobs in the industry falls. Thus, as the industry's sector-specific capital gradually decays or moves elsewhere and the number of jobs in the industry declines, the tariff also gradually falls, inducing further contraction. Cassing and Hillman then demonstrate the possibility of a sudden large contraction in the industry's labour force as its political support is eroded at an increasing rate with an associated rapid fall in protection. While the Cassing and Hillman model admits other possibilities, this particular outcome does reflect the pattern of decline of a number of industries.[6]

In the model of this section, the pressure groups are implicitly dealing directly with the policy makers, and it is a straightforward matter (at least in theory) to define the tariff level as a function of the pressures exerted by the two lobbies. In most democracies, lobbies are operating in a context in which more than one political party has a positive probability of being elected. The party which is elected is not necessarily favourably disposed towards a particular lobby's position, nor does the opposing party's policy necessarily coincide with that of the lobby (e.g. a free-trade lobby may be faced with a protectionist party and a "low tariff" party, but no free-trade party). To couch the analysis of pressure groups in a context of competing parties is an extremely difficult task, given that the minimum number of players is four (with all that implies for possible strategic interactions). Nevertheless, some progress has been made, and some surprising results have been obtained. The next section examines some of these results.

8.3   Lobbies and political parties

Brock and Magee (1978) develop a model in which two political parties are seen as forming tariff "quotations". Each party chooses its tariff quote to maximize its probability of election, taking the other party's tariff quote as given. The outcome is a Nash equilibrium in tariff quotes and election probabilities for each party, from which an equilibrium expected tariff can be calculated. The parties are competing in an environment with two opposing pressure groups, one pro-tariff and the other anti-tariff. Each lobby supports its position by contributing campaign funds to the party whose tariff position is more favourable to it. In the Brock and Magee framework, it does not pay either lobby to contribute to more than one party.[7] A party can increase its probability of winning by (1) attracting more campaign funds from the lobby which supports it (thus enabling it to buy more votes), (2) reducing the funds going to the other party and (3) winning more votes directly by having a low tariff quote (the general voter effect). (1) tends to drive the tariff quotes of the two parties further apart as the "high-tariff party" raises its tariff quote to attract more funds from the protectionist lobby and the "low-tariff party" reduces its tariff quote to attract more funds from the free-trade lobby. (2), on the other hand, tends to drive the two parties' tariff quotes closer together, with, for example, the low-tariff party increasing its tariff quote to stem the flow of protectionist money to the high-tariff party. This effect offers one explanation why "anti-protectionist" parties may support a positive level of protection. Effect (3) works to reduce the tariff quotes of both parties. The whole process can be simplified by writing the probability of winning for either party in a reduced form as a function of the tariff quotes of the two parties. Letting H denote the high-tariff party, L the low-tariff party and T_H and T_L the tariff quotes of the respective parties, party H chooses T_H to maximize its probability of election,

$$P^H \equiv P^H (T_H, T_L)$$

taking T_L as given. Similarly, party L chooses T_L to minimize P^H, taking T_H as given. Because of all the offsetting effects [(1)–(3)] involved in the relationship between P^H and the tariff quotes, the direction of dependence of P^H on T_H and T_L is ambiguous. It is nevertheless possible to gain some insight into the determination of the equilibrium tariff. We begin by assuming that each party faces diminishing marginal returns from raising its tariff quote for any given level of the other party's tariff quote (i.e. $P^H_{HH} \equiv \partial^2 P^H / \partial T_H{}^2 < 0; P^H_{LL} \equiv \partial^2 P^H / \partial T_L{}^2 > 0$). On the other hand, there does not appear to be any good reason for attaching a particular sign to the cross effects ($P^H_{LH} = P^H_{HL} \equiv \partial^2 P^H / \partial T_H \partial T_L$) of a change in one party's tariff quote on the marginal return to the other party from changing its tariff quote. However, let us suppose, for purposes of illustration, that the cross-derivative P^H_{HL} is positive. This means that an increase in L's tariff quote will (by sufficiently alienating the free-trade lobby and voters) increase the marginal benefit (or reduce the marginal cost) to H of increasing its tariff quote, and thus induce H to choose a higher tariff quote [i.e. H's reaction curve $T_H^*(T_L)$ is upward sloping]. At the same time, a higher tariff quote by H will reduce the marginal benefit (or increase the marginal cost) to L of increasing its tariff quote and thus lead L to choose a lower tariff quote [i.e. L's reaction curve $T_L^*(T_H)$ is downward sloping]. Figure 8.6 illustrates the reaction curves for this case. The Nash equilibrium tariff quotes are given by the intersection of the two reaction curves at E_1. The opposite case, in which $P^H_{HL} < 0$, is symmetrically analysed and is left as an exercise for the reader.

Now suppose that, for some reason (e.g. a new leader or a reduction in organization costs) the protectionist lobby becomes more aggressive and that this increases the tariff quote chosen by each party for a given quote by its opponent (e.g. party L raises its tariff quote to reduce the flow of campaign funds from the protectionist lobby to party H). $T_H^*(T_L)$ moves up, and $T_L^*(T_H)$

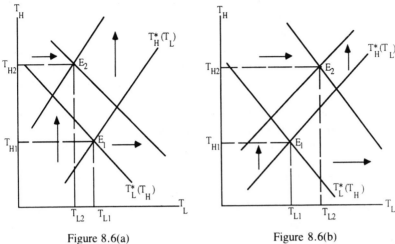

Figure 8.6(a)   Figure 8.6(b)

moves to the right as shown in Figure 8.6. The new equilibrium is at E_2 and, as drawn in Figure 8.6a, admits the interesting possibility that the tariff quotes of the two parties may move further apart, with the free-trade party reducing its quote from T_{L1} to T_{L2} (i.e. becoming more anti-protectionist) and the protectionist party increasing its quote from T_{H1} to T_{H2} (i.e. becoming more protectionist). It is indeed possible that T_L may fall sufficiently to cause the expected tariff level to fall.[8] In other words, a more aggressive stance by the protectionist lobby "polarizes" the party positions, allowing the possibility that the lobby might be worse off as a result.[9,10] Of course, it is also possible that the increased pressure by the protectionist lobby will cause both parties to become more protectionist (Figure 8.6b).

Young and Magee (1986) are able to take the analysis of pressure groups and political parties somewhat further by assuming particular functional forms. In the context of a two-sector HOS model in which the competing lobbies are the two factors, labour and capital, and the parties are respectively pro-labour and pro-capital, they are able to show how some well-known results of trade theory are affected when tariffs are determined endogenously. Because the menu of possible strategic interactions between the players is somewhat large, they make the appealing assumptions that (i) each party is a Stackelberg leader with respect to its own lobby and takes the behaviour of the other party and lobby as given and (ii) each lobby takes the behaviour of the other three players as given. Such an approach appears to sit comfortably with the political arrangements in many countries in which, say, a pro-labour party is very familiar with the responses of organized labour (not least because many party members may be ex-union officials) and thus knows their reaction curve, but is less familiar with the responses of the other party or lobby. Assuming that the importable is capital-intensive and that each lobby uses some of its own factor to exert pressure [with capital (labour) lobbying for a higher (lower) relative price of the importable], each lobby chooses its allocation to lobbying effort to maximize its expected utility, and each party chooses its quoted relative commodity price to maximize its probability of election subject to the particular strategic assumptions (i) and (ii).

The authors then consider the effects of changes in factor endowments. For example, suppose there is an increase in the economy's endowment of capital. Because there are now more units of the factor which stands to gain from, say, tariffs, more pressure is exerted by that lobby. After all the general equilibrium effects have worked through, the final outcome is, as one might expect, a higher tariff on the importable (assuming a tariff is the protective instrument chosen). This leads to an even greater increase in the output of the capital-intensive good than would be predicted by the Rybczynski theorem. Furthermore, this magnified expansion of the capital-intensive sector is accompanied by an increase in the expected return to capital (and a fall in the expected return to labour), a result which runs counter to both the factor price equalization theorem, and the normal response of factor prices to factor supplies in a closed economy. As well as being an interesting result in its own right, it also suggests an interesting dynamic process in an economy in which capital is internationally mobile. If, for some reason, a country's capital stock falls, the associated fall in lobbying pressure by capital implies a fall in capital's expected return which, in turn, implies an outflow of capital from the country. This leads to a repetition of the process and causes the country in question to become increasingly capital-scarce. Young and Magee also demonstrate the possibility that in a lobbying equilibrium, both lobbies could end up worse off than under free trade if they are relatively evenly matched: in such cases, it can be shown that the value of resources wasted in the lobbying process exceeds the expected return for the group.

The models surveyed in the foregoing sections are concerned primarily with the question of how the level of protection is determined by the political process. A related and equally important question that economists are beginning to ask is: what determines the choice between forms of protection? In particular, how do we explain the shift away from price-based instruments such as tariffs to quantitative policies such as quotas and voluntary export restrictions? The next section considers the progress that has been made in answering these questions.

8.4   The choice of protective instrument

In the last two decades, the world economy has witnessed a pronounced shift away from tariffs towards direct quantitative restrictions on trade. It is tempting to explain this shift simply by appealing to constraints imposed on trade by GATT and the success of earlier rounds of trade negotiations (particularly the Kennedy round) in achieving widespread tariff reductions. Certainly, much of the increase in both the relative and absolute importance of quantitative trade barriers can be explained by the history of trade negotiations, in particular the relative ease of defining formulae for tariff (as opposed to non-tariff) reductions. All of this has meant that, to a large extent, other policies have simply been substituted for tariffs.[11] Nevertheless, one is left with a feeling that not all has been explained. To say that quantitative trade barriers have been chosen because negotiations have favoured them is rather like ascribing a particular type of arms control to the treaty that produced it. The real question remains unanswered: insofar as any negotiation produces an outcome which is mutually agreeable to the participants, what determines the policy ranking of the participants? That institutional constraints do not fully explain actual policy choice has been further emphasized by Deardorff (1987), who cites numerous instances in which countries have chosen nontariff forms of protection in situations in which they were not prevented from using tariffs.[12] There is, therefore, some point in turning to the theory in an attempt to explain why certain policies, in particular import quotas, have been favoured by governments.

In previous chapters, we have examined many reasons why tariffs and quotas are not equivalent. We have seen that these two policies differ in their effects (1) in the presence of uncertainty (Chapter 3); (2) in a large-country context, in the presence of retaliation (Chapter 4) and (3) when the protected industry is a monopoly (Chapter 5). It is in situations such as these that political forces will favour selection of one policy in preference to another. We now consider two examples of this political choice process. Both employ the Stigler–Peltzman[13] "reduced form" version of the political support process, which simplifies analysis by avoiding explicit modelling of voters, pressure groups and parties.

Cassing and Hillman (1985) consider the political choice between tariffs and quotas in the presence of domestic monopoly. The choice between the two instruments is made by a policy maker who maximizes political support by trading off the gains to the beneficiary of protection (the domestic producer) against the penalty inflicted on the losers from protection (purchasers of the good). Political support M is assumed to be an increasing function of the protection-induced increment in the monopolist's rents $\Delta \pi$ (relative to free trade) and a decreasing function of the increment in price Δp (relative to free trade). For the time being, assume the revenue derived by the government from either policy does not enter the policy maker's calculations. It is then possible to draw political support indifference curves in the $(\Delta p, \Delta \pi)$ plane as illustrated in Figure 8.7. They are upward sloping because higher producer rents increase political support unless they are offset by a higher price (which reduces support from consumers). Higher indifference curves are associated with higher levels of political support (larger producer rents for a given penalty to the consumer).

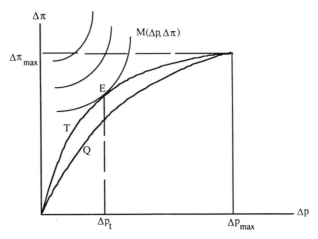

Figure 8.7

Now consider the two policies. With the aid of Figure 8.8 it is possible to graph the locus of combinations of $\Delta\pi$ and Δp embodied in each policy. Figure 8.8a shows the decision problem for a domestic monopolist facing either a tariff or a non-zero quota, and Figure 8.8b shows the monopolist's problem under a zero quota or its equivalent, a prohibitive tariff. As in Chapter 5, D represents the domestic demand curve for importables, MR is its marginal revenue curve and MC is the industry's marginal cost curve while D' is the demand curve net of a quota and MR' is its marginal revenue curve. Returning to Figure 8.7, we note that the origin corresponds to free trade. From there, as domestic price is increased under either policy, producer rents also increase up to a maximum $\Delta\pi_{max}$ which occurs for the case of a zero quota or the maximum usable tariff, either of which can be seen from Figure 8.8b to yield excess producer rents (relative to free trade) of $\Delta\pi_{max} = p_{max}HIJp^*$ at a domestic price of p_{max}.

At any given domestic price between the free-trade price p^* and p_{max}, it is easy to see from Figure 8.8a that producer rents are higher under a tariff than a quota. At price p_Q, rents (relative to free trade) under the quota are p_QABCp^* whereas under the price-equivalent tariff they are given by the larger area p_QEBCp^*. Thus, between the prices p^* and p_{max}, the curve relating $\Delta\pi$ to Δp for a tariff (curve T in Figure 8.7) lies everywhere above the corresponding curve for a quota (curve Q in Figure 8.7), and the policy maker maximizes political support at point E in Figure 8.7 where a political support indifference curve is tangential to curve T (assuming the usual conditions for existence of a unique maximum). The policy chosen is a tariff, which the policy maker prefers to a quota because, for any given penalty to the consumer, the tariff yields higher producer rents and, hence, higher political support. Note that political equilibrium at point E also determines the level of the tariff which is equal to Δp_t.

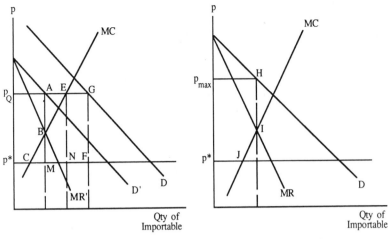

Figure 8.8(a)   Figure 8.8(b)

This result is both simple and persuasive. Unfortunately, it does little to explain the prevalence of quotas in the real world. Cassing and Hillman do show that if the revenue associated with the alternative policies is taken into account by the policy maker, the policy choice can be reversed in favour of a quota. The argument runs as follows. If import licences are auctioned off competitively so that the government captures the full quota rents, then at any price [e.g. p_Q in Figure 8.8a], the quota rents ($AGFM$) exceed the revenue from the price-equivalent tariff ($EGFN$). Because revenue can be used to purchase political support, this advantage of a quota may be sufficient to make it the support-maximizing instrument. The fact remains, however, that quotas are more often given to importers free of charge (or for some nominal fee) than auctioned, and tariff revenue usually exceeds government receipts from quota licence sales. If we are to explain the popularity of quantitative restrictions, it seems we must look beyond the Cassing and Hillman model.

Falvey and Lloyd (1985) consider the choice of policy instrument for maximizing political support in the presence of uncertainty. Although their paper is quite general and is concerned with the derivation of an "optimal" policy (which does not usually correspond exactly to any actual policy), it is illuminating to use their framework to examine a small country's choice between a tariff and a quota in the presence of a fluctuating world price. Not surprisingly, the analysis follows lines similar to the comparison of tariffs and quotas under uncertainty in Chapter 3.

Let us initially use consumer surplus analysis to study the problem. Figure 8.9a illustrates the domestic demand and supply curves for an importable good. Suppose the world price of the commodity in question can take on values $p^* + \varepsilon$ and $p^* - \varepsilon$, each with probability $\frac{1}{2}$.

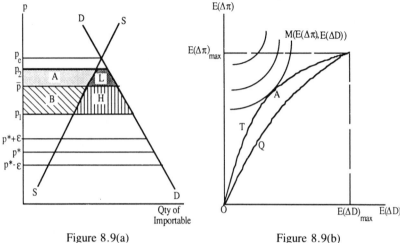

Figure 8.9(a)   Figure 8.9(b)

Consider a tariff policy which yields a domestic price p_1 when the world price is low and p_2 when the world price is high (it is not necessary to be precise about the type of tariff involved; all that matters here is that it transmits foreign price fluctuations to the domestic economy in some way). We now compare this tariff with a quota which yields the same expected rents to the protected industry (we again ignore the distribution of the revenue from either policy).[14]

Let $\bar{p}$ be the (constant) domestic price under this quota, where $\bar{p}$ is such that areas A and B in Figure 8.9a are equal (so that the tariff and the quota each yield the same expected rents to the protected industry). Then it follows that $p_2 - \bar{p} < \bar{p} - p_1$ (since A is everywhere wider than B). Now consider the expected consumer surplus for the two policies. It is easy to see that expected consumer surplus under the quota falls short of expected surplus under the tariff by the area

$$\frac{1}{2}(B + H) - \frac{1}{2}(A + L) = \frac{1}{2}(H - L) > 0$$

since $A = B$ by construction and $H > L$ because H is both wider and higher than L ($p_2 - \bar{p} < \bar{p} - p_1$).

Thus, when the two policies are implemented at levels where both yield the same expected return to producers, the tariff offers a higher expected surplus to consumers. This information is illustrated in Figure 8.9b.

In Figure 8.9b, $E(\Delta\pi)$ denotes the expected increment in producer rents over their level in the free-trade situation, and $E(\Delta D)$ denotes the expected loss of consumer surplus relative to free trade. Political support M is an increasing function of $E(\Delta\pi)$ and a decreasing function of $E(\Delta D)$. As in the previous model, the political indifference curves are upward sloping, and higher curves represent higher levels of political support. $E(\Delta\pi)_{max}$ is the highest level of expected rents which can occur under either policy; it is associated with either a zero quota or a tariff for which the world price + tariff is greater than or equal to the autarky price p_e for both levels of the world price (remember that no protection above p_e is used by a competitive industry). Between the origin and $E(\Delta\pi)_{max}$, $E(\Delta\pi)$ is an increasing function of $E(\Delta D)$ for both policies. Moreover, as we have already seen with the aid of Figure 8.9a, $E(\Delta D)$ is higher under a quota than under a tariff for given $E(\Delta\pi)$. Thus, the "constraint curve" for the quota (curve Q) lies below and to the right of the corresponding curve for the tariff policy (T) in Figure 8.9b. Clearly, in this case, equilibrium will be at a point such as A, with a tariff being the chosen policy.

Now, suppose that consumers, at least, are more risk-averse than is implicit in the use of consumer surplus analysis in this context. To keep things simple, suppose that producers are still risk-neutral. Then for a quota and a tariff to yield the same $E(\Delta\pi)$, we will still have $A = B$ in Figure 8.9a, but if consumers are sufficiently risk-averse, they will attach a higher value to the loss of real income when price rises [$(A + L)$ in the consumer surplus case] and a correspondingly lower value to the gain in real income when price falls [$(B + H)$ in the consumer surplus case]. This gives the result that $E(\Delta D)$ is higher under a tariff than under the $E(\Delta\pi)$-equivalent quota. Consequently, the T curve lies below the Q curve and the quota is the instrument chosen by the policy maker. This will be the outcome, for example, if the coefficient of relative risk aversion is of a size sufficient to make price stabilization socially desirable, and it is under conditions such as these that Falvey and Lloyd show a quota to be the optimal policy when the only disturbance is a fluctuating world price.

Thus, a sufficiently high degree of risk aversion can be advanced as one reason for the adoption of quotas.[15] This may, for example, explain the protectionist response of an economy which has experienced a fall in the world price of one of its traded goods but does not know how far price will fall. In this uncertain environment, it resorts to quantitative trade restrictions if its agents are sufficiently risk-averse.

Quantitative restrictions may also be chosen in declining industries if producers are better informed than consumers about likely future price movements. If producers are fairly certain that price will fall in the subsequent period, but consumers regard world price as random or constant, then producers will lobby strongly for a quota (which completely insulates them from the fall in price). In this situation, it is easy to see that a quota may be adopted even if consumers are not too risk-averse.

One particular type of quantitative restriction which is used by a number of countries (see Chapter 2) is *domestic content protection* (or local content schemes). Such schemes, which have been popular as a means of protecting automobile component sectors, offer a given level of rents to intermediate goods producers at a lower penalty to the user than tariffs or import quotas and may therefore be thought to be favoured by the political support process. On the other hand, they do not offer the government any revenue, and this may lessen their attractiveness.

In this section, we have considered why national governments might prefer to use quantitative trade restrictions rather than trade taxes. However, we have confined our attention to a one-country model in which a policy maker maximizes political support from his electorate. In the last section of Chapter 10 we shall return to this issue and consider how the choice of quotas might be dictated by the mutual political gains which emerge from trade negotiations between two countries.

8.5   Summary

The existence of sub-optimal policies such as tariffs and quotas can be explained by the existence of costs associated with redistributions (preventing the gainers from trade liberalization from fully compensating the losers) and imperfections in political markets. In this chapter, we have considered various models of the political process to explain how protection levels are determined by equilibrium in political markets and why particular policies are chosen in preference to others.

Even in a world where policies are chosen by means of direct majority voting, it is possible for a tariff benefiting only a small subset of the population to be supported by a majority of voters. This can occur if there are fixed costs associated with voting (or information-gathering costs) and the stakes are smaller for the losers than the winners (perhaps because the penalties imposed on the losers are spread more thinly). In such a situation, many of the voters adversely affected by the tariff may choose not to vote (or at least not to vote in an informed way) because the net return from doing so is negative.

Precisely because the net returns from individual action are frequently negative, there is an incentive for individuals to form coalitions or pressure groups to oppose or support particular policies. These groups will tend to be more successful in pushing their chosen position if (i) they are not too large (so that the benefits are not spread over too many members, and there is less incentive for individual members to free-ride), but large enough to be visible, (ii) their members have a well-defined commonality of interest and (iii) their per capita organizational and information-sharing costs are not too high. When a tariff is determined as the equilibrium in a contest between two such opposing groups (each expending resources to influence the government), it is possible to offer simple explanations of protectionist responses to various exogenous changes. For example, the observed tendency for protection to be increased more (reduced less) in periods or areas of economic downturn is readily generated by the pressure-group model if the opposing groups are sufficiently risk-averse. In addition, it is possible to show that industries which are declining because of a falling world price of their good will continue to decline because diminishing marginal returns to political pressure imply that protection will not increase sufficiently to maintain domestic price at a constant level.

It is also possible to allow for interaction between pressure groups and political parties in a two-party political system in which the campaign contributions, media campaigns, and other activities of the lobbies affect the respective parties' probabilities of being elected and, thus, influence their protectionist stands (or "tariff quotes"). An interesting implication to emerge from this type of model is that a more aggressive stand by a protectionist lobby could conceivably lead to a reduced expected level of protection as the two party positions on protection become more polarized.

The political markets approach to protection has also begun to consider what determines the choice of protective instrument; why, for example, are quantitative restrictions so widespread? We consider two such models. One examines the political choice between tariffs and quotas when the protected industry is a monopoly and finds that a tariff will be the chosen instrument if revenue considerations are ignored, but that a quota may be chosen if revenue is taken into account. The other model also looks at the choice between tariffs and quotas, but in the context of foreign price uncertainty. In this case, quotas will be the outcome of the political support process if and only if economic agents are sufficiently risk-averse.

PART IV

Reducing protection

CHAPTER 9

Approaches to reducing protection I: Unilateral reform

As this book has proceeded, various arguments for protection have been considered and found wanting. If one ignores the beneficial effects of trade taxes on a country's terms of trade, there seems to be a good case for dismantling many existing protective barriers. However, even the well-motivated policy maker faces an enormously difficult task here. Pressure groups will strongly oppose tariff reductions, and the process of reform must, to some extent, accede to the political calculus. The political imperatives are important insofar as they prevent the immediate removal of all distortions. This means that the policy maker is necessarily working in a second-best world, attempting to reduce some distortions while others remain firmly in place. As we know from the theory of the second best (Lipsey and Lancaster, 1956; Meade, 1955a), such changes do not necessarily increase welfare. Moreover, the information required to identify and implement second-best policies is likely to be formidable. In a typical economy with many distortions, it would be helpful to have some simple rules telling us "which way is up". Considerations of this kind have led a number of economists to look for simple "piecemeal" reform rules which can be readily understood and implemented by policy makers with some confidence that a welfare improvement will be the outcome. In this chapter we shall explore this literature in detail. The treatment is necessarily mathematical, and the non-technical reader will find this and the next chapter (which deals with similar issues in a multilateral setting) rather more difficult than the rest of the book. Such readers are nevertheless urged to at least peruse the results and attempt to follow the intuitive explanations which accompany most of them.

9.1 Piecemeal tariff reform

In this section we consider the prospects for welfare improvement from a number of piecemeal or partial reforms in a protected economy. Common to all these reforms is that they involve either: (i) removal or reduction of some distortions while other distortions remain in place or (ii) partial reduction of all distortions. In such second-best situations, the implications for welfare depend crucially on the demand and production inter-relationships between the markets in which distortions are being reduced and other distorted markets. The basic

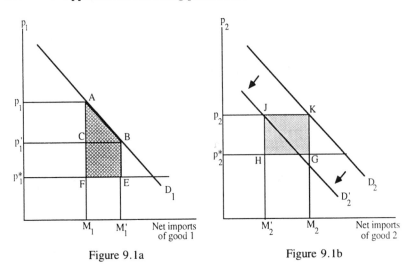

Figure 9.1a   Figure 9.1b

principles are easily explained using a partial equilibrium framework. Figure 9.1 illustrates the markets for two goods in a small open economy which produces and consumes many goods. For purposes of illustration, both goods are assumed to be imported, and both are subject to a tariff on imports. Consumers in this economy are assumed to have identical homothetic preferences.

The diagrams illustrate the excess demands for the goods (net imports M_i) graphed against price p_i (relative to a numeraire good); p_i^* is the world price of good i. We shall now consider the welfare implications of a reduction in the tariff on good 1 (implying a fall in its domestic price from p_1 to p_1' in Figure 9.1a) holding the tariff on good 2 fixed at $p_2^* p_2$ per unit. If D_1 represents the compensated excess demand curve for good 1 (for the utility level after the tariff reduction), then the compensated excess demand for good 1 increases from M_1 to M_1', implying a gain to consumers of $p_1 A B p_1'$. Tariff revenue on good 1 increases by $(CBEF - p_1 A C p_1')$, implying a net gain of $ABEF$. Now suppose that good 2 (Figure 9.1b) is a net substitute for good 1, so the tariff reduction on good 1 shifts the compensated demand curve for good 2 down from D_2 to D_2'. Any change in consumer surplus associated with this shift has already been counted in the area $ABEF$. However, the fall in imports of good 2 from M_2 to M_2' reduces tariff revenue by $JKGH$. This area (and other similar areas for other commodities in the economy), which reflects the by-product distortion in market 2 as M_2 is reduced further below the free-trade level, must be subtracted from $ABEF$ to determine a consumer surplus estimate of the welfare "gain" from the tariff reduction on good 1. Thus the by-product distortion in the market for a substitute good ($JKGH$) reduces any welfare gain accordingly and may even lead to an overall loss from the reform – indeed, this is the substance of the second-best argument for a tax on a good which is a substitute for another taxed good. Nevertheless, there are circumstances in which a welfare improvement may be associated with a reduction of the good 1 tariff. For example, if the tariff on good 1 is particularly high relative to other goods, then the component *CBEF* of *ABEF* tends to be higher (and the area *JKGH* relatively lower), so a net gain is more likely. In addition, if other goods with high tariff rates are complementary to good 1 (i.e. their excess demand rises when the price of 1 falls), there will be relatively large increases in tariff revenue which make an overall gain more likely. For example, if good 2 is a complement to good 1, the demand curve shifts out from, say, D_2' to D_2 with tariff revenue increasing by *JKGH*, which must then be added to *ABEF* (reflecting a reduction in the cost of the distortion in market 2 as M_2 is increased towards its free-trade level). This is more likely to offset losses in revenue for other (substitute) commodities if the tariff rate on good 2 is high. On the other hand, if the complements for good 1 generally have low tariff rates, the gains in tariff revenue are likely to be meagre, while the presence of the complements "dilutes" the substitution away from other goods towards good 1, reducing *ABEF*.

These considerations suggest that piecemeal reforms are more likely to be welfare improving if the following occur:

(i) More extreme distortions are reduced first.
(ii) A good whose tax rate is reduced has, as substitutes, goods with relatively low tax rates and, as complements, goods with relatively high tax rates.

Finally, we note that if the tariff on good 2 is also reduced (in much the same proportion as that on good 1), then the area *JKGH* is reduced, and an additional consumer surplus gain (similar to *ABEF*) will be opened up in market 2. If such a policy is extended to all markets in which there are distortions, we might expect welfare to be enhanced.

Ideas along these lines have provided the motivation for a number of economic theorists to analyse piecemeal reform proposals in a rigorous framework. Although this literature is quite general (applying to any type of distortion), in what follows, we shall be content to present the main results in a model which emphasizes the instruments of trade policy which have been the concern of this book. Nevertheless, the reader should be aware that these results are but part of a wider picture and, in most cases, the generalizations of the results are immediately clear.

Consider a small economy in which n traded goods are produced and consumed, and the only distortions are taxes or subsidies on the country's imports and exports. For simplicity, we assume no non-traded goods though these may be readily incorporated. C_i and X_i denote, respectively, consumption and production of good i ($i = 1, 2, \ldots, n$). To avoid distributional questions, we shall also assume a single consumer (or consumers with identical homothetic preferences) with the (increasing, strictly quasi-concave) utility function

$$u(C) \equiv u(C_1, C_2, \ldots, C_n).$$

On the production side, the n sectoral outputs are constrained by the economy's transformation curve (or production frontier)

$$\phi(X,v) \equiv \phi(X_1, X_2, \ldots, X_n, v) = 0$$

where v is the economy's vector of factor endowments.

In the tradition of duality theory (see e.g. Dixit and Norman, 1980; Woodland, 1982), it is convenient to work with the GNP and expenditure functions. These are defined as follows:

1. *The expenditure function, $E(p, V)$, is the minimum expenditure incurred by the consumer in attaining utility level V when the domestic price vector is p;* that is,

    $$E(p, V) \equiv \min_{C} \{pC : u(C) = V\}.$$

    E can be shown to be continuous, non-decreasing in all arguments, concave in p and homogeneous of degree 1 in p for all V.[1] In addition E has the following useful derivative property:

    $$C_i(p, V) = E_{p_i} \qquad \text{(Shephard's lemma)} \tag{1}$$

    where $C_i(p, V)$ is the Hicksian compensated demand for good i and a subscript p_i denotes a partial derivative with respect to p_i (and similarly for other variables). The linear homogeneity of E with respect to price implies (by Euler's theorem) that

    $$\sum_{i=1}^{n} p_i E_{p_i} = E \qquad \text{and} \qquad \sum_{i=1}^{n} p_i E_{p_i v} = E_v. \tag{2}$$

2. *The GNP function, $g(p, v)$, is the maximum value of domestic output (valued at domestic prices p) satisfying the economy's resource and technology constraints as embodied in the transformation curve;* that is,

    $$g(p, v) \equiv \max_{X} \{pX : \phi(X, v) = 0\}.$$

    The function $g(p, v)$ is continuous and is both convex in p and homogeneous of degree 1 in p for all v. It also has a derivative property similar to Equation (1) and satisfies a homogeneity equation similar to Equation (2):

$$X_i = g_{p_i} \tag{3}$$

$$\sum_{i=1}^{n} p_i g_{p_i} = g. \tag{4}$$

With the (given) world price of good i denoted by p_i^* and the trade tax on good i given by t_i per unit (the taxes may be ad valorem despite being written in specific form), domestic price is related to world price by

$$p_i = p_i^* + t_i. \tag{5}$$

Note that t_i can represent an import tariff or an export subsidy (if it is positive), an import subsidy or an export tax (if it is negative). It can also be the implicit tax associated with a quantitative trade restriction such as an import quota; however, we shall defer consideration of this case until later in this section because it has certain special properties. Finally, we come to the economy's budget constraint. With trade in balance at each point of time, domestic expenditure valued at domestic prices (E) equals domestic factor income (=output), also valued at domestic prices, plus the recycled tax revenue which is assumed to be disbursed (or collected in the case of a subsidy) by costless non-distortionary means. Thus we have

$$E(p, V) = g(p, v) + \sum_i t_i[C_i - X_i]. \tag{6}$$

We now derive an expression for the welfare effects of small changes in the taxes t_i. Substituting Equations (1) and (3) into Equation (6) and taking total differentials yields

$$\sum_j E_{p_j} dt_j + E_v \, dV = \sum_j g_{p_j} dt_j + \sum_i \sum_j t_i[E_{p_i p_j} - g_{p_i p_j}] \, dt_j$$

$$+ \sum_i [E_{p_i} - g_{p_i}] \, dt_i + \sum_i t_i E_{p_i v} \, dV. \tag{7}$$

Using the second equation in (2), we can rearrange Equation (7) to yield

$$\left[\sum_i p_i^* E_{p_i v} \right] dV = \sum_i \sum_j t_i[E_{p_i p_j} - g_{p_i p_j}] \, dt_j = \sum_i \sum_j t_i S_{p_i p_j} \, dt_j \tag{8}$$

where $S \equiv E - g$. Because g is convex in p and E is concave in p, S is concave in p and the matrix (S_{pp}) is therefore negative semi-definite. In addition, the terms

$$E_{p_i v}$$

represent the effects of a change in real income on the demands for commodities i. These will all be positive if there are no inferior goods, a strong assumption which ensures that the term in brackets on the left-hand side of Equation (8) (call it H) is positive. However, it is not necessary to make such a strong assumption. Indeed Hatta (1977a) has shown that a necessary condition for Marshallian stability of equilibrium is that H be non-negative.[2] Thus, if we assume stability and exclude the case in which $H = 0$, the coefficient of dV in Equation (8) is positive, and we need only consider the terms on the right-hand side.

Equation (8) can be used to solve for the second-best level of a particular tax rate, given "unalterable" distortions on some other commodities ($i \in D$, where D is the set of commodities subject to unalterable distortions). Suppose we wish to find the second-best level of the tax on commodity k for given values of the other t_i. Equation (8) then becomes

$$H \frac{dV}{dt_k} = \sum_i t_i S_{p_i p_k} = 0$$

when V is at a maximum. This can then be solved for the second-best optimum value of t_k, viz,

$$t_k = \frac{-1}{S_{p_k p_k}} \left\{ \sum_{i \in D} t_i S_{p_i p_k} \right\}. \tag{9}$$

A number of results can be deduced from Equation (9). The most obvious is the standard second-best conclusion that the best response to unalterable existing distortions may be imposition of another distortion (i.e. $t_k \neq 0$). For example, if all goods are net substitutes for each other (i.e. all the off-diagonal components of the S_{pp} matrix are positive – the diagonal elements are the own-price effects and are clearly negative), and the only distortions are tariffs on imports ($t_i > 0$) which restrict trade below the free-trade level, then Equation (9) tells us that welfare is maximized by imposing a tariff or export subsidy on another traded commodity ($t_k > 0$) which will (by substitution) increase imports of the other taxed commodities in the direction of free trade. In fact, it is possible to show that for the case in which all commodities are substitutes, the optimal alterable second-best taxes or subsidies are an average of the unalterable taxes or subsidies (see Green, 1961; Lloyd, 1974).

An ideal situation would be to use a formula such as Equation (9) to compute the second-best optimal values of those taxes and subsidies which can be changed and thus achieve the best possible outcome subject to the constraints imposed by the existing unalterable distortions. Unfortunately, the informational requirements of such an exercise are rather formidable, and this has led economists to search for simple partial or piecemeal reforms which, though not optimal, can be assessed as welfare-improving on the basis of relatively limited information. We now consider some of these piecemeal reform proposals.

(a)   Proportional reduction of all trade taxes

A simple tariff-cutting formula which is often proposed is the reduction of all trade taxes in the same proportion; that is, $dt_j = -kt_j$ for all j (it is easy to show that ad valorem rates also fall in the same proportion k). This proposal has appeal because of its simplicity and its equitable treatment of various protected sectors. As suggested by our earlier discussion, it also has the desirable property that any "cross-effect" losses are kept to a minimum because all taxes are being reduced in a uniform fashion. In fact, because the relative prices within the group of protected commodities are not changing as trade taxes are reduced, it is possible to aggregate to obtain a two-good model in which one good is protected and the other good is unprotected. It is then clear that proportional reduction of all trade taxes simply reduces the domestic price of the protected good relative to the unprotected good, thus guaranteeing a welfare improvement under the usual conditions which ensure gains from trade (e.g. well-behaved community indifference curves; see Chapter 1). To verify that this reform policy does indeed raise welfare, substitute for dt_j in Equation (8) to obtain

$$H \, dV = -k \sum_i \sum_j t_i S_{p_i p_j} t_j. \tag{10}$$

Because the matrix S_{pp} is negative semi-definite, the quadratic form on the right-hand side of Equation (10) is non-negative, and it is straightforward to show that in most cases it is positive.[3] Thus we have shown that *when all goods are traded and the only distortions are taxes on international trade, an equi-proportionate reduction in all taxes will increase welfare*. Variants of this result (which is but a special case of a more general proposition in public economics) have been proved by many authors, in particular Dixit (1975), Fukushima (1979), Hatta (1977a) and Lloyd (1974). In particular, Fukushima (1979) shows that welfare is improved by an equi-proportional adjustment of all ad valorem tax rates $\tau_j \ (\equiv t_j/p_j^*)$ towards a uniform rate τ^* according to the formula

$$d\tau_j = -k(\tau_j - \tau^*) \tag{11}$$

for all j.[4] The intuition of this result is based on the observation that a uniform tax rate across all goods yields the same relative prices as the complete absence of distortions. Thus a reform which involves an equi-proportionate move towards uniform tax rates on all goods is similar in nature to an equi-proportionate reduction of all rates and raises welfare for the same reasons. Clearly the two reforms are identical when $\tau^* = 0$, with higher rates being reduced more than lower rates. Negative rates (import subsidies or export taxes) are increased, but of course that means a fall in their absolute value; the distortion is still reduced and larger distortions are reduced by a larger amount. When $\tau^* \neq 0$, reform along the lines of Equation (11) may involve some smaller tax or subsidy rates being increased towards the uniform level τ^*.

Before leaving the case of proportional tax changes, it is worth noting the following two contrasting views of the above results:

(i)   Provided a suitable assumption is made about the stability of equilibrium [so that H in Equation (8) is positive], reform of the kind being considered here will necessarily improve welfare. No special assumptions about the properties of the matrix S_{pp} or its components are necessary; the particular complementarity or substitutability relationships between commodities do not matter, provided S_{pp} is negative semi-definite (as would be implied by the usual consumer and producer optimization problems). Of course, more detailed information about the components of S_{pp} is required if we wish to estimate the gains from proportional reforms (see Section 9.3).

(ii)   On the other hand, the welfare gain we have identified can be assured only if a proportional reform of the kind proposed is followed precisely. Such rules require that all distortions be reduced in a uniform or proportional fashion. It is therefore important that all (or at least most) distortions be identified and reduced in the manner described. In principle, there is no problem with including other sorts of taxes and subsidies in the process (these are all readily incorporated into the theorems; see Dixit, 1985). However, some distortions such as those associated with monopoly and various sorts of government regulation may be difficult to identify, and it may be costly to quantify the tax or subsidy implicit in such distortions. In addition, there may be political constraints limiting a government's ability to reduce some distortions. This is not to say that we should be faint-hearted in tackling such problems. However, it does suggest the value of looking for other, simpler types of piecemeal reforms. Certainly, the informational requirements of the above radial reform proposals are considerably greater than is apparent from a cursory reading of the theorems.

We now consider an alternative type of piecemeal reform based on reduction of selected distortions.

(b)   *Reduction of selected trade taxes*

As was clear from the discussion of Figure 9.1, the problem with reducing selected distortions is that cross-effects can result which magnify distortions associated with other commodities or markets. In particular, community welfare may fall if reducing a tax rate on one commodity leads to a fall in demand for substitute commodities with larger per unit distortions. One simple approach which would appear to circumvent such difficulties is *reduction of the most extreme distortion first*. This proposal is often an implicit rule-of-thumb used by actual policy makers, and it has been analysed by a number of theorists (Bertrand and Vanek, 1971; Fukushima, 1979; Hatta, 1977a, 1977b; Lipsey and Lancaster, 1956; Lloyd, 1974; and Meade, 1955a) who have derived conditions under which it is welfare-improving. It may be surprising to many readers that such a reform need not increase welfare. However, if the good with, say, the highest tariff rate has a large number of complements with low tariff rates (so that the by-product gains in these markets are low while the beneficial substitutions to good 1 are reduced by the presence of the complements) and several highly taxed substitutes (with accordingly high cross-effect losses), then it is clear that reduction of the highest tariff rate may make matters worse. Let us therefore consider under what conditions the proposal in question would increase welfare.

Recall that, for any good subject to a fixed tariff, welfare is increased (reduced) if imports of that good are increased (reduced) because the restrictive effect of the tariff on imports is thereby partly offset (reinforced). Moreover, such effects are more pronounced on goods with high tariff rates because the deadweight loss associated with the marginal unit equals the tariff per unit (in terms of Figure 9.1, the area *JKGH* is larger, the higher the tariff on good 2). However, if imports of one good are increased, the balance-of-trade constraint dictates that imports of some other good(s) must fall [or, equivalently, exports of some good(s) must rise]. It therefore seems necessary to make sure that the reduction in the highest tariff causes imports to rise for those goods with higher tariffs, with any falls in imports being associated with the low-tariff commodities (of course, these remarks are illustrative only and are readily generalized to take account of the full range of taxes and subsidies).

There are clearly many possible situations in which the gains and losses just described may be associated with particular commodities in a way which yields a net increase in welfare. Because some of these may be difficult to identify, several authors have sought simpler, more easily recognizable conditions which guarantee welfare improvement. The simplest such scenario involves imports of the good with the highest tariff rate increasing when that tariff is reduced and imports (exports) of all other goods falling (rising) – that is, all other goods subject to tariffs are gross substitutes for the good with the highest tariff rate. The welfare loss on the goods below the maximum tariff is not sufficient to offset the gain on the good with the highest tariff. This result, which is attributed to Bertrand and Vanek (1971), is readily proved as follows.

Let n be the good with the highest tariff rate. Taking total differentials of Equation (6) yields

$$E_{p_n} \, dt_n + E_v \, dV = g_{p_n} \, dt_n + (C_n - X_n) \, dt_n + \sum_i t_i(dC_i - dX_i). \tag{12}$$

Using Equations (1) and (3) and letting $M_i \equiv C_i - X_i$, we find that Equation (12) simplifies to

$$E_v \, dV = \sum_i t_i \, dM_i = \sum_i \tau_i p_i^* \, dM_i \tag{12a}$$

where $\tau_i \equiv t_i/p_i^*$, as previously defined. In addition, we have the balance-of-trade condition

$$\sum_i p_i^* M_i = 0 \tag{13}$$

Differentiating Equation (13), we obtain

$$\tau_n p_n^* \, dM_n = -\sum_{i \neq n} \tau_n p_i^* \, dM_i \tag{14}$$

which we can substitute in Equation (12a) to yield

$$E_v \, dV = -\sum_{i \neq n} (\tau_n - \tau_i) p_i^* \, dM_i. \tag{12b}$$

Thus, if $\tau_n > \tau_i$ and $dM_i < 0$ for all $i \neq n$, then the Bertrand and Vanek result is seen to hold. Let us note a couple of important features of this result:

(i)   It is overly sufficient. It is clear from inspection of Equation (12b) that other configurations of dM_i across commodities (in particular $dM_i > 0$ for some $i \neq n$) are, in principle, consistent with dV being positive; the problem with such weaker conditions is that they depend on the magnitude of the dM_i's and hence are more difficult to verify than the Bertrand and Vanek condition.

(ii) The Bertrand and Vanek condition is based on actual (uncompensated) changes in excess demands for the various goods; to be able to predict these effects requires data which would, in general, be sufficient to compute the effects of a wider range of reform proposals than the simple one being considered here. On the other hand, as Hatta (1977b) has pointed out, whether the condition is satisfied will be automatically apparent after the tax rate τ_n has been reduced. Thus, if the condition is satisfied, the government's reform will have proved to be in the right direction. The difficulty arises if the condition is not met. It is, after all, only a (rather strong) sufficient condition, so its violation does not mean the reform is a failure; moreover, even if that were the correct inference, the government might, for political and administrative reasons, be reluctant to reverse its policy change.

An alternative approach which has been explored by Hatta (1977a, 1977b) and others, is to work with the compensated excess demands. As we shall see, this approach offers more hope for predicting whether a reduction of (say) the highest tariff rate will be a welfare-improving measure. However, it turns out to be beset by a shortcoming similar to the Bertrand and Vanek result: the condition for welfare improvement is so overly sufficient that its violation tells us little.

In working with compensated demands, the intuition of the problem is very similar to that given above. In the previous case, a net increase in welfare was assured if excess demand for the good with the highest tariff (which is the tariff being reduced) increased while excess demands for all other goods fell. These excess demand changes were uncompensated and therefore included income effects. The task of netting out these income effects was accomplished in the move from Equation (7) to Equation (8). Basically, any increase in real income (V) increases both expenditure and income (the latter via increased recycled tariff revenue due to higher imports, assuming non-inferior goods) with the expenditure effect dominating the tariff revenue effect when all goods are non-inferior (or if the Hatta stability condition holds). Thus, netting out the income effects does not make any qualitative difference here. It is then easy to see that, taking each good separately, welfare is increased if and only if the compensated excess demand for that good increases. This compensated analogue of the previous result is summed up in the following alternative form of Equation (8):

$$H \, dV = \sum_i t_i dM_i^c \tag{8a}$$

where the superscript c denotes a compensated (constant V) excess demand. Given that $H > 0$, Equation (8a) is of the same form as Equation (12a) (with uncompensated changes in excess demands replaced by compensated changes), and the associated intuition is along the same lines. In the previous case, we were able to appeal to the balance-of-trade condition to argue that, if imports of one good were to rise, imports of some other goods must fall. However, we cannot use this condition here because the balance of trade involves uncompensated, not compensated, excess demands. Nevertheless, a similar result is implied by the fact that the output and compensated demand functions (and hence the compensated excess demand functions) are homogeneous of degree zero in prices. Applying Euler's theorem to the excess demand function for good n and using the symmetry of the substitution terms in the matrix S_{pp}, we have

$$0 = \sum_i p_i S_{p_n p_i} = \sum_i p_i S_{p_i p_n} = \sum_i p_i \frac{\partial M_i^c}{\partial p_n}. \tag{15}$$

In other words, if the compensated excess demand for any good increases as a result of a fall in p_n (or t_n), Equation (15) implies that some other(s) must fall to hold constant the value of total excess demand evaluated at the initial domestic prices.

We are now able to tell the same story as for the case of uncompensated demands. If a rise in imports for one good must be offset by a fall in imports elsewhere, then it is important that the rises be associated with goods subject to a high tax t_i (for which the marginal gains are higher) and falls be linked to goods with a low tax. As before, many conditions can be constructed to give the desired outcome, but the simplest one involves compensated imports of the good with the highest tax rate increasing when that tax rate is reduced, with compensated imports of all other goods falling. Another way of stating this result (due to Hatta, 1977a, 1977b) is that a reduction in the tariff on good n (which has the highest tariff rate) is welfare-improving if good n is a net substitute for all other goods. Formal proof proceeds as follows.

With $dt_j = 0$ for all $j \neq n$, Equation (8) becomes

$$H \, dV = dt_n \sum_i t_i S_{p_i p_n} = dt_n \sum_i \tau_i p_i^* S_{p_i p_n}. \tag{16}$$

From Equation (15) we have

$$(1 + \tau_n) p_n^* S_{p_n p_n} = -\sum_{i \neq n} (1 + \tau_i) p_i^* S_{p_i p_n}. \tag{17}$$

Multiplying both sides of Equation (17) by t_n, rearranging and substituting in Equation (16) yields

$$H \, dV = dt_n \sum_{i \neq n} p_i^* S_{p_i p_n} \left[\tau_i - \tau_n \frac{(1 + \tau_i)}{(1 + \tau_n)} \right] = \frac{dt_n}{(1 + \tau_n)} \sum_{i \neq n} p_i^* S_{p_i p_n} (\tau_i - \tau_n)$$

$$\tag{18}$$

Thus, as claimed, $dV > 0$ if

(a) $H > 0$ (the stability condition);
(b) $\tau_n > \tau_i$ for all $i \neq n$ and $dt_n < 0$ (i.e. the highest tariff rate is reduced);
(c) $S_{p_i p_n} > 0$ for all $i \neq n$ (i.e. all other goods are net substitutes for n).

Clearly, the condition that the good with the highest tariff rate be a net substitute for all the other goods in the economy is rather strong and is indeed overly sufficient for a welfare improvement. However, it is a relatively simple condition which, if satisfied, enables the policy maker to predict that reducing the highest tariff rate is a welfare-improving reform. If it is not satisfied (e.g. if some goods are net complements for n), then, as in the Bertrand and Vanek case, the reform may still be worthwhile, but the magnitudes of the terms on the right-hand side of Equation (18) would have to be calculated to see if the expression is still positive.

It is also possible to construct various other piecemeal reforms involving a change in tariff rates other than the highest one. To ensure that such reforms are welfare-improving, it is customary to assume that the good whose tariff is reduced is a net substitute for all goods with lower tariff rates and a net complement for all goods with higher tariff rates (see e.g. Dixit, 1975). It is also possible to raise welfare by increasing the lowest tariff rate if the good in question is a substitute for all other goods (Hatta, 1977a). The intuition of such results is along the same lines as that just presented, and simple proofs can be readily constructed by the reader using Equation (18).

These results can be extended to allow for the existence of non-traded goods if it is assumed that non-traded goods are net substitutes for all other goods (see Fukushima, 1979; Hatta, 1977b). With this (admittedly overstrong) substitutability assumption, we are once again assured that excess demand will switch sufficiently towards the good(s) whose tariff(s) has been reduced to yield a net welfare gain.

Finally, we note that the analysis can be extended to the case of many consumers. Diewert, Turunen-Red and Woodland (1989) generalize the main piecemeal tariff reform propositions in a many-consumer economy in which the government can use either consumer-specific lump-sum transfers or commodity taxes (but not both) as instruments.

The preceding analysis has been concerned with the case in which all trade restrictions are explicit taxes or subsidies. We now turn our attention to the case where quantitative trade restrictions are also involved.

(c)   Reform in the presence of quantitative trade restrictions

We know from Chapter 2 that when markets are competitive, a quantitative restriction (e.g. an import quota) is equivalent to its implicit tariff. On the other hand, we saw in Chapter 3 that these instruments, which are equivalent in a static sense, are no longer equivalent in the presence of changing parameters (e.g. shifting demand and supply curves). The relevance of this in the present context can be illustrated as follows. Suppose a tariff on a particular commodity is reduced. Then, as was seen earlier, this shifts the excess demand curves of other goods in the economy (the direction of shift depending on whether they are complements or substitutes). However, the response of any particular market to such a shift differs depending on whether it is protected by a tariff or a quota: under a tariff, the equilibrium excess demand adjusts (a fact which was used in deriving the earlier piecemeal reform propositions) whereas under a quota, the excess demand cannot change, being fixed at the level specified by the quota. An immediate implication is that the existence of quotas in some markets cannot, in itself, be a reason for introducing other distortions elsewhere [as was the case with tariffs; see Equation (9)] because a new distortion can do nothing to change the excess demands in the quota-protected markets in the direction of free trade. In terms of Figure 9.1b, if good 2 is quota-protected, the area *JKGH* is zero, so there is no by-product gain in market 2 from a tariff in market 1. This result, which has been noted by Corden and Falvey (1985) is easily established formally by rewriting Equation (9) with commodities subject to unalterable distortions partitioned into two groups, tariff-protected commodities *T* and quota-protected commodities *R*. The second-best optimum tariff (or tariff-equivalent) for some other good *k* is then given by

$$
t_k = \frac{-1}{K} \left\{ \sum_{i \in T} t_i \left[S_{p_i p_k} + \sum_{j \in R} S_{p_i p_j} \frac{dp_j}{dt_k} \right] + \sum_{i \in R} (p_i - p_i^*) \frac{dQ_i}{dt_k} \right\} \tag{9a}
$$

where

$$
K \equiv S_{p_k p_k} + \sum_{j \in R} S_{p_k p_j} \frac{dp_j}{dt_k}
$$

and Q_i is the import quota on good $i \in R$. Under reasonable assumptions (i.e. the "feedback" effects of changes in the prices of the quota-protected goods do not offset the impact effect of a change in k's own price on its compensated demand) K is negative. Moreover, since Q_i is a given constant, the second group of terms in the brackets is zero, so t_k is only non-zero if $t_i \neq 0$ for some $i \in T$; that is, *the existence of quota-distorted markets does not provide a second-best argument for introducing distortions elsewhere.* On the other hand, we should be careful in interpreting this result. If there is at least one good protected by an unalterable tariff and that good has non-zero cross-elasticities with quota-protected goods, then though a tariff on, say, good *k* does nothing to reduce the cost of the distortion in the quota-protected markets, it does, in general, change the domestic (market-clearing) prices of the quota-protected goods. These price changes then affect the cost of any distortions in markets with unalterable tariffs; that is, the imposition of a tariff on *k* has a quantitatively different effect on the costs of unalterable tariff distortions if some other markets are protected by quotas than if those markets are unprotected. In other words, unless quotas are the only distortions, we cannot simply ignore quota-protected markets when computing the optimal second-best tariff (or implicit tariff) in a particular market: the magnitude of that tariff is affected by the presence of the quotas and the particular commodities on which they are imposed. Thus, where quotas coexist with a range of non-quantitative distortions, the Corden and Falvey result offers no simple short cuts to policy makers. On the other hand, if all existing distortions such as tariffs can be converted to quotas, no new distortions need be introduced. Interpreted in this way, the result provides a reason for preferring quotas to tariffs, despite the clear superiority of tariffs on other grounds.

How does the existence of fixed quotas affect the piecemeal tariff reform proposals discussed above? To answer this question, we again note that a particular set of small tariff changes cannot change excess demands in markets where quotas are fixed and binding. Thus quota-protected commodities are essentially the same as non-traded goods at the margin. This parallel has been noted by Falvey (1988), and it means that the propositions of Hatta (1977b) and Fukushima (1979) concerning piecemeal reform in the presence of non-traded goods can be reinterpreted to apply to quota-protected markets. Specifically, if all quota-protected goods are net substitutes for all other goods, then (given the other relevant assumptions) all the piecemeal reforms considered in this section are welfare-improving. The presence of fixed quotas makes no substantive difference.

Although the presence of fixed quotas does not change the results concerning piecemeal reforms involving taxes or subsidies, piecemeal reforms which involve changes in quotas on particular goods do affect markets which are not protected by quotas. Of course, if all distortions take the form of quantitative restrictions, a relaxation in any one quota must make the community better off because it unambiguously enlarges the economy's consumption set (without amplifying the losses from distortions in related markets). This welfare improvement is demonstrated by writing Equation (12a) as

$$E_v \, dV = \sum_i t_i \, dM_i = \sum_i t_i \, dQ_i \qquad (12c)$$

which is positive if some binding quotas ($t_i > 0$) are relaxed ($dQ_i > 0$) with others remaining fixed ($dQ_i = 0$), and there are no other distorted markets (i.e. $t_i = 0$ for non-quota-protected markets for which $dM_i \neq 0$). Because "the way up" is so clear when all distortions take the form of quantitative restrictions (i.e. simply relax these restrictions one or several at a time), it would appear that the difficulty of identifying welfare-improving piecemeal reforms can be resolved simply by converting all explicit taxes or subsidies to quotas and then gradually relaxing the quotas. As observed by Falvey (1988), such an approach runs counter to the view of reform which is popular with most policy makers, that is, change quotas to tariffs and then set about reducing the tariffs. However, as we have seen elsewhere in this book, quotas have many other disadvantages relative to tariffs, particularly in the presence of monopoly and/or foreign retaliation, and such considerations presumably are what motivate the popular view. Accordingly, assessment of any piecemeal reform proposal which involves replacing tariffs with quotas (or vice versa) should explicitly take account of the relative merits of the two instruments. Until the models of piecemeal reform explicitly incorporate the welfare gains or losses associated with switches between various instruments (as distinct from reductions of given distortions), it is difficult to offer any clear recommendations on how the choice of protective instrument should enter the reform process.

In the simple case just considered, quotas were the only form of distortion. If some other markets are protected by tariffs, relaxation of a quota in one market may (through cross-effects) amplify distortions in some tariff-protected markets by reducing excess demands in those markets. In such a case, it is more appropriate to view the quota as a tariff-equivalent and treat relaxation of the quota as a reduction in the quota's implicit tariff. Such an approach enables quota reform to be analysed in the same way as tariff reform; in particular, it can be shown that a reform which reduces the most extreme distortion (where the implicit tariffs associated with the various quotas are included in the set of distortions being considered) is welfare-improving if (i) the good whose distortion is being reduced is a net substitute for all other goods and (ii) if non-traded goods and goods subject to fixed quotas are net substitutes for all other goods. Indeed, relaxation (tightening) of any quota which has an implicit tariff above (below) the highest (lowest) explicit tariff constitutes a welfare improvement (see Falvey, 1988).

We have now considered a number of piecemeal proposals encompassing a range of types of distortions. Although these proposals only represent an improvement for the economy if certain conditions are met, it is interesting to note that the general thrust of all proposals is a movement towards uniformity of distortions across markets (whether it is achieved by proportional reduction of all distortions or by reducing extreme distortions first). Thus the theory of piecemeal reform lends some rough support to an approach which has often been favoured (if not always explicitly) by policy makers: the idea that reducing disparities in protection across industries improves welfare.[5]

9.2   Tariff reform in the presence of adjustment costs

An aspect of tariff reform which is often emphasized by pressure groups and politicians is the adjustment costs associated with factors which are displaced from the sector(s) whose protection has been reduced and are thus forced to move to other sectors of the economy. Such factors may have to forego income and incur other costs while they search for employment elsewhere and/or undergo retraining. A common view[6] is that the presence of such adjustment costs justifies a "gradualist" approach to reductions in protection with tariffs, and so on, in an industry being phased out over time rather than being eliminated in a single stroke. The validity of this proposition can be shown to depend on whether the tariff cuts are unanticipated at the time they are implemented or whether they are known in advance. In the former case, the pattern of factors across industries can be taken as a bygone and (in the absence of other distortions) immediate tariff elimination is the optimal policy. On the other hand, if (as is often the case) tariff changes are anticipated, the extent of those tariff changes may significantly influence the initial allocation of factors across industries (as well as the subsequent transfer of factors between industries). In such a case, the policy maker is in the position of choosing an optimal future tariff level, given the present (unalterable) tariff level, a second-best problem of the kind considered in the previous section. In such a situation the optimal future tariff may well be positive (i.e. incomplete or gradual tariff reduction). This problem is analysed by Leamer (1980), who considers the production effects of staged tariff reduction. In what follows, we use a variant of the model of the previous section to incorporate the consumer into Leamer's analysis.

Leamer considers a small economy consisting of two sectors A and B (which we denote by appropriate subscripts). A is the importable (subject to a tariff), and B is the exportable. Units of both goods are chosen so that their (given) world prices are unity. Suppose producers and consumers each solve a two-period maximization problem, both using the same discount factor ρ [$=1/(1 + r)$, where r is the common discount rate for both groups of agents]. Further, suppose that good A is subject to an unalterable tariff in period 1 at rate t_1 and that the policy maker is to choose the period-2 tariff rate (t_2) on A to maximize the present value of community welfare; this rate, when chosen, is pre-announced at the beginning of period 1. Thus all agents know the time profile of protection for industry A at the time when they make their decisions regarding consumption, employment and so on. In particular, individuals who decide to work in sector A in the first period also decide at the outset whether to transfer labour from sector A to sector B (and, if so, how much labour to transfer) at the beginning of period 2 when the new tariff rate t_2 takes effect; this decision depends on the level of the second-period tariff. It is assumed that the process of transferring labour involves a period of unemployment as workers search for new jobs. Specifically, we assume that, of T man-hours transferring out of A at the beginning of period 2, only a (constant) proportion $\lambda \leq 1$ actually reaches sector B. When $\lambda < 1$, the transfer of labour involves adjustment costs, while $\lambda = 1$ corresponds to the standard case in which such costs are absent or ignored.

The production side of the economy is as follows. Both goods are produced using a single "mobile" factor (labour), of which the economy's total endowment is L in both periods. Letting L_B denote the period 1 allocation of labour to sector B and T the transfer of labour out of sector A at the beginning of period 2, we can define the GNP function over the two periods as

$$g(p, v, \lambda) \equiv \underset{L_B, T}{\text{Max}}\{(1 + t_1)F(L - L_B) + G(L_B) +$$
$$\rho(1 + t_2)F(L - L_B - T) + \rho G(L_B + \lambda T)\} \tag{19}$$

subject to $T \geq 0,$[7] where $F(\cdot)$ and $G(\cdot)$ are the single-period production functions of A and B, respectively, and the domestic price vector p is given by

$$(p_{A1}, p_{A2}, p_{B1}, p_{B2}) \equiv [(1 + t_1), \rho(1 + t_2), 1, \rho]$$

where p_{Ai} and p_{Bi} are the period i prices of the outputs of sectors A and B, respectively.

What is the effect of a lower second-period tariff on the sectoral outputs in the two periods? The answer to this question depends in part on whether t_2 is sufficiently below t_1 to induce factors to move from A to B at the beginning of period 2. There is a range of values of t_2 immediately below t_1 for which no such factor mobility occurs. This is because the resulting higher period-2 return to labour in sector B is insufficient to cover the loss of income incurred by a unit of labour in the move from A to B. If t_2 is in this interval, then a higher t_2 causes more workers to initially choose sector A (and stay there, since $T = 0$), so the output of A is increased in both periods (and the output of B correspondingly falls in both periods). This unambiguous shift of resources into the protected sector reduces the value of GNP at world prices in both periods and thus reduces the present value of GNP at world prices. There can therefore be no argument for increasing t_2 above the level necessary to deter inter-sectoral factor movements. Of course, it is quite possible that inter-sectoral adjustment costs are so large that no factors move between sectors for any positive value of t_2. In such a case, t_2 should be immediately reduced to zero, and there may even be a case for subsidizing imports ($t_2 < 0$). It follows that, in the present context, there is no case for gradual tariff reduction unless it induces some inter-sectoral movement of factors, some structural adjustment.

Now suppose that there is a positive value of t_2 below which labour moves from sector A to sector B. Reductions of t_2 below this value stimulate inter-sectoral transfers of labour and lead to increased period 1 output of good A but a lower second-period output of that good (because more workers leave the sector at the end of period 1). Similarly, period-1 output of the unprotected good B falls, but period-2 output of B rises. The reason for the apparently perverse output movements in period 1 is that the lower period-2 tariff reduces the net cost of transferring from A to B at the end of period 1 so more labour units decide at the outset to earn a "protected" return in sector A in period 1 and transfer out of A at the end of the period.

We conclude that, in the presence of inter-sectoral factor movements, reducing the second-period tariff reduces GNP at world prices in period 1 (because the production point is moved away from free trade), but increases it in period 2 (for a symmetrical reason). The effect on the present value of GNP at world prices is therefore ambiguous. However, it can be shown that the present value of GNP at world prices is increased by a rise in t_2 in the neighbourhood of $t_2 = 0$; that is, there is a production gain from not eliminating tariffs completely in the second period. This is because, with a positive tariff in period 1 and a zero tariff in period 2, a small increase in t_2 above zero yields a positive gain through the improved mix of period-1 outputs, but only an infinitesimal loss arises from the distortion to period-2 outputs (because at $t_2 = 0$, the marginal deadweight loss from a small increment in the tariff is zero). This is the essence of Leamer's argument for staged tariff reductions: in the presence of adjustment costs and an unalterable first-period tariff, raising the second-period tariff above zero reduces the production loss from the existing first-period distortion more than it costs from the second-period distortion (initially zero in this experiment). It is thus not optimal, from a production point of view to completely eliminate tariffs in one round. The reader can find proofs of all these results in Appendix 5.

Of course, there are also the consumption effects of the tariff to be considered, and we now introduce the representative consumer into the problem.[8] Letting C_{Ai} and C_{Bi} be the period i consumption of A and B, respectively, define the present value of utility as

$$U \equiv u(C_{A1}, C_{B1}) + \rho u(C_{A2}, C_{B2})$$

where $u(\cdot)$ is the single period utility function. Taking total factor supplies as given, we define the expenditure function as

$$E(p, V) \equiv \underset{C_{A_i}, C_{B_i}}{\mathrm{Min}}\{(1 + t_1)C_{A1} + C_{B1} + \rho(1 + t_2)C_{A2} + \rho C_{B2} : U = V\}$$

where E has all the usual properties of an expenditure function (see previous section).

Assuming that the economy in question balances its trade over the two periods of the model, its budget constraint is given by

$$E = g + t_1(C_{A1} - X_{A1}) + \rho t_2(C_{A2} - X_{A2}), \tag{20}$$

where X_{Ai} and X_{Bi} are the period i outputs of A and B, respectively.

It is now straightforward to differentiate Equation (20) totally to solve for the optimal period-2 tariff, given the tariff prevailing in period 1. Using the techniques of the previous section, we obtain

$$H \frac{dV}{dt_2} = t_1[E_{P_{A1}P_{A2}} - g_{P_{A1}P_{A2}}] + t_2[E_{P_{A2}P_{A2}} - g_{P_{A2}P_{A2}}] \tag{21}$$

where

$$H \equiv E_{P_{A1}V} + E_{P_{B1}V} + \rho[E_{P_{A2}V} + E_{P_{B2}V}]$$

is defined similarly to the H in the previous section and can be shown to be positive for stability of equilibrium.

Equation (21) can be used to solve for the optimal second period tariff $(dV/dt_2 = 0)$. This is

$$t_2 = \frac{t_1[g_{P_{A1}P_{A2}} - E_{P_{A1}P_{A2}}]}{[E_{P_{A2}P_{A2}} - g_{P_{A2}P_{A2}}]}.$$ (22)

The denominator is simply the derivative of compensated excess demand for good A in period 2 with respect to its own price in that period and is therefore negative. The numerator is also negative if period-1 good A and period-2 good A are net substitutes; however, it is instructive to look at the individual terms in the numerator. In particular, the term

$$g_{P_{A1}P_{A2}} = \frac{\partial X_{A1}}{\partial t_2} = \frac{\lambda(1 - \lambda)\rho^2 F_1' F_2' G_2''}{\Delta} \leq 0 \qquad (<0 \text{ for } \lambda < 1)$$

(see Appendix 5) captures the production effect identified by Leamer. In the absence of adjustment costs, the term is zero and does not enter the calculation of the second-period tariff. However, when there are adjustment costs, it is strictly negative and, by itself, implies a positive optimal period-2 tariff as claimed earlier (i.e. staged tariff reduction). However, as is clear from Equation (22), this result may be reinforced or offset by the demand effect in the numerator. The term

$$E_{P_{A1}P_{A2}} = \frac{1}{\varrho} \frac{\partial C_{A1}}{\partial t_2}$$

is positive (negative) if and only if period-1 and -2 consumptions of good A are net substitutes (complements). In the case of net substitutes in demand, staged tariff reduction ($t_2 > 0$) is optimal even in the absence of adjustment costs. On the other hand, for the net complements case with zero adjustment costs, the optimal response to the unalterable tariff in period 1 is an *import subsidy* in period 2 ($t_2 < 0$) – an "overshooting" of the ultimate free-trade equilibrium. In such a case, adjustment costs reduce the size of this subsidy, but a positive period-2 tariff is only optimal if the production effect is dominant.

So far we have assumed that workers made their period-1 job choices in full knowledge of the future course of tariffs. If, instead, a tariff reduction is unanticipated at the time it is implemented, then the period-1 tariff t_1 is irrelevant to the government's calculations because workers have already allocated their labour to the two sectors for period 1, and this will not be changed by the choice of t_2. Accordingly, it is proper to drop the first group of terms from Equation (21) to obtain

$$H \frac{dV}{dt_2} = t_2[E_{P_{A2}P_{A2}} - g_{P_{A2}P_{A2}}].$$ (21a)

Now welfare is maximized by complete tariff elimination ($t_2 = 0$). The foregoing argument also applies if workers know the government's tariff plans at the outset but are locked into a particular sector; if the government's ability to influence job choice through its tariff policy is limited, then the best course is to immediately reduce tariffs to zero and obtain the full consumption gains of free trade. Thus the case for gradual reduction of tariffs is seen to depend on whether at the time of implementation (i) the tariff reform is anticipated, and (ii) factors are inter-sectorally mobile. If these conditions are satisfied, then there may well be a good case for staged reduction as explained. Otherwise, an immediate move to free trade is optimal.

In practice, the policy maker is constrained by political pressures from producers who are in the process of entering various long-term contracts and who argue for advance notice of any changes. In addition, change is often anticipated through the usual process of rumour and leaked information. For these and other reasons, the case of pre-announced changes in industry protection may be the most appropriate model. On the other hand, if we bring political factors into the discussion, we should note one of the stronger arguments against gradualism: it gives pressure groups time in which to lobby against any change. For this reason, governments may prefer rapid implementation of their reforms. However, given that such reforms are often the outcome of a rather prolonged and publicly visible discussion (e.g. senate committees and government reports), such an approach may be generally infeasible.

The foregoing analysis assumes that λ, the adjustment cost per labour unit, is a constant; in particular, it does not depend on the speed of tariff reduction. However, it seems likely that employment search costs, and so forth, will increase as the number of unemployed workers increases, so we might expect λ to be a decreasing function of the period-2 tariff. In the presence of such an externality, the policy maker would have to trade off the usual efficiency gains from reduced protection against the increased costs associated with inter-sectoral movement of factors. It is quite possible that the optimal trade-off may involve gradual tariff reduction even if the tariff reduction is unanticipated. Certainly a result along these lines has been obtained by Mussa (1986), using a rather different model from that presented here. In one section of his paper, Mussa considers a policy trade-off between the production efficiency gains from reduced protection and the costs of lost production due to unemployment. He finds that under reasonable assumptions the optimal policy involves the tariff being gradually reduced to its long-run optimal level. Baldwin, Mutti and Richardson (1980) also consider the case for gradualism in the presence of involuntary unemployment (due, for example, to rigid factor prices).

9.3   Measurement of the gains from reduced protection

In the previous two sections of this chapter, various aspects of reform have been analysed in detail. However, so far we have said nothing about measurement of the gains from particular reform proposals. In this section we generalize the simple formulae obtained in Chapter 2 for the two-good case and derive expressions for the gains from particular tariff reforms in a small country. The literature on measurement of deadweight loss is extensive (see e.g. Diewert, 1984; Dixon, 1978; Harberger, 1964; Johnson, 1960; King, 1983), and the treatment here is intended merely as an illustration of the relevant techniques. In particular, we do not consider gains or losses arising from effects such as terms-of-trade changes, economies of scale, reduced rent-seeking costs; all of these should be taken into account in any evaluation of an actual reform proposal. In this respect, the present treatment should be viewed as no more than a starting point (though it is a starting point which has received considerable attention in the literature).

As in Chapter 2, we shall follow the practice of other authors in the tariff area and work in terms of an *equivalent variation* (EV) measure of the gains from tariff reduction (or deadweight loss from tariff increase). The measure defines the EV net of production and tariff revenue effects and corresponds to the "generalized equivalent variation" of Chipman and Moore (1980), the "equivalent gain" of King (1983) and the "Hicks–Boiteux loss" of Diewert (1984). Specifically, the equivalent variation measure of the deadweight loss from a given increase in a set of tariffs is the amount of net income (i.e. allowing for changes in GNP and tariff revenue) which would have to be taken away from consumers at the initial prices to make them as well off as they would be at the new set of prices; that is,

$$\text{EV} \equiv E(p_1, V_1) - E(p_0, V_1) - [g(p_1, v) - g(p_0, v)] - [TR(p_1, V_1) - TR(p_0, V_1)] \tag{23}$$

where TR denotes tariff revenue. Subscripts 1 and 0 denote variables in the new and initial situations, respectively.

Using Equation (6), we can rearrange Equation (23) to give

$$\text{EV} = E(p_0, V_0) - E(p_0, V_1)$$

which corresponds to the definition used by Diewert (1984) and King (1983). The "composition" of EV when there are two goods is illustrated in Figure 9.2 for the case of a move from free trade to a positive tariff; EV_G in the diagram denotes the "gross" EV:

$$E(p_1, V_1) - E(p_0, V_1).$$

We start by deriving an expression for the gain from complete elimination of all tariffs (i.e. the deadweight loss of the tariff system relative to free trade). Thus $p_1 = p$, the actual price vector under the tariff system, and $p_0 = p^*$, the free-trade price vector. Using a Taylor series expansion of Equation (23) about $p = p^*$, we obtain the following approximation of EV:

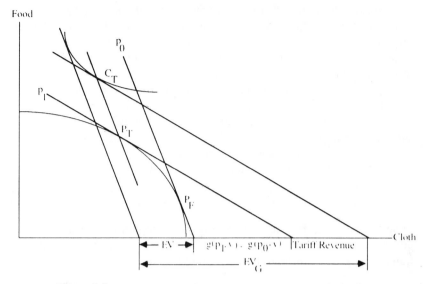

Figure 9.2

$$EV = -\frac{1}{2} \sum_i \sum_j S_{p_i p_j} t_i t_j = -\frac{1}{2} \sum_i \sum_j \left[\frac{\partial C_i(p^*, V_1)}{\partial p_j} - \frac{\partial X_i(p^*)}{\partial p_j} \right] t_i t_j$$

(24)

where the second expression contains the usual decomposition of the cost of protection into consumption and production components. Equation (24) can also be manipulated to yield the following expression for EV as a proportion of GNP (Y):

$$\frac{EV}{Y} = -\frac{1}{2} \sum_i \sum_j r_i r_j \eta_{ij} \, \alpha_i$$

(25)

where r_i is t_i/p_i, the tariff rate expressed as a proportion of the tariff-distorted price; η_{ij} is the compensated elasticity of demand for imports of good i with respect to p_j; and α_i is $p_i M_i^c / Y$, the share of imports of good i in GNP. If we assume zero cross-elasticities of demand and supply,[9] then $\eta_{ij} = 0$ for $i \neq j$, and we obtain the following expression, which is a more general form of the simple formula derived in Equation (4) of Chapter 2:

$$\frac{EV}{Y} = -\frac{1}{2} \sum_i r_i^2 \eta_{ii} \alpha_i.$$

(25a)

It is worth emphasizing that these formulae are only approximations of the deadweight loss of the tariff system. They are used when there is insufficient information for an exact measure of welfare change to be derived (see Hausman, 1981), or when rough estimates are all that is required. The need to resort to approximations is greater when the changes being evaluated are large changes (such as the removal of all tariffs) because correct estimation requires knowledge of the full demand curve. However, valuation of small or incremental changes is not subject to this limitation; point estimates of elasticities are sufficient to compute the relevant welfare gains or losses. Accordingly, we now move on to consider the gains from various small changes in an existing set of tariffs. Total differentiation of Equation (23) yields

$$\frac{dEV}{Y} = -\frac{1}{Y} \sum_i \sum_j t_i S_{p_i p_j} dt_j = \sum_i \sum_j r_i \eta_{ij} \alpha_i \frac{dt_j}{p_j}. \tag{26}$$

Suppose that all tariffs t_i are reduced in the same proportion k (recall that such a uniform tariff reduction is necessarily welfare-improving if the tariffs in question are the only distortions in the economy). Then,

$$dt_i = -kt_i \quad \forall_i \quad k > 0$$

and the gain from tariff reduction as a percentage of GNP is

$$\frac{dEV}{Y} = k \sum_i \sum_j r_i r_j \eta_{ij} \alpha_i. \tag{27}$$

An alternative (but similar) tariff reduction rule involves reducing all the r_i in the same proportion. This is considered by Dixon (1978) and is defined as

$$dr_i = -kr_i \quad \forall_i \quad k > 0.$$

Now from the definition of r_j, we have[10]

$$\frac{dt_j}{p_j} = -\frac{kr_j}{1 - r_j}$$

which can be substituted in Equation (26) to yield the following expression for the gain from tariff reform as a percentage of Y:

$$\frac{dEV}{Y} = k \sum_i \sum_j \frac{r_i r_j \eta_{ij} \alpha_i}{1 - r_j}. \tag{28}$$

Equation (28) has much the same properties as Equation (27) and is a more general version of the formula derived as Equation (5) in Chapter 2. For the two-good model, a linear approximation yields the formula given in Chapter 2.

Finally, we consider the effect of reducing the highest tariff rate. Since the rates r_i are ranked in the same order of magnitude as the ad valorem rates τ_i, it is convenient to work in terms of reducing the highest r_i, say r_n. The methods used to derive Equation (18) are also applied here. Equation (26) becomes

$$\frac{dEV}{Y} = \frac{dt_n}{Y} \sum_i t_i S_{p_i p_n}$$

$$= \frac{dt_n}{Y} \sum_i r_i p_i S_{p_i p_n}$$

$$= \frac{dt_n}{Y} \sum_{i \neq n} (r_i - r_n) p_i S_{p_i p_n}$$

$$= \frac{dt_n}{p_n} \sum_{i \neq n} (r_i - r_n) \eta_{in} a_i \qquad (29)$$

which is an expression along the same lines as Equation (18) [and would resemble Equation (18) more closely if expressed in terms of τ_i rather than r_i].

Note that the formulae derived in this section all include compensated demand elasticities. Because such elasticities are not directly observable, they must either be approximated (by using elasticities of the uncompensated demands) or be constructed from the uncompensated substitution elasticities and income elasticities using the Slutsky equation. For a discussion of these two approaches, the reader is referred to Boadway and Bruce (1984). Alternatively, if there is sufficient information, the full compensated demand curve can be generated from the ordinary demand curve using duality methods.

The various formulae for welfare gains derived here are generalizations of the simple "triangle analysis" of Chapter 2 to the case of n goods. In fact, as we noted at the beginning of this section, various other gains and losses should be taken into account in any actual evaluation project. One effect which is readily taken into account in this framework is adjustment costs. As Leamer (1980) has pointed out, if adjustment costs arise in the context of voluntary unemployment (as analysed in the previous section), then correct estimation should yield a short-run supply curve which embodies any costs associated with inter-sectoral factor mobility. This would mean that any such adjustment costs are fully taken into account in the compensated import demand elasticities η_{ij}.

9.4   Summary

Given the political constraints on policy makers, it is inevitable that all tax reform will be taking place in a second-best world (i.e. one in which there are some "unalterable" distortions). One possible approach to reducing protection in such a situation is to set the variable tariffs or subsidies, at their second-best optimal levels given the levels of the unalterable distortions. Unfortunately, such an approach requires considerable information and there is no guarantee that the policy maker will arrive at the correct tariff levels. This difficulty has prompted a search for simple piecemeal rules which are known to be welfare improving for a wide range of parameter values, even though they may be a long way from a Pareto optimum. Two rules which have received particular attention are (i) equi-proportionate reduction of all trade taxes (or the *uniform reduction rule*) and (ii) reduction of the highest trade tax first (or the *harmonization rule*). Both are framed with the object of avoiding some of the more costly cross-effects which can occur in markets related to those subject to tax reduction. The uniform reduction rule is welfare improving under fairly innocuous conditions precisely because it reduces all distortions together and so also reduces the magnitude of any cross-effect losses. On the other hand, it does require that all distortions be reduced proportionately, and this may be difficult both for political reasons and because of the difficulty of identifying and/or quantifying all of the major distortions. More stringent conditions are required for the harmonization formula to be welfare improving. In the tariff case, these amount to the assumption that a reduction of the highest tariff causes net imports (compensated or uncompensated) to expand for those goods with higher tariff rates and to fall for goods with lower tariff rates. In this way, the by-product costs in related markets are minimized. A simple sufficient condition for the harmonization rule to have the desired outcome is that the good with the highest tariff be a net substitute for all other goods; this will ensure that the direct gain in the market in which the tariff is reduced swamps the other by-product costs in related markets. The condition is excessively strong, but its informational requirements are relatively slight. On the other hand, its violation tells us little; the rule might still work. Despite these reservations, it is encouraging that these piecemeal rules offer broad support for what has become a rule-of-thumb of many governments; the principle of systematically moving towards a more uniform tax structure.

Another important aspect of protection and tax reform is the question of how gradual the reform should be. In particular, do inter-sectoral adjustment costs justify incomplete or gradual reduction of tariffs? This question is a standard application of the theory of the second best and is succinctly framed in a two-period two-sector framework as follows: given an unalterable tariff in the importables sector in period 1 and assuming that workers lose labour time in moving between sectors (adjustment costs), at what level should the government set the tariff in period 2? If the tariff reduction in period 2 is unanticipated or if it is extremely difficult for factors to move between sectors, the answer is easy: by the end of period 1, allocation of workers between sectors is a bygone, so the optimal policy is complete tariff elimination in period 2 (i.e. tariff reduction in period 2 cannot affect the cost of an existing distortion in period 1, so there are no second-best considerations to worry about). On the other hand, if the tariff reduction is pre-announced and if factors are inter-sectorally mobile, the reduction will affect the allocation of factors between sectors in period 1 as well as period 2, and the choice of the period 2 tariff must take this cross-effect into account. It can then be shown that in the presence of adjustment costs, tariffs should not be eliminated completely in the second period provided the degree of complementarity between consumption in the two periods is not too high.

CHAPTER 10

Approaches to reducing protection II:
Multilateral reform

In this chapter, we turn from questions of unilateral reductions of protective barriers to the potentially more complex questions of multilateral reform. The literature on multilateral reform is extensive, ranging far beyond the scope of the present chapter. Here we shall reflect the emphasis in the theory and confine our attention to issues of tariff reform. In this respect, the theory has itself reflected the emphasis in the various rounds of GATT-sponsored trade negotiations, which have been notably more successful in securing tariff cuts than in removing (or, indeed, preventing the spread of) non-tariff barriers. Some reasons for this have already been offered in a political economy context in Chapter 8.

It is interesting to note that multilateral tariff reductions (MTRs) seem to have received considerably more attention in the literature than unilateral tariff reductions (UTRs). There are several reasons for this. In particular, while the simple idea of the gains from UTR can be succinctly stated in a model with one importable, the more interesting case of many goods and distortions was not thoroughly analysed until the 1970s when duality theory facilitated the developments surveyed in Section 9.1. On the other hand, problems of MTR (in particular the theory of customs unions) appeared less amenable to a unified framework. Indeed, such problems are inherently taxonomic, given the range of possible patterns of international trade and the sensitivity of results to the number of countries involved and the pattern of trade among them. For this reason, a voluminous literature developed examining various possible cases and issues (see Johnson, 1962; Kemp, 1969b; Lipsey, 1970; Meade, 1955b; Vanek, 1965; Viner, 1950).

The literature on MTR was given further impetus by the setting up of the European Economic Community (EEC) and by the various rounds of trade negotiations (the Kennedy round, the Tokyo round) conducted under the auspicies of GATT, with the high public interest and supply of research funds which these developments implied. In addition, there has been a pervasive feeling that MTR is more easily accomplished than UTR, and this has led trade policy theorists to devote considerable resources to an area in which they felt something might be accomplished. To some extent, the view of MTR as the "path of least resistance" was encouraged by the presence of institutional structures conducive to its achievement. However, ultimately such institutions must be a reflection of underlying views (and relative bargaining strengths) of countries (which are, in turn, a reflection of the views and relative strengths of pressure groups in those countries – see Chapter 8). For example, a government which reduces a tariff loses some support from the domestic import-competing industry protected by the tariff. However, if it can secure a reciprocal reduction in a foreign tariff, the resulting higher price (and/or greater market share) obtained by a domestic exporting industry induces greater support from the exporting lobby, and thus, at least partly offsets the loss of political support from the import-competing group.

Finally, there is the simple point that, in the context of trade between large countries, a country loses by unilaterally reducing its tariffs below their Nash-optimal level(s) (because of the resulting terms-of-trade deterioration); this is true even if all countries are in a Nash equilibrium in which all are worse off than under free trade. In such a case, gains can only be realized by a cooperative solution (i.e. MTR). It is therefore not surprising that, in a world economy dominated by a few large economies, MTR is a favoured approach which has received considerable attention from economic theorists.

Despite this emphasis in the literature, the main questions of multilateral reform can be dealt with by using the same analytical framework applied to questions of unilateral reform in Chapter 9. Here, we must allow for more than one country, but that is essentially the same as allowing for more than one consumer, something which is readily incorporated into the simpler model. It is also convenient to substitute one type of complexity for another; here we are less interested in the details of the tariff structure in each economy (fundamental to questions of piecemeal reform) and more concerned with differences in protection across countries. We also wish to allow trade taxes to differ according to the source (destination) of the imports (exports); however, this can be accomplished within our existing framework simply by classifying goods traded with different countries as different goods. In short, we are looking at essentially the same problem as was considered in the previous chapter: given that some tariffs (or other trade distortions) may be difficult to change (e.g. the external tariff imposed by the members of a customs union), what changes in other tariffs are welfare-improving for individual countries and/or groups of countries and/or the world as a whole?

Suppose the world consists of n economies, each with a single (or suitably aggregated) consumer. Each economy has its own preferences, production set (or transformation curve), expenditure and GNP functions (which satisfy the conditions stated in Section 9.1) and its own set of trade taxes. Functions, prices, taxes, and so on, for economy k are denoted by a k superscript; t_i^k is country k's tariff per unit on good i, while τ_i^k is the associated ad valorem tariff rate. In addition, each country k may or may not be constrained to balance its trade:

$$E^k(p^k, V^k) = g^k(p^k, v^k) + \sum_i t_i^k [C_i^k - X_i^k] \tag{1}$$

where p^k is the domestic price vector for country k, V^k is that country's utility, and so on. Equation (1) applies for each country only if lump-sum transfers between countries are not or cannot be used to achieve some desired equilibrium for a group of countries or the world as a whole. As before, the domestic price of good i in country k is related to the world price of good i by

$$p_i^k = p_i^* + t_i^k \qquad \forall_{i,\ k}. \tag{2}$$

Finally, we must add the following market-clearing condition for each good:

$$\sum_k S_{p_i}^k(p^k, V^k) = 0 \qquad \forall_i. \tag{3}$$

We shall begin by using this model to identify some welfare-improving tariff reform rules for the world economy. It is perhaps not surprising that the familiar rules of uniform tariff reduction and reducing the highest distortion first should appear once again.

10.1   Welfare-improving tariff-cutting formulae

Suppose that we wish to identify tariff reductions which are a Pareto improvement for the whole world economy and that lump-sum transfers between countries can be used to support such an improvement. Then individual countries' budget constraints of the form of Equation (1) are not relevant. To obtain the effects of changes in trade taxes, take total differentials of Equation (3) and use Equation (2) to obtain

$$\sum_k \sum_j S_{p_i p_j}^k [dp_j^* + dt_j^k] + \sum_k S_{p_i v} dV^k = 0 \qquad \forall_i. \tag{4}$$

Now assume, as in Hatta and Fukushima (1979), that there are n countries but only two commodities, goods 1 and 2. Let good 1 be the numeraire and suppose that the countries are numbered in increasing order of the tariff rate on good 2 – that is, country 1 has the lowest ad valorem tariff and country n the highest. Because only the tariffs and prices associated with good 2 are relevant, we shall omit the 2 subscript from these variables in this sub-section. Now, suppose that the utility levels of all countries except arbitrarily chosen country m are fixed and use Equation (4) to evaluate the effects of tariff reforms on the welfare of country m (bearing in mind that we have lump-sum taxes and subsidies at our disposal to prevent the other countries' utilities from falling). Setting

$$p_1^* = 1, \qquad p_2^* \equiv p^*, \qquad t_1^k = 0, t_2^k \equiv t^k, \qquad \forall_k$$
and $dV^k = 0$ for $k \neq m$.

We reduce Equation (4) to two equations determining the variables dV^m and dp^* as functions of the changes in the tariff rates dt^k. The solution for dV^m is derived in Appendix 6. We now consider the two most obvious types of reforms.

(a)   Equi-proportional reduction of all tariffs

Suppose $dt^k = -\alpha t^k$ for all k (where α is a positive constant). Then it is straightforward to show (see Appendix 6) that

$$dV^m = -\frac{\alpha}{\Delta} \sum_k \sum_{h<k} S^k_{p_2 p_2} S^h_{p_2 p_2} [t^k - t^h]^2 > 0 \tag{5}$$

where $\Delta < 0$ is the determinant of the system represented by Equation (4). Thus, an equi-proportional reduction of all tariffs represents a Pareto improvement for the world as a whole. The same is true for an equi-proportional reduction in all tariff rates (see Hatta and Fukushima, 1979).

(b)   Reduction of the highest tariff rate

If we set $dt^n < 0$, where country n is defined as having the highest tariff rate ($\tau^n \equiv t^n/p^*$), we obtain (see Appendix 6)

$$dV^m = \frac{p^* dt^n}{\Delta} \left\{ S^n_{p_2 p_2} \sum_h S^h_{p_2 p_2} (\tau^n - \tau^h) \right\} > 0 \tag{6}$$

since $\tau^n > \tau^h \; \forall_{h \neq n}$ by definition. Thus, reducing the highest tariff rate constitutes a Pareto improvement for the world economy.

Although we have only considered the case of two goods, it is possible to generalize these results to the case of many goods (see Fukushima and Kim, 1989; Turunen-Red and Woodland, 1987). It would also be nice to be able to show that results of this kind to not depend on the use of intercountry transfers; however, results along these lines have proved rather more elusive. Certainly, the foregoing analysis lends some rough theoretical support to the approaches which have been adopted in international trade negotiations such as the Kennedy and Tokyo rounds in which rules of this type were explicitly considered and debated (see Cline et al., 1977).

Of course, the process of negotiating reforms on a world scale is extremely difficult, requiring participation of all major trading countries. If, for example, countries with high levels of protection refuse to play their part in implementing a particular tariff-cutting rule, there is no guarantee that application of that rule to a cooperative subset of countries would yield a Pareto improvement. On the other hand, given the difficulties of securing agreement at the world level, it is not surprising that smaller groups of countries get together to reduce protective barriers on trade within the group while maintaining protection on trade with countries outside the group. We now turn to a consideration of how such preferential reductions in protection might affect the welfare of the participating countries and the world as a whole.

10.2   Preferential tariff reduction

Preferential reduction of protection can take many forms. It may simply involve a number of countries trading with each other at rates of protection lower than those applying to trade with countries outside the group. Because an arrangement of this type encompasses all classes of preferential trade, it is usual to describe such a group of countries as a *preferential trading club*. The British Commonwealth and the associated Commonwealth Preference System is a good example of a preferential trading club in the loosest sense. If we go further and require complete removal of trade barriers within the group but allow the countries in the group to set their own tariffs (or other restrictions) on trade with outside countries, we have what is known as a *free-trade area*. Real-world examples of free-trade areas include the European Free Trade Association (EFTA) and the Latin American Free Trade Area (LAFTA). A free-trade area in which all of the member countries impose a common set of tariffs on trade with outside countries is a *customs union*. The European Economic Community (EEC) is by far the best known example of a customs union; the East African Community (EAC) also fits into this category. If a customs union has no impediments to factor mobility between member countries then it is termed a *common market;* the EEC is in the process of moving into this category. An *economic union* is all of these with a central economic authority pursuing a common fiscal and monetary policy for the group; countries with a federal system of government (e.g. the United States, Canada and Australia) are clearly economic unions though they go further in having a central political authority (the federal government).

In what follows, we shall adhere to the tradition in the literature and confine our attention to customs unions. There are several good reasons for the emphasis given to customs unions. Essentially they are viewed as an attainable configuration with advantages not possessed by free-trade areas. The main difficulty with a free-trade area is that its members may have very different external tariff rates for the same commodity; if the countries in a group are in relatively close geographic proximity (e.g. Europe), such an arrangement may lead to commodity arbitrage within the group. It would thus appear that free-trade areas are really only sustainable where there are substantial costs (e.g. transport) associated with international arbitrage of commodities. In the absence of such costs, we might expect a free-trade area to evolve to something approximating a customs union with the emergence of a *common external tariff* (CET). Of course, the prominence of the EEC in policy discussions has also made the customs union the appropriate vehicle for analysis.

We therefore consider the following question. Can a group of countries, $k = 1, 2, \ldots, K$, gain (relative to an initial tariff-ridden equilibrium) by eliminating tariffs on trade among themselves and imposing a CET on trade with countries outside the group – that is, by forming a customs union? As Ohyama (1972) and Kemp and Wan (1976) have shown, the answer is in the affirmative if there are no restrictions on lump-sum transfers between the countries in the group and if the group's CET can be chosen appropriately. The idea is surprisingly simple. Suppose the group chooses a CET which yields the pre-union volume of trade (for each commodity) between the union as a whole and the outside world,[1] what Vanek (1965) refers to as the "compensating common tariff". In such a situation, market clearing for good i can be written

$$\sum_{k=1}^{K} S_{p_i}^k(p^k, V^k) = x_i(p^*) \qquad \forall_i \tag{7}$$

where $x_i(p^*)$ is the rest of the world's aggregate exports of good i in the pre-union situation, and p^* the pre-union vector of world prices.[2] Because p^* is unchanged, countries outside the union are made no worse off by the formation of the union. In addition, the customs union faces the same "endowment" of goods [the external trade vector $x(p^*)$] as before the union was formed. Assuming conditions which ensure the existence of a Pareto optimum, we know that such an optimum can be achieved at an internal price vector p^c, which is the same for all agents in the union – that is, free trade within the union. Given that potential losers can be compensated by lump-sum transfers within the union, this outcome will, in general, represent a Pareto improvement relative to the pre-union situation in which the group of countries faced the same initial endowment vector.[3] Thus, provided the CET can be chosen appropriately, and inter-country lump-sum transfers can be effected,[4] a customs union represents a Pareto improvement. The compensating common tariff equals $(p^c - p^*)$ per unit.

Kemp and Wan note a further interesting implication of this argument. Consider enlarging an existing customs union to include an additional country. Then Equation (7) can be written with the sum on the left-hand side extending from $k = 1$ to $k = K + 1$, and the exports of the remaining countries set at their level before the additional country was admitted to the union. Then the previous argument can be replicated to show that, in general, a Pareto improvement is the outcome of enlarging the membership of the union. Viewed in this way, the formation and expansion of a customs union can be viewed as a welfare-improving path towards free trade at a world level.

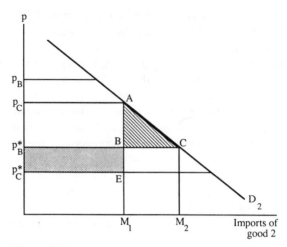

Figure 10.1

Although such results are reassuring, there is some reason to doubt that groups of countries can agree on the correct CET. In practice, the CET is usually derived as some sort of average of the countries' pre-union tariff rates, probably as the equilibrium outcome of a political contest between pressure groups in the different countries. It is not obvious that such a political equilibrium will involve a tax structure for which the customs union represents a Pareto improvement over the pre-union equilibrium. There would therefore appear to be some merit in considering the welfare effects of customs union formation taking the CET as given. Indeed, this has been the dominant approach in the literature dating back to the work of Viner (1950). One of the difficulties encountered by this literature has been the plethora of special cases and results which arise because of the need to specify the particular pattern of trade. The early models assumed three countries [two (A and B) in the union, one (C) outside] and two commodities. Subsequently, a model with three countries and three goods was developed by Meade (1955b) and refined by Vanek (1965) and Lipsey (1970). For a useful discussion of the relative properties of the 3 × 2 and 3 × 3 models, the reader is referred to Corden (1984) (pp. 112–124). Although most of our discussion will involve the Meade–Vanek–Lipsey model, the two-good model is a convenient starting point for introducing the much-discussed concepts of trade creation and trade diversion. Although these concepts were initially the subject of a rather protracted semantic debate, the ideas now seem quite straightforward and are readily explained here with the aid of Figure 10.1.

Country A (which exports good 1) has an import demand curve D_2 for good 2. Good 2 is produced under constant cost conditions in countries B and C with the unit cost being lower in C(p_C^* compared with p_B^*). Initially there are tariffs on A's imports from both B and C (p_B and p_C are the respective tariff-inclusive prices) with country A purchasing all of its imports of good 2 (M_1 in the diagram) from the low-cost country C. Now suppose the removal of the tariff on imports from the partner country B reduces the price faced by A's consumers and producers from p_C to p_B^*, leading to higher consumption, reduced production and higher imports of good 2 (M_2) in A. This is the so-called *trade creation effect*. It has an associated welfare gain which is given by the usual triangular area (*ABC*) associated with a domestic tariff reduction. On the other hand, the price fall in A means that good 2 is now imported entirely from B, the higher-cost source, at a higher c.i.f. import price to A (p_B^* rather than p_C^*); this is the *trade diversion effect* with a welfare cost to A equal to the original imports of good 2 times the increased cost per unit ($p_B^*BEp_C^*$ in Figure 10.1). Country A is then seen to benefit from the union if the trade creation effect outweighs the trade diversion effect (i.e. $ABC > p_B^*BEp_C^*$).

Having illustrated these concepts using the two-good model, we shall now move on to the richer possibilities offered by the 3 × 3 model. Although other variants of this model (assuming different trade patterns) have been developed (see Berglas, 1979; Collier, 1979; and Riezman, 1979), here we shall be content to use the Meade model to illustrate the main themes which have emerged in the literature. The interested reader is referred to Lloyd (1982) for a useful survey and synthesis of the various 3 × 3 models.

The model assumes that both countries in the customs union are small in world markets. There are no inter-country lump-sum transfers, so the trade balance condition of Equation (1) must hold for all countries. Each country in the union is completely specialized, producing one of the three goods and importing the other two. Letting A and B be the two partner countries in the customs union and C the outside country, suppose that A produces only good 1 (importing good 2 from B and good 3 from C), while B produces only good 2 (importing 1 from A and 3 from C). This trade pattern is symmetric, with each of the union partners importing one good from its partner and a common good (good 3) from the outside country. Thus, the question of whether union formation is welfare improving for each member country can be analysed in the same way for both members of the union. Here, we choose to look at the problem from the point of view of country A.

The basic principles are illustrated in Figure 10.2. Figure 10.2a shows country A's demand for imports of good 2 while Figure 10.2b shows A's demand for imports of good 3 (from country C). Suppose that in the pre-union equilibrium, A imposes tariffs on both goods, yielding domestic prices of p_2^A and p_3^A for goods 2 and 3, respectively (p_2^* and p_3^* being the respective world prices), and associated imports of M_{2D} and M_{3D}, respectively. Now, let countries A and B form a customs union, eliminating tariffs on their trade with each

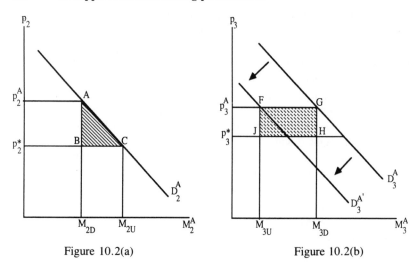

Figure 10.2(a)   Figure 10.2(b)

other but leaving the tariff on imports of good 3 (all of which come from the outside country) at its original level. Thus, in country A, the domestic price of good 2 falls to p_2^* while the price of good 3 remains p_3^A. In the case illustrated, goods 2 and 3 are net substitutes so that the fall in the price of good 2 shifts country A's compensated demand curve for imports of 3 to the left (from D_3^A to $D_3^{A'}$). A's imports of goods 2 and 3 change to M_{2U} and M_{3U}, respectively. Clearly, this is just a piecemeal reform exercise of the kind considered in the previous chapter (Figure 10.2 is formally identical to Figure 9.1). Whether country A gains or loses from the exercise depends on whether the net gain in consumer surplus resulting from the fall in p_2 (*ABC* in Figure 10.2a) is large enough to offset any increase in the cost of unaltered distortions on substitute goods (area *FGHJ* in Figure 10.2b if good 3 is a substitute). This, in turn, depends on the relative heights of the pre-union tariffs on goods 2 and 3 and the degree of substitutability or complementarity between the two markets (indeed, one advantage of the three-good model is that possibilities of complementarity enter the picture). The analysis of the first section of Chapter 9 applies exactly here, and all that is required is a reinterpretation in terms of the customs union problem.

At this stage, a word is in order about how the trade creation and trade diversion effects can be defined in the three-good case. So far as the terms have any meaning outside the two-good paradigm, it seems reasonable to define gain *ABC* in Figure 10.2a as the trade creation effect (the gain attributable to the fall in A's domestic price of good 2 and the associated increase in A's imports of that good from B), and area FGHJ in Figure 10.2b as the three-good version of the trade diversion effect. Where goods 2 and 3 are net substitutes (the case illustrated), this measures the welfare cost of the trade diverted from the outside country. However, if goods 2 and 3 are complements, then, in fact, trade between A and C is increased and the term *trade diversion* is misleading. Having noted this connection to the traditional literature, it is less confusing to eschew use of these terms and to follow the approach of McMillan and McCann (1981) (and, indeed the piecemeal reform literature) in emphasizing the complementarity or substitution relationships between the goods.

We now consider the effect on the welfare of country A of a small reduction in A's tariff on good 2 (t_2^A), holding the tariff on good 3 fixed[5] (we assume that both A and B impose the same initial tariff, t_3, on good 3 which automatically becomes the CET when the customs union is formed). Although this is an identical problem to that solved in Chapter 9, here we emphasize some different aspects of the results. Taking total differentials of Equation (1), we obtain the following variant of Equation (8) in the previous chapter:

$$H \frac{dV^A}{dt_2^A} = [t_2^A S_{P_2 P_2}^A + t_3 S_{P_3 P_2}^A] \tag{8}$$

where H is as defined in the previous chapter (with the summation extending from $i = 1$ to 3), and is positive if the Hatta stability condition is assumed. Note that the first term in brackets on the right-hand side of Equation (8) is always negative and represents the direct gain in the market where the tariff reduction has occurred (an incremental version of the triangle *ABC* in Figure 10.2a), while the second term tends to offset (reinforce) this welfare gain if goods 2 and 3 are net substitutes (complements).

Using the homogeneity of the compensated demand for good 2 [see Equation (15) in Chapter 9], Equation (8) can alternatively be written in terms of the ad valorem tariff rates, τ_3 and τ_2^A, as

$$H \frac{dV^A}{dt_2^A} = -\frac{1}{1 + \tau_3} [p_1^* \tau_3 S_{P_2 P_1}^A + p_2^* S_{P_2 P_2}^A (\tau_3 - \tau_2^A)]. \tag{8a}$$

Note that Equations (8) and (8a) relate to small reductions in the tariff on good 2 whereas a customs union involves elimination of that tariff.[6] Nevertheless, the two equations can be used to derive sufficient conditions for customs union formation to improve the welfare of country A.

Because we are interested in the conditions under which a complete removal of A's tariff on good 2 will raise welfare in A, it is not sufficient that dV^A/dt_2^A be negative – we require that the integral of this derivative (evaluated from the initial value of t_2^A to 0) be negative. Here we content ourselves with deriving sufficient conditions for $dV^A/dt_2^A < 0$ for all relevant t_2^A. Because the first term in brackets on the right-hand side of Equation (8) is negative (being the own-price effect), an obvious (but far too strong) sufficient condition for welfare improvement is that goods 2 and 3 be net complements. Indeed, such a condition is immediately obvious from the analysis of Figure 10.2; if goods 2 and 3 are net complements, then the demand curve in Figure 10.2b shifts out and the area *FGHJ* is an additional gain. In such a situation there is no "trade diversion" and no loss.

A less stringent condition can be obtained from Equation (8a); dV^A/dt_2^A is < 0 for all relevant t_2^A if

$$(p_1^* S_{p_2 p_1}^A + p_2^* S_{p_2 p_2}^A)\tau_3 > p_2^* S_{p_2 p_2}^A \tau_2^A \qquad \text{for all } \tau_2^A > 0. \qquad (9)$$

A sufficient condition for Equation (9) to hold is

$$p_1^* S_{p_2 p_1}^A > -p_2^* S_{p_2 p_2}^A. \qquad (9a)$$

In other words, the union makes A better off if goods 1 and 2 (the two goods figuring in intra-union trade) are sufficiently strong net substitutes over the relevant range of prices of good 2.

Of course, these conditions are overly sufficient, so their violation does not automatically imply that a customs union would make country A worse off. Nevertheless, the general thrust of the results is clear. Formation of the union is more likely to be beneficial to its members the closer net substitutes are to the goods traded within the union or the weaker the net substitutability is between the goods traded within the union and the good imported from the outside country. This accords with both the intuition of Figure 10.2 and the general wisdom in the literature; it is often said (see e.g. Johnson, 1962) that customs union formation will be more successful the more "similar" are the union members (i.e. if they produce goods which are close net substitutes for each other) and the greater the dissimilarity there is between the union members and the rest of the world (i.e. the weaker the net substitutability between goods produced in the union and goods produced outside).

Note that a welfare improvement can be achieved with weaker net substitutability between goods 1 and 2 if the pre-union value of τ_2^A exceeds τ_3. Inspection of Equation (8a) reveals that if $(\tau_3 - \tau_2^A)$ is initially negative, there is a range of values of τ_2^A for which the last term in brackets in Equation (8a) is positive, contributing to a welfare improvement for A when τ_2^A is reduced, thus lessening (but not removing) the net substitutes requirement on goods 1 and 2. The gain which is captured here has been identified by Corden (1976). It derives from the move towards a more uniform tariff structure represented by reducing τ_2^A to the level of τ_3. Of course, as τ_2^A is reduced below τ_3, this creates a new non-uniformity of tariff rates with an associated welfare loss [the last term in Equation (8a) being negative for $(\tau_3 - \tau_2^A) > 0$]. The degree of net substitutability required between goods 1 and 2 then depends on the initial dispersion of tariff rates, the level of τ_3 and the value of the own-price effect for good 2.

In the event that the move to a full customs union reduces the welfare of the participants, it is interesting to ask what, if any, tariff concessions are optimal behind the wall of a CET.[7] In particular, for country A, given t_3, what is the optimal value of t_2^A? Setting $dV^A/dt_2^A = 0$ in Equation (8), we obtain the second-best value of t_2^A as

$$t_2^A = -\frac{t_3 S_{P_3 P_2}^A}{S_{P_2 P_2}^A}. \tag{10}$$

Since the denominator of Equation (10) is negative, A's optimal tariff on imports from B is positive if and only if the good imported from B is a net substitute for the good imported from the rest of the world. To see whether any tariff concession at all benefits A, set $dV^A/dt_2^A = 0$ in Equation (8a) to obtain

$$\tau_3 - \hat{t}_2^A = -\frac{p_1^* t_3 S_{P_2 P_1}^A}{p_2^* S_{P_2 P_2}^A}. \tag{11}$$

Equation (11) tells us that if τ_3 and τ_2^A are initially equal, preferential trade benefits A if and only if the goods traded between A and B are net substitutes. Thus, even for small policy changes, complementarity of goods traded between particular countries works against gains from preferential trade between those countries.

So much for the effects of customs union formation and preferential trade on the welfare of country A. As indicated earlier, symmetric results apply for country B. Although this is reassuring, because it implies a likely commonality of interest between the potential union partners (particularly if they have similar preferences, etc.), it does raise a rather awkward question. If a country can gain by unilaterally reducing or eliminating its tariffs on imports with B, why should it go further and form a customs union with B (with the limits that such a union may impose on its future actions)? A popular answer to this question is that customs unions are formed for political reasons. Although there is no doubt much truth in this assertion, it is not a complete explanation, given that political motives often reflect economic forces. The question of why formation of a customs union might benefit the participant countries more than UTR was reopened by Wonnacott and Wonnacott (henceforth W&W) (1981) using a two-good model. Essentially, their point amounts to the usual argument for MTRs: a country which unilaterally reduces its tariff(s) worsens its own terms of trade, whereas if its tariff reduction is reciprocated by its trading partner, this adverse shift in its terms of trade is lessened or even reversed. Thus a customs union offers both participating countries a better terms of trade than either could expect from UTR.

Here the basic W&W argument is presented in the context of the Meade model. We begin by comparing a customs union with a preferential UTR (i.e. the UTR only involves reduction of the tariff on imports of the "partner"

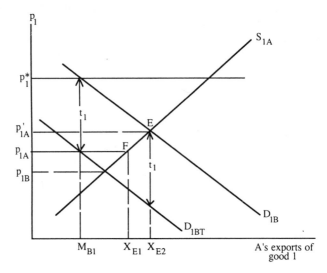

Figure 10.3

country's good). First, we must modify the Meade model to allow for terms-of-trade effects between A and B. As in W&W, we continue to assume that country C is large enough to determine the world prices at which A and B trade goods 1 and 2, so long as the good in question is traded with C. However, terms-of-trade effects involving these goods may arise if, say, a tariff reduction by A or B changes the pattern of trade with all exports of the good in question shifting to the partner country (i.e. the country which has reduced its tariff on the good). This outcome is possible if C's imports of the good are also subject to a tariff and/or transportation cost. Figure 10.3 illustrates this possibility and the associated gain to the exporting country.

The diagram graphs quantity against producer price for good 1. S_{1A} is country A's supply curve of exports of good 1, D_{1B} is country B's demand for imports of good 1 when its tariff on that good is zero, and D_{1BT} is its tariff-distorted demand curve. The world price of good 1 is determined by country C and is p_1^*. Suppose transport costs of shipping to C and C's tariff on imports of good 1 add up to t_1 per unit. For simplicity, we assume that this is the same as the tariff imposed by country B. Thus, in this initial distorted situation, country A receives p_{1A} per unit of good 1 if it sells some to C at price p_1^*, whereas it would only receive p_{1B} per unit if it confined its exports to B. Accordingly, it will sell at the world price p_1^*, exporting X_{E1} units, M_{B1} of them to B and the remainder to C.

Now let B remove its tariff. Its demand curve for imports of good 1 shifts up to D_{1B} so that A can now get p_{1A}' per unit (determined by the intersection of S_{1A}

and D_{1B} at E) if it sells all its exports (X_{E2}) to B. Thus, given the presence of the transport costs or tariff associated with exports to C (which hold the producer price from sales to C down to p_{1A}), the pattern of trade changes, with A exporting only to B at an improved terms of trade ($p'_{1A} > p_{1A}$) and an associated welfare gain given by area $p'_{1A}EFp_{1A}$ in Figure 10.3. This area represents an additional gain for A from bilateral tariff reduction and customs union formation compared with preferential unilateral tariff reduction. Of course, this is just a terms-of-trade gain resulting from a tariff reduction by a trading partner, and it would be commonplace in a standard large-country context (or if A and B never trade with C anyway). The interesting feature of the present example is the role of country C's tariff and/or transport costs, which are such as to exclude C as a trading partner with A so long as B does not also impose excessive impediments to trade. W&W cite the example of trade between the United Kingdom and Germany (countries A and B) with the United States (country C). Because the transport costs associated with shipping from Germany to the United States are higher than the costs of shipping from Germany to the United Kingdom, then ceteris paribus, Germany would do better to sell to the United Kingdom, particularly if the United States imposes tariffs. Such an advantage may not be realized if United Kingdom tariffs are too high, but will be realized if United Kingdom tariffs are removed. This implies that countries in close geographic proximity can gain by forming a customs union because they are then able to avoid the resource cost of shipping to more distant markets (and incurring the cost of tariffs imposed by large outsiders). Similar remarks could be made about Canada and the United States in terms of their trade with a country such as Japan, or about Australia and New Zealand in terms of their trade with the United States and Europe. Interestingly, Canada and the United States, and Australia and New Zealand have recently signed bilateral free-trade agreements.

The foregoing analysis compares a customs union with preferential UTR. If UTR is non-preferential (as it is usually taken to be in the literature on this issue, see Cooper and Massell, 1965), then it has the advantage of removing the tariff on imports from C (this is pure gain if we make the usual assumption that C is large enough to determine the price of its exports). Then the question of whether UTR is superior to a customs union depends on whether this advantage outweighs the intra-union terms-of-trade advantage of a customs union which we identified earlier. Clearly both outcomes are empirically (and theoretically) possible.[8]

Note that we have assumed that neither A nor B is large enough to influence its external terms of trade with country C. Nevertheless, it is possible that formation of a customs union by a group of countries may give them collective market power with respect to the outside world, which they do not possess as individual countries. This market power can be exercised by appropriate choice

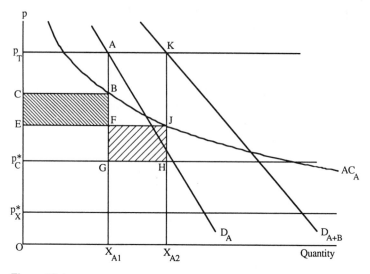

Figure 10.4

of the common external tariff to achieve additional gains for the member countries. Recall that appropriate choice of the CET was at the heart of the Kemp and Wan argument discussed earlier.

The preceding model also assumed competitive markets. If markets are oligopolistic, then, in the light of the rent-shifting effects of tariffs discussed in Chapter 6, there would appear to be additional gains (in the form of rents conceded by a country's union partner) from bilateral tariff reduction when compared with UTR. This aspect of "market swapping" does not appear to have been given a detailed treatment in the customs union literature, but its relevance in the present context should be clear.

Another aspect of non-competitive markets which is clearly important is economies of scale. Indeed, as we saw in Chapter 6, increased economies of scale are an empirically significant source of gain from reduced protection. To date they do not appear to have received much attention in the customs union literature, notable exceptions being Corden (1972); Johnson (1962); Pearson and Ingram (1980); and Viner (1950). Here we follow the approach of Corden in considering economies of scale which are internal to the firm. The effects of customs union formation in the presence of these scale economies is illustrated in a partial equilibrium framework in Figure 10.4. Clearly the natural taxonomy of customs union problems could be stretched even further here, but the particular case illustrated seems adequate to capture the main ideas. The new element introduced by the presence of scale economies is the reduction in unit cost which may occur if either A or B can expand production by selling to its partner country. On the other hand, the unit cost at which the partner country buys the good is still higher than if that country had imported it from C (a standard trade diversion effect) or had produced it itself with its producer earning positive rents (a rent-shifting effect).[9] Figure 10.4 illustrates the relevant trade-off for the union as a whole in the case in which the good is initially produced in country A but not in country B.

p_C^* is the (fixed) price at which the good in question can be imported from C (we continue to assume that countries A and B are small in world markets), and p_T is the tariff-inclusive price of those imports (for simplicity both A and B are assumed to impose the same pre-union tariff on imports of the good; the tariff on imports from C remains at this level after formation of the customs union). The f.o.b. price for exports to C (p_X^*) is assumed to be so low that such exports would never occur. In the pre-union situation, the good is produced by a monopolist in A but is not produced in B, which imports it from the lower-cost source (C). AC_A is the average cost curve in A, D_A is A's demand curve for the good and D_{A+B} is the horizontal sum of A's and B's demand curves.

Thus, the pre-union output of the good in A is X_{A1}, which is sold to A's consumers at price p_T yielding profits to A's producer of $p_T ABC$. B imports its supplies from C, with associated tariff revenue of $AKHG$. Formation of a customs union between A and B means that B no longer faces a tariff on imports from A; however, A's monopolist can capture the entire B market by pricing marginally below p_T. Assuming p_T to be the price charged by A, A's output increases from X_{A1} to X_{A2} (where p_T intersects D_{A+B}) with an associated fall in the unit cost of production to OE. Thus the rents accruing to the A producer increase by the area ($CBFE + AKJF$). On the other hand, B is unambiguously worse off because it is now paying p_T rather than p_C^* for each unit it imports – this loss equals B's foregone tariff revenue $AKHG$. Of this, the rectangle $AKJF$ is a transfer to rents in A. The net outcome for the customs union as a whole is a gain equal to ($CBFE - FJHG$); that is, the union gains via what Corden terms the "cost reduction effect" $CBFE$ but loses via the diversion of trade from the low-cost source C (at p_C^* per unit) to the higher-cost A (at OE per unit). Formation of the union only results in an overall welfare gain if the cost reduction effect outweighs the trade diversion effect. If this is the case, A would then have to bribe B to join such a union; in the absence of such transfers, B is unambiguously worse off as a result of lowering its tariff on imports from A.

On the other hand, even if adequate side-payments cannot be made, it is possible that the two countries may agree to form a union if B also has a decreasing cost industry which can expand its sales to A when tariffs are removed. This would be the case, for example, if there is intra-industry trade in differentiated products (see Chapter 7); however, it is a possibility in any situation in which both union partners have potential export industries exhibiting economies of scale. Then, whether a particular country elected to join the union would depend on whether the increase in its rents from exporting to its partner was sufficient to offset the loss of tariff revenue on its (diverted) imports. Considerations of this type are taken into account in a study by Pearson and Ingram (1980) of the economic effects of formation of a customs union involving Ghana and the Ivory Coast. Using a variant of the Corden model which also allows for significant domestic distortions in each country's good and factor markets, they estimate that both countries would reap significant welfare gains from such a union – a welfare gain for Ghana of about 33 per cent of GNP and the for the Ivory Coast about 22 per cent of GNP.

We have considered two approaches to multilateral tariff reform: the search for welfare-improving rules for tariff reduction and preferential tariff reduction among a group of countries. Of course, any such reforms have to be negotiated among the relevant parties, so it is appropriate that we now consider what outcomes might emerge from the negotiation process.

10.3   Negotiated tariff reductions

Despite the vast literature on the various rounds of trade negotiations, very little has been written on the theory of tariff negotiations[10] (notwithstanding the large body of relevant microeconomic theory – for example, game theory, the theory of the core). In this section we use the model of Mayer (1981) to say something about the types of reforms which are likely to be favoured by the negotiation process.

Assume a two-good world consisting of two large countries, each of which chooses its Nash-optimal tariff (i.e. taking the other country's tariff as given). Figure 10.5a, which is based on Figure 4.5, illustrates the two countries' reaction curves in tariff space, where t^A and t^B are the tariffs of countries A and B, respectively, $t^A(t^B)$ is country A's reaction curve, and so on. There is assumed to be a unique non-cooperative Nash equilibrium in tariffs at N with the indifference curves through N labelled u^{AN} and u^{BN} for countries A and B, respectively.

It is clear from Figure 10.5a that both parties can gain from negotiation. Since u^{AN} and u^{BN} intersect at right angles, there is a non-empty area of tariff combinations which are Pareto-superior to N. These are the points to the southwest of N bounded by u^{AN}, u^{BN} and the locus CC – that is, the area NEF in Figure 10.5a. CC represents the locus of Pareto optimal combinations of t^A and t^B. Clearly, the free-trade point O must lie on CC as must all points for which domestic relative prices are the same in both countries. To maintain domestic relative prices equal in the two countries, an increased tariff in one country cannot be accompanied by a higher tariff in the other country (because this would drive the domestic relative prices further apart), it must be associated with an increased import subsidy in the other country. Thus CC passes through

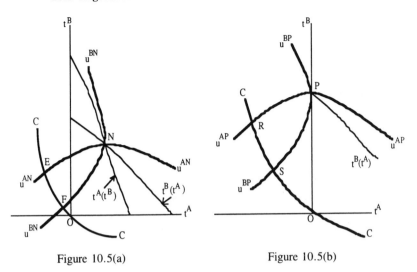

Figure 10.5(a)   Figure 10.5(b)

O and is negatively sloped.[11] EF represents the segment of CC which is attainable by collusion between the two countries bargaining from point N. Note that free trade may or may not be an attainable outcome. In Figure 10.5a, O is excluded from the attainable set; this corresponds to the situation noted in Chapter 4 in which one country (in this case B) gains from a tariff war.

Assuming that collusion is successful in extracting all the available gains, the final outcome is somewhere on the curve segment EF. This means that if free trade is not attained, the outcome involves one country imposing a tariff and the other country imposing an import subsidy. This observation has interesting implications if one of the countries, say country A, is small. Then its non-cooperative Nash-optimal tariff is zero, and its reaction curve is the vertical axis in Figure 10.5b. The non-cooperative Nash equilibrium is then at P with country B imposing its optimal tariff. In this case, a cooperative solution lies on the curve segment RS, bounded by the indifference curves u^{AP} and u^{BP} through P. Such an outcome necessarily involves the small country subsidizing its imports in exchange for tariff reduction by the large country. This is in marked contrast to the usual result that the optimal tariff for a small country is zero, a result which is derived in the context of a noncooperative game.

In fact, outcomes such as those predicted by this analysis are rarely observed. The major rounds of trade negotiations have favoured the use of tariff cutting formulae of the kind analysed in Section 10.1, and, indeed, an important part of these negotiations has been to reach agreement on which rule should be used. There are many possible reasons for this approach. The most obvious reason is that each national government is constrained by pressure groups in its own country and is therefore forced to opt for a simple piecemeal rule of some

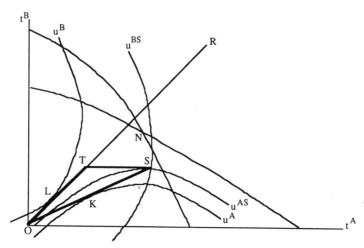

Figure 10.6

kind. Two such alternative proposals which were prominent in the Kennedy and Tokyo rounds of trade negotiations were (i) reduction of all tariffs by the same percentage and (ii) larger percentage reduction of higher tariff rates. As we saw in Section 10.1, both types of rules are a Pareto improvement in a two-good world in which there are no impediments to inter-country transfers. Figure 10.6 illustrates how the use of such rules may affect the outcome in a collusive equilibrium without lump-sum transfers between countries.

As before, N is the non-cooperative Nash equilibrium; however, the two countries' initial tariff point is at S (possibly arrived at in previous negotiations). Here we assume that the basis of the negotiations is that tariffs will not be increased above their levels at S. This means that S is the "threatpoint" for the players, and N is irrelevant to the outcome. For purposes of illustration it is assumed that country A has higher tariffs than country B (i.e. S is below and to the right of the 45° line through the origin). The ray SKO is the locus of tariff combinations satisfying a uniform (or linear) reduction rule of the form

$$dt^k = -\alpha t^k \qquad \text{for } k = \text{A, B}$$

as considered in Section 10.1. In contrast, locus $STLO$ represents a tariff-cutting rule in which the highest (in this case, higher) tariff is reduced to the level of the second highest (the move from S to T) and then both countries' tariffs are reduced in the same proportion (along ray OT).[12] It is immediately clear that country A will argue for adoption of the uniform reduction rule SKO because it allows A to attain higher utility levels (lower indifference curves u^A) than are possible along the locus $STLO$. Similarly, B may be seen to prefer the rule which reduces the highest tariffs first. Interestingly, as noted by Mayer, this corresponds to the positions taken by the United States and the E.E.C. in the

Kennedy and Tokyo rounds. The United States, with a higher average tariff rate, favoured the uniform–linear tariff reduction rule, whereas the E.E.C. pressed for faster reduction of higher tariffs.

Now suppose that the parties have agreed on the tariff-cutting rule which is to be used, but have yet to negotiate the size of the cuts under the rule (e.g. the magnitude of α in the uniform reduction rule). What outcomes are likely? Unfortunately, the answer to this question depends very much on the curvature of each country's indifference curves, the position of the initial point S, and so on. Nevertheless, it seems likely that only a part of the locus for each rule will be a collusive equilibrium. Segments on either locus where there are mutual gains from moving along the locus are not equilibrium points. In the case illustrated, if the uniform reduction rule (SKO) is used, both countries stand to gain by reducing tariffs along the segment SK. At point K, A's welfare is maximized subject to the rule (i.e. u^A is tangent to SKO at K). Thus, tariff combinations along the segment OK are possible equilibria in the sense that neither country can be made better off without making the other country worse off.

On the other hand, if the rule of reducing the highest tariff first ($STLO$) is applied, then in Figure 10.6 as drawn, country A stands to lose from any tariff reduction (i.e. any point to the left of S), while both countries stand to lose from tariff reductions in the segment OL where L is B's rule-constrained optimum. Thus, the cooperative equilibrium lies along the segment LTS. The case illustrated has another interesting feature: it appears to yield a dominant rule. Because A can only lose from the implementation of the harmonization rule whereas both countries can gain under the uniform reduction rule, we would expect the uniform reduction rule to be adopted. In general, however, both rules (and indeed, other rules) offer a region of gains for both parties, so the choice of rule is not so straightforward.

It is clear from the foregoing analysis that the constraints imposed by tariff-cutting rules of the type commonly considered in major trade negotiations reduce the set of likely outcomes to a range of positive tariff rates (and possibly free trade). The tariff and import subsidy combinations identified in Figure 10.5 are ruled out here, and the resulting collusive equilibria more closely resemble what is actually observed. Of course, what the theory has not explained is why tariff-cutting rules of this kind should be the outcome of the negotiating process and/or the political process within countries; after all, if these real-world rules were omitted from the model, the final outcome would be less realistic. We know (Section 10.1) that, under certain conditions, rules of the kind being considered here are a Pareto improvement over an initial distorted equilibrium; however, that does not guarantee that they will be adopted or even considered. Why they should be favoured in international trade negotiations is a further interesting question for endogenous protection theorists.

In the preceding analysis, we have confined our attention to tariff reform. This emphasis is not misplaced because, to date, trade negotiations have had considerable success in achieving tariff cuts, while they have conspicuously failed to attack non-tariff barriers to trade. Indeed, as tariffs have been negotiated to extremely low levels, non-tariff distortions have become increasingly widespread and pernicious. In Chapter 8 we attempted to explain why the political process might favour the adoption of non-tariff barriers such as import quotas and VERs, with risk aversion on the part of economic agents emerging as the most likely reason. Of course, the analysis in Chapter 8 was confined to a unilateral political-markets view of protection. We now consider the same question from a bilateral point of view using an extension of the Mayer model due to Copeland (1989).

To allow for the presence of several types of trade restrictions (rather than just tariffs) we relabel the axes in Figure 10.5, with the two countries' tariff levels replaced by their respective "protection levels", a composite measure of the protection offered by the whole range of available instruments. It then follows that mutual gains can be realized by moving from the non-cooperative Nash equilibrium N to a cooperative equilibrium on the curve segment EF in Figure 10.5a – a negotiated reduction in each country's protection level. However, because of information and transactions costs, it is unlikely that countries will negotiate reductions in the levels of all instruments. Instead, they will agree to reduce those alterable distortions which are less costly at the margin and leave more costly distortions to be set non-cooperatively. For purposes of illustration, suppose that tariffs are less costly than quotas and that the two countries agree on binding tariff cuts. Because the national governments are now constrained in their ability to use tariffs to protect their domestic industries, they will resort to use of quotas. However, because the marginal cost of protection under quotas is higher than it was under tariffs, the level of protection used will be lower than it was before tariff levels were constrained by an international agreement. Put simply, the purpose of the negotiations is to restrict the use of one group of instruments, thereby forcing governments to resort to more costly distortions which they will be reluctant to set at such high levels. The levels of the negotiated instruments are set in anticipation of the subsequent non-cooperative game involving the unconstrained instruments. The outcome is lower protection levels even though it may appear that the negotiations are "not working" because one set of trade restrictions is being replaced by another. This explanation of events offers an appealing resolution of the mystery of why governments have systematically negotiated tariff cuts only to put VERs, import quotas and similar restrictions in their place.

10.4   Summary

In this chapter, we have seen how the piecemeal reform approach to tariff reduction can be extended to the area of multilateral reform. In particular, equi-proportional reduction of all tariffs and reduction of the highest tariff first were seen to yield a Pareto improvement for a two-good, many-country world. This offers some theoretical support for the prominence of formulae of this type in the Kennedy and Tokyo rounds of trade negotiation.

Given the many difficulties associated with reducing protection at a world level, smaller numbers of countries will frequently find it to their advantage to form preferential trading clubs. The most widely analysed such arrangement is the customs union, in which free trade among the member countries is combined with a common external tariff (CET) imposed on imports from outside the group. If there are no impediments to lump-sum transfers between countries, it is always possible for a group of countries to achieve a Pareto improvement by forming a customs union, provided the common external tariff is set at an appropriate level. Where political and other considerations constrain the choice of the external tariff, it is possible that formation of a customs union may lead to a lower level of welfare than in the pre-union distorted situation. Such a possibility is a simple consequence of the theory of the second best; faced with an unalterable distortion (the external tariff), removal of other distortions (the internal tariffs) can reduce welfare. In the presence of a given CET, formation of a customs union is more likely to be beneficial to its members if the goods they produce are close substitutes for one another and poor substitutes for goods produced by countries outside the union. Finally, it is to be noted that the presence of economies of scale is likely to considerably enhance the benefits from union formation.

A further interesting question in the context of multilateral reform is what types of policies are likely to be the outcome of trade negotiations, that is, what does a cooperative equilibrium look like? In a two-country model, if there are no constraints on the choice of tariff levels and the initial equilibrium is a non-cooperative Nash equilibrium, all of the available gains from collusion will be exploited either by free trade or by one country imposing a tariff and the other country an import subsidy. In addition, if one of the countries is small, that country can gain by agreeing to subsidize its imports, a result in marked contrast to the standard prescription for non-cooperative optimality for small countries (i.e. a zero tariff). In practice, trade negotiations seem to proceed by considering a limited number of tariff-cutting formulae. If this approach is used, the negotiated outcome is quite different from that just described, with positive tariff levels likely for both countries. An interesting unanswered question is why the participants in tariff negotiations choose to constrain the bargaining set by supporting particular reform rules.

A peculiar anomaly of world protectionism in the 1970s and 1980s is the way in which systematic negotiated tariff reductions have been accompanied by a proliferation of other forms of protection, most notably quantitative trade restrictions. One explanation of this phenomenon is that agreeing to restrict use of less costly forms of trade restriction (e.g. tariffs) drives up the marginal cost of protection (by forcing governments to resort to instruments with a higher marginal social or political cost) and thus leads to a mutually beneficial reduction in overall protection levels for all countries.

Appendices

The two-sector trade model

(a)   Consumers

The model assumes that the community's utility is given by a strictly concave function $u(C_F, C_C)$ of aggregate consumption of food and cloth (C_F and C_C, respectively) which is strictly increasing in both arguments; u is also assumed to have continuous second-order partial derivatives.

Optimization by consumers leads to C_F and C_C being chosen to maximize u subject to the budget constraint

$$Y = p_F C_F + p_C C_C \tag{A1}$$

where p_F and p_C are the prices of food and cloth faced by consumers (and producers), and Y is national income valued at domestic prices.

(b)   Production

The economy produces food (X_F) and cloth (X_C) using capital and labour. K_i and L_i denote the capital and labour inputs into sector i (i = F, C). Both sectors have strictly concave production functions (F and H for food and cloth, respectively) which are homogeneous of degree 1 in the inputs (constant-returns-to-scale) and have continuous second-order partial derivatives. These production functions are given by

$$X_F = F(L_F, K_F) = L_F f(k_F) \tag{A2}$$

$$X_C = H(L_C, K_C) = L_C h(k_C) \tag{A3}$$

where $k_i \equiv K_i/L_i$ (i = F, C), and the functions f and h represent the outputs of food and cloth per unit of labour input. Their use in Equations (A2) and (A3) reflects the assumption of constant-returns-to-scale. The properties assumed for F and G imply that f and g have the following standard derivative properties:

$$f', h' > 0 \qquad f'', h'' < 0.$$

The economy has given factor endowments of L units of labour and K units of capital. It is assumed that labour and capital can both move freely between the two sectors. Thus, the conditions for full employment of both factors are

$$L_F + L_C = L \tag{A4}$$

$$K_F + K_C = K. \tag{A5}$$

Factor markets are assumed to be competitive, so labour and capital are allocated between the two sectors so as to equate the value of the marginal product of a particular factor in both sectors to the price of the factor; that is,

$$w = p_F[f(k_F) - k_F f'(k_F)] = p_C[h(k_C) - k_C h'(k_C)] \tag{A6}$$

$$r = p_F f'(k_F) = p_C h'(k_C) \tag{A7}$$

where w is the wage rate and r is the rental rate per unit of capital. Equations (A6) and (A7) imply the following equations for the wage–rental ratio ($\omega \equiv w/r$):

$$\omega = [f(k_F) - k_F f'(k_F)]/f'(k_F) = [h(k_C) - k_C h'(k_C)]/h'(k_C) \tag{A8}$$

Differentiating Equation (A8) with respect to ω yields

$$\frac{dk_i}{d\omega} > 0, \qquad i = F, C$$

which establishes a positive slope for the relationship between capital–labour ratios and relative factor prices illustrated in Figure 1.5.

The assumption of competitive product markets implies that in long-run equilibrium, profits are zero. These zero-profit conditions can be written in terms of the f and g functions as

$$p_F f(k_F) = w + r k_F \tag{A9}$$

$$p_C h(k_C) = w + r k_C. \tag{A10}$$

Finally, we consider how national income is derived from the producer problem. Equations (A2) through (A7) can, in principle, be solved to obtain the locus of efficient outputs for the economy (i.e. the production possibilities frontier). This can be written in the form

$$\phi(X_F, X_C, K, L) = 0 \tag{A11}$$

where it can be shown that ϕ is a strictly convex function of X_F and X_C if $k_F \neq k_C$. Given that competitive producers all face the same prices, their optimizing behaviour will be to choose the allocation of outputs between sectors so as to maximize the total value of output subject to Equation (A11), for the given prices p_F and p_C and the economy's given factor endowments K and L. In the absence of any taxes, subsidies and so on (and associated transfers), Y in the consumer budget constraint will then be equal to the GNP function which is defined as

$$g(p_F, p_C, K, L) \equiv \max_{X_F, X_C} \{p_F X_F + p_C X_C : \phi(X_F, X_C, K, L) = 0\}. \quad (A12)$$

To solve the problem implicit in Equation (A12), we define the Lagrangean

$$\mathcal{L} = p_F X_F + p_C X_C + \lambda \phi(X_F, X_C)$$

where λ is the Lagrange multiplier attached to the economy's production feasibility constraint, Equation (A11). The first-order conditions for this optimization problem are

$$\frac{\partial \mathcal{L}}{\partial X_F} = p_F + \lambda \phi_F = 0 = p_C + \lambda \phi_C = \frac{\partial \mathcal{L}}{\partial X_C},$$

where

$$\phi_F \equiv \frac{\partial \phi}{\partial X_F}, \phi_C \equiv \frac{\partial \phi}{\partial X_C}$$

which implies

$$\frac{p_F}{p_C} = \frac{\phi_F}{\phi_C}$$

that is, the condition that the MRT in production equals the ratio of producer prices, as reflected in the tangency between the production frontier and the producer price ratio. Using the envelope theorem, we also obtain

$$\frac{\partial g}{\partial p_F} = X_F \qquad \frac{\partial g}{\partial p_C} = X_C \qquad (A13)$$

a frequently used property of the GNP function which we use in a more general form in Chapters 9 and 10. Differentiating Equation (A13) with respect to p_F and p_C and using the first-order conditions and the strict convexity of ϕ, we can show that g is a strictly convex function of the prices (p_F, p_C). Using Equation (A13) and Euler's theorem, we can also show that g is homogeneous of degree 1 in (p_F, p_C); that is,

$$p_F \frac{\partial g}{\partial p_F} + p_C \frac{\partial g}{\partial p_C} = p_F X_F + p_C X_C = g.$$

(c)   General equilibrium and community welfare

We assume no distortions such as taxes or subsidies. Also, let cloth be the numeraire so that $p_C \equiv 1$. Let $p_F \equiv p$. Then, with the GNP function as defined in Equation (A12) substituted into the economy's budget constraint for Y, the consumer optimization problem may be written as

$$\max_{C_F, C_C} u(C_F, C_C) \qquad \text{subject to} \qquad pC_F + C_C = g(p, K, L). \qquad (A14)$$

The Lagrangean for this problem is

$$\mathscr{L} = u(C_F, C_C) + \mu[g(p, K, L) - pC_F - C_C]$$

where μ is the Lagrange multiplier attached to the economy's budget constraint. The first-order conditions to this problem are

$$\frac{\partial \mathscr{L}}{\partial C_F} = u_F - \mu p = 0 = u_C - \mu = \frac{\partial \mathscr{L}}{\partial C_C} \Rightarrow \frac{u_F}{u_C} = p,$$

where

$$u_F \equiv \frac{\partial u}{\partial C_F}, \ u_C = \frac{\partial u}{\partial C_c}$$

which is the usual tangency condition for consumers (i.e. MRS = price ratio). Note also that $\mu = u_F/p > 0$.

Now define the following reduced-form indirect utility function

$$V(p, K, L) \equiv \max_{C_F, C_C} \{u(C_F, C_C) : pC_F + C_C = g(p, K, L)\}.$$

The strict convexity of g and the strict concavity of u can be used to deduce that V is strictly convex in p. In addition, using the envelope theorem in the consumer problem, we obtain

$$\frac{\partial V}{\partial p} = \mu \left(\frac{\partial g}{\partial p} - C_F \right) = \mu(X_F - C_F) \gtrless 0 \text{ according to whether } X_F \gtrless C_F.$$

$$(A15)$$

It follows from Equation (A15) and the strict convexity of V that the autarky equilibrium (where $X_F = C_F$ and hence $\partial V/\partial p = 0$) is a utility minimum – that is, any change in relative prices away from the level required to clear each domestic market makes the community better off. This is a simple demonstration of the gains from trade which were illustrated in Figure 1.3b. Equation (A15) also shows how an economy benefits by an increase in the relative price of its exportable (i.e. an improvement in its terms of trade); if cloth is the exportable, then $X_F < C_F$ and $\partial V/\partial p < 0$, implying that a rise in the relative price of cloth (a fall in p) raises community welfare.

(d) The Stolper–Samuelson theorem:

Dividing the zero-profit conditions, Equations (A9) and (A10), by p_F yields

$$f(k_F) = \frac{w}{p_F} + k_F \left(\frac{r}{p_F} \right) \tag{A9a}$$

$$h(k_C) = p \left[\left(\frac{w}{p_F} \right) + k_C \left(\frac{r}{p_F} \right) \right] \tag{A10a}$$

which are the respective equations of the *FF* and *CC* curves in Figure 1.6. *FF* is seen to have slope $(-k_F)$ while *CC* has slope $(-k_C)$, verifying the form of the curves in the diagram. Differentiating Equations (A9a) and (A10a) with respect to p and using Equation (A7) yields

$$\frac{d(w/p_F)}{dp} + k_F \frac{d(r/p_F)}{dp} = 0$$

$$p \frac{d(w/p_F)}{dp} + p k_C \frac{d(r/p_F)}{dp} = - \frac{h(k_C)}{p}.$$

Solving these two equations, we obtain

$$\frac{d(w/p_F)}{dp} = \frac{k_F h(k_C)}{p^2 (k_C - k_F)} < 0 \qquad \text{since } k_F > k_C$$

$$\frac{d(r/p_F)}{dp} = \frac{-h}{p^2 (k_C - k_F)} > 0.$$

Thus an increase in the relative price of food reduces the real return to labour and increases the real return to capital. It is left to the reader to check that these results are unaffected if the real factor returns are measured in cloth units.

(e) Factor endowments and outputs:

The factor employment conditions, Equations (A4) and (A5), can be rewritten as

$$\frac{1}{f(k_F)} \left(\frac{X_F}{L} \right) + \frac{1}{h(k_C)} \left(\frac{X_C}{L} \right) = 1 \tag{A4a}$$

$$\frac{k_F}{f(k_F)} \left(\frac{X_F}{L} \right) + \frac{k_C}{h(k_C)} \left(\frac{X_C}{L} \right) = k \equiv \frac{K}{L} \tag{A5a}$$

where k_F and k_C are fixed since fixed p implies fixed w and r. Differentiating Equations (A4a) and (A5a) with respect to k gives the following solutions:

$$\frac{d(X_F/L)}{dk} = \frac{f(k_F)}{k_F - k_C}; \qquad \frac{d(X_C/L)}{dk} = - \frac{h(k_C)}{k_F - k_C}. \tag{A16}$$

First, note that if both goods are produced, then $k_F > k > k_C$. Second, if L is constant, then X_F and X_C move in the same direction as X_F/L and X_C/L, respectively. Then $k_F > k_C$ implies that X_F rises and X_C falls in response to a rise in the economy's capital stock (Rybczynski's theorem). More generally, we can deduce from Equation (A16) that

$$\frac{d(X_F/X_C)}{dk} = \frac{1}{(X_C/L)^2} \left[\frac{X_C}{L} \frac{d(X_F/L)}{dk} - \frac{X_F}{L} \frac{d(X_C/L)}{dk} \right]$$

$$= \frac{1}{(X_C^2/L)} \frac{1}{k_F - k_C} [X_C f(k_F) + X_F h(k_C)] > 0 \qquad \text{since } k_F > k_C.$$

Thus a rise in k causes the output of the capital-intensive sector to increase relative to that of the labour-intensive sector as claimed in the text.

(f)   Trade-indifference curves

Let $M_F = C_F - X_F \equiv$ imports of food; $E_C = X_C - C_C \equiv$ exports of cloth. Define

$$B(M_F, E_C, K, L) \equiv \max_{C_i, X_i} \{u(C_F, C_C) : M_F = C_F - X_F, E_C = X_C - C_C,$$
$$\phi(X_F, X_C, K, L) = 0\}$$

as the *Meade trade utility function* derived from u. For given K and L we shall omit the factor endowments as arguments. Then $B(M_F, E_C) = u$ (constant) is a *trade-indifference curve* derived from the consumption-indifference curve, $u(C_F, C_C) = u$. If we apply the envelope theorem to the Lagrangean for the constrained optimization problem defining B, we find that $B_M = u_F$, $B_E = -u_C$ ($B_M \equiv \partial B / \partial M_F$, etc.) and

$$\left(\frac{dM_F}{dE_C} \right)_{B=u} = \frac{u_C}{u_F} > 0 \qquad\qquad\qquad (A17)$$

So the trade-indifference curves are upward sloping in the (E_C, M_F) plane. In addition, differentiating Equation (A17), we obtain

$$\left(\frac{d^2 M_F}{dE_C^2} \right)_{B=u} = \frac{1}{(u_F)^3} [u_F, \ u_C] \begin{bmatrix} -u_{CC} & -u_{CF} \\ -u_{FC} & -u_{FF} \end{bmatrix} \begin{bmatrix} u_F \\ u_C \end{bmatrix} > 0$$

which, given the usual assumptions used to guarantee strict concavity of u [$u_{CC}, u_{FF} < 0$ and $(u_{CC}u_{FF} - u_{CF}u_{FC}) > 0$], is a positive definite quadratic form. Hence, $d^2 M_F/dE_C^2 > 0$ along $B = u$. Thus the trade-indifference curves possess the convex form shown in Figure 1.10 in the text.

(g)   Offer curves

The offer curve is derived by choosing quantities traded so as to maximize utility subject to the balance of trade constraint:

$$pM_F - E_C = 0.$$

This problem can be stated as

$$\max_{M_F, E_C} B(M_F, E_C) \quad \text{subject to} \quad pM_F - E_C = 0.$$

The Lagrangean for this problem is

$$\mathcal{L} = B(M_F, E_C) + \lambda(pM_F - E_C)$$

with associated first-order conditions,

$$-\frac{B_M}{p} = \lambda = B_E \Rightarrow p = -\frac{B_M}{B_E}. \tag{A18}$$

Equation (A18) defines the home country's offer curve as the locus of tangencies between the trade-indifference curves and terms-of-trade lines. From the balance of payments constraint it can also be written (omitting subscripts from exports and imports) as

$$\frac{E}{M} = -\frac{B_M}{B_E} \tag{A18a}$$

and, as such, defines the offer curve as a locus in the (E, M) plane.

With the balance-of-payments constraint and the implicit relationship $E = R(M)$, defined by Equation (A18a), it is straightforward to determine the slope of the offer curve $[R'(M)]$ in terms of the elasticity of demand for imports.

Differentiating the balance-of-payments constraint, we have

$$M + p\frac{dM}{dp} - R'(M)\frac{dM}{dp} = 0.$$

That is,

$$R'(M) = \frac{M}{dM/dp}[1 - \varepsilon_M], \quad \text{where} \quad \varepsilon_M \equiv -\frac{p}{M}\frac{dM}{dp}.$$

Assuming food to be non-inferior, we have $dM/dp < 0$ (see text). It then follows that

$$R'(M) \gtreqless 0$$

according to whether $\varepsilon_M \gtreqless 1$ as claimed in the text.

Optimal policies in the presence of "non-economic" objectives

We now go beyond the simple two-good model analysed in Appendix 1 and consider an economy which produces n traded goods in quantities $X_1, \ldots, X_n$ and consumes them in quantities $C_1, \ldots, C_n$. The economy wishes to choose the C_i and the X_i and, if it is a large country the world prices of these goods, $p_1^*, p_2^*, \ldots, p_n^*$, to maximize the community utility function

$$u(C_1, C_2, \ldots, C_n)$$

subject to a number of constraints. These are the following:

i. *The economy's balance-of-trade constraint:*

$$\sum_{i=1}^{n} p_i^* (C_i - X_i) = 0. \tag{A19}$$

ii. *The economy's transformation function:*

$$\phi(X_1, X_2, \ldots, X_n) = 0. \tag{A20}$$

iii. *A "non-economic" objective:*
This is an objective which constrains the variables $C_1, \ldots, C_n$ and $X_1, \ldots, X_n$ in some (as yet unspecified) way; that is,

$$K(C_1, \ldots, C_n, X_1, \ldots, X_n) \geq 0. \tag{A21}$$

iv. *A market-clearing condition for each good:*

$$C_i - X_i = R^i(p_1^*, p_2^*, \ldots, p_n^*) \tag{A22}$$

where R^i is the rest of the world's net export function for good i (equivalently the import supply curve faced by the home country). Note that if the home country is small, it can buy or sell as much as it likes at the given world prices $p_1^*, p_2^*, \ldots, p_n^*$ (i.e. R^i is perfectly elastic), so Equation (A22) is redundant and therefore drops out of the problem for the small-country case.

The Lagrangean for the general problem is

$$\mathscr{L} = u(C_1, \ldots, C_n) + \lambda_1 \left[\sum_{i=1}^{n} p_i^*(C_i - X_i) \right] + \lambda_2 \phi(X_1, \ldots, X_n)$$

$$+ \mu K(C_1, \ldots, C_n, X_1, \ldots, X_n) + \sum_{j=1}^{n} \omega_j [C_j - X_j - R^j(p_1^*, \ldots, p_n^*)]$$

and the first-order conditions are that for all i,

$$\frac{\partial \mathscr{L}}{\partial C_i} = u_i + \lambda_1 p_i^* + \mu K_{C_i} + \omega_i = 0 \qquad (A23)$$

$$\frac{\partial \mathscr{L}}{\partial X_i} = \lambda_2 \phi_i - \lambda_1 p_i^* + \mu K_{X_i} - \omega_i = 0 \qquad (A24)$$

$$\frac{\partial \mathscr{L}}{\partial p_i^*} = \lambda_1(C_i - X_i) - \sum_{j=1}^{n} \omega_j R_i^j = 0 \qquad (A25)$$

where

$$R_i^j \equiv \frac{\partial R^j}{\partial p_i^*}, \quad u_i \equiv \frac{\partial u}{\partial C_i}, \quad \phi_i \equiv \frac{\partial \phi}{\partial X_i}, \quad K_{C_i} \equiv \frac{\partial K}{\partial C_i}, \quad K_{X_i} \equiv \frac{\partial K}{\partial X_i}.$$

From Equations (A23) and (A24), we have the following equations involving marginal rates of substitution in consumption (u_i/u_j) and marginal rates of transformation in production (ϕ_i/ϕ_j):

$$\frac{u_i}{u_j} = \frac{p_i^* + \beta K_{C_i} + T_i}{p_j^* + \beta K_{C_j} + T_j} \qquad (A26)$$

$$\frac{\phi_i}{\phi_j} = \frac{p_i^* - \beta K_{X_i} + T_i}{p_j^* - \beta K_{X_j} + T_j} \qquad (A27)$$

where

$$\beta \equiv \frac{\mu}{\lambda_1} \text{ and } T_i \equiv \frac{\omega_i}{\lambda_1}.$$

We shall now use Equations (A26) and (A27) to derive optimal policies in different situations. It is instructive to consider the small- and large-country cases separately. This serves to highlight the different aspects of the problem considered in Chapters 2 and 4, respectively.

(a)   Small-country case

When the home country is small, it cannot treat the world prices as variables. Thus, the constraint (A22) and Equation (25) are dropped. In particular, this implies that ω_i can be set equal to zero; hence T_i disappears from Equations (A26) and (A27) which can now be written in the simpler form:

$$\frac{u_i}{u_j} = \frac{p_i^* + \beta K_{C_i}}{p_j^* + \beta K_{C_j}} \tag{A26a}$$

$$\frac{\phi_i}{\phi_j} = \frac{p_i^* - \beta K_{X_i}}{p_j^* - \beta K_{X_j}}. \tag{A27a}$$

Equations (A26a) and (A27a) embody the basic principle of targeting the instrument(s) to the variable(s) to be constrained under the non-economic objective, Equation (A21). The relevant taxes or subsidies depend on which derivatives of K appear in Equations (A26a) and (A27a) to distort u_i/u_j and ϕ_i/ϕ_j away from free-trade relative prices. In the absence of any non-economic objectives, the partial derivatives of K drop out of Equations (A26a) and (A27a), making it optimal to equate the MRS in consumption and the MRT in production to relative world prices for each pair of goods; that is,

$$\frac{u_i}{u_j} = \frac{\phi_i}{\phi_j} = \frac{p_i^*}{p_j^*} \tag{A28}$$

so no taxes or subsidies are optimal in such a case. We now consider some examples of particular non-economic objectives.

(i)   *Output objective in a particular sector*

Suppose it is desired to achieve a minimum level of output $\bar{X}_i$. Then

$$K \equiv X_i - \bar{X}_i \geq 0$$

with

$$K_{C_i} = 0 \; \forall_i, \qquad K_{X_i} = 1, \qquad K_{X_j} = 0 \; \forall_{j \neq i}.$$

Thus Equations (A26a) and (A27a) become

$$\frac{u_i}{u_j} = \frac{p_i^*}{p_j^*} \tag{A29}$$

$$\frac{\phi_i}{\phi_j} = \frac{p_i^* - \beta}{p_j^*}. \tag{A30}$$

Note that from Equation (A23), $\lambda_1 < 0$, so that $\beta \equiv \mu/\lambda_1 < 0$ when the constraint of Equation (A21) is binding. Thus, as claimed in the text, the optimal policy in this case is a subsidy of β per unit to producers of good i.

With the same approach, it is straightforward to show that a constraint on consumption of good i of the form

$$\bar{C}_i - C_i \geq 0$$

is best achieved by imposing a consumption tax on good i.

(ii) Constraint on the value of a class of imports:

Now suppose it is desired to constrain the value of imports of goods in a certain set $\Omega \subseteq \{1, 2, \ldots, n\}$ to be below some target level V. Then

$$K \equiv V - \sum_{i \in \Omega} p_i^*(C_i - X_i)$$

with $K_{C_i} = -p_i^*$ for $i \in \Omega$ (0 otherwise) and $K_{X_i} = p_i^*$ for $i \in \Omega$ (0 otherwise). Thus Equations (A26a) and (A27a) become

$$\frac{u_i}{u_j} = \frac{p_i^*(1 + t)}{p_j^*} = \frac{\phi_i}{\phi_j} \quad \text{for} \quad i \in \Omega, j \notin \Omega \tag{A31}$$

with Equation (A28) holding for $i, j \notin \Omega$. $t = -\mu/\lambda_1 > 0$ when the imports constraint is binding. Equation (A31) tells us that the optimal policy to constrain the value of a class of imports is to apply a uniform ad valorem tariff at rate t to all goods in the class and to apply no distortions elsewhere.

(iii) Constraint on the volume of a class of imports

Suppose that the objective is to restrict the total volume of imports of goods in the set Ω below some target level M. Then the constraint function K is

$$K \equiv M - \sum_{i \in \Omega} (C_i - X_i) \geq 0$$

with $K_{C_i} = -1$ for $i \in \Omega$ (0 otherwise), and $K_{X_i} = 1$ for $i \in \Omega$ (0 otherwise). Equations (A26a) and (A27a) become

$$\frac{u_i}{u_j} = \frac{p_i^* + T}{p_j^*} = \frac{\phi_i}{\phi_j} \quad \text{for} \quad i \in \Omega, j \notin \Omega \tag{A32}$$

with Equation (A28) holding for $i, j \notin \Omega$ and $T = -\mu/\lambda_1 > 0$ when the imports constraint is binding. Thus, in this case, the optimal policy is a uniform specific tariff of T per unit applied to all goods in the restricted set Ω and no distortions elsewhere.

(b) Large-country case

When the home country is large, it will also be able to employ policy instruments to affect the value of the world prices $p_1^*, p_2^*, \ldots, p_n^*$ which clear the world's goods markets [Equation (A22)]. In this case, the more general optimality conditions, Equations (A26) and (A27), apply. Note that these equations extend the basic principle previously established that the instruments chosen should be those which directly affect the target variables. Instrument β is used to achieve the non-economic objective, Equation (A21), with its form depending on the nature of the objective (i.e. the values of the partial derivatives of K). On the other hand, the T_i's affect domestic consumer and producer prices equally – they are therefore trade taxes (tariffs or export taxes). Clearly, they are used to exploit the country's ability to determine its terms of trade [they were absent from Equations (A26a) and (A26b)]. Rearranging Equation (A25), we see that the optimal set of trade taxes must satisfy

$$\sum_{j=1}^{n} t_j p_j^* R_i^j = R^i \tag{A33}$$

where $t_j \equiv T_j/p_j^*$ is the ad valorem tariff (or the tariff equivalent of an export tax) applied to good j. For the simple case of two goods with a tariff on the importable (say, good i), Equation (A33) can be rearranged to yield the following simple formula for the optimal tariff expressed in terms of the elasticity of the foreign supply curve:

$$t_i \frac{\partial R^i}{\partial p_i^*} = \frac{R^i}{p_i^*}$$

so that $t_i = 1/\varepsilon_i$, where $\varepsilon_i \equiv (p_i^*/R^i)(\partial R^i/\partial p_i^*)$ is the elasticity of supply of imports.

The Cournot–Nash model
of Sections 6.1 and 6.2

We present an algebraic version of the Brander and Spencer model of trade policy under oligopoly. The primary aim of this appendix is to show how the Nash stability conditions can be used to derive the comparative static results of Figures 6.1 and 6.3. We confine our attention to the two-firm problem and do not consider any wider general equilibrium or welfare implications of the model.

Using the notation of the text, we write the profit functions of the home and foreign firms, respectively, as

$$\pi = xp(x + y) - cx + x^*p^*(x^* + y^*) - cx^* + sx^* - F$$

$$\pi^* = yp(x + y) - (c^* + t)y + y^*p^*(x^* + y^*) - c^*y^* - F^*$$

where t is the tariff per unit imposed on imports (y) into the home market, and s is the export subsidy per unit applied to home country exports to the foreign market (x^*). The home firm chooses x and x^* to maximize π, whereas the foreign firm chooses y and y^* to maximize π^*. The first-order conditions for these two maximization problems are

home market: $\quad A(x, y) \equiv MR^H(x, y) - c = 0$ (A34)

$\qquad\qquad\quad A^*(x, y) \equiv MR^F(x, y) - c^* - t = 0$ (A35)

foreign market: $\quad B(x^*, y^*) \equiv MR^H(x^*, y^*) - c + s = 0$ (A36)

$\qquad\qquad\quad B^*(x^*, y^*) \equiv MR^F(x^*, y^*) - c^* = 0$ (A37)

where $MR^H(x, y)$ ($= p + xp'$) is the home firm's marginal revenue from sales to the home market, $MR^F(x, y)$ is the foreign firm's marginal revenue from its sales to the home market and $MR^H(x^*, y^*)$ [$MR^F(x^*, y^*)$] is the home (foreign) firm's marginal revenue from sales to the foreign market. Equations (A34) and (A35) define the Cournot–Nash equilibrium in the home market, and Equations (A36) and (A37) define the corresponding equilibrium in the foreign market.

In what follows, we shall assume that an increase in one firm's sales to a particular market reduces both the profits and the marginal revenue of its rival in that market. This assumption and the second-order conditions for a maximum imply that the partial derivatives of the A and B functions have the following signs:

$$A_x < 0, \qquad A_y < 0, \qquad B_{x^*} < 0, \qquad B_{y^*} < 0$$

where

$$A_x \equiv \frac{\partial A}{\partial x}, \qquad B_{y^*} \equiv \frac{\partial B}{\partial y^*}, \qquad \text{etc.}$$

It is straightforward to derive the slopes of the reaction curves in the home and foreign markets. Totally differentiating Equations (A34) through (A37), we obtain

$$\text{slope of } x(y) \text{ in Figure 6.1} = \left(\frac{dy}{dx}\right)_{A=0} = -\frac{A_x}{A_y} < 0$$

$$\text{slope of } y(x) \text{ in Figure 6.1} = \left(\frac{dy}{dx}\right)_{A^*=0} = -\frac{A_x^*}{A_y^*} < 0$$

$$\text{slope of } x^*(y^*) \text{ in Figure 6.3} = -\frac{B_{x^*}}{B_{y^*}} < 0$$

$$\text{slope of } y^*(x^*) \text{ in Figure 6.3} = -\frac{B_x^*}{B_y^*} < 0.$$

A sufficient condition for stability of the Cournot–Nash equilibrium in the home market is

$$\Delta \equiv \begin{vmatrix} A_x & A_y \\ A_x^* & A_y^* \end{vmatrix} > 0. \tag{A38}$$

It is straightforward to show that Equation (A38) amounts to the condition that the reaction curve $x(y)$ in Figure 6.1 is steeper than curve $y(x)$, as claimed in the text. Verification is left as an exercise for the reader. The corresponding stability condition for the Cournot equilibrium in the foreign market [Equations (A36) and (A37)] is

$$\Delta^* \equiv \begin{vmatrix} B_{x^*} & B_{y^*} \\ B_x^* & B_y^* \end{vmatrix} > 0. \tag{A39}$$

Assuming these conditions to hold, we now can easily derive the comparative static results obtained in the text. Differentiating Equations (A34) and (A35) with respect to t and solving yields

$$\frac{dx}{dt} = -\frac{A_y}{\Delta} > 0 \qquad \frac{dy}{dt} = \frac{A_x}{\Delta} < 0$$

which, using the envelope theorem, implies

$$\frac{d\pi}{dt} = \frac{\partial \pi}{\partial y} \cdot \frac{dy}{dt} > 0 \qquad \frac{d\pi^*}{dt} = \frac{\partial \pi^*}{\partial x} \cdot \frac{dx}{dt} - y < 0$$

as claimed in the text. Similarly, differentiating Equations (A36) and (A37) with respect to s yields

$$\frac{dx^*}{ds} = -\frac{B_y^*}{\Delta^*} > 0 \Rightarrow \frac{d\pi^*}{ds} = \frac{\partial \pi^*}{\partial x^*} \cdot \frac{dx^*}{ds} < 0 \qquad \text{and}$$

$$\frac{dy^*}{ds} = \frac{B_x^*}{\Delta^*} < 0 \Rightarrow \frac{d\pi}{ds} = \frac{\partial \pi}{\partial y^*} \cdot \frac{dy^*}{ds} + x^* > 0.$$

Derivation of results in Section 8.2

Let p^* denote the (given) world relative price of the importable in terms of the exportable. Consumers and firms are assumed to have upward-sloping, strictly convex lobbying cost functions (measured in units of utility) given by $H(x_C)$ ($H' > 0$, $H'' > 0$) for consumers and $J(x_F)$ ($J' > 0$, $J'' > 0$) for firms. Suppose also that all of the individuals in a given group (firms or consumers) have identical homothetic preferences (though preferences can differ between groups) and that neither group's welfare is noticeably affected by changes in the (recycled) tariff revenue. Then each group's utility can be written as a (reduced form) function of the domestic relative price of the importable, $p = p^* + T(x_C, x_F)$. We denote the consumer group's utility as $V^C(p)$ with V_p^C ($\equiv \partial V^C / \partial p$) < 0 and the producer group's utility as $V^F(p)$ with $V_p^F > 0$ (indicating that consumers lose and producers gain from a rise in the relative price of the importable). We assume nothing at this stage about the curvature of these utility functions. Now suppose that the consumer group chooses its lobbying effort, x_C, to maximize its utility net of lobbying costs, taking the firms' lobbying effort, x_F, as given; that is,

$$\max_{x_C} V^C(p^* + T(x_C, x_F)) - H(x_C)$$

for given x_F.

Similarly, firms choose their lobbying effort to maximize their utility net of lobbying costs taking consumers' lobbying as given; that is,

$$\max_{x_F} V^F(p^* + T(x_C, x_F)) - J(x_F)$$

for given x_C.

The first-order conditions for a maximum for the two problems are

$$M(x_C, x_F, p^*) \equiv V_p^C T_C - H' = 0 \tag{A40}$$

$$N(x_C, x_F, p^*) \equiv V_p^F T_F - J' = 0. \tag{A41}$$

Equations (A40) and (A41) define the Nash equilibrium levels of lobbying effort for the two groups. We now consider the comparative static effects of a change in p^* on this equilibrium. Differentiating Equations (A40) and (A41) with respect to p^*, we obtain

$$
\begin{bmatrix} M_{x_C} & M_{x_F} \\[2mm] N_{x_C} & N_{x_F} \end{bmatrix}
\begin{bmatrix} \dfrac{dx_C}{dp^*} \\[4mm] \dfrac{dx_F}{dp^*} \end{bmatrix}
= \begin{bmatrix} -M_{p^*} \\[2mm] -N_{p^*} \end{bmatrix}
\tag{A42}
$$

where the subscripts on M and N denote partial derivatives with

$$
M_{x_C} \equiv \frac{\partial M}{\partial x_C} = V_{pp}^C (T_C)^2 + V_p^C T_{CC} - H'' < 0 \qquad \text{by second-order}
$$

conditions for a maximum

$$
M_{x_F} = V_{pp}^C T_C T_F + V_p^C T_{CF}
$$

$$
N_{x_C} = V_{pp}^F T_F T_C + V_p^F T_{FC}
$$

$$
N_{x_F} = V_{pp}^F (T_F)^2 + V_p^F T_{FF} - J'' < 0 \qquad \text{by second-order conditions}
$$

for a maximum

$$
M_{p^*} = V_{pp}^C T_C \qquad N_{p^*} = V_{pp}^F T_F.
$$

Substituting these expressions into Equation (A42) and solving using Cramer's Rule, we obtain

$$
\frac{dx_C}{dp^*} = \frac{1}{\varDelta} \, [V_{pp}^C T_C J'' - V_{pp}^C V_p^F T_C T_{FF} + V_{pp}^F V_p^C T_F T_{CF}]
\tag{A43}
$$

$$
\frac{dx_F}{dp^*} = \frac{1}{\varDelta} \, [V_{pp}^F T_F H'' - V_{pp}^F V_p^C T_F T_{CC} + V_{pp}^C V_p^F T_C T_{FC}]
\tag{A44}
$$

where $\varDelta$ is the determinant of the coefficient matrix of the system of Equations (A42) and is assumed positive to ensure stability of the Nash equilibrium. Totally differentiating the tariff function T and using Equations (A43) and (A44), we obtain the following expression for the effect of a change in world price on the domestic tariff level:

$$
\frac{dT}{dp^*} = \frac{1}{\varDelta} \, \{ T_C V_{pp}^C \, [T_C J'' - V_p^F T_C T_{FF} + V_p^F T_F T_{FC}]
$$

$$
- T_F V_{pp}^F \, [V_p^C T_F T_{CC} - T_F H'' - V_p^C T_C T_{CF}] \}
$$

which is ambiguous in sign if $T_{FC} = T_{CF} \neq 0$. However, if $T_{CF} = T_{FC} = 0$ and if we assume that V_{pp}^F and V_{pp}^C both have the same sign, then it follows from the properties of T and V that dT/dp^* also has this same sign. Thus, if all individuals are strongly risk-averse, we would have $V_{pp}^i < 0$ ($i = C, F$) (see Turnovsky, Shalit and Schmitz, 1980), in which case

$$
\frac{dT}{dp^*} < 0
$$

that is, a fall in the world price of the importable implies an increase in the tariff per unit. Clearly, this result can be reversed if individuals are not very risk averse ($V_{pp}^i > 0$) or if the political influence process has a strong marginal bias towards one group or the other ($T_{FC} \neq 0$). However, although a fall in p^* has an ambiguous effect on the equilibrium tariff level, it is straightforward to show that it implies a definite fall in the domestic price of the importable. Using the above expression for dT/dp^* and the definition of Δ, with some manipulation we obtain

$$\frac{d(p^* + T)}{dp^*} = \frac{1}{\Delta} \{V_p^C V_p^F [T_{CC} T_{FF} - (T_{CF})^2] - V_p^C T_{CC} J'' - V_p^F T_{FF} H'' + H'' J''\}$$

$$> 0$$

which is the Hillman result that a declining industry will continue to decline. Note that the result does not depend on the sign or the magnitude of T_{CF} nor does it depend on the curvature of the utility function. It follows directly from the assumptions of diminishing marginal returns to political effort ($T_{FF} < 0$, $T_{CC} > 0$, J'', $H'' > 0$).

Derivation of results in Section 9.2

Domestic producers will choose L_B and T to maximize

$$\mathscr{L} = (1 + t_1)F(L - L_B) + G(L_B) + \rho(1 + t_2)F(L - L_B - T)$$
$$+ \rho G(L_B + \lambda T) + \mu T.$$

The first-order conditions for a maximum are

$$\frac{\partial \mathscr{L}}{\partial L_B} = -(1 + t_1)F'(L - L_B) + G'(L_B) -$$

$$\varrho(1 + t_2)F'(L - L_B - T) + \varrho G'(L_B + \lambda T) = 0 \quad \text{(A45)}$$

$$\frac{\partial \mathscr{L}}{\partial T} = -\varrho(1 + t_2)F'(L - L_B - T) + \lambda\varrho G'(L_B + \lambda T)$$

$$+ \mu = 0. \quad \text{(A46)}$$

From Equation (A45) and the concavity of F and G, we have

$$0 > -(1 + t_1)F'_2 + G'_2 - \varrho(1 + t_2)F'_2 + \varrho G'_2$$

where $F'_2 \equiv F'(L - L_B - T)$ and $G'_2 \equiv G'(L_B + \lambda T)$ (i.e. the second-period values of F' and G'). It follows that

$$F'_2 > \frac{G'_2 (1 + \varrho)}{(1 + t_1) - \varrho(1 + t_2)}. \quad \text{(A47)}$$

From Equations (A46) and (A47) we have

$$\mu > G'_2 \left[\frac{\varrho(1 + \varrho)(1 + t_2)}{(1 + t_1) - \varrho(1 + t_2)} - \varrho\lambda \right].$$

Thus, $\mu > 0$ if the expression in brackets is non-negative, that is,

$$1 + t_2 \geq \frac{\lambda}{1 + \varrho(1 - \lambda)} (1 + t_1). \quad \text{(A48)}$$

For $\lambda < 1$, $1/[1 + \varrho(1 - \lambda)] < 1$ also, so that Equation (A37) is satisfied for an interval of values of t_2 below t_1. Thus, as claimed in the text, factors will not move between sectors ($\mu > 0$ and $T = 0$) for a range of second-period tariffs below the first-period tariff.

When $T = 0$, L_B is given by Equation (A45), and differentiation of Equation (A45) yields

$$\frac{\partial L_B}{\partial t_2} = \frac{\varrho F'(L - L_B)}{\partial^2 \mathcal{L}/\partial L_B^2} < 0.$$

Thus, when t_2 is sufficiently high to deter factor movements from A to B, higher values of t_2 cause the unprotected sector (B) to contract in both periods.

When $T > 0$ $(\mu = 0)$, differentiation of Equations (A45) and (A46) yields

$$\frac{\partial L_B}{\partial t_2} = \frac{\lambda \varrho^2 (\lambda - 1) F'_2 G''_2}{\Delta} \geq 0 \qquad (>0 \text{ if } \lambda < 1)$$

$$\frac{\partial T}{\partial t_2} = \frac{\varrho F'_2 [(1 + t_1) F''_1 + G''_1 + (1 - \lambda) \varrho G''_2]}{\Delta} < 0$$

$$\frac{\partial (L_B + T)}{\partial t_2} = \frac{\varrho F'_2 [(1 + t_1) F''_1 + G''_1 + \varrho (1 - \lambda)^2 G''_2]}{\Delta} < 0$$

where subscripts on the F and G functions refer to the time period; for example,

$$G''_2 \equiv G''(L_B + \lambda T), \qquad G''_1 \equiv G''(L_B), \qquad \text{etc.}$$

and Δ is the Hessian determinant of $\mathcal{L}$, which will be positive if the second-order conditions hold. Thus, when t_2 is low enough for factors to move from A to B, a higher value of t_2 will cause period-1 output of the protected good to fall [since $dX_{A1}/dt_2 = -F'_1(dL_B/dt_2)$] and period-2 output of that good to rise (since $L_B + T$ falls).

Finally, we note the effect of an increase of t_2 on the present value of GNP at world prices. Let

$$Y^* \equiv F(L - L_B) + G(L_B) + \varrho F(L - L_B - T) + \varrho G(L_B + \lambda T).$$

Then

$$\frac{\partial Y^*}{\partial t_2} = [t_1 F'_1 + \varrho t_2 F'_2] \frac{\partial L_B}{\partial t_2} + \varrho t_2 F'_2 \frac{\partial T}{\partial t_2}$$

$$= t_1 F'_1 \frac{\partial L_B}{\partial t_2} + \varrho t_2 F'_2 \left[\frac{\partial (L_B + T)}{\partial t_2} \right].$$

Clearly, when $T = 0$, sgn $\partial Y^*/\partial t_2 = $ sgn $\partial L_B/\partial t_2 < 0$, so that Y^* is reduced by raising t_2 above the level which just deters transfers. For lower values of t_2 $(T > 0)$, increasing t_2 may increase or decrease Y^* depending on the values of parameters. However, when $t_2 = 0$, $\partial Y^*/\partial t_2 = t_1 F_1'(\partial L_B/\partial t_2) > 0$ for $\lambda < 1$ (and $= 0$ for $\lambda = 1$). Thus, in the presence of adjustment costs, the present value of GNP at world prices will be higher under staged tariff reduction than with full tariff elimination. However, if such adjustment costs are absent ($\lambda = 1$), Y^* will be maximized by complete removal of tariffs in the second period.

Derivation of Equations (5) and (6) in Chapter 10

For the two-good case being considered, the system of Equations (4) in Chapter 10 can be written in matrix form as

$$
\begin{bmatrix} S^m_{p_1v} & \sum_k S^k_{p_1p_2} \\ S^m_{p_2v} & \sum_k S^k_{p_2p_2} \end{bmatrix} \begin{bmatrix} dV^m \\ dp^* \end{bmatrix} = - \begin{bmatrix} \sum_k S^k_{p_1p_2} dt^k \\ \sum_k S^k_{p_2p_2} dt^k \end{bmatrix}. \tag{A49}
$$

Also, from the homogeneity of the compensated demand functions [see Equation (15) in Chapter 9], we have

$$
S^k_{p_1p_2} = -(p^* + t^k)S^k_{p_2p_2}.
$$

Substituting in Equation (A49) yields

$$
\begin{bmatrix} S^m_{p_1v} & -\sum_k (p^* + t^k)S^k_{p_2p_2} \\ S^m_{p_2v} & \sum_k S^k_{p_2p_2} \end{bmatrix} \begin{bmatrix} dV^m \\ dp^* \end{bmatrix} = \begin{bmatrix} \sum_k (p^* + t^k)S^k_{p_2p_2} dt^k \\ -\sum_k S^k_{p_2p_2} dt^k \end{bmatrix}. \tag{A50}
$$

Using Cramer's rule, we obtain

$$
dV^m = \frac{1}{\Delta} \sum_k \sum_h S^k_{p_2p_2} S^h_{p_2p_2} (t^k - t^h) dt^k \tag{A51}
$$

where

$$
\Delta \equiv \sum_k S^k_{p_2p_2} [S^m_{p_1v} + (p^* + t^k)S^m_{p_2v}] < 0 \qquad \text{if stability is assumed.}
$$

(a) Proportional reduction of all tariffs

Substituting $dt^k = -\alpha t^k$ in Equation (A51) yields

$$
dV^m = \frac{-\alpha}{\Delta} \sum_k \sum_h S^k_{p_2p_2} S^h_{p_2p_2} (t^k - t^h) t^k
$$

276

$$= \frac{-\alpha}{\Delta} \sum_{k} \sum_{h<k} S^{k}_{p_2 p_2} S^{h}_{p_2 p_2} [(t^k - t^h)t^k + (t^h - t^k)t^h]$$

which, on rearrangement, yields Equation (5) in Chapter 10.

(b)   Reduction of the highest tariff rate

Substituting $dt^n < 0$, $dt^k = 0$ for $k \neq n$, in Equation (A51) yields

$$dV^m = \sum_{h} S^{n}_{p_2 p_2} S^{h}_{p_2 p_2} (t^n - t^h)\, dt^n = \sum_{h} S^{n}_{p_2 p_2} S^{h}_{p_2 p_2} (t^n - t^h) p^*\, dt^n$$

which is Equation (6) in Chapter 10.

Notes

Chapter 1

1. Samuelson (1956) exhibits the general non-existence of a community indifference map. He does however also show that (i) given the assumption that an ordinal social-welfare function defines society's preferences as a function of individual utilities and (ii) given the assumption that a given aggregate income is always distributed among consumers so as to optimize social welfare (by means of "last minute" lump-sum transfers), then a well-defined social ordering over aggregate quantities of goods can be defined. Chipman (1974) shows that if consumers possess identical homothetic preferences and incomes that are a constant proportion of total income, then one can define a meaningful aggregate utility ordering. Interested readers should also see the seminal papers by Eisenberg (1961) and Gorman (1953). For a useful survey of the literature on this topic, see Woodland (1982), chapter 6. Tower (1979) provides a useful geometric exposition of the various rationales for community indifference curves.
2. For a rigorous definition of the production frontier and derivation of its properties, see Woodland (1982), chapter 3.
3. This is a simplified version of the standard gains-from-trade argument (for which see Kemp, 1969a; Samuelson, 1938, 1962). The basic argument has been developed and refined considerably over the years. Useful surveys and syntheses are to be found in Chipman and Moore (1978); Dixit and Norman (1980), chapter 3; and Woodland (1982), chapter 9.
4. In fact, the slope of sector i's zero-profit locus is easily seen to be $(-k_i)$ (see Appendix 1).
5. However, it should be noted that such a conclusion implicitly assumes that (i) the government does not or cannot use the revenue from the tariff to achieve a different distributional outcome and (ii) the imposition of the tariff does not improve the country's terms of trade. This latter possibility, which arises if the country imposing the tariff is large (analysed in detail in Chapter 4), could enable the government to redistribute the tariff revenue so that both factors are better off under the tariff (i.e. the losers are compensated by the gainers). For the case in which the country is small, no such Pareto improvement is possible (see Chapter 2). Certainly, in the event that the government's ability to use the tariff revenue as a compensatory vehicle is limited, one factor would gain from protection and the other would lose.
6. KK and LL have the equations

$$a_{KF}X_F + a_{KC}X_C = K \tag{1}$$

$$a_{LF}X_F + a_{LC}X_C = L \tag{2}$$

where a_{Ki} is the capital employed per unit of output in sector i, a_{Li} is the labour per unit of output employed in sector i and K and L are the economy's respective endowments of capital and labour. As noted in the text, the input–output coefficients (a_{Ki} and a_{Li}) are constant, given our assumption of fixed product prices.
7. From Equations (1) and (2) in note 6, the slope of KK is seen to be $(-a_{KC}/a_{KF})$, and the slope of LL is $(-a_{LC}/a_{LF})$.

8. Slope of KK − slope of $LL = -\dfrac{a_{KC}}{a_{KF}} + \dfrac{a_{LC}}{a_{LF}} = \dfrac{a_{LC}}{a_{KF}} \left(\dfrac{a_{KF}}{a_{LF}} - \dfrac{a_{KC}}{a_{LC}} \right) = \dfrac{a_{LC}}{a_{KF}} (k_F - k_C) > 0.$

278

Chapter 2

1. Another measure of welfare loss which has gained some prominence is the so-called Allais–Debreu loss (see Diewert, 1984).
2. Our analysis ignores administrative-collection-disbursement costs. After these are introduced there may be a much stronger argument for a tariff which is a single instrument in preference to a tax-subsidy combination which may increase the administrative costs involved.
3. The principle that, when cross-elasticities of demand are zero, an optimal commodity tax structure will involve taxes being set inversely to goods' own-price elasticity of demand was first enunciated by Ramsey (1927). For a discussion of this and related results see Dixit (1970).
4. For an analysis of value-based content schemes see Grossman (1981) and Mussa (1984).
5. The production-side DWL (EKL) equals area $X_F KE X_Q$ (the cost of increasing component output from X_F to X_Q) minus $X_F KL X_Q$ (the fall in payments to foreign exporters). Similarly, the consumption-side DWL (GRT) equals area $C_Q GT C_F$ (the loss of benefits to purchasers relative to free trade) minus $C_Q RT C_F$.
6. A more general result is that a tax on all balance-of-payments debits is symmetric to a tax on all balance-of-payments credits (see Kaempfer and Tower, 1982). This result holds even when the balance of payments is not in equilibrium, because the nature of balance-of-payments accounts implies that each debit begets an identically sized credit. Clearly the Lerner result is a special case of this result, holding when the only debits are imports and the only credits are exports (i.e. no capital flows, interest payments etc. or accommodating transactions).
7.

$$r = \frac{p_T - p^*}{p^*} \cdot \frac{p^*}{p_T} = \tau(1 - r), \qquad \text{so that } r = \frac{\tau}{1 + \tau},$$

where $\tau \equiv (p_T - p^*)/p^*$ is the usual ad valorem tariff rate.
8. From Figure 2.10 we see that the fall in DWL as a percentage of GNP is approximated by

$$-\frac{\Delta DWL}{Y} = \frac{1}{2}(p_T - p'_T)\frac{\Delta M'}{Y} + (p'_T - p^*)\frac{\Delta M'}{Y}$$

$$= \frac{1}{2}\frac{\Delta M'}{Y}[(p_T - p^*) + (p'_T - p^*)]$$

$$= \frac{1}{2}\eta_M \frac{p_T - p'_T}{p_T}\alpha(\tau_0 + \tau_1)$$

where $\Delta M'$ is the absolute value of the change in imports associated with the fall in price from p_T to p'_T (see Figure 2.14).
   Now,

$$k \equiv \frac{r_0 - r_1}{r_0} = \frac{p^*(p_T - p'_T)}{p'_T(p_T - p^*)} \Rightarrow \frac{p_T - p'_T}{p_T} = kr_0\frac{p'_T}{p^*} = \frac{kr_0}{1 - r_1}.$$

Substituting this into the preceding expression for $-\Delta DWL/Y$ yields Equation (5).
9. See Cline et al. (1977), particularly their Table 2.3, p. 58.
10. A reasonable approximation for Canada or some EEC countries, but the figures are considerably lower for the United States (approx. 7 per cent) or Australia (14 per cent) (see International Monetary Fund, 1984). Of course the percentage of GDP actually protected by tariffs will be even lower.
11. This was the figure selected by Johnson in 1960, but today the average tariff rate in developed countries is considerably lower. For example, the average nominal tariff rate for manufacturing

industry is about 16 per cent for Australia, 11 per cent for Canada and lower again for the United States.

12. Magee adds to this figure another $1.2 billion per year of tariff-equivalent revenue lost to foreigners.

13. See Cline et al. (1977), table 3–8, p. 99.

14. The maximum gain here occurs for the Canadian proposal, which was that a tariff on a good would be cut to 40 per cent of the pre-existing U.S. tariff on the good if the initial tariff rate exceeds 5 per cent. Tariffs under 5 per cent would be eliminated altogether.

15. See Brown and Whalley (1980), table 10, p. 859.

16. Although, as Corden notes (1975, p. 60), this cost "is small in relation to GNP, but a justified source of indignation. There are many good things that can be done with £250 million per annum."

17. Hartigan and Tower (1982), table 1, simulation 1.1.

18. Hartigan and Tower (1982), table 3, simulation 3.2.

19. Hartigan and Tower (1982), table 3, simulation 3.11.

20. The model used by Hartigan and Tower (1982) assumes domestic and foreign goods to be perfect substitutes.

21. In other words, normative questions are best analysed using nominal rates of protection. In this context at least, effective rates offer no advantages that are not also offered by nominal rates and use of effective rates introduces unnecessary complications and data requirements. This view appears to have been first enunciated by Vanek (1971). It was subsequently presented in a more general and rigorous form by Bertrand (1972) and was forcefully reiterated by Ethier (1977). Similar conclusions have been reached independently by Ray (1980).

22. Using the symbols as defined in the text, we have

$$\sum_i v_i X_i = \sum_i \left(p_i - \sum_j p_j a_{ji} \right) X_i$$

$$= \sum_i p_i X_i - \sum_i \sum_j p_j a_{ji} X_i$$

$$= \sum_i p_i X_i - \sum_i \sum_j p_i a_{ij} X_j$$

$$= \sum_i p_i \left(X_i - \sum_j a_{ij} X_j \right) = \sum_i p_i Y_i.$$

23. The interested reader is referred to Ethier (1977), Jones (1971b) and Woodland (1977) for a more detailed analysis of how ERPs can be defined and calculated in the presence of input substitutability.

Chapter 3

1. Of course, their reduced effort may be revealed by a lower output in the high-crop state of the world, in which case there is no moral hazard problem.

2. This implicitly assumes that the distribution of income does not affect social welfare or that a socially optimal distribution can be always attained at zero cost. The usual condition for social welfare to be independent of wealth or income distribution is that individuals have identical homothetic preferences (see also Woodland, 1982).

3. This is not to suggest that such lobbying is not important – indeed, it usually accounts for greater use of resources than the "distortion-triggered" lobbying being considered here.

4. If bribery is viewed merely as a transfer, then it should not be counted as a cost. However, insofar as bribery affects the income of government officials, it may divert excessive resources

into the government sector and thus involve some inefficiency. On the other hand, as noted by Bhagwati (1982, footnote 4), if the salaries of government officials reflect the expectation that they will be able to "top up" their incomes with bribes, then for a given number of government employees, the bribes may replace distortionary taxes which would have otherwise been required to finance higher government salaries. In such a case, bribery may well represent a net benefit. Because this issue remains unresolved, it is probably safest to treat bribery as a costless transfer.

5. Bhagwati and Srinivasan (1980) show that the Rybczynski curve will have the form $\mathcal{R}_1$ if the lobbying sector is more labour (capital)-intensive than the exportables sector which is in turn more labour (capital)-intensive than the importables sector. Our example of a lobbying sector which uses only labour and a labour-intensive exportables sector is clearly a special case of their condition.

6. With a different lobbying technology (a higher Rybczynski curve for example), the price under the quota with rent seeking may have been lower than under the tariff, making the quota the superior policy.

7. For this result to occur, it is necessary that the lump-sum transfer be an increasing function of the total tariff revenue. No welfare improvement is possible if the lump-sum transfer component is fixed in dollar terms.

8. It is inefficient to estimate P_T because we would still have to determine P_F. P_R and P_F are sufficient to compute the production cost of a tariff.

Chapter 4

1. The case of a large exporter using an optimal export tax can be similarly analysed using a version of the standard monopoly diagram. This is left as an exercise for the student. Recall that a tariff and an export tax are equivalent via the Lerner symmetry theorem (Chapter 2).

2. On the other hand, for cases where the tariff revenue function is not single-peaked, this result may not hold. See Tower (1977) for a more complete analysis.

3. In the case with multiple equilibria, Johnson (1953) demonstrates the interesting possibility that the country initiating the tariff war may lose, relative to free trade, while the other country may gain.

4. The same outcome should also have been achieved by an export quota of ON with an associated home country offer curve of OBA.

5. The reasons for the popularity of these policies are discussed in a political markets context in Chapter 8.

6. See Takacs (1978) for an analysis of various monopoly cases.

7. See Lizondo (1984) for a discussion of how the pattern of expenditure of the tariff revenue or export licence revenue affects the domestic price.

8. Another special case in which the exporting country may be worse off under a VER than a tariff (or import quota) is to be found in Brecher and Bhagwati (1987). They show that if a large importing country (country H) is pursuing a policy to maintain a target domestic price of its importable good, then the exporting country (A) may be worse off under the VER if H's exportable is sufficiently inferior in consumption.

9. The so-called newly industrialized countries (NICs) include, among others, Brazil, South Korea, Taiwan, Singapore, Mexico, Spain, Portugal, Greece and Yugoslavia.

Chapter 5

1. The f.o.b. export price may be significantly below the c.i.f. import price if transport costs are very high or if the good is subject to high foreign tariffs.

2. To the right of F, MC > MR, so profits will be increased by reducing output, whereas to the left of F, MC < MR, implying that profits will be increased by raising output. Thus Q_2 is the monopolist's profit-maximizing output in this case.

3. The necessary tariff is $p_M p_S$ per unit while the quota is simply the target import level.

4. It is, of course, futile to try and replicate E by considering a fixed tariff at the desired level because the firm is optimizing subject to a variable tariff. This is a potential source of confusion.

5. An apparent corollary of this observation is that, in an industry in which the "natural" number of firms in the domestic industry exceeds one, higher tariffs may induce more firms to enter. This case and the possibility it presents of "inefficient entry" will be considered in an explicit oligopoly framework in the next chapter.

6. An obvious exception to this outcome is the case of a (binding) positive import quota in which some of the good will always be imported. Import quota protection of the monopolist is discussed briefly later in this section.

7. This equals the loss of consumer surplus ($p_D A C p_B$) minus the increased producer rents ($p_D A K p_B - KCLF$).

8. It is worth noting however that Tower (1983) derives this same result (that an import subsidy may be optimal depending on the curvature of the demand curve) in a competitive markets model in which the foreign government is a Stackelberg follower with its tariff (see, in particular, his Propositions 7 and 9).

Chapter 6

1. If the rent shifting illustrated in Figure 6.1 were the only effect, clearly it would pay the home country to push the tariff up to the prohibitive level, driving the foreign firm's reaction curve down to $y_p(x)$.

2. Letting (x_T, y_S) and (x_S, y_S) be the values of (x, y) under the tariff and the subsidy, respectively, we have

$$\pi_0 = x_T p(x_T + y_T) - cx_T - F = x_S p(x_S + y_S) - cx_S + sx_S - F.$$

Hence,

$$V_0 \equiv x_T p(x_T + y_T) - cx_T = x_S p(x_S + y_S) - cx_S + sx_S$$

and, since $x_S > x_T$,

$$\frac{V_0}{x_T} = p(x_T + y_T) - c > p(x_S + y_S) - c + s = \frac{V_0}{x_S}.$$

Thus, $p(x_T + y_T) - p(x_S + y_S) > s > 0$.

3. With entry deterrence, the foreign firms's profits are given by

$$\pi_D^* = y_D p(y_D) - (c^* + t)y_D$$

whereas at the Stackelberg equilibrium, they are

$$\pi_S^* = y_S p(y_S + x(y_S)) - (c^* + t)y_S.$$

Differentiating and using the envelope theorem, we obtain

$$\frac{\partial(\pi_S^* - \pi_D^*)}{\partial t} = y_D - y_S > 0.$$

4. See Brander and Spencer (1981) for proof.

5. It is possible that there are further gains (from rent shifting) as the tariff is increased further above t^*.

6. Consider the home market. Let x_A be the autarky level of x and let x_F, y_F be the free-trade (Cournot) levels of x and y, respectively. We then have

$$x_A p'(x_A) + p(x_A) = c = x_F p'(x_F + y_F) + p(x_F + y_F)$$
$$> (x_F + y_F)p'(x_F + y_F) + p(x_F + y_F).$$

If we take $zp'(z) + p(z)$ to be a decreasing function of z (downward sloping MR in the home market), the above inequality implies that $x_A < x_F + y_F$. Hence, $p(x_A) > p(x_F + y_F)$.

7. There is an extensive literature on the conditions for gains from trade to occur in the presence of imperfect competition and increasing returns to scale. A good survey of this literature is to be found in Helpman (1984). The reader interested in more technical detail is referred to Markusen (1981) and Markusen and Melvin (1984).

8. An exception is the special case in which all industry outputs are unchanged by the uniform rate of subsidy. In such a case, free trade is clearly as good as the subsidy. Dixit and Grossman also show that a uniform specific subsidy always leaves industry outputs unchanged and merely effects a transfer from profits to scientists without changing total welfare.

9. Indeed, Brander and Spencer (1984) and Krugman (1984) are careful to point out that their theories should not be taken as support for protectionist policies.

10. See Markusen and Venables (1988) for a proof of this result for the case of linear demand. Their paper considers many other cases, managing to confer on this complex subject the taxonomy it deserves.

11. If the two goods were perfect substitutes (as in the Venables model), with integrated markets, a small tariff or export subsidy by one country would drive firms in the other country out of business. The problem is therefore rather uninteresting unless the goods are assumed to be imperfect substitutes.

12. See Eastman and Stykolt (1960, 1967); also Corden (1974), pp. 210–11.

13. Indeed, the Harris and Cox model of the perfectly competitive case is along the same lines as the applied general equilibrium models surveyed in Chapter 2. It also shares some of the shortcomings of these models. For example, Harris and Cox employ the Armington assumption which may imply excessive terms-of-trade losses from unilateral trade liberalization (see Chapter 2), and this is reflected in unduly low estimates of the gains from reduced protection.

14. The more so when he assumes less international capital mobility and lower trade elasticities than Harris and Cox and lessens the importance of Eastman-Stykolt pricing.

Chapter 7

1. The current interest in intra-industry trade was stimulated by the work of Gray (1973), Grubel (1967) and Grubel and Lloyd (1975). Since then, much has been written on the subject, with some economists (e.g. Finger, 1975) arguing that observed intra-industry trade is merely a reflection of the particular way in which commodity aggregates are obtained. However, the volume of intra-industry trade appears to be too large to be explained by inappropriate aggregation and, indeed, there is evidence of significant intra-industry trade within commodity groups with quite a low level of aggregation (see Greenaway and Milner, 1983). For a survey of the empirical work see Tharakan (1985).

2. It will later be shown that, because of the symmetric nature of the product varieties, the representative individual consumes the same amount of each (c) at the same price (p). If the individual's income equals the wage, w, then utility from consumption of n varieties is

$$nv(c) = nv\left(\frac{w}{pn}\right).$$

Then

$$\frac{dnv(c)}{dn} = v(c) - nv'(c)\left(\frac{w}{pn^2}\right) = v(c) - cv'(c) > 0$$

using the fact that $v'' < 0$ and $v(0) \geq 0$. This establishes that the consumer benefits from greater variety.

3. For variety i,

$$v'(c_i) = \lambda p_i \qquad\qquad\qquad (*)$$

where λ is the Lagrange multiplier associated with the consumer's budget constraint and is also the marginal utility of income which we are assuming to be unaffected by changes in individual prices (when n is large). Differentiating with respect to p_i yields

$$\frac{dc_i}{dp_i} = \frac{\lambda}{v''(c_i)}.$$

It follows from Equation (*) that

$$\varepsilon \equiv -\frac{dc_i}{dp_i} \cdot \frac{p_i}{c_i} = -\frac{v'(c_i)}{v''(c_i)c_i}.$$

Note also that because prices other than p_i do not enter Equation (*), the cross-price elasticity of demand for each good is also zero when the number of varieties n is large (for n small, cross-price effects would enter via changes in λ).

4. From Equation (*) of note 3, we obtain

$$c_i = \left(\frac{\lambda}{\theta}\right)^{1/(\theta-1)} p_i^{1/(\theta-1)}.$$

Substituting in the consumer's budget constraint, this yields

$$\frac{\lambda}{\theta} = \frac{w^{\theta-1}}{\left(\sum_j p_j^{\theta/(\theta-1)}\right)^{\theta-1}}.$$

Substituting this expression for (λ/θ) back into Equation (*) and manipulating yields the following solution for c_i:

$$c_i = \frac{w p_i^{1/(\theta-1)}}{\sum_j p_j^{\theta/(\theta-1)}}.$$

Differentiating this expression with respect to p_i then yields the following expression for the own-price elasticity of demand ε_i:

$$\varepsilon_i = \frac{1}{1-\theta} - \frac{1}{n} \cdot \frac{\theta}{1-\theta} \to \frac{1}{1-\theta} \quad \text{as } n \to \infty.$$

5. If two firms were to produce the one variety, one firm could drive the other out of business by expanding its output and reducing its unit costs (and increasing the other firm's unit costs).

6. In this context, there are economies of scope if the average cost of a multi-variety firm's typical product falls as the number of varieties produced by the firm increases.

7. If fixed costs are very high relative to the size of the market, the industry will only consist of a small number of firms. In such a case, we would expect to observe positive profits in long-run equilibrium. If another firm were to enter the industry, profits for the marginal firm would be

negative. This outcome arises because the number of firms in the industry is an integer. When the equilibrium number of firms in the industry is large, the difference in profits associated with the entry of the marginal firm is relatively small so that long-run profits will be approximately zero. In other words, the fact that the number of firms is an integer matters less when the number of firms is large (as is the case under monopolistic competition).

8. Differentiating (8a) with respect to L yields

$$\frac{dn}{dL} = \frac{1}{(\alpha + \beta cL)^2} \left\{ \alpha + \beta cL - \beta L \left(c + L \frac{dc}{dL} \right) \right\}$$

$$= \frac{1}{(\alpha + \beta cL)^2} \left\{ \alpha - \beta L^2 \frac{dc}{dL} \right\} > 0 \quad \text{since } \frac{dc}{dL} < 0.$$

9. The conclusions of this section have been obtained on the assumption that all varieties are symmetric substitutes. However, it is possible that imported varieties may not be symmetric substitutes for domestic varieties even if the varieties in each group are symmetric substitutes (e.g. domestic varieties are symmetric to other domestic varieties). In such a case, we would expect demand elasticities to differ between foreign and domestic varieties. It is then possible to construct cases in which trade lowers welfare in the home country if it results in foreign varieties with a higher elasticity of demand displacing some less elastic domestic varieties (see Venables, 1982; also section III of Dixit and Stiglitz, 1977). The implication is that prohibition of trade may be beneficial because it results in the provision of socially desirable varieties (those with less elastic demand).

10. More rigorous treatments of the subject (e.g. Helpman, 1981) find it convenient to represent the specifications as points around the circumference of a circle. This has the analytical advantage that every variety has other products on both sides of it, whereas in the line representation, the products at the ends of the line only sell to one half-market. For the sort of heuristic analysis employed in this chapter, the line representation is quite adequate.

11. See Lancaster (1984), p. 147.

12. Consumers may, however, switch their expenditure towards a good produced by another industry in the economy. We have deferred explicit discussion of other sectors in the economy until Section 7.4.

13. This is why an increased number of products is consistent with increased outputs of domestically produced varieties. The higher price of imported varieties causes their market width to contract and the market width of domestic varieties to expand. In the limit, as the tariff becomes prohibitive, the imported goods have zero market width and are suddenly unavailable in the economy which had previously imported them.

14. Helpman (1981) and Lancaster (1980) use the Lancaster approach, whereas Krugman (1982); Lawrence and Spiller (1983) and Venables (1982) use the SDS formulation. Helpman and Krugman (1985) provide an excellent synthesis of this rather difficult literature.

15. An explicit general equilibrium formulation is provided in Falvey and Kierzkowski (1987).

16. A general equilibrium analysis reveals that, rather than a point such as α_1, there is an interval of values of α around α_1 which divides the two markets. This is because the discrete difference between r and r^* implies a jump in the marginal cost of quality when switching from one country's good to the other at α_1. Thus, a consumer switching from a foreign supplier of α_1 to a domestic supplier faces a sudden drop in the marginal cost of quality (from r^* to r) and accordingly demands a higher quality than α_1. See Falvey and Kierzkowski (1987).

17. The reader can perform a rough check of stability by taking any point away from P and assuming r adjusts to move the system onto EE (i.e. r adjusts to clear the home country's capital market), while r^* adjusts to clear the foreign country's capital market, thus moving the system onto E^*E^*. A sequence of alternating adjustments along these lines is seen to take the system towards P.

18. See Falvey (1981), p. 504.

Chapter 8

1. For a good overview of the theoretical literature, see Hillman (1989) and Magee, Brock and Young (1989). In addition, there is a growing body of empirical research on the determinants of both the level of protection and the choice of protective instrument. See Anderson (1980); Anderson and Baldwin (1981); Caves (1976); Godek (1985); Honma and Hayami (1986) and Ray (1981).
2. Becker (1983) considers a contest between a "taxed" group and a "subsidized" group. This can be analysed similarly to the model of this chapter; however, it should be noted that, in the context of a tariff, Becker's subsidized group receives the tariff revenue as well as producer rents.
3. The cross derivatives of a typical T function may be positive for some values of x_F and x_C and negative for others.
4. In fact, it is possible to show that T will fall so long as it satisfies the conditions in Equation (1) and $T_{CF} = T_{FC} = 0$. Cases in which political influence is consumer-biased ($T_{CF} < 0$) or producer-biased ($T_{CF} > 0$) yield less clearcut results. See Appendix 4 for details.
5. Corden attributes such a social objective to a number of factors, in particular social concepts of fairness, risk aversion and a desire for social harmony.
6. The authors cite the U.S. shoe and toy industries as examples and suggest that the same pattern is emerging in the U.S. steel, shipbuilding and automobile industries.
7. See Brock and Magee (1978), p. 248. This result is proved rigorously in Magee, Brock and Young (1989).
8. That is, T_L and T_H weighted by the parties' probabilities of election.
9. It is possible that the protectionist lobby may be better off if the reason for its increased pressure is a fall in its costs, due to, say, better organization (Brock and Magee, 1978 p. 249).
10. This type of phenomenon is observed in many political contests; for example, a more militant stance by unions may cause opposing parties to move their industrial relations platforms further apart, allowing the possibility that the expected outcome for unions is tougher anti-union legislation.
11. For a cogent statement of this view, see McCulloch (1987), p. 219.
12. See Deardorff (1987), pp. 195–6.
13. Peltzman (1976), Stigler (1971).
14. This may be justified if the industry in question is not too large and the revenue from the protective policy is spread thinly across the community. In such a case, the benefits to any one individual from this revenue are probably less than the cost to that individual of entering the political contest.
15. Note that this might equally well be interpreted as a reason for the use of variable import levies (see Chapter 4) since these are equivalent to an import quota when the only disturbance is external to the economy.

Chapter 9

1. See Woodland (1982) for a more complete analysis of the GNP and expenditure functions and their properties. Appendix 1 also offers some guidance in the derivation and the properties of the GNP function for the two-good case. A similar approach can be adopted for the expenditure function.
2. Note that this condition can be dispensed with if we allow the economy to run a balance-of-trade surplus (see Diewert, Turunen-Red and Woodland, 1989). Because a balance-of-trade

surplus is tantamount to a reduction in the consumer's income, the government can use such a surplus as an instrument in conjunction with "overall inferiority" ($H < 0$) to produce the same sort of outcome as if H were positive.

3. See, for example, Dixit (1985), p. 344.

4. In terms of the tax per unit, this can be written as

$$d\left(\frac{t_j}{p_j^*}\right) = -k\left(\frac{t_j}{p_j^*} - \tau^*\right)$$

that is, $dt_j = -k(t_j - \tau^*p_j^*)$.

Substituting in Equation (8) yields

$$HdV = -k \sum_i \sum_j t_i S_{p_i p_j}(t_j - \tau^*p_j^*)$$

$$= -k \sum_i t_i \sum_j S_{p_i p_j}[t_j - \tau^*p_j + \tau^*t_j]$$

$$= -k \sum_i t_i \sum_j S_{p_i p_j} t_j(1 + \tau^*) \qquad \text{since } \sum_j S_{p_i p_j} p_j = 0$$

using the homogeneity of degree zero of excess demands. Thus,

$$HdV = -k(1 + \tau^*) \sum_i \sum_j t_i S_{p_i p_j} t_j \geq 0$$

as previously.

5. See, for example, Industries Assistance Commission (1982), p. 10.

6. See Industries Assistance Commission (1982) (especially p. 56) for a statement and critical assessment of this view at the policymaking level; also Lloyd (1978) who discusses gradualism in the context of the historical development of Australian tariff policy.

7. In general, T could be either positive or negative (i.e. transfers could go either way). However, here we are only concerned with the possibility of resources moving away from the protected sector at the beginning of period 2.

8. The assumption of a single consumer or identical consumers necessitates some care when discussing the allocation of labour between sectors. We are assuming implicitly that the consumer chooses what proportion of his/her labour to sell to each sector in each period and what proportion to transfer between sectors at the beginning of period two.

9. Such an assumption can only be viewed as a convenient approximation because it violates the condition that the compensated demands be homogeneous of degree zero in prices; that is,

$$\sum_j p_j S_{p_i p_j} = 0$$

which implies $\sum_j \eta_{ij} = 0$.

10. Differentiating $r_j p_j = t_j \Rightarrow p_j dr_j + r_j dt_j = dt_j$, since $dt_j = dp_j$. Thus $dt_j(1-r_j) = -kr_j p_j$. The result follows immediately.

Chapter 10

1. Note that the vectors of trades between each country in the union and the outside world differ in general from their pre-union values because their individual pre-union external tariffs differ from the common external tariff imposed by the union.

2. Taking the taxes imposed by the outside countries as given, the utility levels of those countries can be obtained as functions of p^*, using their respective trade balance conditions – hence x_i can be written as a function of p^* alone.

3. A trivial exception to this result is the case in which the initial (pre-union) equilibrium is already a Pareto optimum. However, this is not the case in the usual situation in which agents in the different countries in the union face different pre-union prices for some goods.

4. Dixit and Norman (1980) sketch a proof that the Kemp and Wan result holds in the absence of lump-sum transfers between countries. They propose a system of commodity taxes combined with the CET to achieve productive efficiency for the union as a whole and to maintain the pre-union external trade vector (see also Dixit, 1985).

5. The analysis for country B (for a reduction of the tariff on good 1) is the same and will not be presented here. This symmetry is a consequence of the symmetric trade pattern of the Meade model and the reader is again referred to Lloyd (1982) for a discussion of other possibilities.

6. Note that we are using the narrower definition of customs union as involving free trade among the member countries. Some writers (e.g. Lipsey, 1970; McMillan and McCann, 1981) use the term in the broader sense to describe any mutual tariff reductions among a group of countries subject to a common external tariff.

7. Note that a positive second-best tariff $\hat{t}_2{}^A$ does not mean that A cannot gain by forming a customs union. V^A is increased relative to the pre-union situation if the gain from reducing t_2^A to its second-best level exceeds the loss associated with reducing t_2^A the rest of the way from its second-best level to zero.

8. The polar case in which A and B do not trade with C when their tariffs are zero (but C's tariffs are non-zero) is an instance in which the customs union trivially dominates non-preferential UTR. See Wonnacott and Wonnacott (1981).

9. This cost of liberalization will be converted into a gain if the partner country (say B) was originally producing the good at a unit cost higher than its supply price from A after the union is formed (presumably because the pre-union tariff in B was relatively high). This is the case considered by Pearson and Ingram (1980), which explains why their model does not yield losses from trade diversion.

10. Notable exceptions are to be found in Caves (1974), Johnson (1965), Kemp (1969b) and Mayer (1981).

11. Letting p^* denote the world relative price of country A's importable, the domestic relative prices of A's importable are $p^A = p^*(1 + t^A)$ and $p^B = p^*/(1 + t^B)$, respectively; $p^A = p^B$ if and only if

$$(1 + t^A)(1 + t^B) = 1.$$

This is the equation of CC, which is seen to have a negative slope.

12. Our choice of rules here was motivated solely by a desire for uniformity with Section 10.1. Mayer considers an alternative rule in which higher tariffs are cut at a faster rate than lower tariffs, which yields a smoother version of our path $STLO$, but otherwise has the same general properties. His version of the rule is defined by the formula

$$dt^k/t^k = -t^k, \qquad k = A, B$$

which was one of the rules explicitly advanced for consideration in the Tokyo round (see Cline et al., 1977). It is represented by a concave locus joining S to O and it has the advantage that it embodies an iterative application of the "reduce the highest tariff first" approach.

References

M. Anam (1982), "Distortion-triggered Lobbying and Welfare", *Journal of International Economics* **13**, 15–32.

K. Anderson (1980), "The Political Market for Government Assistance to Australian Manufacturing Industries", *Economic Record* **56**, 132–44.

K. Anderson and R. E. Baldwin (1981), "The Political Market for Protection in Industrial Countries: Empirical Evidence", World Bank Staff Working Paper No. 492 (World Bank: Washington DC).

K. J. Arrow (1970), *Essays in the Theory of Risk Bearing* (Amsterdam: North-Holland).

A. J. Auerbach (1985), "The Theory of Excess Burden and Optimal Taxation", in A. J. Auerbach and M. Feldstein (eds), *Handbook of Public Economics, Vol. I* (Amsterdam: North-Holland), pp. 61–127.

B. Y. Aw and M. J. Roberts (1986), "Measuring Quality Change in Quota-Constrained Import Markets: The Case of U.S. Footwear", *Journal of International Economics* **21**, 45–60.

R. E. Baldwin (1984), "Trade Policies in Developed Countries", in R. W. Jones and P. B. Kenen (eds.), *Handbook of International Economics: Vol. I* (Amsterdam: North–Holland), pp. 571–619.

R. E. Baldwin, J. H. Mutti and J. D. Richardson (1980), "Welfare Effects on the United States of a Significant Multilateral Tariff Reduction", *Journal of International Economics* **10**, 405–423.

G. S. Becker (1983), "A Theory of Competition among Pressure Groups for Political Influence", *Quarterly Journal of Economics* **98**, 371–400.

E. Berglas (1979), "Preferential Trading Theory: The *n* Commodity Case", *Journal of Political Economy* **87**, 315–31.

T. J. Bertrand (1972), "Welfare Indexes with Interindustry Flows: Comment", *Journal of Political Economy* **80**, 796–800.

T. J. Bertrand and J. Vanek (1971), "The Theory of Tariffs, Taxes and Subsidies: Some Aspects of the Second Best", *American Economic Review* **61**, 925–31.

J. N. Bhagwati (1980), "Lobbying and Welfare", *Journal of Public Economics* **14**, 355–63.
(1982), "Directly Unproductive, Profit-seeking (DUP) Activities", *Journal of Political Economy* **90**, 988–1002.

J. N. Bhagwati and T. N. Srinivasan (1969), "Optimal Intervention to Achieve Non-economic Objectives", *Review of Economic Studies* **36**, 27–38.
(1980), "Revenue Seeking: A Generalization of the Theory of Tariffs", *Journal of Political Economy* **88**, 1069–87.

R. W. Boadway and N. Bruce (1984), *Welfare Economics* (New York: Blackwell).

R. W. Boadway and J. Treddenick (1978), "A General Equilibrium Computation of the Effects of the Canadian Tariff Structure", *Canadian Journal of Economics* **11**, 424–46.

J. A. Brander and P. R. Krugman (1983), "A 'Reciprocal Dumping' Model of International Trade", *Journal of International Economics* **15**, 313–21.

J. A. Brander and B. J. Spencer (1981), "Tariffs and the Extraction of Foreign Monopoly Rents under Potential Entry", *Canadian Journal of Economics* **14**, 371–89.

289

(1984), "Tariff Protection and Imperfect Competition", in H. Kierzkowski (ed.), *Monopolistic Competition in International Trade* (Oxford: Oxford University Press), pp. 194–206.

(1985), "Export Subsidies and International Market Share Rivalry", *Journal of International Economics* **18**, 83–100.

R. A. Brecher and J. N. Bhagwati (1987), "Voluntary Export Restrictions versus Import Restrictions: A Welfare-theoretic Comparison", in H. Kierzkowski (ed.), *Protection and Competition in International Trade* (New York: Blackwell), pp. 41–53.

T. F. Bresnahan (1981), "Duopoly Models with Consistent Conjectures", *American Economic Review*, **71**, 934–45.

W. A. Brock and S. P. Magee (1978), "The Economics of Special Interest Politics: The Case of the Tariff", *American Economic Review* **68**, 246–50.

D. K. Brown (1987), "Tariffs, the Terms of Trade and National Product Differentiation", *Journal of Policy Modelling* **9**, 503–26.

F. Brown and J. Whalley (1980), "General Equilibrium Evaluations of Tariff-Cutting Proposals in the Tokyo Round and Comparisons with More Extensive Liberalization of World Trade", *Economic Journal* **90**, 838–66.

J. M. Buchanan and G. Tullock (1962), *The Calculus of Consent* (Ann Arbor: University of Michigan Press).

J. H. Cassing and A. L. Hillman (1985), "Political Influence Motives and the Choice Between Tariffs and Quotas", *Journal of International Economics* **19**, 279–90.

(1986), "Shifting Comparative Advantage and Senescent Industry Collapse", *American Economic Review* **78**, 516–23.

R. E. Caves (1974), "The Economics of Reciprocity: Theory and Evidence of Bilateral Trading Arrangements", in W. Sellekaerts (ed.), *International Trade and Finance, Essays in Honour of Jan Tinbergen* (New York: White Plains), pp. 17–54.

(1976), "Economic Models of Political Choice: Canada's Tariff Structure", *Canadian Journal of Economics* **9**, 278–300.

J. H. Cheh (1974), "United States Concessions in the Kennedy Round and Short-Run Labour Adjustment Costs", *Journal of International Economics* **4**, 323–40.

J. S. Chipman (1974), "Homothetic Preferences and Aggregation", *Journal of Economic Theory* **8**, 26–38.

J. S. Chipman and J. C. Moore (1978), "The New Welfare Economics, 1939–1974", *International Economic Review* **19**, 547–84.

(1980), "Compensating Variation, Consumer's Surplus and Welfare", *American Economic Review* **70**, 933–49.

A. H. Chisholm and R. Tyers (1985), "Agricultural Protection and Market Insulation Policies: Applications of a Dynamic Multisectoral Model", in J. Piggott and J. Whalley (eds.), *New Developments in Applied General Equilibrium Analysis* (Cambridge: Cambridge University Press), pp. 189–220.

W. R. Cline et al. (1977), *Trade Negotiations in the Kennedy Round: A Quantitative Assessment* (Washington: The Brookings Institution).

P. Collier (1979), "The Welfare Effects of Customs Unions: An Anatomy", *Economic Journal* **89**, 84–95.

C. Collyns and S. Dunaway (1987), "The Cost of Trade Restraints", *IMF Staff Papers* **34**, 150–75.

C. A. Cooper and B. F. Massell (1965), "A New Look at Customs Union Theory", *Economic Journal* **75**, 742–7.

B. R. Copeland, (1990), "Strategic Interaction Among Nations: Negotiable and Non-Negotiable Trade Barriers", *Canadian Journal of Economics*, forthcoming.

W. J. Corcoran (1984), "Long-run Equilibrium and Total Expenditures in Rent Seeking", *Public Choice* **43**, 89–94.

W. M. Corden (1966a), "Protection: Review of the Vernon Report", *Economic Record* 42, 129–38.

(1966b), "The Structure of a Tariff System and the Effective Protective Rate", *Journal of Political Economy* 74, 221–37.

(1967), "Monopoly, Tariffs and Subsidies", *Economica* 34, 50–8.

(1971), *The Theory of Protection* (Oxford: Oxford University Press).

(1972), "Economics of Scale and Customs Union Theory", *Journal of Political Economy* 80, 465–75.

(1974), *Trade Policy and Economic Welfare* (Oxford: Clarendon Press).

(1975), "The Costs and Consequences of Protection: A Survey of Empirical Work", P. B. Kenen (ed.), *International Trade and Finance* (Cambridge: Cambridge University Press), pp. 51–91.

(1976), "Customs Union Theory and the Nonuniformity of Tariffs", *Journal of International Economics* 6, 99–106.

(1984), "The Normative Theory of International Trade", in R. W. Jones and P. B. Kenen (eds), *Handbook of International Economics: Vol. I* (Amsterdam: North-Holland), pp. 63–130.

W. M. Corden and R. E. Falvey (1985), "Quotas and the Second Best", *Economics Letters* 18, 67–70.

W. W. Csaplar, Jr., and E. Tower (1988), "Trade and Industrial Policy under Oligopoly: Comment", *Quarterly Journal of Economics* 103, 599–602.

A. V. Deardorff (1987), "Why Do Governments Prefer Nontariff Barriers?", *Carnegie-Rochester Conference Series on Public Policy* 26, 191–216.

W. E. Diewert (1984), "The Measurement of Deadweight Loss in an Open Economy", *Economica* 51, 23–42.

W. E. Diewert, A. H. Turunen-Red and A. D. Woodland (1989), "Productivity and Pareto Improving Changes in Taxes and Tariffs", *Review of Economic Studies* 56, 199–216.

A. K. Dixit (1970), "On the Optimum Structure of Commodity Taxes", *American Economic Review* 60, 295–301.

(1975), "Welfare Effects of Tax and Price Changes", *Journal of Public Economics* 4, 103–23.

(1985), "Tax Policy in Open Economies", in A. J. Auerbach and M. Feldstein (eds.), *Handbook of Public Economics, Vol. I* (Amsterdam: North-Holland), pp. 313–74.

(1987a), "Trade and Insurance with Moral Hazard", *Journal of International Economics* 23, 201–20.

(1987b), "Tariffs and Subsidies under Oligopoly: The Case of the U.S. Automobile Industry", in H. Kierzkowski (ed.), *Protection and Competition in International Trade* (New York: Blackwell), pp. 112–27.

A. K. Dixit and G. M. Grossman (1986), "Targeted Export Promotion with Several Oligopolistic Industries", *Journal of International Economics* 21, 233–49.

A. K. Dixit and V. Norman (1980), *Theory of International Trade* (Cambridge: Cambridge University Press).

(1986), "Gains from Trade without Lump-Sum Compensation", *Journal of International Economics* 21, 111–22.

A. K. Dixit and J. E. Stiglitz (1977), "Monopolistic Competition and Optimum Product Diversity", *American Economic Review* 67, 297–308.

P. B. Dixon (1978), "Economies of Scale, Commodity Disaggregation and the Costs of Protection", *Australian Economic Papers* 17, 63–80.

P. B. Dixon et al. (1981), *ORANI: A Multi-Sectoral Model of the Australian Economy* (Amsterdam: North-Holland).

A. Downs (1957), *An Economic Theory of Democracy* (New York: Harper and Row).

H. Eastman and S. Stykolt (1960), "A Model for the Study of Protected Oligopolies", *Economic Journal* 70, 336–47.

(1967), *The Tariff and Competition in Canada* (Toronto: Macmillan).

J. Eaton and G. M. Grossman (1985), "Tariffs as Insurance: Optimal Commercial Policy when Domestic Markets Are Incomplete", *Canadian Journal of Economics* **18**, 258–72.

(1986), "Optimal Trade and Industrial Policy under Oligopoly", *Quarterly Journal of Economics* **101**, 383–406.

E. Eisenberg (1961), "Aggregation of Utility Functions", *Management Science* **7**, 337–50.

W. Ethier (1977), "The Theory of Effective Protection in General Equilibrium: Effective Rate Analogues of Nominal Rates", *Canadian Journal of Economics* **10**, 233–45.

W. J. Ethier (1982), "Dumping", *Journal of Political Economy* **90**, 487–506.

R. E. Falvey (1979), "The Composition of Trade within Import-Restricted Product Categories", *Journal of Political Economy* **87**, 1105–14.

(1981), "Commercial Policy and Intra-Industry Trade", *Journal of International Economics* **11**, 495–511.

(1988), "Tariffs, Quotas and Piecemeal Policy Reform", *Journal of International Economics* **25**, 177–83.

R. E. Falvey and H. Kierzkowski (1987), "Product Quality, Intra-Industry Trade and Imperfect Competition", in H. Kierzkowski (ed.), *Protection and Competition in International Trade* (New York: Blackwell), pp. 143–61.

R. E. Falvey and P. J. Lloyd (1985), "Uncertainty and the Choice of Protective Instrument", Working Paper No. 125 (Australian National University).

R. Feenstra (1984), "Voluntary Export Restraint in U.S. Autos, 1980–81: Quality, Employment, and Welfare Effects", in R. Baldwin and A. Krueger (eds.), *The Structure and Evolution of Recent U.S. Trade Policy* (Chicago: University of Chicago Press, NBER), pp. 298–325.

R. Findlay and S. Wellisz (1982), "Endogenous Tariffs, the Political Economy of Trade Restrictions and Welfare", in J. N. Bhagwati (ed.), *Import Competition and Response* (Chicago: University of Chicago Press) pp. 223–38.

J. M. Finger (1975), "Trade Overlap and Intra-Industry Trade", *Economic Inquiry* **13**, 581–9.

G. Fishelson and A. Hillman (1979), "Domestic Monopoly and Redundant Tariff Protection", *Journal of International Economics* **9**, 47–55.

T. Fukushima (1979), "Tariff Structure, Nontraded Goods and Theory of Piecemeal Policy Recommendations", *International Economic Review* **20**, 427–35.

T. Fukushima and N. Kim (1989), "Welfare Improving Tariff Changes: A Case of Many Goods and Countries", *Journal of International Economics* **26**, 383–8.

I. Gibbs and V. Konovalov (1984), "Volume Quotas with Heterogeneous Product Categories", *Economic Record* **60**, 294–303.

P. E. Godek (1985), "Industry Structure and Redistribution through Trade Restrictions", *Journal of Law and Economics* **28**, 687–703.

W. M. Gorman (1953), "Community Preference Fields", *Econometrica* **21**, 63–80.

H. P. Gray (1973), "Two-Way International Trade in Manufactures: A Theoretical Underpinning", *Weltwirtschaftliches Archiv.* **109**, 19–39.

H. A. J. Green (1961), "The Social Optimum in the Presence of Monopoly and Taxation", *Review of Economic Studies* **29**, 66–78.

D. Greenaway and C. R. Milner (1983), "On the Measurement of Intra-Industry Trade, *Economic Journal* **93**, 900–8.

D. Gros (1987), "Protectionism in a Framework with Intra-Industry Trade", IMF Staff Papers **34**, 86–114.

G. M. Grossman (1981), "The Theory of Domestic Content Protection and Content Preference", *Quarterly Journal of Economics* **96**, 583–603.

(1983), "Partially Mobile Capital: A General Approach to Two-Sector Trade Theory", *Journal of International Economics*, **15**, 1–17.

H. G. Grubel (1967), "Intra-Industry Specialization and the Pattern of Trade", *Canadian Journal of Economics and Political Science* **33**, 347–88.

H. G. Grubel and P. J. Lloyd (1975), *Intra-Industry Trade: The Theory and Measurement of International Trade in Differentiated Products* (New York: John Wiley and Sons).

C. Hamilton (1985), "Economic Aspects of Voluntary Export Restraints", in D. Greenaway (ed.), *Current Issues in International Trade: Theory and Policy* (London: Macmillan), pp. 99–117.

A. Harberger (1964), "Taxation, Resource Allocation and Welfare", in *The Role of Direct and Indirect Taxes in the Federal Reserve System*, National Bureau of Economic Research (Princeton: Princeton University Press).

R. Harris (1984), "Applied General Equilibrium Analysis of Small Open Economies with Scale Economies and Imperfect Competition", *American Economic Review* **74**, 1016–32.

   (1985), "Why Voluntary Restraints Are 'Voluntary'", *Canadian Journal of Economics* **18**, 799–809.

R. G. Harris and D. Cox (1984), *Trade, Industrial Policy and Canadian Manufacturing* (Toronto: Ontario Economic Council).

J. C. Hartigan and E. Tower (1982), "Trade Policy and the American Income Distribution", *The Review of Economics and Statistics* **64**, 261–70.

T. Hatta (1977a), "A Theory of Piecemeal Policy Recommendations", *Review of Economic Studies* **44**, 1–21.

   (1977b), "A Recommendations for a Better Tariff Structure", *Econometrica* **45**, 1859–69.

T. Hatta and T. Fukushima (1979), "The Welfare Effect of Tariff Rate Reductions in a Many Country World", *Journal of International Economics* **9**, 503–11.

J. A. Hausman (1981), "Exact Consumer's Surplus and Deadweight Loss", *American Economic Review* **71**, 662–76.

E. Helpman (1981), "International Trade in the Presence of Product Differentiation, Economies of Scale, and Monopolistic Competition: A Chamberlin–Heckscher–Ohlin Approach", *Journal of International Economics* **11**, 305–40.

   (1984), "Increasing Returns, Imperfect Markets and Trade Theory", in R. W. Jones and P. B. Kenen (eds.), *Handbook of International Economics: Vol. I* (Amsterdam: North-Holland), pp. 325–65.

E. Helpman and P. R. Krugman (1985), *Increasing Returns, Imperfect Competition and International Trade* (Cambridge: MIT Press).

J. R. Hicks (1946), *Value and Capital*, 2nd ed. (Oxford: Clarendon Press).

A. L. Hillman (1982), "Declining Industries and Political-Support Protectionist Motives", *American Economic Review* **72**, 1180–7.

   (1989), *The Political Economy of Protection* (Chur: Harwood).

A. L. Hillman and E. Katz (1984), "Risk-averse Rent Seekers and the Social Cost of Monopoly Power", *Economic Journal* **94**, 104–110.

M. Honma and Y. Hayami (1986), "Structure of Agricultural Protection in Industrial Countries", *Journal of International Economics* **20**, 115–29.

I. J. Horstmann and J. R. Markusen (1986), "Up the Average Cost Curve: Inefficient Entry and the New Protectionism", *Journal of International Economics* **20**, 225–47.

Industries Assistance Commission (1980), *Passenger Motor Vehicles: Import Restrictions and Quota Allocation* (Canberra: Australian Government Publishing Service).

   (1982), *Approaches to General Reductions in Protection*, Industries Assistance Commission Report No. 301 (Canberra: Australian Government Publishing Service).

International Monetary Fund (1984), *International Financial Statistics Yearbook: 1984*.

M. Itoh and Y. Ono (1982), "Tariffs, Quotas and Market Structure", *Quarterly Journal of Economics* **96**, 295–305.

D. G. Johnson (1975), "World Agriculture, Commodity Policy and Price Variability", *American Journal of Agricultural Economics* **57**, 823–8.

H. G. Johnson, (1953), "Optimum Tariffs and Retaliation", *Review of Economic Studies* **21**, 142–53.

(1960), "The Costs of Protection and the Scientific Tariff", *Journal of Political Economy* **68**, 327–45.

(1962), "The Economic Theory of Customs Union", in H. G. Johnson (ed.), *Money, Trade and Economic Growth* (London: George Allen and Unwin), pp. 46–74.

(1965), "An Economic Theory of Protectionism, Tariff Bargaining and the Formation of Customs Unions", *Journal of Political Economy* **73**, 256–83.

R. W. Jones (1971a), "A Three-Factor Model in Theory, Trade and History", in J. Bhagwati et al. (eds.), *Trade, Balance of Payments and Growth* (Amsterdam: North-Holland), pp. 3–21.

(1971b), "Effective Protection and Substitution", *Journal of International Economics* **1**, 59–81.

(1975), "Income Distribution and Effective Protection in a Multicommodity Trade Model", *Journal of Economic Theory* **11**, 1–15.

(1987), "Trade Taxes and Subsidies with Imperfect Competition", *Economics Letters* **23**, 375–9.

R. E. Just, A. Schmitz and D. Zilberman (1979), "Price Controls and Optimal Export Policies under Alternative Market Structures", *American Economic Review* **69**, 706–14.

W. H. Kaempfer and E. Tower (1982), "The Balance of Payments Approach to Trade Tax Symmetry Theorems", *Weltwirtschaftliches Archiv.* **118**, 148–65.

H Katrak (1977), "Multinational Monopolies and Commercial Policy", *Oxford Economic Papers* **29**, 283–91.

M. C. Kemp (1967), "Notes on the Theory of Optimal Tariffs", *Economic Record* **43**, 395–403.

(1969a), *The Pure Theory of International Trade and Investment* (Englewood Cliffs, NJ: Prentice-Hall).

(1969b), *A Contribution to the General Equilibrium Theory of Preferential Trading* (Amsterdam: North–Holland).

M. C. Kemp and H. Y. Wan (1976), "An Elementary Proposition Concerning the Formation of Customs Unions", *Journal of International Economics* **6**, 95–7.

(1986), "Gains from Trade with and without Lump-Sum Compensation", *Journal of International Economics* **21**, 99–110.

M. A. King (1983), "Welfare Analysis of Tax Reforms Using Household Data", *Journal of Public Economics* **21**, 183–214.

E. Kleiman and J. J. Pincus (1981), "The Cyclical Effects of Incremental Export Subsidies", *Economic Record* **57**, 140–9.

(1982), "The Australian Export Expansion Grants Scheme", *Australian Economic Papers* **21**, 85–105.

K. Krishna (1989), "Trade Restrictions as Facilitating Practices", *Journal of International Economics* **26**, 251–70.

A. O. Krueger (1974), "The Political Economy of the Rent-seeking Society", *American Economic Review* **64**, 291–303.

P. Krugman (1979), "Increasing Returns, Monopolistic Competition and International Trade", *Journal of International Economics* **9**, 469–79.

(1980), Scale Economies, Product Differentiation and the Pattern of Trade", *American Economic Review* **70**, 950–9.

(1982), "Trade in Differentiated Products and the Political Economy of Trade Liberalization", in J. N. Bhagwati (ed.), *Import Competition and Response* (Chicago: University of Chicago Press), pp. 197–208.

(1984), "Import Protection as Export Promotion: International Competition in the Presence of

Oligopoly and Economies of Scale", in H. Kierzkowski (ed.), *Monopolistic Competition in International Trade* (Oxford: Oxford University Press), pp. 180–93.

K. J. Lancaster (1979), *Variety, Equity and Efficiency* (New York: Columbia University Press).

—— (1980), "Intra-Industry Trade Under Perfect Monopolistic Competition", *Journal of International Economics* **10**, 151–75.

—— (1984), "Protection and Product Differentiation", in H. Kierzkowski (ed.), *Monopolistic Competition and International Trade* (Oxford: Oxford University Press), pp. 137–56.

C. Lawrence and P. T. Spiller (1983), "Product Diversity, Economies of Scale, and International Trade", *Quarterly Journal of Economics* **98**, 63–83.

E. E. Leamer (1980), "Welfare Computations and the Optimal Staging of Tariff Reductions in Models with Adjustment Costs", *Journal of International Economics* **10**, 21–36.

A. P. Lerner (1936), "The Symmetry between Import and Export Taxes", *Economica* **3**, 306–13. Reprinted in R. E. Caves and H. G. Johnson (eds.), (1968), *Readings in International Economics* (Homewood, Ill.: Richard D. Irwin).

R. G. Lipsey (1970), *The Theory of Customs Unions: A General Equilibrium Analysis* (London: Weidenfeld and Nicholson).

R. G. Lipsey and K. Lancaster (1956), "The General Theory of the Second Best", *Review of Economic Studies* **24**, 11–32.

J. S. Lizondo (1984), "A Note on the Nonequivalence of Import Barriers and Voluntary Export Restraints", *Journal of International Economics* **16**, 183–7.

P. J. Lloyd (1974), "A More General Theory of Price Distortions in Open Economies", *Journal of International Economics* **4**, 365–86.

—— (1978), "Protection Policy" in F. H. Gruen (ed.), *Surveys of Australian Economics* (Sydney: George Allen and Unwin).

—— (1982), "3 × 3 Theory of Customs Unions", *Journal of International Economics* **12**, 41–63.

N. V. Long and N. J. Vousden (1987), "Risk-averse Rent Seeking with Shared Rents", *Economic Journal* **97**, 971–85.

R. McCulloch (1973), "When Are a Tariff and a Quota Equivalent?", *Canadian Journal of Economics* **6**, 503–11.

—— (1987), "Why do Governments Prefer Nontariff Barriers? A Comment on Deardorff", *Carnegie-Rochester Conference Series on Public Policy* **26**, 217–22.

R. McCulloch and H. G. Johnson (1973), "A Note on Proportionally Distributed Quotas", *American Economic Review* **63**, 726–32.

J. McMillan and E. McCann (1981), "Welfare Effects in Customs Unions", *Economic Journal* **91**, 697–703.

Stephen P. Magee (1972), "The Welfare Effects of Restrictions on U.S. Trade", *Brookings Papers on Economic Activity*, 645–701.

S. P. Magee (1978), "Three Simple Tests of the Stolper–Samuelson Theorem", in P. Oppenheimer (ed.), *Issues in International Economics* (London: Oriel Press), pp. 138–53.

S. P. Magee, W. A. Brock and L. Young (1989), *Black Hole Tariffs and Endogenous Policy Theory* (Cambridge: Cambridge University Press).

J. R. Markusen (1981), "Trade and the Gains from Trade with Imperfect Competition", *Journal of International Economics* **11**, 531–51.

J. R. Markusen and J. R. Melvin (1984), "The Gains-from-Trade Theorem with Increasing Returns to Scale", in H. Kierzkowski (ed.), *Monopolistic Competition and International Trade* (Oxford: Oxford University Press), pp. 10–33.

J. R. Markusen and A. J. Venables (1988), "Trade Policy with Increasing Returns and Imperfect Competition: Contradictory Results from Competing Assumptions", *Journal of International Economics* **24**, 299–316.

J. R. Markusen and R. M. Wigle (1989), "Nash–Equilibrium Tariffs for the U.S. and Canada: The Roles of Country Size, Scale Economies and Capital Mobility", *Journal of Political Economy* **97**, 368–86.

W. Mayer (1974), "Short-Run and Long-Run Equilibrium for a Small Open Economy", *Journal of Political Economy* **82**, 955–67.

(1981), "Theoretical Considerations on Negotiated Tariff Adjustments", *Oxford Economic Papers* **33**, 135–53.

(1984), "Endogenous Tariff Formation", *American Economic Review* **74**, 970—85.

J. E. Meade (1952), *A Geometry of International Trade* (London: Allen and Unwin).

(1955a), *Trade and Welfare* (Oxford: Oxford University Press).

(1955b), *The Theory of Customs Unions* (Amsterdam: North-Holland).

M. Michaely (1977), *Theory of Commercial Policy* (Chicago: University of Chicago Press).

S. Mohammed and J. Whalley (1984), "Rent Seeking in India: Its Costs and Policy Significance", *Kyklos* **37**, 389–413.

M. Mussa (1974), "Tariffs and the Distribution of Income: The Importance of Factor Specificity, Substitutability and Intensity in the Short and Long Run", *Journal of Political Economy* **82**, 1191–203.

(1984), "The Economics of Content Protection", National Bureau of Economic Research Working Paper No. 1457, National Bureau of Economic Research (Cambridge, Mass.).

(1986), "The Adjustment Process and the Timing of Trade Liberalization", in A. M. Choksi and D. Papageorgiou (eds.), *Economic Liberalization in Developing Countries* (New York: Blackwell).

J. P. Neary (1978), "Short-Run Capital Specificity and the Pure Theory of International Trade, *Economic Journal* **88**, 488–510.

D. M. G. Newbery and J. E. Stiglitz (1984), "Pareto Inferior Trade", *Review of Economic Studies* **51**, 1–12.

M. Ohyama (1972), "Trade and Welfare in General Equilibrium", *Keio Economic Studies* **9**, 37–73.

M. Olson (1965), *The Logic of Collective Action* (Cambridge Mass: Harvard University Press).

Y. Ono (1984), "The Profitability of Export Restraint", *Journal of International Economics* **16**, 335–43.

S. R. Pearson and W. D. Ingram (1980), "Economies of Scale, Domestic Divergences, and Potential Gains from Economic Integration in Ghana and the Ivory Coast", *Journal of Political Economy* **88**, 994–1008.

M. D. Pelcovits (1976), "Quotas versus Tariffs", *Journal of International Economics* **6**, 363–70.

S. Peltzman (1976), "Toward a More General Theory of Regulation", *Journal of Law and Economics* **19**, 211–40.

J. Pincus (1975), "Pressure Groups and the Pattern of Tariffs", *Journal of Political Economy* **83**, 757–78.

G. Pursell and R. H. Snape (1973), "Economies of Scale, Price Discrimination and Exporting", *Journal of International Economics* **3**, 85–91.

F. P. Ramsey (1927), "A Contribution to the Theory of Taxation", *Economic Journal* **37**, 47–61.

A. Ray (1980), "Welfare Significance of Nominal and Effective Rates", *Australian Economic Papers* **19**, 182–90.

E. J. Ray (1981), "The Determinants of Tariff and Nontariff Trade Restrictions in the United States", *Journal of Political Economy* **89**, 105–21.

M. Richardson and S. Wilkie (1986), "Incremental Export Subsidies", *Economic Record* **62**, 88–92.

R. Riezman (1979), "A 3×3 Model of Customs Unions", *Journal of International Economics* **9**, 341–54.

J. Riley (1970), "Ranking of Tariffs under Monopoly Power in Trade: An Extension", *Quarterly Journal of Economics* **84**, 710–12.

C. A. Rodriguez (1974), "The Non-Equivalence of Tariffs and Quotas Under Retaliation", *Journal of International Economics* **4**, 295–98.

G. P. Sampson and R. H. Snape (1980), "Effects of the EEC's Variable Import Levies", *Journal of Political Economy* **88**, 1026–40.

P. A. Samuelson (1938), "Welfare Economics and International Trade", *American Economic Review* **28**, 261–6.

(1956), "Social Indifference Curves", *Quarterly Journal of Economics* **70**, 1–22.

(1962), "The Gains from International Trade Once Again", *Economic Journal* **72**, 820–9.

A. M. Spence (1976), "Product Selection, Fixed Costs and Monopolistic Competition", *Review of Economic Studies* **43**, 217–35.

G. J. Stigler (1971), "The Economic Theory of Regulation", *Bell Journal of Economics* **2**, 3–21.

(1974), "Free Riders and Collective Action", *Bell Journal of Economics* **5**, 359–65.

R. Sweeney, E. Tower and T. D. Willett (1977), "The Ranking of Alternative Tariff and Quota Policies in the Presence of Domestic Monopoly", *Journal of International Economics* **7**, 349–62.

W. E. Takacs (1978), "The Nonequivalence of Tariffs, Import Quotas, and Voluntary Export Restraints", *Journal of International Economics* **8**, 565–73.

P. K. M. Tharakan (1985), "Empirical Analyses of the Commodity Composition of Trade", in D. Greenaway (ed.), *Current Issues in International Trade: Theory and Policy* (London: Macmillan), 63–79.

E. Tower (1975), "The Optimum Quota and Retaliation", *Review of Economic Studies* **42**, 623–30.

(1976a), "The Maximum Revenue Tariff", *Malayan Economic Review* **21**, 104–11.

(1976b), "The Optimum Tariff, Retaliation and Autarky", *Eastern Economic Journal* **3**, 72–5.

(1977), "Ranking the Optimum Tariff and the Maximum Revenue Tariff", *Journal of International Economics* **7**, 73–9.

(1979), "The Geometry of Community Indifference Curves", *Weltwirtschaftliches Archiv.* **115**, 680–700.

(1983), "On the Best Use of Trade Controls in the Presence of Foreign Market Power", *Journal of International Economics* **15**, 349–65.

G. Tullock (1967), "The Welfare Costs of Tariffs, Monopolies and Theft", *Western Economic Journal* **5**, 224–32.

(1980), "Efficient Rent Seeking", in J. M. Buchanan, R. D. Tollison and G. Tullock (eds), *Toward a Theory of the Rent-Seeking Society* (College Station: Texas A&M Press), pp. 97–112.

S. J. Turnovsky (1986), "Optimal Tariffs in Consistent Conjectural Variations Equilibrium", *Journal of International Economics* **21**, 301–12.

S. J. Turnovsky, H. Shalit and A. Schmitz (1980), "Consumer's Surplus, Price Instability and Consumer Welfare", *Econometrica* **48**, 135–52.

A. H. Turunen–Red and A. D. Woodland (1987), "On Strict Pareto Improving Multilateral Reforms of Tariffs", University of Sydney Econometrics Discussion Paper #87-03.

A. L. Vandendorpe (1974), "On the Theory of Noneconomic Objectives in Open Economies", *Journal of International Economics* **4**, 15–24.

J. Vanek (1965), *General Equilibrium of International Discrimination: The Case of Customs Unions* (Cambridge Mass.: Harvard University Press).

(1971), "Interindustry Flows and Meade's Second Best Index", *Journal of Political Economy* **79**, 345–50.

A. J. Venables (1982), "Optimal Tariffs for Trade in Monopolistically Competitive Commodities", *Journal of International Economics* **12**, 225–42.

(1985), "Trade and Trade Policy with Imperfect Competition: The Case of Identical Products and Free Entry", *Journal of International Economics* **19**, 1–20.

J. Viner (1923), *Dumping: A problem in International Trade* (Chicago: University of Chicago Press).

(1950), *The Customs Union Issue* (New York: Carnegie Endowment).

N. J. Vousden (1987), "Content Protection and Tariffs under Monopoly and Competition", *Journal of International Economics* **23**, 263–82.

J. Whalley (1986), "Impacts of a 50% Tariff Reduction in an Eight Region Global Trade Model", in T. N. Srinivasan and J. Whalley (eds.), *General Equilibrium Trade Policy Modelling* (Cambridge, MA: MIT Press).

R. Wigle (1988), "General Equilibrium Evaluation of Canada–U.S. Trade Liberalization in a Global Context", *Canadian Journal of Economics* **21**, 539–64.

P. Wonnacott and R. Wonnacott (1981), "Is Unilateral Tariff Reduction Preferable to a Customs Union? The Curious Case of the Missing Foreign Tariffs", *American Economic Review* **71**, 704–14.

R. J. Wonnacott and P. Wonnacott (1967), *Free Trade Between the United States and Canada: The Potential Economic Effects* (Cambridge, Mass.: Harvard University Press).

A. D. Woodland (1977), "Joint Outputs, Intermediate Inputs and International Trade Theory", *International Economic Review* **18**, 517–33.

(1982), *International Trade and Resource Allocation* (Amsterdam: North-Holland).

L. Young and J. E. Anderson (1980), "The Optimal Policies for Restricting Trade Under Uncertainty", *Review of Economic Studies* **46**, 927–32.

(1982), "Risk Aversion and Optimal Trade Restrictions", *Review of Economic Studies* **49**, 291–305.

L. Young and S. P. Magee (1986), "Endogenous Protection, Factor Returns and Resource Allocation", *Review of Economic Studies* **53**, 407–19.

Index